ADVANCE PRAISE FOR *GLAUCON'S*

MW00658138

"Jacob Howland's fascinating new book about Plato's *Republic* is beautifully written, original, and profound. Providing evidence from the *Timaeus*, the *Critias*, and the *Charmides* as well as from other historical sources, Howland demonstrates Socrates' rivalry with the tyrannical Critias for the soul of Glaucon, the likely failure of Socrates' pedagogy, and Plato's grave reservations about the philosophic rigor and scientific control in the city in speech. Illuminating the *Republic*'s drama and philosophy by situating the dialogue in Athens' political history, Howland's work is a masterful introduction for those reading Plato for the first time and a challenge for seasoned classical scholars." —MARY NICHOLS, Professor Emerita of Political Science, Baylor University

"In *Glaucon's Fate*, Jacob Howland reveals exquisitely how Plato's thought was formed by his lived experience. Through close attention to the historical personalities in the circle of Socrates, Howland shows how memory of Glaucon—Plato's brother, who also figures in Xenophon's *Memorabilia of Socrates*—provided a foil for Plato to construct his ideal philosopher-ruler. Our reading of the *Republic* is richly informed by this book." —MARK MUNN, Professor of Ancient Greek History and Greek Archaeology, The Pennsylvania State University

"*Glaucon's Fate* presents a stunning new reading of Plato's *Republic*. Like some previous commentators, Howland argues that the 'city in speech' Socrates sketches does not constitute his idea of the best political order. It represents an *ad hominem* argument designed particularly to persuade Plato's older brother to jettison his tyrannical ambitions and become a philosopher. However, building on recent historical research that indicates Glaucon died fighting for the Thirty Tyrants, Howland maintains that Socrates failed. Philosophy could be saved and perpetuated only as beautified by Plato's poetic art." —CATHERINE ZUCKERT, Nancy Reeves Dreux Emerita Professor of Political Science, University of Notre Dame

"In this provocative new study of Plato, Jacob Howland entertains the possibility that Glaucon's disappearance from the historical record stems from the fact that he died in 403, fighting on behalf of the tyrannical regime imposed on Athens by his kinsmen Critias and Charmides. In what amounts to a *tour de force*, Howland re-reads not only the *Republic* but also the dialogues in which Critias and Charmides appear in light of the hypothesis that Plato presupposes his reader's awareness that, as an educator, Socrates in this instance failed. Despite Socrates' valiant attempt to bring home to his chosen companion and chief interlocutor the limits of politics and the horrors to which political idealism can lead, the young man succumbed to the totalitarian temptation proffered by Critias. Within Platonic studies and the study of Athenian history, this book opens up new vistas." —Paul A. Rahe, Professor of History and Charles O. Lee and Louise K. Lee Chair in the Western Heritage, Hillsdale College

"Despite Plato's meticulous efforts to locate his dialogues in particular places and to populate them with actual historical persons, most scholars abstract Plato's philosophy from its precise historical setting. Howland offers an essential corrective by persuasively showing how Greek political history illuminates Plato's dialogues (especially the *Republic*) and by showing how Plato's dialogues illuminate Greek history. Howland's interweaving of historical background and textual foreground is masterful. Plato's *Republic* is haunted by the fate of Glaucon." —James Murphy, Professor of Government, Dartmouth College

"This captivating book develops Leo Strauss's insight that, far from being a blueprint for dictatorship or a metaphysical stairway to heaven, Plato's *Republic* depicts Socrates' attempt to save Glaucon's soul from tyranny and injustice. Astutely using the historic backdrop of the *Republic*, Jacob Howland proves that the notorious Critias is the invisible interlocutor against whose ideas and influence Socrates must contend. Writing with a deep appreciation of the unrequited risks and unseen rewards of practicing philosophy, Howland brings the *Republic* down from the clouds and shows us its true context. He reveals the timeless meaning and startling contemporary relevance of this famously elusive work." —Nalin Ranasinghe, Professor of Philosophy, Assumption College

"*Glaucon's Fate* is a *tour de force*. Howland argues through historical consideration of character and myth in the *Republic* that the Callipolis is the fulfillment of Glaucon's baser desires. He suggests that Socrates appeals to these desires in order to tame Glaucon's tyrannical spirit, and his failure presses questions of why and who philosophy fails and what philosophy's responsibility is to those it fails. I won't be able to read Plato's *Republic* the same way after reading this book." —Adriel M. Trott, Associate Professor of Philosophy, Wabash College

"Did even Plato regard Socrates as a corrupter of the youth? In particular, did he present the Socrates of the *Republic* as the corrupter of Plato's beloved brother Glaucon? In this rich, original, and provocative study, Jacob Howland argues that far from having won over Glaucon to philosophy, Socrates had failed signally to do so. Relying on circumstantial evidence and certain features of the *Republic* itself, he contends that Glaucon had died at Munychia in 403 BCE fighting beside his kinsman Critias and the Thirty Tyrants. He thus represented not a triumph but a disaster for Socratic philosophy. This stunning new reading of the *Republic* and elaboration of a Platonic critique of Socrates is bound to attract much discussion. Hovering over *Glaucon's Fate* is the sinister figure of Critias, whom Howland presents as both the inspiration and the target of the dystopic *callipolis* of the *Republic*." —Clifford Orwin, University of Toronto and Berlin Thucydides Center

Glaucon's Fate

History, Myth, and Character in Plato's *Republic*

Jacob Howland

PAUL DRY BOOKS
Philadelphia 2018

First Paul Dry Books Edition, 2018

Paul Dry Books, Inc.
Philadelphia, Pennsylvania
www.pauldrybooks.com

Paul Dry Books gratefully acknowledges the generous grant from the University of Tulsa which made the publication of this book possible.

Cover: *King David* by Mandy Sand, used by permission of Agy Sand.

Reprint rights have been granted for the following:

"Stemma: Plato," from Debra Nails, *The People of Plato: A Prosopography of Plato and Other Socratics* (Indianapolis and Cambridge: Hackett Publishing Company, 2002), p. 244.

Jacob Howland, "Storytelling and Philosophy in Plato's *Republic*," *American Catholic Philosophical Quarterly* 79.2 (2005), pp. 213–32, parts of which are adapted in Chapter 4.

Jacob Howland, "Glaucon's Fate: Plato's *Republic* and the Drama of the Soul," *Proceedings of the Boston Area Colloquium in Ancient Philosophy* 29.1 (2014), pp. 113–36, parts of which are adapted in Chapters 1 and 7.

Printed in the United States of America

Library of Congress Control Number: 2018951844

ISBN: 978-1-58988-134-1

For Ada Lynn Howland
who gave us all new life

PLATO'S FAMILY

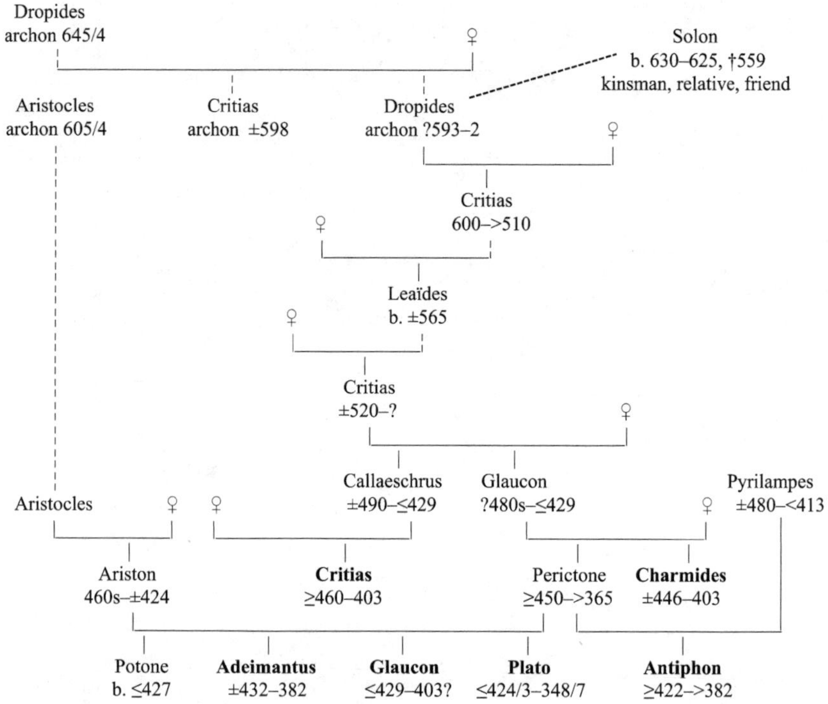

dialogues' characters in **boldface**
legal marriages and birth ————
other relationships ------------------------
hypothetical or dubious links – – – – – – –
woman of unknown name ♀

Adapted from "Stemma: Plato," in Debra Nails, *The People of Plato: A Prosopography of Plato and Other Socratics* (Indianapolis and Cambridge: Hackett Publishing Company, 2002), 244.

CONTENTS

Glaucon's Fate

ABBREVIATIONS

For authors other than Plato, I have adopted the standard abbreviations listed in *The Oxford Classical Dictionary*, 4th ed., rev., ed. Simon Hornblower, Antony Spawforth, and Esther Eidinow (Oxford: Oxford University Press, 2012). Texts are cited by the divisions or subdivisions (book, chapter, page number, line number, etc.) used by the author or introduced by later editors.

Fragmentary writings of pre-Socratic authors are drawn from Hermann Diels, *Die Fragmente der Vorsokratiker*, 6th ed., rev., ed. Walther Kranz, 3 vols. (Berlin: Weidmann, 1952), abbreviated DK.

Platonic texts are cited by Stephanus pages, using the following abbreviations:

Alc.	*Alcibiades*	*Menex.*	*Menexenus*
Ap.	*Apology*	*Phdo.*	*Phaedo*
Chrm.	*Charmides*	*Phdr.*	*Phaedrus*
Cleit.	*Cleitophon*	*Stsm.*	*Statesman*
Crat.	*Cratylus*	*Prm.*	*Parmenides*
Criti.	*Critias*	*Prt.*	*Protagoras*
Epist.	*Epistles*	*Rep.*	*Republic*
Euthphr.	*Euthyphro*	*Symp.*	*Symposium*
Grg.	*Gorgias*	*Soph.*	*Sophist*
Lach.	*Laches*	*Tht.*	*Theaetetus*
Leg.	*Laws*	*Tim.*	*Timaeus*

INTRODUCTION

Saving the Myth

THE EPIC STRUGGLE AND COSMIC VOYAGE OF THE *REPUBLIC*

Perhaps the best measure of the richness and complexity of Plato's *Republic,* the most influential work of political philosophy in the Western tradition, is the remarkably broad spectrum of intellectual accomplishments it has inspired over the centuries. These range from scientific discoveries of cosmic significance to tragic meditations on revolutionary politics.

The astronomer Nicholas Copernicus studied Plato's writings in the original Greek, and found in him a kindred spirit. In his main work, *On the Revolutions of the Heavenly Spheres,* Copernicus draws on what the philologist František Novotný describes as Plato's "metaphysical heliocentric argument from the *Republic*"—his characterization of the sun as the god and ruler of the visible sphere and image of the Good, the unifying source and highest principle of reality. In defense of his most famous assertion, *In medio vero omnium residet Sol* ("But in the middle of everything sits the Sun"), Copernicus writes reverently of the architectural splendor of the cosmos:

> For who in this most beautiful of temples would have placed this lamp in any other or better place than one, from which it might illuminate the whole at once? Some indeed have not improperly called the Sun the lantern of the world, its soul, or its ruler. Trismegistus calls it "the visible god" and Sophocles' Electra terms it "all-seeing."

> And thus the sun resting as upon a royal throne rules the circling family of stars.[1]

A perfect counterpoint to Copernicus's almost mystical awe before the grandeur of the universe can be found in Florian Henckel von Donnersmarck's film *The Lives of Others*. Like Yevgeny Zamyatin's dystopian novel *We*, which was denied publication by the censors of the Soviet Union, *The Lives of Others* repeatedly evokes the philosophic and scientific totalitarianism of Callipolis, the Beautiful City of the *Republic*, in telling the story of the repression of writers and artists in communist East Germany. The film includes a Platonic joke about Erich Honecker, East Germany's head of state and Party General Secretary:

> Honecker comes to his office early in the morning and opens the window. He sees the sun and says: "Good morning, dear sun." The sun replies: "Good morning, dear Erich." Honecker works and goes at noon to the window and says: "Good day, dear sun." The sun replies: "Good day, dear Erich." In the evening Erich closes up and goes once more to the window and says "Good evening, dear sun." The sun does not respond. Honecker again says: "Good evening, dear sun. What's the matter with you?" The sun answers: "Lick my ass, I'm in the West now."[2]

In his ideological conceit, the leader of the DDR supposes that the sun revolves around him and his political work. Copernicus delights in the heliocentric universe, whereas Honecker tries to lord it over the very source of light and life on earth, as though the constructions of dialectical materialism could subdue the Good itself. And in a way, he succeeds: the joke's dark humor is that he intimidates even the most regal of celestial bodies.

While Henckel von Donnersmarck reflects the fundamental tension between the *Republic*'s teaching on the Good and the tyranny of Callipolis, the logician Karl Popper is uncompromising in his criticism of Plato. Popper's book *The Open Society and its Enemies*, conceived on the day in March of 1938 when he learned of Nazi Germany's *Anschluss* with Austria, traces the origins of totalitarianism directly to the *Republic*.[3] Students of Plato behind the Iron Curtain—where *The Open Society* was known, but banned—quickly reached a similar conclusion, and later totalitarian regimes have looked to the dialogue as a model. Cambodia's Khmer Rouge, led by a Marxist who was radicalized while studying in Paris, appear to have followed almost to the letter Socrates' advice to purify the old regime and initiate the new one by sending everyone over the age of ten to the country (540e–41a). The medieval Shiite philosopher Al-Farabi argued for an Islamic version of Callipolis, ruled by a philosophical prophet and lawgiver; a millennium later, Ayatollah Khomeini looked to the *Republic* in founding his revolutionary theocracy, in which power is concentrated in a Supreme Leader and a Council of Guardians.[4]

How has the *Republic* managed to inspire tyrannical hubris as well as reflective openness, thumotic pusillanimity as well as erotic expansiveness? (For Plato, the philosopher is distinguished by *erōs* or love of wisdom; *thumos* or "spirit" is the part of the soul that loves victory and flares with anger at insult and injustice.) Is the *Republic* primarily a work of philosophical inquiry, or ideological dogmatism? Are its political proposals serious, or ironic? Does it celebrate, or condemn, what Nietzsche's Zarathustra teaches is "the coldest of all cold monsters"—the State that sees all with "a gaze," as Yeats writes, "blank and pitiless as the sun"?[5] It is unsurprising that these questions remain unresolved, for the intellectual energy and dramatic tension of Plato's most famous dialogue spring from its fundamental ambiguity.[6]

In the Myth of Er with which the *Republic* concludes, Socrates teaches that philosophy is the indispensable source of virtue and happiness, while injustice and misery are the predictable consequences of an unexamined life. Nor is moral luck—the good fortune to live in a well-ordered regime, where decency becomes second nature—an adequate substitute for thoughtfulness: Er observes a soul that had in its former life participated in virtue only "by habit, without philosophy" pitifully lamenting its hasty choice to be reincarnated as a tyrant (619b–c). Er's story supports an erotic reading of the *Republic* as a quest for individual salvation through philosophy. Why, then, does Socrates insist on the supreme excellence of Callipolis, whose rulers alone are allowed to pursue, not philosophy as such, but only a part of it—a formal and systematic metaphysics? Worse, doesn't he do injustice to his companions in recommending a regime that exercises almost total control over the behavior of its citizens?

These questions are of more than theoretical interest to Plato, and not just because they concern the moral and intellectual character of the teacher he immortalizes in his dialogues. The *Republic* is historically as well as philosophically significant. It tells the story of Socrates' attempt to keep Plato's brother Glaucon from the path of tyranny—a path on which Plato himself began to embark when, in the immediate aftermath of the Peloponnesian War, his influential relatives championed a kind of ideological absolutism that promised to promote the cause of justice in Athens (*Epist.* 324d–25a). When I wrote my first book on the *Republic* twenty-five years ago, I took it for granted that Socrates succeeded in convincing Glaucon of the superiority of the life of philosophy and justice.[7] At some point in teaching and thinking about the dialogue, however, I began to try to justify what I had previously assumed, and instead found myself stirring up doubts. I now strongly suspect something that would have shocked my earlier self, and will doubtless shock many of my readers: that Glaucon *did* choose tyranny over philosophy. I cannot say whether my argument for this hypothesis—which the historian Mark Munn seems to have been the first to propose—will persuade skeptical students of Plato. But I am convinced that it is a case well worth making. For it opens up unsuspected depths of meaning in the *Republic*, and sheds fresh light on a neglected but crucial dimension of the Platonic dialogues: Socrates' rivalry with Critias, the cousin of Plato's mother Perictone.

Glaucon's story is part of a well-known political tragedy that swept up many of Plato's friends and fellow citizens, including Socrates. The evidence for his personal tragedy, however, is deeply embedded in the text. Like a three-dimensional image hidden within a two-dimensional picture, it requires a special adjustment of the eyes to perceive. To bring it into focus, we must trace the primary threads of which the *Republic* is woven: history, myth, and character.

Glaucon and the Thirty

Plato's dialogues situate historical characters in a partially fictionalized past. This historical fiction invites readers to view Socrates' conversations in the light of actual events and circumstances, and vice versa.[8] While Plato does not hesitate to fabricate conversations that never took place, his literary inventions spring from, and illuminate, historical realities. We know, for example, that Socrates associated with Alcibiades and Critias, men the Athenians rightly blamed for many of their political ills. What was the nature of Socrates' relationship with these individuals? What was the gist of their conversations? Plato offers informed, imaginative answers to these questions in dialogues like the *Symposium* and the *Charmides.*

Two features of the *Republic* directly link this work with Plato's personal experience. The first is the fact that Glaucon and Adeimantus, Socrates' main interlocutors, are Plato's older brothers. Why, one wonders, is the *Republic* framed almost entirely as a conversation between Plato's teacher and his siblings? Why does Glaucon in particular command so much of Socrates' attention? Could it be that the central subject of the dialogue, the choice between the just life and the unjust life, is especially relevant to him? The second is that Plato structures the *Republic* in a way that foreshadows the violent civil strife in Athens in the aftermath of the Peloponnesian War—violence for which his own relatives were largely responsible.

The *Republic,* which is set during the war, is saturated in the bloody history of the Thirty, the Spartan-backed oligarchy that came to power after the Athenian surrender in 404. The Thirty, led by Plato's older cousin Critias and (in a lesser office) his uncle Charmides, governed Athens for eight months in 404–403 and put to death roughly 1,500 Athenians. Of the eleven men Socrates identifies by name in the dialogue, all of whom are actual historical persons, the Thirty executed Niceratus and possibly Cleitophon, robbed and murdered Polemarchus, and were defeated by an army that Lysias (Polemarchus's brother) supplied with shields and mercenaries. Socrates' indictment and execution under the restored democracy in 399 is attributable partly to his association with Critias—even though the Thirty tried to silence him, and even though he bravely defied their order to arrest Leon of Salamis, as he tells us in Plato's *Apology* (32c–d). Critias and Charmides were killed and the Thirty dealt a fatal blow by a democratic coalition in the Battle of Munychia in 403. This battle occurred on the very road, and at roughly the same spot, where Socrates and Glaucon are playfully arrested in the Piraeus by Polemarchus at the beginning of the *Republic.*[9]

Might the political violence that looms on the horizon of the *Republic* be connected with the centrality of Glaucon in its argument and action? In a rich study of the intellectual ferment and political rivalries of Athens in the last decades of the fifth century, Mark Munn offers an astonishing conjecture: Glaucon died fighting for the Thirty at Munychia.[10] The evidence for Munn's hypothesis is circumstantial, but suggestive: Xenophon's testimony regarding Glaucon's extreme political ambition; the centrality and vividness of Glaucon's character in the *Republic* and the location of the opening scene at the site of the Battle of Munychia; a poem about Glaucon's courage in battle that was written by his lover (possibly Critias); the dialogue's concluding image of Er, a "bold warrior slain in battle"; and Glaucon's absence from the trial of Socrates—a fact that suggests he was no longer alive in 399.[11]

Plato scholars rarely ask whether Socrates had any lasting effect on Glaucon, and the few who have done so almost always suppose that, by the end of the dialogue, Socrates did manage to persuade him that the just life is preferable to the unjust one.[12] Munn's historical hypothesis casts the *Republic* in a radically new light, endowing it with a moral urgency that shades into tragedy. For if he is right, the *Republic* is haunted by Glaucon's death, and by how far his life of politics and ideology fell short of the philosophical life he might have led. If he is right, Plato's intelligent and courageous brother—suspended as he was between the corruption of Athenian politics and the integrity of Socratic inquiry, between kinsmen who were leaders of the Thirty and a just friend who fell afoul of them—could not be saved even by the age's most capable advocate of virtue and philosophy.

History and Drama in the Republic

Assuming that it can be substantiated, Munn's hypothesis has two general interpretative consequences. First, the *Republic* and the dialogues most closely related to it—the *Timaeus-Critias* (two texts that present a continuous conversation) and *Charmides*—turn out to be more significant sources of information about the experiences of Plato and his family than has previously been recognized. But if these dialogues are historically significant, the converse is also true:

Plato's philosophical writings can be fully understood only by attending closely to Athenian history. Literary text and historical context are essentially related and mutually illuminating. Although this notion has long been familiar to classicists, and has in recent decades been popularized by practitioners of the New Historicism, it has yet to take hold in Plato studies.[13]

Second, the *Republic* turns out to possess a heretofore unrecognized complexity of perspective. Seen from the vantage point of Socrates as he recounts yesterday's trip to the Piraeus to an unknown audience—perhaps Plato, if we take "day" metaphorically—the conversation at the home of Polemarchus is a moral drama in which a timeless inquiry of universal relevance may decide the urgent particular matter of Glaucon's fate.[14] Read in the hindsight of history, the *Republic* is a poignant literary memorial that lets us glimpse who Glaucon might have been, while allowing us to infer who he came to be in the company of Critias and Charmides. It is also a disappointing test of Socrates' pedagogical capability. For although he commands Glaucon's attention, Socrates is unable to save him from abandoning philosophy for a life of tyrannical rule. It is not that he fails to persuade him of certain opinions pertaining to philosophy and politics; indeed, he seems to succeed *only* in transmitting doctrine. It is rather that he cannot bring Glaucon to embrace his life of philosophical dialogue, even in the subordinate role of a companion and public defender of the philosopher.

What blame does Socrates bear for Glaucon's self-destruction in the service of Critias? Is Socrates, too, guilty of some sort of tragic *hamartia*, an unintended and harmful missing of the mark at which one aims? If he cannot bring Glaucon into the life of philosophy, much less recruit him as an ally or auxiliary of his own philosophizing, who will receive and preserve his legacy? The *Republic*, I propose, is the means by which Plato replies to these questions, making intelligible not only what Socrates wanted to communicate to Glaucon, but the meaning of his failure to do so. In thus reclaiming Socrates' gift of philosophy for the *Republic*'s readers, Plato claims it for himself. Repaying with interest the moral and intellectual debts of his philosophical father, he reveals himself to be the spiritual heir Socrates had hoped to find in Glaucon.

Glaucon and Socrates

The *Republic* moves in fits and starts of interruptions and insights, and contains many new beginnings. This book follows Socrates' example in repeatedly circling back to central themes and problems. It proceeds in a manner more conversational than systematic, as is appropriate to a text in which the pulse of human life and history is as strong and vital as it is in the *Republic*.[15] It will therefore be useful to begin by briefly mapping the terrain I intend to cover.

Chapter 1 explores the historical and literary evidence concerning Glaucon, including the *Seventh Letter*, in which Plato writes of his own brief involvement with the Thirty; Xenophon's *Memorabilia*, which portrays Socrates' initial attempt to rein in Glaucon's extreme political ambition; and the *Symposium* and *Parmenides*, in which Glaucon also appears. The remainder of the chapter discusses the main ways in which the *Republic*, starting with its opening scene, exhibits Glaucon's brilliant but flawed nature and anticipates his fate.

In the *Republic* as elsewhere, Socrates applies the medicine of philosophy to companions sick with culturally-induced vices.[16] If he is to treat Glaucon, he must diagnose his condition; but because Glaucon's whole soul needs healing, he must determine in the most fundamental sense who he is. I show in Chapter 2 that he conducts his diagnostic inquiry in a musical and experimental way, trying to find some philosophically and politically authoritative measures of goodness and virtue to which Glaucon will allow himself to be attuned. Socrates communicates these measures by sequentially describing the lives of different, paradigmatic communities and the formations of soul that correspond to them. If this process does not in Glaucon's case prove to be therapeutic as well, it at least allows Socrates to take the measure of his psyche—his mind and character, pleasures and passions—and so to estimate pedagogical possibilities and plan his next moves.

Socrates' music, and Glaucon's resistance to it, generates waves of discourse: peaks of goodness and virtue (including the True City of book 2) followed by troughs of excess and dissolution (the Feverish City). The birth of the philosopher in the third wave of book 5 is one such peak; the city of philosopher-kings that follows, one such trough. Glaucon evidently lacks the philosopher's pure, powerful *erōs* to see and associate with being and truth, and so cannot fully share in the music of true philosophy. Socrates nevertheless excites him by giving him cause to imagine that, in Callipolis, he could be not just an acclaimed warrior, enjoying the Homeric excess of food, sex, violence, and honor with which the regime rewards its most disciplined and courageous combatants, but perhaps even a philosopher-king. Callipolis, as Socrates states explicitly, is *Glaucon's* city (527c); its measures of moral and intellectual virtue are deeply incoherent, but sufficiently in tune with Glaucon's corrupted natural excellence that he would be willing to submit to them. Far from being Socrates' or Plato's idea of the best regime—as many scholars, following Popper, continue to insist[17]—the Noble or Beautiful City (*kallipolis*) is merely the sort of city that Glaucon, who is incompetent to judge such things, is inclined to regard as best.

Socrates and Critias

Socrates' relationship with Glaucon has its own dynamic. Yet neither this relationship nor Callipolis's combination of nobility (*to kalon*) and baseness (*to aischron*) can be fully understood independently of Critias son of Callaeschrus, whose personal, political, and intellectual gravitas exercises a kind of tidal influence over the movement of the *Republic*.

Glaucon's older, once-removed first cousin plays a major role in three Platonic dialogues, the *Charmides*, *Timaeus*, and *Critias*. We also know a good deal about him from the historical record and the surviving fragments of his writings, which include dramas, poems, and an appreciation of the Spartan regime. The examination of these materials in Chapter 3 brings to light Socrates' long-standing rivalry with Critias, whose seductive union of apparent knowledge and virtue with social status and political influence is anchored in a history of familial distinction going back to Solon, the great sixth-century Athenian lawgiver and poet. Socrates competes with Critias—with little initial success—for the attention of noble and ambitious young Athenians like Alcibiades, whose notorious hubris and violence led Socrates' accusers to compare him with Critias; Charmides, one of the so-called Ten who ruled under the Thirty in the Piraeus; and

Glaucon.[18] A few observations may begin to convey the deceptive and manipulative turn of Critias's mind and character.

A speech attributed to Sisyphus in an unidentified drama by Critias praises the anonymous man who stopped the secret injustice of human beings by inventing the fear of gods supposedly able to "hear everything that is said among mortals, and . . . [to] see everything that is being done." Although he contemplates the heavens as a physicist or natural scientist, this wise thinker and poet "conceal[s] the truth," as Sisyphus says, "with a false speech."[19] Plato shows that Critias considers himself to be just the sort of scientifically educated, poetically gifted, and politically clever man Sisyphus praises. In the *Critias,* he remarks on "the inexperience and extreme ignorance" of human beings regarding the gods (107b); in the *Timaeus,* he fashions a marvelously inventive pseudo-history of Athens that depicts Saïs—Athens' Egyptian sister-city, whose regime is alleged to resemble that of the very first Athenians—as ruled by a cadre of scientific priests who cloak their knowledge in the garb of religion. One of these priests chides Critias's ancestor, the legendarily wise Solon, for ignorantly trusting in ancient myths. He then explains the meteorological phenomena of floods and fires that periodically reduce the Greeks to illiteracy, giving rise to childish legends like the one about Phaethon driving the chariot of the Sun into the earth (22b–23b).

Plato's *Charmides,* in which Socrates and Critias compete for the soul of Charmides—then an ephebe, or youth on the verge of manhood—highlights the vast difference between these two men. In the *Charmides,* Critias comments on the phrase "Know thyself" that is inscribed on the exterior wall of the temple of Apollo at Delphi (164d–65a). Socrates takes this divine injunction much to heart, but Critias asserts that only the ignorant many suppose that "Know thyself" is the advice of a god. It is, rather, a cryptic greeting exchanged by the few human beings who know the temple from the inside. In Critias's esoteric interpretation, the words of the god are literally and figuratively an exoteric invention of the wise. Later in the *Charmides,* Critias enthusiastically embraces the dream of a city in which everything is done in accordance with scientific knowledge, one governed by a ruling meta-science that would allow no mere opinion to direct any part of human affairs (171d–73d). But Socrates is unsure whether human beings would do and fare well if everything were done scientifically, perhaps because such an arrangement would rule out philosophy: the mere quest for knowledge.

The Influence of Critias

The contrast between Socrates and Critias, a philosophical original and his spurious image, is stark. Socrates is plebian, while Critias is aristocratic. Socrates' soul is erotic and musical; Critias's is thumotic and polemical. Socrates offers young souls an escape through philosophy from the Cave of the city; Critias offers them a path to rule. Socrates' path is reliant on the knowledge of one's ignorance and neediness; Critias's is rooted in the presumption of an abstract and impersonal perfection. Socrates seeks truth; Critias supposes he already possesses it. Yet despite the ethical and intellectual chasm that separates him from Socrates, Critias's ideas stand at the heart of the *Republic*.

Chapter 4 traces the connections between Critias's thought and that of Thrasymachus and Glaucon. Critias's aristocratic pride and technical understanding of politics are echoed in Thrasymachus's account of the science of rule in book 1, while his atheism and predilection for esoteric mythmaking are reflected in Glaucon's defense of injustice in the Ring Myth of book 2. What is more, Callipolis looks like a child born of the intellectual union of Thrasymachus and Glaucon. Until its inevitable political collapse, the regime rests on a combination of political expertise and poetic esotericism with which Critias would feel entirely at home. Callipolis's citizens, if that is the right word, are crafted by rulers who possess an ostensibly precise and scientific knowledge of what is.[20] These philosopher-kings tightly control all forms of creative eroticism: sex is mathematically regulated, and poets are employed to fabricate religious myths and medicinal lies so as to conceal this fact. Strangely, however, political repression coexists in Callipolis with individual license; stranger still, this corrupting, Gygean license is the exclusive reward of those warriors the regime considers to be most courageous and self-controlled.

In constructing Callipolis, Socrates disgraces philosophy as well as virtue—and he knows it, as the fears and regrets that frame the *Republic*'s central books make clear. Socrates alludes in these books to a cluster of myths and historical tales that implicitly identify Callipolis's kings as philosophical bastards: lame souls that fail to inherit, develop, or transmit the legitimate love of wisdom. (Critias, too, is a philosophical bastard in Socrates' terms.) At the same time, he clarifies the nature of genuinely philosophical *erōs* through multiple prophetic images. What Socrates reveals about the Good allows us to discern just how the education of the philosopher-kings in Callipolis produces a decayed philosophy that is ultimately indistinguishable from political ideology. Chapters 5 and 6 explore all of this: Socrates' misgivings and forebodings, the noble beauty of his erotic, philosophical song, and the shameful ugliness of Callipolis.

The Problem of Socrates

Socrates' contradictory behavior in the *Republic* is deeply puzzling. He argues that the unjust life is toilsome, fearful, and wretched, and that genuine virtue and happiness belong to the philosopher alone. He furthermore demonstrates in deed the justice and moderation of the philosopher, displaying in particular a distinctly ethical kind of piety—an exemplary openness to other individuals that is rooted in humble subordination to the divine, as when he says that it would be impious not to come to the defense of justice while he can still breathe (368b–c). Yet he also professes admiration for a regime that anticipates the political program of the Thirty, to say nothing of late-modern totalitarian states that are themselves rooted in supposedly scientific ideologies.

Consider the regulation of speech in Callipolis. Poets produce state-mandated content, including "marriage" hymns celebrating ephemeral sexual unions that are secretly dictated by eugenic science; their poems, certainly including depictions of the regime itself, are also subject to censorship (459e–60a; cf. 377b–c). But in Callipolis, censorship extends far beyond poetry. Because philosophical argumentation tends to induce lawlessness among its practitioners, Socrates proposes that only those thirty and older who have proved to be unusually steadfast in studies should be allowed to share in dialectical inquiry (537d–e). His defense of this measure makes it clear that *any* speech that calls into question the goodness of the regime's laws and customs, or the decency and truthfulness of its founders and rulers, will be suppressed. To ensure compliance with its dictates, the regime keeps all citizens under its omnipresent and often invisible eye: all rooms are subject to search by anyone at any time (416d).[21]

History leaves no doubt about the deplorable consequences of such tyrannical measures. In a regime like Callipolis, Socratic conversation and Platonic writing would be driven underground and forced to communicate in cryptic ways.[22] In such a regime, as Henckel von Donnersmarck makes clear in *The Lives of Others*, even true believers among the ruling class would be susceptible to corruption by the concentrated power of lying and spying placed in their hands—the political equivalent of the anonymous invisibility that is praised by Critias's Sisyphus and rediscovered by the protagonist of Glaucon's Ring Myth.

Why does Socrates lend his authority to such an ugly and ignoble regime? What was he hoping to achieve when he accompanied Glaucon to the Piraeus, and what does he in fact accomplish in the *Republic*? What responsibility does he have for Glaucon's fate? These are my book's guiding questions. Investigating them will deepen our appreciation of both the ideality of philosophy and the reality of the philosopher—of the pure philosophical soul Socrates describes in speech, and the noble yet impure one (prone to error, like all mortal natures) he displays in deed.

Studying the *Republic* in the light of Glaucon's fate will also help to unlock the meaning of Plato's obscure and ambiguous pronouncement that his writings are "of a Socrates grown beautiful and young" (*Epist.* 314c). The *Republic* leaves no doubt that its protagonist—a wide-open soul and erotic lover of wisdom, profoundly aware of his ignorance—is morally and intellectually superior to those thumotic souls, including Critias and the kings of Callipolis, who claim actually to *possess* wisdom. Plato's rejuvenation and ennobling of Socrates is nowhere more evident than in the Myth of Er, a philosophical correction and cosmic expansion of the argument and action of the *Republic* that is the focus of Chapter 7. But the truth about Glaucon, communicated in the *Republic* with the delicate indirection demanded by brotherly affection and decency of feeling, also raises questions about Plato's own philosophical and psychological development.[23] To what extent is the *Republic* his appropriation of his teacher's philosophizing, and to what extent is it his repudiation of it? Does the *Republic* represent Plato's liberation from his relatives? Or has he embraced and transformed not just the flawed example of Socrates, but also the intellectual and spiritual patrimony of his paradigmatically Athenian family? It is my hope that the big, exciting questions raised in this book will motivate readers to join me in exploring the artful interweaving of history, myth, and character in the *Republic*.

Interpretative Frames and the Voyage of the Soul

The *Republic* concerns what Stanley Crouch has identified as the fundamental issue of epic literature: "the judgment and drama of human conduct."[24] Socrates' epic struggle for the soul of Glaucon plays out in the shadowy space between history and eternity, cosmos and city, truth and illusion. Plato uses a variety of literary techniques to map this uniquely human domain, and to frame the *Republic* as a philosophical voyage of the soul through life and death, light and darkness.

To begin with, the *Republic* contains a sequence of temporally distinct interpretative frames, nested within one another in such a way that later ones, broader in scope, illuminate earlier ones. Yesterday, as Socrates informs us in the dialogue's first words, he went down to the Piraeus with Glaucon; today, he narrates the story to an unknown audience; tomorrow, we read his narrative with the benefit of historical hindsight. This way of putting the matter is not *quite* right, because past, present, and future are relative to the observer, and shift as one moves from the innermost frame to the outermost one. Nor do I mean to imply that the *Republic* is the accurate record of an actual conversation. Socrates remarks that he and his interlocutors are "men mythologizing in a myth" (376d), and although the *muthos* or story of the dialogue reveals essential truths, it is Plato's poetic construction. My point is rather that Socrates internalizes the meaning of "yesterday's" dialogue. He recollects yesterday's conversation and puts it into his own words, achieving thereby a deeper and broader understanding than is immediately available on the level of the conversation itself. A still larger perspective, however, is available to Plato's readers, who can study the text of the *Republic* within the context of subsequent historical events. While only Plato's first readers could appreciate all of the ways the text resonates against the soundboard of history, an informed historical imagination may nevertheless help today's readers to grasp much more than Socrates' interlocutors could in hearing his words.

Plato also draws extensively on primal images and familiar myths in connecting Glaucon's story with the cosmic voyage of the human soul. In the *Republic,* the instability of Becoming—the material and historical medium into which the soul and its sunlike eye (the mind) are plunged through incarnation—is evoked by the sea, a teeming and turbulent broth of spawn and scum, nourishment, waste, and putrefaction, whose briny spray almost instantly rots timbers and rusts metal. The particular voyage of Socrates and his companions in the *Republic,* a literary microcosm of the soul's journey through the Whole as described in the Myth of Er, unfolds in speech; Socrates accordingly compares the argument to rolling depths that he and his interlocutors swim through, climb out of, fall or jump into, and are inundated by. Their philosophical seafaring mimics the difficult homecoming of Homer's Odysseus—his return, significantly enough, from a long, pan-Hellenic conflict (the Trojan War) to fight in a civil war that is both precipitated by that conflict and concluded, as in Athens, by oaths of amnesty between the warring parties. One pregnant example of the connection between these Homeric and Platonic epics deserves special mention: three waves of increasing magnitude give birth to Callipolis and its godlike philosopher-kings, just as three similar waves sweep Odysseus, naked as a newborn, onto an island ruled by the godlike Alcinous, King Mighty-Mind. (The Greek word *kuma,* "wave," can also mean "fetus.")[25]

Other images Socrates uses to describe the inquiry of the *Republic* include descending and ascending, climbing and slipping, military skirmishing, and running a race. The motif of descent and ascent runs from the dialogue's opening words through the Ring Myth and the Cave Image to the Myth of Er at its very end. The palindromic voyage of the soul through death and reincarnation that Socrates describes in the Myth of Er is formally echoed in the *Republic*'s ring structure—its composition, in Eva Brann's words, "on the plan of concentric rings," so that "themes on the diameter reappear in reverse order as if they were reflected through a central axis."[26] The soul's voyage is also symbolically reproduced in the ritual backdrop of the *Republic*'s discussion. Thracian religion emphasized immortality, and the all-night festival in honor of Bendis and relay race on horseback, with torches as batons, are enactments, as Bruce Rosenstock has written, "of the continuing life of the sun's light and the promise of the sun's renewal after its descent into the realm of perpetual night."[27] While the relay race symbolically evokes the transmission of life from generation to generation (cf. *Laws* 776b), the Myth of Er describes the endless cycle of reincarnation to which our immortal souls are subject. In returning us to the cosmic perspective of its ritual beginning, the *Republic*'s mythical conclusion reinforces our sense that the journey of Socrates and Glaucon to the Piraeus exemplifies the voyage of the embodied soul through space and time.

Finally, the homecoming or *nostos* of Socrates in the *Republic*—a word derived, like *nous* or intellect, from the Indo-European root **nes-*, meaning something like "return to light and life"—reenacts the round trip of sun and soul. Socrates and Glaucon follow the procession of Bendis down from the ceremonial hearth of Athens in the agora. They are detained in the Piraeus early enough to have dinner at Polemarchus's house and return for the torch race at sunset, which in the summer month of Thargelion, when the festival took place, is around 9:00 p.m. At roughly 88,000 Greek words, the *Republic* would take about ten hours to narrate; the original conversation took perhaps an hour longer to complete. When Socrates informs us at the very end of the dialogue that Er awakened on his funeral pyre at dawn, it is about 5:30 a.m., the sun is just peeking over the horizon, and the all-night festival is ending. Socrates then walks back to Athens (a four-mile journey) and narrates the dialogue. We may thus imagine that he finishes recounting the conversation of the *Republic* approximately twenty-four hours—one earthly day, equivalent to the cosmic rotation of the soul through life and death—after he and Glaucon set out from Athens.[28]

A Spirited and Erotic Race

Just before the end of the *Republic*, Socrates gives us a further clue about the path the argument has traversed. He compares a human life to a race run round a pole and back again, where the starting line is also the finish line. "Clever and unjust men," he says, "run well from the lower end, but not from the upper" (613b). Socrates' argument has precisely this form, for it reverses direction at the *Republic*'s exact center as measured by Stephanus pages, the standard pagination of Plato's Greek text for the past four centuries. The turning point of the dialogue is the third wave of book 5: the assertion that the ills of the cities will not cease unless philosophers become kings or kings philosophers.[29]

Although the ancients wrote on scrolls, one can visualize the *Republic*'s ring structure by imagining the midpoint of the text as a hinge along which its two halves may be folded. Book 1 would then line up roughly with book 10, book 2 with book 9, and so forth. (What is more, the corpse of Er that reawakens to life on its funeral pyre 0.3 pages from the dialogue's end would be superimposed on the road where Socrates and Glaucon are arrested 0.3 pages from its beginning—"the same road," as Munn writes, "that soaked up the blood of the seventy devotees of Critias.")[30] If we think of the third wave as the *Republic*'s hinge, it becomes clear that the dialogue resembles a relay race in which the unjust runner hands off to the just. The action of the *Republic* mimics the simultaneous race of Bendis, which is itself a ritual imitation of the passage of the soul through life. The conversation rounds the post in the middle of the night, just as the sun begins its upward journey toward morning.

Discounting local peaks and valleys, the first half of the *Republic* displays a process of moral and political degeneration: a sinking of soul and city that is only briefly arrested by the political assertion of spirit, and is later accelerated when *thumos* teams up in Callipolis with its cognate, *epithumia* or appetite. This process is characterized by an escalating struggle between, and finally a toxic mixture of, unjust excess and political coercion. But the birth of the philosopher in the third wave opens up the possibility that the love of wisdom may allow a soul to turn around and advance toward the sunlit uplands of truth and being. While the *Republic*'s first half proceeds increasingly in the spirit of political autocracy exemplified by Critias, the second half begins with the description of a soul's ascent toward the light of the Good in the mode of *erōs*, the love of wisdom.

Myth and Tragedy in the *Republic*

In the *Republic* as in tragedy, however, the way up is inseparable from the way down. Socrates' presentation of the possibility of individual salvation through philosophy takes place in the shadow of politics, a shadow Plato fills in with the density of myth. Especially in the dialogue's central books, Socrates and Glaucon allude to the violent Theban legends of Cadmus and his descendants, including Oedipus and his sons Polynices and Eteocles; to the fall of the Heraclids in Lydia, brought about by Gyges' murder of Candaules; and, by way of the myth of Arion, to the ill-fated history of the Cypselids of Corinth, culminating in the vicious tyranny of Periander. These and other tales about failed lines of descent, political bastardy, and intellectual lameness, including (in the *Timaeus* as well as the *Republic*) the myth of Phaethon, and (in the *Critias*) the myth of Atlantis, frame our understanding of the political and philosophical catastrophe of Callipolis and anticipate that of the Thirty. More important, they underscore the difficulty Socrates faces in attempting to transmit his understanding of the nature and goodness of philosophy to other individuals.

Socrates' Cave Image depicts the educational ascent of a soul from phantasms or distorted images of what is to the reality of being and goodness. I have suggested that the argument of the *Republic* is itself a cave or a turbulent sea from which Socrates' interlocutors and Plato's readers must strive to emerge. Glaucon will have to work his own way out, as will we all; for we must each choose, time and again, between justice and injustice, philosophy and the unexamined life. In some mysterious way, these past and present choices both determine our character as existing individuals and reveal, at bottom, who we really are.

In suggesting that individual human lives are somehow the product of character *and* destiny, freedom *and* fate, the concluding Myth of Er embraces the ambiguity at the heart of Greek tragedy. Heraclitus captures this ambiguity in his enigmatically reversible saying *ēthos anthrōpōi daimōn estin*: "Character for a human being is destiny" or "Destiny for a human being is character" (DK frag. 119; a *daimōn* in this context is a favorable or hostile deity). On the first reading, we bear responsibility for the lives we live; we make our choices and reap the consequences. On the second, a power beyond our control determines who we are and how we live. If character is destiny, goodness is rewarded by happiness (*eudaimonia*), and wickedness by misery (*kakodaimonia*). If destiny is character, our wise or foolish choices, and our lives of good or evil, are expressions of divine or demonic forces that pull and push us like puppets. Tragedy dwells in the murky middle ground between these alternatives.[31]

The *Republic* nevertheless ends with Socrates expressing the hope that tragedy can in certain cases be decisively overcome, or that the *muthos* Er saves—a tale that teaches the necessity of philosophy for salvation—may in turn individually "save us" if we are persuaded by it (621b–c). Socrates seems to exemplify the triumph of character: the possibility of determining one's own destiny by choosing the life of philosophy. Yet if I am right, he fails to prevent Glaucon from pursuing tyranny, just as Callipolis fails to achieve and sustain genuinely philosophical rule. These dramatic failures teach that philosophical salvation cannot be worked out through political institutions. This is a lesson human beings seem doomed to forget, as we are perpetually threatened by new extensions of old forms of tyranny. Individual existence is another matter, for Socrates succeeded brilliantly in reproducing philosophy in the person of Plato. In writing the *Republic*, Plato furthermore turns his family's tragedy into an occasion for the possible salvation of others. But the question of whether he places philosophy on a more secure footing than Socrates was able to discover can be answered only by the struggles of individual readers as they choose, or fail to choose, an examined life. Of course, one must also reckon with the historical legacy of the view that Callipolis is not just Plato's vision of the best regime, but what is more, a positive recommendation for political action. The first step in this reckoning is to show, as I hope to do in the following pages, that this interpretation involves a fundamental misunderstanding of the dialogue.

The *Republic*'s indefinite combination of grammatical moods, the hopeful optative and the hard indicative, captures both the weight of historical actuality in shaping human possibilities and the necessary openness of a still undecided future. It is above all this openness—the essential condition of responsibility and freedom, and thus of human existence—that makes the *Republic* immediately relevant to every new generation of readers.

CHAPTER 1

Glaucon's Fate

THE HISTORICAL AND LITERARY EVIDENCE

In *Leviathan*, Thomas Hobbes compares the nature of war to "the nature of foul weather," which "lieth not in a shower or two of rain, but in an inclination thereto of many days together" (xiii.8). In human affairs, however, some gathering storms are visible only in hindsight. For Plato's readers, the violent rule of the Thirty and the civil war they precipitated loom darkly on the horizon of the *Republic*, and charge its atmosphere with anxious electricity.

The Revolution of 404

In 405, almost the entire Athenian navy was wiped out by the Spartan general Lysander in the battle of Aegospotami. Lysander subsequently used his ships to blockade the Piraeus and starve the Athenians into submission. In the spring of 404, the Athenian Assembly agreed to Sparta's terms, including the destruction of the Long Walls that connected the city with the seaport of Piraeus. With the surrender to Lysander that summer of Samos, the last remaining member of the Athenian alliance, the Peloponnesian War was over (Xen. *Hell.* 2.1.21–2.3.9).

Critias was one of a small group of oligarchic Athenians known as "Ephors" after the powerful Spartan officials of the same name. Following the Athenian surrender, the Spartan general Lysander helped these men to push through the Assembly a proposal to elect a commission that was charged with composing ancestral laws according to which they would govern. This was the group we know as the Thirty. Instead of publishing the laws as they had been charged to do, the Thirty appointed a Council of 500 and filled the magistracies as they saw fit. This was not an unwelcome development from the viewpoint of the Athenian aristocracy, especially given the record of overheated ambition and ignominious defeat that was the legacy of democratic Athens. According to Lysias, the oligarchy proposed "to purge the city of unjust men, and to turn the rest of the citizens toward virtue and justice" by resurrecting the Athenian ideals of an earlier era (12.5). Since the defeat of Xerxes in the Battle of Salamis in 480, the core of the Athenian armament had consisted in a fleet of triremes powered by wage-earning rowers. As long as the Athenians depended on their navy, they would have to allow the many to share in political power. The disastrous defeat at Aegospotami, followed by the demolition of the Long Walls, removed this necessity. The Thirty were committed to what was essentially an aristocratic political program on the model of Sparta, one in which the political ascendancy of a land-warrior elite went hand in hand with the subordination of the poor and ostensibly unruly multitude.[1]

Xenophon tells us that the oligarchy began to consolidate power by arresting and executing "those who everyone knew made a living in the democracy by informing [the so-called 'sycophants'] and were burdensome to the aristocrats." These initial measures were widely approved by the Athenians. It is unclear whether the Thirty then requested and received from Sparta a garrison of 700 troops, who were stationed on the Acropolis to keep watch over the city, or whether they did so only after the start of the civil war. In any case, they next proceeded to arrest and execute not simply "base men of little account," but also those "preeminent in wealth and birth and reputation" whose opposition they feared and whose wealth they coveted.[2]

Thus began a reign of terror during which the Thirty disarmed, disenfranchised, and evicted Athenian citizens, summarily judged and executed innocent men, robbed and murdered resident aliens (metics), purged internal opponents, and put to death the men of Eleusis in order to make that neighboring city a base of operations against the rebellious democratic exiles. Like so many others in a similar position, the oligarchs were corrupted by extreme power;

Lysias, who witnessed many of these events, makes it clear that the tyrannical injustice praised in the *Republic* by Thrasymachus and Glaucon—injustice that hides behind a mask of justice, is motivated by extreme greed, and has no fear of the gods or respect for the sanctity of custom or the boundaries of private life—was realized in all of its essential details by the Thirty.[3]

The Thirty and the Sons of Ariston

What did Socrates think of the oligarchic revolution? Did Plato and his brothers support it? While the historical record includes some valuable information about Socrates' response to the Thirty, Plato documents his own rapidly changing attitudes in his *Seventh Letter.* Read in connection with Xenophon's characterization of Glaucon in the *Memorabilia* and the evidence of the *Apology* and the *Republic* concerning Adeimantus, Plato's letter allows for some probable inferences about his brothers' responses as well.

Given the original intentions of the Thirty, it is unsurprising that Socrates—a critic of democracy who was known to praise the laws, habits, and character of the Spartans—does not seem to have initially opposed the regime. There is little reason to doubt his assertion in the *Apology* (32c–d) that his concern "to commit no unjust or impious deed" caused him to disobey the Thirty's command to arrest Leon of Salamis. Nor were the oligarchs well-disposed toward Socrates: they drafted a law against "teaching the art of words" that was formulated with him in mind, and explicitly forbade him from conversing with anyone under thirty years of age. Yet Socrates seems at least tacitly to have accepted the oligarchy when it first came to power: he did not leave the city when the democrats fled, and he was apparently one of the 3,000 Athenians the Thirty selected to share in the government.[4]

We do not know how Socrates' initial acquiescence to the rule of the Thirty might have influenced his companions. But in his *Seventh Letter,* Plato makes it clear that he at first enthusiastically supported the new regime:

> When I was a young man I was affected in the same way as many others. I thought that as soon as I became my own master, I would im-

> mediately enter into the public life of the city. And certain chances in the affairs of the city fell to me in the following way. The regime then in existence, which was reviled by many, was overthrown, and some fifty-one men presided as leaders of the revolution, eleven in the city and ten in the Piraeus—each of these dealing with the market and as many things as it was necessary to administer in the city—and thirty stood over them as absolute rulers of all. Some of these men happened to be relatives and familiars of mine, and moreover they immediately called me to join them in what seemed fitting deeds. And I was affected in an entirely unsurprising way, owing to my youth. I thought they would indeed govern the city by leading it from some unjust life onto the path of justice, so I was greatly attentive to them, to see what they would do. And of course, having seen these men quickly demonstrate that the previous regime was a thing of gold . . . I was disgusted, and I drew back from the evils of that time. (*Epist.* 324d–25a)

Plato tells us that his attitude and ambition were typical of young Athenians. Like many others, he was eager to pursue a political career. Like many, he scorned the democracy that had led the Athenians to ruin, and he was convinced the oligarchy would save the city. That his relatives were among the leaders of the Thirty, and that they encouraged his participation in the regime, seemed to him to be a lucky break indeed. Finally, Plato makes it clear in this passage that he ceased to participate in the affairs of the Thirty not because he opposed their antidemocratic ideals, which were surely well known to him, but because he was shocked by their vicious deeds.

The experience of Plato's brothers in the initial days of the revolution could not have differed much from his. Glaucon and Adeimantus evidently shared Plato's aristocratic political preferences, for in the *Republic* they participate enthusiastically in planning their own deeply antidemocratic regime.[5] Being older than Plato, and of sufficient prowess in battle to have been praised in song by Glaucon's lover as "Sons of Ariston, godlike offspring of a famous man" (*Rep.* 368a), they were almost certainly also invited by their relatives to join the regime.

Whatever enthusiasm Adeimantus might have had for the political project of the oligarchy, however, must have been short-lived.

The fact that he appears in the *Apology* (34a) strongly suggests that he supported the Thirty no more than Plato did, for otherwise his presence at Socrates' trial would have been detrimental to his brother's friend and teacher. The *Republic* furthermore presents Adeimantus as a natural ally of justice. He is indignant at the spectacle of injustice, and fervently rejects speeches that "vulgarly" praise its power (367a–b, 378b). He seems to be one of the few who recoil from doing injustice on account of their "divine nature" (366c)—someone who, in Plato's pun, would indeed be "so adamant [*adamantinos*] as to stick by justice" even if he possessed Gyges' ring, and would "cling adamantly [*adamantinōs*]" to the opinion that the most important choice "in life and death" is the one between justice and injustice (360b, 618e–19a).

Glaucon is another matter. If Plato was as politically ambitious as most other young Athenian gentlemen, Xenophon makes it clear in the *Memorabilia* that Glaucon carried this ambition to an embarrassing extreme:

> When Glaucon the son of Ariston was attempting to harangue the people, as he longed to be a leader of the city although he was not yet twenty years old, and none of his other relatives and friends was able to stop him from being dragged and laughed down from the platform [in the Assembly]—then Socrates alone, being well-disposed toward him on account of Charmides the son of Glaucon and on account of Plato, was able to make him stop. (3.6.1)

Glaucon would have been ridiculed simply because he was still an ephebe, a youth who had not yet passed the threshold of citizenship. His insistence on putting himself forward as an advisor to the Assembly was presumptuous to the point of scandal. Yet he was so bold, or so convinced of his own worth, that this consideration failed to give him pause.

The rest of Xenophon's discussion of Glaucon is equally revealing. It is unclear whether Socrates had anything to do with Glaucon prior to his intervention on behalf of his relatives; notably, while Charmides and Plato stand in the background of this story (the latter barely a teenager, but already a companion of Socrates), Adeimantus goes unmentioned. In any case, Socrates seems to recognize with whom he is dealing when he does speak to Glaucon. His strategy is to build him up and then break him down by showing that he is ignorant of the knowledge he needs in order "to be held in good repute and be admired in the city" (3.6.18). He begins by calling Glaucon's ambition to rule beautiful or noble (*kalon*), adding that, if he succeeds in being a leader of the city,

> you yourself will be able to get whatever you want and will be capable of helping your friends, and you will raise up your father's house, and will augment your fatherland, and make a name for yourself first in the city, then in Hellas, and perhaps just like Themistocles also among the barbarians; and wherever you are, you will be admired of all observers. (3.6.2)

This list of the benefits of political power presumably reflects Socrates' (or Xenophon's) impression of the order of Glaucon's priorities: fulfilling his appetites, helping his friends, exalting his family and city, and becoming known in ever-widening circles. At any rate, Socrates' speech hits the mark: "On hearing these things Glaucon swelled with pride, and gladly lingered" (3.6.3).

In the sequel, however, Glaucon proves to be almost entirely ignorant of economic and military matters; on these subjects, he vaguely observes only that "it is possible for the city to obtain wealth from its enemies." Woefully unprepared for political leadership, he bemoans the "enormous task" of acquiring the knowledge he will need to benefit the city (3.6.7, 13). Toward the end of the conversation, he makes it clear that he wishes to impress Charmides, insisting that "I should indeed be able to benefit my uncle's house, if only he would listen to me" (3.6.15). At this point, Socrates notes that he can hardly hope to make all of the Athenians heed his advice if he cannot even persuade his uncle to do so:

> Be on your guard, Glaucon, lest your desire to be held in good repute should come to the opposite. Or don't you see how unsafe it is for one to say or do what one does not know? Think of others whom you know to be the sort of men who manifestly say and do what they do not understand: do they seem to you to meet with praise rather than blame, and to be admired rather than despised? . . . You will discover that in every sort of work those who have good reputations and are admired come from the men with the most knowledge, while those

> who are held in ill repute and are despised come from the most ignorant. So if you desire to be esteemed and admired in the city, try as much as possible to gain the knowledge of what you wish to do. For if you surpassed the others in this respect and attempted to do the business of the city, I would not be surprised if you obtained what you desire very easily. (3.6.16–18)

It is significant that Socrates does not try to dissuade Glaucon from seeking honor and power. He presumably understands that the youth must be very headstrong indeed to be undaunted by the sort of public humiliation from which his relatives have been trying to protect him. Instead, he points out that Glaucon lacks the knowledge he needs if he is to fulfill his ambition; in doing or saying things in ignorance, he therefore runs the risk of being reviled and despised. Socrates seems already to have sensed the dangerous potential of Glaucon's desire, for to fall into misfortune by acting ignorantly in the pursuit of a noble goal is the very definition of tragic error.[6]

Glaucon and Alcibiades

The story Xenophon tells about Socrates' first encounter with Glaucon closely resembles the one Plato tells about the philosopher's first encounter with Alcibiades, another intelligent and courageous young Athenian (but a generation older) endowed with high birth, powerful connections, wealth, and physical beauty. Socrates employs a similar pedagogical strategy in both cases: he grants the validity of his interlocutors' political ambitions, but observes that they lack the knowledge to achieve their aims. Pausing to compare these stories will help us to understand Socrates' conduct in the *Republic*.

Like Glaucon, Alcibiades is not yet twenty at the time Socrates approaches him in Plato's *First Alcibiades*, on the eve of the Peloponnesian War.[7] Socrates converses with Alcibiades much more intimately than with Glaucon; he has been observing him for many years, and he describes himself as the young man's first and most faithful lover (103a). Like Glaucon, Alcibiades is highly ambitious and supremely confident of his own excellence. Socrates shows that Alcibiades is ignorant of what he needs to know in order to advise the city, and he, too, balks at undertaking the necessary studies. But while Socrates focuses on Glaucon's ignorance of economic and military matters, he emphasizes Alcibiades' ignorance of "the just, noble, good, and advantageous things" (118a). And while he is content merely to encourage Glaucon's goal of being "esteemed and admired in the city," he pointedly flatters Alcibiades and inflames his ambitions. He very specifically presents himself as the sole means by which Alcibiades may obtain greater honor and power than any other man has ever enjoyed, and satisfy a greater erotic longing than anyone else has ever felt (104e–05e, 124b). Socrates' entire seductive performance aims to bag his prey by thrilling and intriguing him.

Plutarch reports that Alcibiades' shield "bore no ancestral device, but Eros wielding a thunderbolt."[8] Socrates seems to have hoped that this erotically and thumotically supercharged young man, pursuing philosophy first as a means to power and honor, would ultimately come to value it as an end in itself. We shall see in due course that he deals with Glaucon in the *Republic* in a similar way. At the end of the *First Alcibiades*, his interlocutor pledges to care for justice and to keep company with Socrates from that day forward. But Socrates receives these pledges with foreboding: "seeing the strength of the city," he tells Alcibiades, "I fear it may overcome both me and you" (135e).[9]

Socrates' fear turns out to be justified. Years later, in Plato's *Symposium*, Alcibiades admits to being too weak to resist what Socrates has taught him is the empty honor of the many. His shame before the philosopher's preeminent virtue and strength of soul causes him to wish that Socrates were dead—"often I would gladly see him no longer in the company of human beings"—and yet, he admits, "I know well that if that were to happen, I would be much more greatly distressed" (216b–c). Hurled forward by his powerful longings, Alcibiades splits in two on the rock of Socrates, and finds himself fluctuating violently between disdainful pride and self-loathing, cheap satisfaction and frustrated longing. He compares Socrates to the legendary Sirens, whose alluring song of otherwise inaccessible knowledge—"we know everything that happens over the all-nourishing earth," they sing—transfixes seafarers to the point of death.[10] Wounded and destabilized by his direct acquaintance with a superior existence that exceeds his grasp, Alcibiades is the most spectacular philosophical casualty in the Platonic dialogues.

Socrates must have approached Glaucon with Alcibiades in mind. In the *Republic,* as we shall see, he expresses serious concerns about his effect on Glaucon. Why he does so, and whether *those* fears turn out to be justified, remains to be determined.

The Road to Town and the Problem of Dramatic Chronology

Besides the *Republic,* Glaucon appears in Plato's *Symposium* and *Parmenides.* All of these dialogues are narrated for unidentified audiences, and the framing narratives of both the *Symposium* and the *Parmenides* implicitly refer to the *Republic.* Taken together, these three dialogues tell a reasonably coherent story about Glaucon's developing relationship with Socrates, but one that is complicated by Plato's strong tolerance for historical anachronism.

The story of Glaucon would seem to begin in the *Symposium*: in the *Republic,* Socrates recounts the events of "yesterday"; in the *Symposium,* Apollodorus begins by speaking of "the day before yesterday" (172a). Both dialogues use the same language in prefacing their narratives with nearly identical stories. Socrates begins the *Republic* by explaining what happened when he and Glaucon started walking from the Piraeus back up toward "the town," Athens:

> Catching sight of us from a distance as we were heading homeward, Polemarchus the son of Cephalus ordered his slave to run and order us to wait. And the boy took hold of my cloak from behind and said "he bids you to wait." (327b)

The *Symposium* is Apollodorus's reply to a question about a celebration that occurred when Agathon won the prize for the best tragedy in 416. Apollodorus is prepared to tell the whole story, for he has just rehearsed it:

> The day before yesterday I happened to be going up to town from my home in Phaleron. Then a man I knew caught sight of me from behind at a distance, and playfully summoning me, he called "Hey Phalerian, you there, Apollodorus! Won't you wait?" (*Symp.* 172a)

The man is Glaucon, and he wants "to learn all about Agathon's party, and what Socrates and Alcibiades and the others who were then present at the banquet said about erotic love [*erōs*]." Glaucon has received an unsatisfactory account of the conversation from a man who "had nothing clear to say," and has sought out Apollodorus in the belief that he was present at Agathon's party. The sharp reply this mistake elicits establishes that Glaucon is not very familiar with Socrates and his companions:

> Don't you know that Agathon has not been in Athens for many years, and it is not yet three years that I have spent time with Socrates and made my concern every day to know whatever he says or does? Before then, running around in whatever way I chanced and thinking that I was doing something, I was more wretched than anyone, not less than you are now, thinking you must do all things rather than philosophize. (*Symp.* 172c–73a)

Considered in connection with Xenophon's testimony, the framing narratives of the *Republic* and the *Symposium* chart Glaucon's changing relationship with Socrates. In Xenophon's *Memorabilia*, Glaucon rushes to harangue the Athenians; in Plato's *Symposium*, he inquires into the speeches of others. Formerly ambitious and impatient, Glaucon has become curious and methodical. By "the day before yesterday," he had begun to reflect on his longings, and was eager to learn what Socrates and Alcibiades might be able to teach him concerning erotic matters. Yet he was still an outsider to the Socratic circle, and it is fitting that he hails Apollodorus from a distance below him as he walks up from the coastal neighborhood of Phaleron toward Athens, where Socrates lives.

The *Republic* supplies the next chapter of Glaucon's story. As of "yesterday," he had risen into the company of Socrates himself, and it is now Polemarchus who stands on the periphery of Socratic philosophizing. But what happens next? Where is Glaucon *today*? In the narrative frame of the *Symposium*, a similar question arises in connection with Aristodemus, the ultimate source of Apollodorus's information about Agathon's party. Apollodorus's comment that Aristodemus was "a lover of Socrates, among those most smitten with him at that time" (*Symp.* 173b) implies that he is no longer around. He seems also to have been absent from the trial of Socrates, as he is not named in the *Apology*. Did he die? Or did he fall out of love with Socrates? Did he long for more than Socrates was able to provide—perhaps like Cleitophon, who ultimately came to prefer the company of Thrasymachus, and the promise of a scientific articulation of knowledge? "To a human being who has not yet been exhorted," Cleitophon tells Socrates, "you are worth everything, but to one who has been exhorted, you are almost even an impediment to arriving at the goal of virtue and becoming happy" (*Cleit.* 410e).

Did Glaucon, too, ultimately turn away from Socrates and the life of philosophy? Did he return to the life of politics on which he had initially hoped to embark—the shining, illusive life lived by Alcibiades, whose understanding of erotic longing is of such great interest to him in the *Symposium*? It is tempting to think that the *Parmenides* can answer these questions, because Plato implicitly connects it with the *Republic*: the dialogue is narrated by a philosopher named Cephalus, and Glaucon and Adeimantus appear in its opening scene. Much as Glaucon sought out Apollodorus, Cephalus and his companions have traveled from Clazomenae in Ionia to hear Plato's half-brother Antiphon recite the story of Socrates' youthful encounter with Parmenides and his student Zeno. Adeimantus warmly welcomes the visitors and brings them to Antiphon, but Glaucon remains silent, as if to suggest a certain coldness toward Socratic inquiry. Adeimantus remarks that Antiphon once memorized by heart Socrates' conversation with Parmenides, but now "spends most of his time with horses" (*Prm.* 126c); perhaps Glaucon, too, had lost interest in philosophy by the time of the *Parmenides.*

While these are plausible speculations, it is not obvious where to locate the *Parmenides* within the larger story Plato tells about Glaucon. For one thing, it is unclear exactly when its frame narrative is supposed to have occurred. Debra Nails suggests the dramatic date of 382, asserting that "Antiphon II is described as no longer a young man but now like his grandfather."[11] But this claim is unwarranted: Adeimantus says merely that "as a stripling," Antiphon "took great care" memorizing the conversation that Socrates had with Parmenides, "but now, like his grandfather of the same name, he spends most of his time with horses." In fact, we cannot tell just how old Antiphon is, or when he lost interest in philosophy.

One might reply that the *Parmenides* must at any rate be set after 399, as Cephalus would have attempted to speak with Socrates himself if he had still been alive at the time of his arrival in Athens. This would seem not only to confirm the dramatic order *Symposium-Republic-Parmenides,* but also to prove that Glaucon outlived Socrates. Yet there are two problems with this view. First, it is by no means clear that Socrates is dead at the time of the *Parmenides.* As Catherine Zuckert observes, Cephalus might regard Antiphon, who heard the story of Parmenides' visit from Zeno's companion Pythodorus, as a more reliable source than Socrates.[12] Second, the dialogues in which Glaucon appears are riddled with anachronisms. The *Symposium*'s frame narrative cannot plausibly be set before 404, but Glaucon is not yet in the circle of Socrates. Can Plato really have wanted us to suppose that the conversation of the *Republic* occurs at a still later date, but before the rise of the Thirty the same year? To complicate matters further, the *Republic* contains so many conflicting chronological clues that it seems to be set at various times throughout the Peloponnesian war. Yet it depicts a continuous conversation over the course of a single night![13]

In sum, we are forced to acknowledge that Plato does not respect the chronological conventions of modern historical fiction. Indeed, he is so unconcerned with chronological impossibility that he occasionally revives the dead: in the *Menexenus,* he portrays a revenant Socrates; in the *Republic,* an apparently revenant Cephalus.[14] This is not to say that Plato is unconcerned with history. Like myth, the story of Glaucon's relationship with Socrates develops independently of historical time, but not of historical context. The basic facts of the Athenian experience are by no means irrelevant to the meaning Plato wishes to convey, for Glaucon's story cannot be understood apart from the backdrop of war, revolution, and civil strife against which it unfolds. Situating Glaucon's relationship with Socrates within its historical context is, in fact, the key to grasping its inner moral truth.

The *Republic*'s Opening Scene

The evidence for Glaucon's involvement with the Thirty and his death at Munychia runs throughout the *Republic,* from its opening scene to its mythical conclusion. My aim in the remainder of this chapter is to bring forth enough of this evidence to merit the reader's continued attention. The case I sketch here will deepen and solidify when we later explore Glaucon's serious engagement with Critias's thought, and trace the dark political myths woven into the action and argument of the *Republic*'s central books.

According to Socrates, "the beginning is the greatest part of every work" (*Rep.* 377a). The *Republic*'s opening scene maps the whole, helping to attune readers to the religious and mythical framework of the dialogue's drama and to the political and historical dimensions of its argument and action. Most important, it emphasizes Socrates' special pedagogical relationship with Glaucon, and anticipates the deformation of this relationship under various internal and external pressures. It thereby establishes a pattern of argument and action that is repeated throughout the *Republic*: the generation, and subsequent deterioration, of distinct forms of virtue and goodness within souls and communities.

The *Republic*'s first words set Socrates and Glaucon apart from everyone else in the dialogue:

> I went down yesterday to the Piraeus with Glaucon, the son of Ariston, to pray to the goddess, and at the same time I wanted to observe [*theasasthai*] how they would conduct the festival, as they were now holding it for the first time. Now the procession of the native inhabitants seemed to me to be fine, but the one the Thracians conducted appeared no less fitting. Having prayed and observed [*theōrēsantes*], we went off toward town. (327a–b)

The cult of Bendis had been introduced in the late fifth century by Thracian metics, and was at some point officially institutionalized by the Athenians. The Athenians ordered the Thracians to conduct a ritual procession from the city's hearth in the Athenian agora to the Piraeus, where a sacred precinct, an altar, and perhaps a temple had already been dedicated to her.[15] It is this procession, along with one conducted simultaneously by Bendis's Athenian worshippers, that Socrates and Glaucon follow down from the city (cf. 354a).

In the *Republic*, the descent of the soul—whether it be into a chasm opened by an earthquake, the Cave of the city, the sea of Becoming, or the underworld where injustice is punished—is a dangerous business laden with moral and metaphysical significance. "I went down [*katebēn*] into the house of Hades," Odysseus tells Penelope in Homer's *Odyssey* (23.252); in beginning the *Republic* with Odysseus's very word, Socrates indicates that he has entered a dark realm in which phantasms eclipse reality and an insubstantial existence is mistaken for the fullness of human life (cf. 516c–d). But the attempt to ascend from this realm is equally risky, as it may lead to the corruptions of absolute power no less than the achievement of intellectual illumination: Gyges' ancestor emerges from the earth to seize the throne of Lydia, while in Callipolis the most promising youths enter into the light of knowledge and wisdom and the office of philosopher-king "just as some are said to have gone up from Hades to the gods" (521c). Socrates' vivid and detailed recollection of yesterday's adventure emphasizes the careful reflection called for at every stage of the human journey.

Glaucon's Socratic education in the *Republic* starts with his participation in the rites of Bendis. Both he and Socrates, we are told in two different ways, observed the festival; *theasthai* is to contemplate with a sense of wonder, while *theōrein* originally meant to serve as an envoy sent on a mission (called a *theōria*) to consult an oracle, make an offering, or attend a religious festival.[16] Socrates will later use all of these terms to refer to the philosophical contemplation of the whole and the highest things (486a, 511c, 529b). In the present instance, theory—in the sense not of a speculative construction or model, but a primary act of intellectual seeing—is oriented by the healthy practice of communal worship: Socrates and Glaucon enter the dialogue as members of an integrated religious and political community. Glaucon's day of religious observance and philosophical observation in the company of Socrates lifts him, however briefly, out of his everyday existence. This experience offers him an opportunity to purify himself of dross and distraction, much as souls are purified in the afterlife described by Er. It is a wholesome preparation for a discussion about philosophy and justice.

But Socrates and Glaucon are unexpectedly detained in the Piraeus, and the conversation at the home of Polemarchus must take the place of the private one they would have had while they returned to the city. Socrates tells us that they were spotted going up to Athens by Polemarchus, Adeimantus, Niceratus (the son of Nicias, the general who led the ill-starred Athenian expedition to Syracuse in 415) and some unnamed others, all of whom are primed for a night of partying at the festival of Bendis. Adeimantus and Niceratus are

Athenian aristocrats, and Polemarchus is a wealthy metic; they and their companions nevertheless constitute a relative "many," as Polemarchus jokes at 327c, prepared to force Socrates and Glaucon to remain in the Piraeus. What does this mean?

In the context of late fifth-century Athens, the many (*hoi polloi*), the multitude (*to plēthos*), the few (*hoi oligoi*), and the lesser number (*hoi elattones*) were political terms that reflected vastly different judgments, depending on the speaker, about the virtues and vices of the groups thus designated.[17] In the *Republic*, however, the opposition of many and few also denotes a fundamental difference on the level of the soul, a difference that may or may not be filtered through the lens of politics. When in book 4 Socrates contrasts "the few and more decent" men who are "best by nature and best educated" with "the foul [*phaulois*] many" (431c–d), he speaks the partisan and antidemocratic language of the Athenian aristocracy. But he transcends ordinary political distinctions in asserting in book 6 that genuine philosophers are a few among the few, because the influence of the non-philosophical many corrupts and destroys the philosophical nature in "many" of the "few" who possess it (490e–91a, 492b). Those whose excellence of intellect or character make them members of the few by nature may belong contingently to an association, political or otherwise, that obscures this excellence; thus when Socrates observes that "it is impossible for a multitude to be philosophical" (494a), he underscores the relinquishment of individual judgment that frequently occurs in groups. Socratic education undertakes to separate such individuals from the multitude so that they can think for themselves.

Yet the opening scene allows us only briefly to glimpse essential distinctions on the level of the soul. The restless troupe from the Piraeus dangles before the two who are making for Athens the prospect of an all-night party, and it is Glaucon who, demonstrating the propensity to jump out in front of older men that Xenophon also observes, peremptorily decides that he and Socrates will stay right where they are (328b). Diverted by friends and family, and distracted from the soul-searching rigors of Socratic inquiry by the pleasures of food, drink, and the spectacle of athletic competition, the would-be philosophical few are absorbed by the non-philosophical many. This leveling of aims subtly vulgarizes the few, as Socrates suggests by implicitly comparing the newly-formed group to the Athenian Assembly.[18] Most important, it underscores the confusion of philosophical aspiration and political ideology that runs throughout the *Republic* and reaches its highest pitch in Callipolis.

The politicization of the philosophical distinction between the few and the many is evident in another way in the opening scene. Polemarchus and Niceratus are well-known victims of the Thirty, and Adeimantus, as we have seen, must be presumed at least to have refrained from actively supporting them. Polemarchus's joke that Socrates and Glaucon must "prove stronger than these [many] men, or stay here" (327c) reminds us of the coalition of foreigners and democratic Athenians that would in 403 do battle with the oligarchs, defeating them at roughly the place where the two groups of men now stand. It also seems significant that Socrates and Glaucon are twice said to be heading back up to "the town" (*to astu*, 327b, c): those who remained in Athens under the regime of the Thirty were referred to as *hoi ex asteōs*, "the party of the town," while their democratic opponents, who left for the Piraeus or sought refuge in other cities, were known as *hoi ek Peiraiōs* (Lys. 12.92; cf. *Menex.* 243e).

The sequel strengthens our expectation that Socrates will need to reckon with the gravitational attraction of politics as well as the satisfactions of appetite if he is to keep Glaucon from slipping off the steep path of wisdom and virtue. At Polemarchus's home, he and Glaucon encounter, among unnamed others, the metic's brothers Euthydemus and Lysias (a well-known writer of forensic speeches), the Chalcedonian teacher of rhetoric Thrasymachus, and the Athenian politician Cleitophon. This particular assembly is not coincidental, for Plato connects Thrasymachus with Lysias in the *Phaedrus* (266c, 269d) and with Cleitophon in the *Cleitophon* (406a, 410d). Unlike Polemarchus and his leisured friends, these men are directly involved in the serious business of politics; their group resembles a political association or *hetaireia*.[19]

If Socrates is to recapture Glaucon's undivided attention, he must try to steer his companions toward the pleasures of reflective inquiry. His strategy is to draw them into an extended conversation, one that succeeds in displacing the promised night on the town because it combines the vicarious satisfaction of a wide range of appetites with the excitement of the pursuit of wisdom. Things nevertheless fall apart in the *Republic,* and must repeatedly be put back together. The unanimity reflected in the participation of Socrates and Glaucon in the rites of Bendis must repeatedly be recovered in the dialogue's argument and action, because it cannot be preserved on either level. The minor drama that ensues when Polemarchus and his friends playfully threaten to resort to force to keep Socrates and Glaucon in the Piraeus imitates, somewhat comically, the descent of a political community into factional strife. This playfulness is soon succeeded by Thrasymachus's vicious attack against Socrates and his understanding of justice, the seriousness of which is not entirely eclipsed by the fact that Socrates finally manages to tame his ferocious interlocutor. And while the civic concord achieved in the celebration of Bendis anticipates the simple goodness of the first city of book 2, Glaucon derides the life of this city as one fit for pigs (372d).

As the foregoing examples suggest, the activities of seeing and speaking are quickly separated in the *Republic* from the turn of character on which their goodness ultimately depends (cf. 518d–19a). Thrasymachus's defense of tyranny as theoretically perfect injustice, the silent contemplation of injustice by Gyges' invisible ancestor in Glaucon's Ring Myth, and the secret observation and control of citizens by the rulers of Callipolis are all variations on this theme. Socrates' attempt to lead Glaucon to the life of philosophy is thus also a dramatic exploration of the consequences of the detachment of philosophy from its mooring in the proper orientation of the soul.

The Vulnerabilities of a Second-Best Nature

Plato makes it clear in the *Republic* that Glaucon's nature and character, while admirable in important respects, fall short of perfection. Glaucon's Ring Myth offers ample evidence of an imaginative and poetically creative intelligence, and he is knowledgeable about mathematics as well as music.[20] Socrates describes him as "most courageous in everything" (357a), and the political self-assurance of which Xenophon speaks is matched in the *Republic* by the boldness of his case for injustice. His distinguished service in combat (cf. 368a) indicates that he has the discipline and toughness needed to meet the extreme physical and mental challenges of hoplite warfare. Combining courage and self-discipline, the essential virtues of any warrior, he has proved more than capable of mastering fear, enduring pain, and setting aside yearnings for ease and comfort.

Yet when at leisure from the rigors of warfare, Glaucon's tastes run toward cultivated and aristocratic excess. He deplores the lack of conventional luxuries, including couches and fine foods, in what Socrates calls the "true" and "healthy" city (372d–e)—a city characterized by the harmony of soul and modesty of appetite that distinguish genuine moderation (*sōphrosunē*) from mere self-control (cf. 431e–32a).[21] He breeds hunting dogs and "noble cocks" for fighting (459a). His erotic love of boys is strong, and so indiscriminate, Socrates suggests, "as to reject none of those who glow with the bloom of youth" (475a).[22] Adeimantus notes that in his love of victory, Glaucon resembles the timocrat—the second-best man of the second-best city, fathered by the best (548d). On the whole, it seems appropriate that Socrates at various points identifies Glaucon as a son of Ariston, "The Best."[23]

Glaucon complains at the beginning of book 2 that he has been persuaded neither by Thrasymachus's praise of injustice in book 1 nor by Socrates' refutation of him (358c–d). His restatement and improvement of Thrasymachus's argument in the Ring Myth indicates that he now stands in a kind of moral no man's land. Adeimantus then comes to his defense in a way that underscores the risk of corruption he faces. He explains that good-natured and intelligent youths, especially those who (like his younger brother) possess "some power of soul, or money, or body, or family," would inevitably conclude from the bad education that is prevalent in the Greek cities that injustice is more choiceworthy than justice (365a–b, 366c). The only exceptions are those who (like himself) are divinely and adamantly opposed to doing injustice, or who keep away from it because they have acquired knowledge (366c). While the very best natures would combine these attributes, Glaucon enjoys neither of these moral protections.

Socrates twice returns in conversation with Adeimantus—albeit first only implicitly—to his concern about Glaucon's attraction to injustice. Glaucon is in both cases portrayed as being pulled in opposite directions in a contest for his soul, one that pits a decent, philosophical man (like Socrates) against relatives who want to draw him into political contests.

In book 6, Socrates observes that the virtues of the few philosophical natures—"I mean courage, sound-mindedness, and all that we went through"—make them peculiarly vulnerable to corruption, especially when they are connected with "the so called goods" of "beauty, wealth, strength of body, and relatives who are powerful in a city" (491b–c). In general, Socrates remarks, the most "vigorous" natures (*neanikēs*, a word composed of the Greek terms for "youth" and "victory") are also most vulnerable to corruption by bad nurture and pedagogy (491d–e). Glaucon does not precisely fit Socrates' description of "one who is going to become perfectly philosophical" (491a–b): while he is endowed with self-control and considerable intelligence, he falls short of real moderation, and his love of wisdom is less powerful and focused than that of the most philosophical natures. But these relative deficiencies in fact make him *more* vulnerable to corruption than he would otherwise be. For Socrates makes it clear that genuine philosophers are intensely concentrated on the attainment of wisdom (485d, 490a–b), and are to that extent protected from the powerful agitations of soul that characterize the frenzied competition of non-philosophers for merely apparent goods (cf. 516c–e). The odds that "a philosophic nature . . . will remain in its practice and reach the end" are in any case extremely low, especially if the young man in question "should happen to be from a big city, where he is wealthy and noble in birth, and is furthermore good-looking and tall." Such a man would be flattered by "kinsmen and fellow citizens" who would want to use him for their own purposes; he would consequently imagine himself managing the affairs of barbarians as well as Greeks, and be "full of pretension and empty thoughts, without intelligence." Adeimantus agrees that, if "someone" told this sort of person "the truth"—that "he has no intelligence in him, but he needs it, and that it cannot be gotten unless one has slaved for its acquisition"—it would be very difficult for him to hear (494a–d).

Commentators tend to assume that the preceding remarks refer to Alcibiades,[24] but the immediate sequel leaves little doubt that Socrates is thinking particularly of Glaucon:

> But if, I said, on account of his good nature and kinship with such speeches, he [the young man] should in some way perceive and be

> turned and drawn toward philosophy, what do you think those will do who believe they are losing his use and companionship [*hetaireian*]? Won't they do and say anything concerning him, so that he won't be persuaded, and concerning the one persuading, so that he won't be able to persuade, and won't they plot against him in private and establish public trials? (494d–e)

This passage closely anticipates the subsequent history of Athens. *Hetaireiai* were aristocratic political clubs of the sort that helped Critias and his oligarchic collaborators gain control of the city. After the Thirty made it illegal to teach the art of words, Socrates openly criticized the regime; in response, Critias and Charicles forbade him to converse with the young, whom they defined as anyone under the age of thirty. Critias, the kinsman and fellow citizen who above all hoped to make political use of Glaucon and his brothers, may well have intended by means of these measures to prevent the sons of Ariston in particular from being influenced by Socrates. This was in any case not the only blow directed at him by the Thirty. At his trial, Socrates mentions his refusal of their order to arrest Leon of Salamis as proof of his courage and justice in the face of powerful antagonists. The Thirty presumably selected him to arrest Leon intending, among other things, to neutralize his pedagogical effectiveness: had he complied with their order, he would have been unable to persuade anyone of the justice of the philosophical life. In brief, the Thirty's actions in relation to Socrates exemplify precisely the sorts of public "trials" or "struggles" (*agōnes*) powerful relatives might use to ensure that a philosopher "won't be able to persuade" and that his young companions "won't be persuaded."[25]

Socrates and Adeimantus return in book 8 to the danger Glaucon faces at the hands of his relatives. In the context of a discussion of the devolution of regimes and their corresponding characters, Adeimantus asserts that the timocratic or honor-loving man, the inferior character that rises to rule Callipolis when the philosophical aristocracy fails to maintain the purity of its line, resembles Glaucon with respect to the love of victory.[26] Socrates agrees, although he maintains that the timocrat is more stubborn that Glaucon, and less musically apt and rhetorically skilled (548d–49a). In fact, Socrates' description of the genesis of the timocrat—the second-best man after the "good and just" individual who resembles the aristocratic city (cf. 544e), and who is himself succeeded by the oligarchic man—makes it clear that his connection with Glaucon runs deep.

In appealing to Socrates in book 2 to "blame injustice and praise justice" in the same manner as he himself blames justice and praises injustice (358d), Glaucon positions himself in between the tyrannical life extolled by Thrasymachus and the philosophical life exemplified by Socrates. Just so, Socrates characterizes the future timocrat as a youth who is initially pulled in opposite directions by a "good" father who "minds [his] own business, "always turns his mind to himself," and "is willing to be gotten the better of, so as not to be bothered," and a mother and household servants who complain about his father's indifference to status and wealth, urging him to punish his father's enemies and "to be more of a man" than he (549c–d). This nicely describes the two fundamental influences that contend for the soul of Glaucon: the philosophical life of Socrates—who never takes anyone to court, does not believe that justice involves harming enemies, and is famously indifferent to insults—and the manly achievement of respect through victory and domination exemplified by his mother's blood relatives Critias and Charmides.[27]

The future timocrat's mother's criticisms of his father are amplified when he "hears and sees other similar things" outside his home, finding that "those who mind their own business in the city are called simpletons and held in small account"—a remark that recalls Callicles' criticism of philosophy as unmanly and childish (*Grg.* 484c–85e)—while those who don't are "honored and praised" (550a). Socrates explains that the young man, who "does not have the nature of a bad man, but has kept bad company with others," ultimately turns his soul over to "the part that loves victory and is spirited" and becomes "a lofty-minded man who loves honor" (549c–50b). His rejection of the example of his father, who "water[s] the rational part in his soul," in favor of his mother and "the others" who nourish "the appetitive and spirited parts" (550a–b) is coincident with his being abandoned by the "best guardian" and the "only savior of virtue throughout life"—"argument [*logos*] mixed with music" (549b), which is precisely what Socrates offers Glaucon in the *Republic*.[28] Socrates' description of the timocratic man as a lover of music who is nevertheless more stubborn and less musical than Glaucon is furthermore consistent with the possibility that he was much like Glaucon in his youth, when he *did* keep company with "the true Muse accompanied by arguments and philosophy" (548b–c).

When he is finished discussing the timocratic man, Socrates asks whether "we shall, with Aeschylus, speak of 'another man stationed against another city'" (550c). This allusion to Aeschylus's *Seven Against Thebes,* a tale of civil war in which Oedipus's son Polynices leads an invading army against his brother Eteocles, gives the story Socrates has just told an undertone of tragic violence. And it is only one of several references to Aeschylus that seem to presage Glaucon's involvement with the Thirty.

A Good Man Gone Bad

In book 2, Glaucon and Adeimantus launch a more powerful attack against Socrates' defense of justice than Thrasymachus was able to muster. The vehicle of Glaucon's attack is the Ring Myth. When Adeimantus later begins to defend Glaucon by pointing out the corrupt teaching of the poetico-religious tradition, Socrates remarks "let a man stand by his brother"; when he finishes his apologia, Socrates quotes from the poem Glaucon's lover wrote about the brothers' bravery in battle (362d, 368a). Yet the theme of brothers-in-arms is already implicit in the context of the Ring Myth, where Glaucon twice refers to Aeschylus's *Seven.* He describes the just person as "a man simple and noble, who according to Aeschylus wishes not to seem, but to be good" (361b). Nevertheless, he insists, "it is much more correct to apply the saying of Aeschylus to the unjust man," who, "because he practices a thing dependent on truth and does not live with an eye to opinion, wishes not to seem unjust but to be so, 'reaping a deep furrow in his mind, from which springs the fruit of careful deliberations'" (362a; cf. Aesch. *Sept.* 593–95). Glaucon refers here to Amphiaraus, one of the champions who fought alongside Polynices in his attack Thebes—a "most sound-minded man," Aeschylus writes, "who wishes not to seem best, but to be so" (*Sept.* 568, 592).

Particularly given the setting of the *Republic,* Glaucon's references to the *Seven* bring to mind the Athenian civil war. A specific connection with Munychia is suggested by the fact that, in the very passage to which Glaucon refers, Amphiaraus foretells his own death in the ensuing engagement, "a seer interred beneath enemy soil" (*Sept.* 588): the seer of the army of democratic exiles that sought to overthrow the Thirty also famously predicted his own death just before the battle.[29] But Polynices is no liberator, and Eteocles describes Amphiaraus as a virtuous man, "moderate, just, good, [and] reverent," who is, however, guilty of "mixing with impious, bold-mouthed men against his better judgment" (*Sept.* 610–12). Amphiaraus had allowed himself to be persuaded by his wife—who had herself been bribed for the task—to join Polynices' seditious army. Recognizing too late his grievous error, Amphiaraus tells Polynices that his cause is neither pious nor just. "Is such a deed dear to the gods," he asks him, "and is it noble for men who come after to hear and tell that you besiege your paternal city and native gods, having brought in an army from abroad?" (*Sept.* 580–84). He could just as well have been speaking to Critias, who used Spartan hoplites to shore up his power. What is more, the worry that motivates Adeimantus's apologia, and that is more generally reflected in Socrates' account of the corruption of philosophical souls in book 6 and the formation of the timocratic man, is that this courageous and good-natured young man might also succumb to his relatives' corrupting influences.[30]

Amphiaraus reappears in connection with Glaucon in book 9. In the course of an argument to the effect that doing base deeds results in the enslavement of the tame part of our souls to the savage part, Socrates asks Glaucon whether one who takes money unjustly "is not therefore wretched, and does he accept a bribe of gold for a destruction far more terrible than Eriphyle's accepting the necklace for her husband's life?" "Far more [terrible] indeed," Glaucon replies, "for I will answer you on behalf of that man" (589d–90a). The antecedent of "that man" might be anyone who damages his soul by taking money unjustly, or it could be Eriphyle's husband, who happens to be Amphiaraus. It is striking that Glaucon is once again connected with the Argive seer—a good man corrupted by bad and impious ones, and manipulated, like the timocrat, by a female relative.[31]

The Myth of Glaucos

So far, we have considered some suggestive hints concerning Glaucon's fate. The *Republic*'s opening scene unfolds at the location of the battle in which Critias and Charmides both fell, and this scene implicitly associates Glaucon with the supporters of the Thirty. Socrates repeatedly suggests that Glaucon is peculiarly vulnerable to corruption at the hands of influential relatives, especially on his mother's side of the family; his description of the likely behavior of these relatives furthermore agrees with what we know of Critias's actions while he led the Thirty. Finally, Glaucon is on several occasions linked with the tragic character of Amphiaraus, a man of good nature who was lured into injustice by his companions and relatives, and who fell in a civil war in circumstances reminiscent of the Battle of Munychia. But the *Republic* contains still more ominous presentiments of Glaucon's fate. Some of these are clustered at the end of book 10; Plato introduces others at the beginning of book 5.

Socrates' concern for Glaucon is reflected in his choice to address him directly, in particular in the last sections of the dialogue: his argument for the immortality of the soul, the Myth of Er and its theodicy, and his final exhortation to philosophize and live justly.[32] Glaucon is amazed when Socrates asks him if he hasn't perceived that "our soul is immortal and never destroyed": "And he looked me in the face with wonder and said, 'No, by Zeus. Can you say that?'" (608d). Socrates' argument, which seems to satisfy Glaucon, turns on the claim that the soul is not destroyed by the evil or baseness peculiar to it—"injustice, licentiousness, cowardice, and ignorance"—even though disease and traumatic injury do destroy the body (609a–11a). Indeed, the soul "in its truest nature" is by no means "full of much variety, dissimilarity, and difference" (611b). Socrates explains, however, that the immortal soul is weighed down by "countless evils" in becoming embodied, so that its original nature is difficult to discern.

Socrates illustrates the corrupting effect of embodiment on the soul in a striking manner. At 611d, he refers to "the sea Glaucos"—a phrase that, appearing in the text in the accusative case (*ton thallation Glaukon*), contains a verbal echo of Glaucon's name. This association is reinforced when Socrates utters his name in the vocative case—*ō Glaukōn*—just a few lines later. Long exposure to the briny depths has caused this Glaucos/Glaucon to be marred, broken, worn down, and covered with "shells, seaweed, and rocks, so as to resemble any beast more than what he was by nature." Just so, the soul we see at present is "maimed by community with body and other evils."

We can only conjecture what it would be like if it were carried by the love of wisdom "out of the sea in which it now is," and "the stones and shells" that now disfigure it were "hammered off" (611b–12a).

The Sea Glaucos (*Glaukos Pontios*) is the title of a lost drama by Aeschylus. Its eponymous protagonist is a fisherman who sees a fish that he has landed become revitalized by eating some grass; he eats the grass himself, jumps into the sea, and becomes "a sea-god with prophetic powers."[33] Aeschylus's Glaucos is notable both for the curious divinity he achieves and the bestialization with which he pays for it. His is the antithesis of the Socratic perspective. While Socrates teaches that we must try to emerge whole and clean from the sea of existence, Glaucos takes to these perilous waters in a way that permanently disfigures his humanity. For Socrates, the scouring, cathartic medicine of philosophy helps the embodied soul to restore its purity (cf. *Soph.* 226b–31b); it also offers a means, we learn in the Myth of Er, by which it may protect itself against future depredations (618b–19b). But Glaucos turns his back to the light of what is, seeking in the depths an immortality that Socrates maintains we already possess.

The scholium on 611d sheds further light on the tragic mistake of Glaucos and its significance for understanding the character and fate of Glaucon:

> They say that the [sea] Glaucos is the son of Sisyphus and Merope, and came to be a sea god [*daimona*]. For this one encountered the immortal water, went down into it, and achieved immortality; but when he was unable to demonstrate this to some, he threw himself into the sea. And he goes around all the seashores and the ships once a year together with the big fish. And he divines all bad things. For the sailors look out for him by night, during which he shouts to them with much clatter, and plunging down into the hold of the ship as it turns—for the *daimōn* is invisible to them—they burn [incense], praying for deliverance from the things he is pronouncing. And he, having swum forward to the rock, laments his immortality in an Aeolian Greek voice, and predicts the destruction of animals and harvests. And they pray for deliverance, being hungry and thirsty.

In the scholiast's version of the story, Glaucos, the son of the legendarily cunning Sisyphus, leaps into the sea so that he may prove he is immortal. His achievement of a kind of bestialized divinity connects his story with that of the ancestor of Gyges, a barbarian shepherd who also goes down in a moral sense in order to jump up in the estimation of others. Glaucon is fascinated by the figure of Gyges' ancestor, and in particular by his crafty and brutal deployment of the ring of invisibility to live as "the equal of a god" (360c). Socrates' play on his name in connection with Glaucos hints that he, too, may succumb to the attractions of a certain sort of dehumanizing and Sisyphean godhood.[34]

Forever trapped in his new form and element, Glaucos is transformed into a prophet, and his story becomes a prophecy of doom. In this respect he resembles Amphiaraus, who foretells his own death in a cause he recognizes to be unjust. Read in the context of the *Republic,* the lament of Glaucos is a powerful warning against sacrificing one's soul in the quest for a merely relative divinity. His fate anticipates Er's observation of the choice to be reincarnated as animals made by the misanthropic souls of Ajax and Agamemnon—men who, as Homer and the tragedians relate, inflicted great suffering on themselves and others for the sake of preeminence in honor and power (620a–b). And his shouts of doom, which so terrify the sailors, echo in the roar that prevents tyrants and others of those who "have greatly gone wrong" (*tōn megala hēmartēkotōn*) from leaving the underworld in which they have already been punished for injustice for a thousand years (615d–e).

An Unwilling Murderer and a Willing Victim

The clearest piece of evidence for Glaucon's fate is also the weightiest. The atmosphere of tragic doom that intermittently descends on Glaucon in the *Republic* is thickest at the beginning of book 5, where it envelops Socrates as well. Socrates' forebodings in this context bear comparison with those he articulates at the end of the *First Alcibiades.* In the *Republic,* however, he confesses to fearing that he *himself* will do injustice to his interlocutors, seriously harming them when he wishes only to help. It is evident from the context that he is thinking especially of Glaucon.

Book 5, which accomplishes the transition to Callipolis—a regime Socrates explicitly associates with Glaucon (at 527c he speaks of "the men in your [Glaucon's] beautiful city," *tēi kallipolei*)—is the dramatic and substantive pivot of the *Republic.* Near the beginning of this book, Socrates and Glaucon fall into a sea of shocking and seemingly ridiculous arguments from which they seek to rescue themselves. The imagery is Homeric, although not exclusively so; at 453c–d (discussed in Chapter 5), Socrates implicitly compares himself to the poet and singer Arion, who was forced by robbers to jump into the sea. In book 5 of the *Odyssey,* Poseidon whips up a storm that destroys Odysseus's raft and strips him of his clothing; Socrates and Glaucon are similarly dumped and exposed by the argument, which shreds the protections of *nomos* (law, custom, conventional opinion) in requiring women to exercise in the nude, dissolving the family, and installing philosophers as kings. Odysseus is pushed by three great waves onto the Phaeacian island of Scheria (*Od.* 5.366, 393, 425); three waves of paradox toss Socrates and Glaucon onto the shores of Callipolis. The naked Odysseus emerges from the sea into a strange new world; the third and most paradoxical wave gives birth to the philosopher, without whose rule Callipolis could not exist. The third wave breaks at the center of the text, and Plato makes it clear that book 5 is also the turning-point of Glaucon's Socratic education—the tragic fulcrum where the way up and the way down, as Heraclitus says, are one and the same, and character reveals itself as destiny, destiny as character (DK frags. 60, 119).

In a way, the conversation of the *Republic* begins anew in book 5. Socrates has just finished describing the Virtuous City of courageous and self-controlled warriors and guardians, and explaining the analogy between this city and the virtuous soul. Having had a "hard swim," as he says, he and Glaucon have at the end of book 4 climbed up to a "lookout," from which Glaucon is able to affirm that a good life requires a just and well-ordered soul (441c, 445a–c). Socrates seems to have brought Glaucon up from a sea of arguments and onto solid moral ground, but this success turns out to be temporary. Having gone through the "good" and "right" city and soul, Socrates intends in book 5 to discuss the various "bad" and "mistaken" ones (449a). He is instead arrested (450a) and compelled to launch into a long digression that spans books 5 through 7. In a reprise of the *Republic*'s opening scene, Polemarchus sets matters in motion by grasping Adeimantus's cloak from behind and whispering in his ear.

Adeimantus then accuses Socrates of "robbing us of a whole division of the argument" (449c). Once again, Socrates faces a superior multitude that is implicitly likened to the Athenian Assembly: Glaucon and Thrasymachus, who claims to speak for everyone, join forces in approving Adeimantus's "resolution" that Socrates go through the arrangements pertaining to women and children (449d–450a). Philosophical discussion must again bend to the forceful expression of popular desire.

But this new beginning also differs in a significant way from the original one, for the many of book 5 seem to speak for philosophy. They have at any rate appropriated Socrates' characteristic language: Thrasymachus asks Socrates whether he supposes that "these men have come here now to look for fool's gold and not to listen to arguments," and when he protests that philosophical speeches must be "measured," Glaucon—who now emerges as the leader of this rebellious coalition—replies that "the proper measure of paying attention to such arguments is a whole life" (450b; cf. 344d–e).[35] It is obvious, however, that they insist on hearing about women because they are motivated by curiosity about sex, the "maddest" of desires (403a; cf. 329c), as much as by a longing for wisdom. Socrates' remark about measure thus reminds us that the goodness of philosophical speech is dependent on the moral orientation of those who employ it. The combination of sexual and intellectual eroticism that drives this new coalition anticipates what will turn out to be the essential incoherence of Callipolis, a profoundly immoderate regime that is only superficially governed by the measures of philosophy.

Socrates at first strongly resists the entreaties of his companions. Speaking specifically to Glaucon, whom he addresses as "you happy man," and, a little later, "best of men" (450c, d), he warns that what he is about to say might not be possible; even if it is, it might not be best. He therefore hesitates to launch into the account of women and children "lest it seem to be a prayer" (450c–d)—an ambiguous statement that might mean making impossible things seem possible, or bad things seem good (and thus worth praying for). Glaucon tries to encourage Socrates by insisting that his audience won't be "unreflective or distrustful or ill-willed"; their openness to his speeches, however, is precisely what worries him:

> If I trusted myself to speak with knowledge, your exhortation would be beautiful. For among prudent men and friends, to speak knowing the truth about what is greatest and dear is both safe and heartening. But to make speeches when one is in doubt and seeking, which is just what I am doing, is frightening and slippery. It's not being laughed at I fear—that's childish—but that in slipping from the truth, concerning which one ought least of all to trip up, I'll not only fall myself but also pull my friends down with me. I prostrate myself before Adrasteia, Glaucon, for what I am about to say. For I expect that it is a lesser error [*hamartēma*] to be an involuntary murderer of someone than a deceiver about noble, good, and just things in laws. It's better to run this risk among enemies rather than friends, so you've done well in exhorting me.[36] (450d–51b)

The tone of this passage is unusually dark. Socrates seems to fear that Glaucon in particular might take his words to heart without thoroughly examining them. The word he uses in this context is a synonym for the morally culpable error (*hamartia*) on which the fate of the protagonist turns in a tragic drama. Adrasteia is an epithet of Nemesis, a goddess who punishes acts of hubris and violations of the sacred order. According to an anonymous epigram, "Nemesis warns us by her cubit-rule and bridle [objects with which she is depicted on ancient coins] neither to do anything without measure [*ametron ti poiein*] nor to be unbridled in our speech."[37] Socrates implies that, if he *does* deceive Glaucon about noble, just, and good laws, both men may suffer divine retribution (and perhaps also legal punishment)—Glaucon because he acts in ignorance, and Socrates because he inadvertently encourages him to do so. Indeed, retribution would in that case seem to be inevitable; the name of the goddess implies that there is nothing (*a-*) "to be done" (*drasteos*).[38] As Sonja Tanner observes, Socrates' reference to Adrasteia also suggests a connection with two men named Adrastus: one a king of Argos (and Eriphyle's brother), "the famous co-conspirator in the attack on the city of Thebes as told in Aeschylus' *Seven Against Thebes*," the other an ill-starred Phrygian in Herodotus's *History*, who "is said to have created the first shrine to Nemesis, inscribed with the dedication to 'Adrasteia,'" and who was "guilty twice-over" of involuntary manslaughter (in the first instance, that of his brother).[39]

The immediate sequel is remarkable: "And Glaucon laughed and said 'But, Socrates, if under the power of the argument we should experience any discord, we will release you just like a man who is purified [*katharos*; and so 'guiltless'] of murder'" (451b). Glaucon's reply sounds like a formal indemnification of Socrates for the crime of homicide. And here is a shocking fact: under the laws of Athens, such indemnification could be granted only by the victim himself, in the time before he died.[40] For Plato's readers, Glaucon's laughter sounds sardonic. Socrates will not kill him, but he seems to be on the verge of doing something even worse: corrupting his soul. Of all of the clues in the *Republic* concerning Glaucon's fate, this is the most ominous.

Why, then, does Socrates call Glaucon a "happy man" and "best of men"? Seen from one angle, these expressions are ironic: Socrates would certainly deny that he who is mistaken about essential moral truths could be either happy or good. Yet he might also be taken to imply that Glaucon is *just now* (that is, prior to falling into book 5's sea of arguments) both happy *and* good. Earlier, in reply to Adeimantus's accusation that the warriors of the Virtuous City would not be happy, Socrates had asserted that "it would not be surprising if these men, even as they are, are happiest" (420b). We may surmise that the regime of guardians and auxiliaries he has just finished describing is one in which Glaucon would be, while perhaps not the best simply, as good and happy as a man of his nature and upbringing could be.

But why would the regimen of the Virtuous City best suit Glaucon? How do the laws and practices introduced in book 5 contribute to the Virtuous City's moral and political decay? Most important, why does Socrates, despite his misgivings, proceed to put Glaucon at risk by depicting a decadent regime as a Noble and Beautiful City? Let us approach these questions by observing the natures of both men as they come to light within the unfolding pedagogical drama of the *Republic*.

CHAPTER 2

Socrates' Music

GLAUCON AND THE MEASURES OF THE *REPUBLIC*

If the central action of the *Republic* consists in Socrates' attempt to lead Glaucon onto the path of justice and philosophy, the dialogue's opening scene prefigures a recurrent problem: others come between them, eroding the educational foundations he has laid and compelling him to adjust his pedagogy to his companion's wayward desires. The opening scene introduces a pattern that is repeated throughout the *Republic*: the establishment and subsequent corruption of metaphysical, moral, and political *archai*. (The meanings of the word *archē* range from "origin" or "beginning" to "first principle" and "ruling office.") This pattern is cosmic and universal as well as historical and particular. The Myth of Er presents the infinite loop of birth and death, remembering and forgetting, as the basic structure of life itself; the rhythms of generation and decay are reflected as well in the rise and fall of communities and individuals as they oscillate between truth and illusion, good and evil.

The *Republic*'s multiple beginnings—necessitated by the unruly impulses of Glaucon and his spirited and erotic companions, but also by Socrates' experimental soundings of Glaucon's soul—reenact the perpetually renewed human quest to reproduce the stability of Being within the sea of Becoming. The conversation at the home of Polemarchus eventually touches on all of the main expressions of this quest: physical procreation; religious myth and ritual; the establishment and transmission of laws or customs, written or unwritten;

memorialization in song, verse, sculpture, and painting; scientific inquiry into the natural world; and the philosophical discovery and communication of the structures of history and eternity. The opening scene, however, reminds us of what is announced in the title of the *Republic*: all of these attempts at stabilization occur within the highly fluid framework of a *politeia* (regime), a particular form of community, way of life, and distribution of offices.[1]

The shared life of a *polis* or city like Athens cannot be exhaustively specified; concrete and complex, it is a microcosm of the Whole that is both natural and constructed. In the *Republic*, Plato chooses to show dramatically what cannot be said discursively. Glaucon is central to this display, for he is a paradigmatic Athenian, shaped by democratic desires and popular imperialistic longings even as he prides himself on possessing the high birth, beauty, courage, and self-discipline of the *kaloi k'agathoi*, men "noble and good." In Plato's depiction of his character, we see a psychological reflection of the contest between the few and the many that would erupt violently at the end of the Peloponnesian War. Glaucon's responses to Socrates tell a story not only about the strengths and deficiencies of his nature, but also about the limits of the virtues peculiar to his time and place.

In the *Republic*, Socrates describes three modes of order and harmony for souls and cities—moral and political measures that might, at best, attune his companions to exemplary ways of life, but will in any case help to reveal Glaucon's nature and diagnose his sickness. These criteria of goodness and virtue, composed in the musical alphabet of Socrates' soul and united in his wholesome nature, succeed one another in a cyclical repetition of the aforementioned pattern of generation and decay:

(1) The peaceful and harmonious *measures of nature* emerge in Socrates' narration of the spontaneous growth of the first city in speech, the True City of book 2. Glaucon rejects the natural goodness of this city, its moderation and simple community, in favor of the life he knows: one swollen with luxuries and afflicted with war. Socrates' subsequent attempt to purge the illness of the Feverish City that Glaucon prefers—or rather of one part of it, its army of professional soldiers—leads him to introduce new, artificial, and specifically political standards of virtue.

(2) The martial and spirited *measures of virtue*, inculcated by a rig-

orous, distinctively Spartan mode of nurture, training, and civic education, come to light in the Virtuous City, the regime ruled by guardians and auxiliaries that Socrates describes in books 2 through 4. The warriors of the Virtuous City are educated, as Glaucon has been, to display courage and self-discipline in battle; yet they, too, are never entirely purified of moral and political sickness. This sickness floods back into city and souls alike in book 5: Callipolis offers opportunities for sexual and aggressive license, appetitive excess, and personal aggrandizement that Glaucon finds irresistible, and that fuel his longing to see this regime realized in deed. While the decay of the Virtuous City exposes tensions within Glaucon's soul, it also reflects the inadequacy of the Spartan educational regimen, and so of the political vision of Laconophiles like Critias.

(3) The cosmic and contemplative *measures of philosophy*—of a soul erotically ordered, through inquiry and reflection, to the intelligible structures of the Whole—are introduced at the end of book 5. Once again, however, Glaucon falls short of Socrates' criteria: he lacks the intellectual eroticism and psychic wholeness of the natural-born philosopher. Socrates responds to these deficiencies in a manner reminiscent of the education in virtue by which he tried to purge the Feverish City. The rigorous intellectual training of Callipolis's future kings turns warriors with stable and courageous dispositions into systematic metaphysicians, even if they lack genuinely philosophical natures.

Gravity moves the tides and bends light. Just so, Socrates' interlocutors repeatedly curve the path of his exposition. The birth of Callipolis in the three waves of paradox of book 5 reproduces the movement of the dialogue as a whole: from beginning to end, the *Republic*'s argument and action unfold in waves propagated by the interactions of nature and custom, order and desire, and shaped by Socrates' efforts to carry Glaucon in particular to the safe harbor of a good and happy life.

Socrates' Ethical Piety

The *Republic*'s first criteria of goodness are set forth against the backdrop of Socrates' conversation with Cephalus at the beginning of book 1, and the notions of piety and sacrifice articulated therein.

It will be helpful briefly to recall this conversation before we turn to the measures of nature and the primal prayers of thanksgiving in the True City. Doing so will also illuminate the philanthropic care for others through dialogue that constitutes Socrates' peculiarly philosophical piety.

At Polemarchus's home Socrates encounters Cephalus, his host's very aged father, who is crowned with a wreath because he has just performed a sacrifice in the courtyard. Noting that Cephalus stands on the threshold of death, Socrates prods him to speak about old age, and to illuminate "a road that we, too, will perhaps have to travel" (328c–e). But Socrates will *never* travel this particular road: Cephalus reveals that he spent his most vital years gratifying a multiplicity of uncontrolled appetites, and his conduct while a slave of "very many mad masters" (329d) cannot have been beyond reproach. The old man nevertheless does not seem to regret his wild youth; and while the poets' tales of punishment in the afterlife might occasionally cause him to wake up in a sweat (330d–e), he is confident that he can square his debts with the gods. The family business, the manufacture of arms, has made him a man of substance, and he has found that wealth is a perfectly adequate substitute for character in the moral economy of conventional piety. Wealth, he claims, makes it unnecessary for one "to cheat or lie to someone against one's will"—a necessity with which Socrates, a poor man (cf. *Ap.* 23b–c), is nevertheless unfamiliar—"or to depart for that place [Hades] in fear because one owes some sacrifices to a god or money to a human being" (331b).

Later in book 1, Thrasymachus defends Cephalus's implicit identification of happiness with the gratification of tyrannical *erōs*, while rejecting the fears aroused by the poets. After Socrates refutes Thrasymachus's arguments, Glaucon restates his defense of injustice in the Ring Myth of book 2, and Adeimantus, having come to the aid of his brother, joins him in urging Socrates to praise justice as they have praised injustice. But Socrates is at a loss as to how to proceed. On the one hand, he claims that he is incapable of helping out. His proof is that they didn't accept it when he showed Thrasymachus that justice is better than injustice. On the other hand, he says,

> I am afraid that it would not be pious for me to be present while justice is being spoken badly of, and to give up and not to help while I

> am still breathing and able to utter a sound. So the best thing is to help her to the extent that I am able. (368b–c)

As even this brief remark makes clear, Socrates' conceptions of character, justice, and piety are radically distinct from those of Cephalus. He agrees to the brothers' request because he feels a sacred duty to act even in the face of what reason declares to be impossible. Piety demands that he defend justice, particularly because Adeimantus has just asserted that intelligent young men are led by what is commonly said and done to infer that the gods either do not exist, do not care for human affairs, or are so unconcerned with justice that they can be bought off with sacrifices (365a–66b). Indeed, Socrates fears that anything less than absolute dedication to the cause of justice would be impious. Only death can discharge his obligation.

But who or what does Socrates feel called upon to help? The Idea of Justice—justice in itself or its intrinsic being—surely cannot be harmed by slander, but the disposition of human beings with respect to justice might well be. Socrates thus comes to the aid of justice in the souls of others, which is to say that he comes to the aid of his companions. In order to help them, however, he must come to know them; he must test his inferences about their character (cf. 368a–b) by taking their measure in philosophical conversation. While Cephalus's piety is entirely self-serving, that of Socrates, manifested in a receptivity and availability to others in dialogue, is fundamentally ethical.[2]

The Measures of Nature: Community and Sound-Mindedness

The city in book 2 that Socrates calls "true" and "healthy" (372e) is the first city in speech of the *Republic*. Socrates' account of this True City (369b–72d) is immediately followed by a description of the Feverish City (372e–73e). In narrating the growth of the True City, Socrates uncovers the original natures of man and political community as modes of being and being together that come to fruition through the social development of moderate and sensible means for satisfying basic needs. In the all-too-human life of the Feverish City, however, these wholesome modes of being are eclipsed by a sickening excess of material and poetic production.

The True City emerges from Socrates' suggestion that justice in the soul might be easier to see in the context of the city, just as letters are easier to read when they are "bigger and in a bigger place" (368d). He accordingly proposes to display the nature of justice in the soul by both "contemplating" and "making" a city in speech "from the beginning [*ex archēs*]" (369a, c). His language in this context merits close attention. The beginning of the True City is nature (*phusis*), which Socrates implicitly contrasts both with law or custom (*nomos*) and with artful human production (*poiēsis*, also the word for "poetry"). The city, a "common settlement [*sunoikia*] of partners and helpers" (369c), grows to fullness through a process of social development that is structured by the intrinsic requirements of the kind of being we are. Households (*oikoi*) are the primary locus of material production in the ancient world, and Socrates confines his discussion of the city to *oikonomia* or economics, which addresses the body's need for nourishment and protection from the harshness of the elements. He says nothing about specifically political concerns like the distribution of ruling offices or the exercise of power. Speaking only of what Nicole Loraux calls "the city of anthropologists," which "operates . . . in the repetitive time of social practices" and "renews its identity in the atemporal return of ritual gestures," Socrates completely ignores the hyper-masculine "city of classical historians," a city whose "life is military and political" and whose "history deals with constitutions and wars."[3] The True City is by classical measures an effeminate one.

The True City is distinguished by its modesty in material and poetic production as well as sexual reproduction. The basic needs served by a common settlement are food, shelter, and clothing, in that order; the "most necessary" city would thus consist of four or five people—a farmer, a house builder, a weaver, a shoemaker (369d). But the idea of specialization then occurs to Socrates and Adeimantus, as it must have occurred at a similarly early stage to human beings in the distant past: the farmer who practices only farming will do a finer job than the one who also makes his own tools.

The newly-discovered need of carpenters, smiths, and many other craftsmen will make the city more populous, but still not very big, even with the addition of herdsmen to provide animals for plowing and hauling as well as hides and wool for weavers and cobblers (370d–e). What is more, the city will require merchants and sailors to import certain necessary items, and additional farmers and craftsmen to produce excess goods for export (370e–71a). It will also require a market, coined currency, and tradesmen, and will include wage-earners who hire their bodies out for labor. And with that, Socrates asks, "has our city already grown so as to be complete [*telea*]?" (371e). Has it, in other words, reached the natural end or *telos* of efficiently satisfying the limited original needs of human beings?

Socrates goes on to consider the leisurely way of life this rudimentary but not undeveloped economy makes possible:

> Will they produce anything other than bread and wine and cloaks and shoes? And although they have built houses, in the summer they will work for the most part naked and shoeless, but in winter sufficiently clothed and shod. And they will prepare, and be nourished on, barley-meal and wheat-flour, baked or kneaded. Setting out noble cakes and loaves on some reeds or clean leaves, and reclining on rushes strewn with yew and myrtle, they and their children will feast, afterwards drinking wine and, crowned with wreaths, singing hymns to the gods, having sweet intercourse with one another [*sunontes allēlois*], but not producing children beyond their means, being wary of poverty and war. (372a–c)

Because the needs of these people are truly modest, their productive activities are minimal; they therefore have ample time to savor what Rousseau describes as the "sweet" feelings of sociability.[4] They work and live outdoors, under the sun—the heavenly body Socrates later describes as "a child of the Good, and most similar to it" (506e). Their bodies feel good; nourished by healthy food, and exercised by moderate labor in fresh air, they are healthy, fit, and tanned.

The basic mode of existence in the True City is *sunousia* or being together, the pleasurable sharing of men and women, parents and children, in a common life. This simple human community is not merely sexual, but broadly erotic; it involves various modes of fellowship, including eating, drinking, singing, and all else that is involved in a common life. What is more, this fellowship produces a joy that is its own end. Wreathed like champions in the game of life, the inhabitants of this city express gratitude for the manifest goodness of their existence by singing hymns or odes to the gods—a ceremony of thanksgiving, Socrates implies, that constitutes the original form of worship in a well-ordered community. (This is his considered reply to the selfish, petitionary piety of the wreathed Cephalus.)[5] Indeed, Socrates suggests that the regular, celebratory unanimity of the citizens in feasting and worshiping is *itself* the crowning goodness of their happy lives.

Socrates states that the residents of this city will not make children (the verb is *poiein*) "beyond their *ousia*," a word that can mean "substance" in the sense of wealth or property but also, in a more philosophical register, "being" or "essence" (cf. 485b). (Socrates' earlier question about Cephalus's "great *ousia*" [330d] is thus pointedly ambiguous.) Both meanings are in play here. Although we are given to understand that the inhabitants of this first city will live within their means, resource management and population control are the least of it. In the cultural formation of habits and dispositions, they will also respect the intrinsic measures of *human being*, the fundamentally social being that is inseparable from the being-together (*sun-ousia*) of individuals in the shared life of the city. Put simply, the poetic or productive decorum of the True City with regard to music, poetry, pastime, and the manufacture and consumption of material objects is such that it exemplifies the natural criteria of what it is to be a self-sufficient human community and a member of such a community.

In the *Republic*, the consonance of the True City furnishes the definitive natural measure of the goodness of all other human communities and human souls. This city is a happy child of the Good, before which the souls of its men and women are just as naked and visible as their sun-kissed bodies. The True City's simple and wholesome life of peace and health exemplifies the fundamental virtue that Socrates will later identify as *sōphrosunē*, the moderation or soundness of mind that he describes as a kind of singing in unison (432a). As true, the city exhibits the authentic form (*eidos* or *idea*) of the *polis*, and of human beings as members of a *polis*; as healthy, it establishes a diagnostic measure of the dissonance and sickness of individual souls as well as of the Feverish City, the Virtuous City, and Callipolis.[6]

This is the point at which Glaucon, interrupting what had been a conversation between Socrates and Adeimantus, has finally had enough. "You make these men [*poieis tous andras*] feast without relishes," he complains. A celebrated warrior and a lover of victory, Glaucon exemplifies the perspective of *andres*, politicized Greek males. Socrates might have replied that the first city does not produce *men*, but human beings; instead, he pretends to misunderstand Glaucon, as if to provoke him with the paradox of a *polis* that does not practice politics in the ordinary sense at all. He replies that they will have salt, olives, cheese, and the like, and will eat and drink in measure. "And so living their life in peace and with health, as is likely," he concludes, "they will die in old age and hand down another, similar life to their offspring" (372d).

Glaucon must be deeply shocked. From his perspective, Socrates' city lacks the very things that make life most worth living—the thrill of competition, battle, victory, and the hunt, the resplendence of glory, and the cultivated excesses of aristocratic cosmopolitanism. The True City is not just an explicit rejection of his accustomed existence; it is an assault on his dignity. Glaucon's response to Socrates—"If you were providing for a city of sows, on what else would you feed them than this?"—is deeply revealing. While the inhabitants of this city look up toward the gods, he looks down, as he supposes, on them. To Socrates' well-formed intuition of what is and grows by nature, Glaucon opposes the inflated perspective of Athenian custom. When Socrates asks him how the inhabitants of the first city ought to feast, he replies "as is conventional [*haper nomidzetai*]"—in just the way, in other words, that accords with *nomos*. "For I suppose men who aren't going to be wretched recline on couches and eat from tables and have relishes and desserts like men nowadays" (372d–e). Glaucon has in mind the equipment of symposia, where men recite poetry and discuss politics.

Socrates yields immediately to Glaucon's objection, probably because he realizes that it is pointless to argue with him. He could not have reasonably expected that Glaucon's soul would resonate to the measures of the True City, and so must continue to sound him out. "Now the true [*alēthinē*] city seems to me to be the one we just described—a healthy one, as it were. But if you wish, let us also contemplate a feverish [or 'swollen': *phlegmainousan*] city" (372e). *Lēthē* is "oblivion"; the *a-lēthinē polis* is the forgotten city that, having been uncovered through an act of intellectual imagination, has been rescued from oblivion. It is recoverable only because it constitutes the hidden or forgotten core of all actual cities, one that may still be glimpsed in the domestic satisfactions of a happy family and the intimacy of friendship, including the philosophical kind. While Glaucon's resistance obscures this healthy core, we shall see directly that the True City furnishes a general model according to which Socrates proceeds to purge the luxurious and inflamed one that he constructs in accordance with his interlocutor's desires (cf. 399e).

Socrates mimics the explosive excess of production and desire in the Feverish City by generating an ever-expanding list of commodities, artisans, and artifices that will be needed if people are to live as they do nowadays, a proliferation that recalls the stages of the True City's natural growth. The first wave of luxuries consists of couches, tables, relishes, perfumes, incenses, courtesans, cakes, painting, embroidery, gold, and ivory. While almost all of these things are adornments of the indispensable requirements of human life—food, housing, and clothes—Socrates is just getting started: "the city must be made bigger yet again, for that healthy city is no longer sufficient, but it must be filled up with a mass [*onkos*] and multitude, which are not in the cities because of necessity." The word *onkos* has a range of meanings from "bulk" or "mass" (cf. "oncology") to "dignity," "pride," and "pretension"; all of these meanings are operative in the present passage. This unhealthy mass includes "all the hunters and imitators—many concerned with figures and colors, and others with music, and poets and their helpers, rhapsodes, actors, choruses, [and] contractors" (373b–c). These hunters and imitators bring about a significant transformation, for they represent the city to itself in painting, song, poetry, drama, and dance. Such modes of creative self-conception introduce a new weight of civic self-consciousness: individuals begin to regard the city as a special, perhaps even unique entity, and to consider its particular goals and projects as essential to their own identity. The multitude of imitators, Socrates implies, is the real beginning of the sickness of the cities. Glaucon, for one, is weighed down by his conception of how real men are supposed to live; the customs and opinions that have shaped his soul stiffen his resistance to Socrates and make him hard to move.

This is not all. Socrates adds that we will need teachers, wetnurses, governesses, beauticians, barbers, relish makers, cooks, and swineherds in the luxurious city (373c). Pigs are used in sacrifices (cf.

378a); the introduction of swineherds thus hints at a fundamental transformation of religious practice from a joyful and natural theology of thanksgiving to the anxious petitionary prayer of Olympian culture. It is at this point that the manly city of history emerges from the womb of the city of anthropology. "Will we not then need to cut off a piece of our neighbor's land," Socrates asks, "if we are going to have enough to pasture and to plow, and they in turn of ours, if they, too, let themselves go to the unlimited acquisition of possessions, overstepping the bounds of the necessary?" (373d). It is not the condition of natural scarcity that pushes human beings into war, Socrates teaches, but desires, habits, and opinions that are liberated from the natural measures of human being and community. "Let us say just this much," he adds, "that we have in turn discovered the origin of war in the things whose presence in the cities most of all produces ills both public and private" (373e).

The Feverish City that Socrates has just midwifed, and that he will attempt to purge in establishing the Virtuous City, is the prototype of democratic Athens, whose ethos of unlimited expansion reached its peak in the Sicilian Expedition of 415–13.[7] It is only in relation to the True City that we can see at what a great distance we, too—the late-moderns heirs of the Athenian legacy of restless appetitive and material inflation, amplified by technical expertise—stand from nature and from one another. Yet the community of dialogue that springs up around Socrates in the *Republic* is nevertheless a temporary vestige within the Feverish City of the paradigmatic erotic fellowship of the original human community.[8]

The Measures of Virtue: Courage and Self-Control

It is in the domain of music that the essential difference between the True City and the Virtuous City is most readily apparent. The song of the True City is spontaneous and joyful, while that of the Virtuous City is deliberately imitative and regimented. "Fittingly imitating the sounds and modulations of one who is courageous in warlike action and every violent deed," as well as one who acts intelligently and measuredly in persuading or being persuaded by others, its harmonies, pitches, and rhythms aim to inculcate habits of steadiness, reliability, and cooperation in war and peace alike (399a–c). This new, specifically *political* music underscores the fact that the inhabitants of the True City are good, but not virtuous. For the interdependent notions of virtue (*aretē*), citizen (*politēs*), and regime (*politeia*) are part of a single conceptual web that is bound together by what we might call political poetry. Virtue in the Greek city is the deliberate product of a regimen of schooling—including the nurture and rearing of infants and children and the civic education (*paideia*) and military training of youths and young adults—that molds souls and bodies with myths, tunes, exercises, diets, rituals, contests, and trials of all sorts, so as to produce citizens who will embrace, sustain, and transmit the constitutive practices and beliefs of a particular regime. There is simply no need for such political poetry in the True City, which is not, properly speaking, a regime; the purposeful cultivation of virtue becomes necessary only when nature no longer suffices to generate good men and women.

Like Sparta, which it closely resembles, the Virtuous City establishes conditions under which its citizens can enjoy an active, healthy, and basically happy life of camaraderie and competition, song and sport.[9] To an ear attuned to the measures of the True City, this new city's controlled and manly harmonies are far more pleasing than the slack dissonance of the Feverish City. Yet the Virtuous City can never be more than second-best, for its very existence is an admission of corruption. In the True City, all are perfected by nature; in the Virtuous City, only some—the warriors—are perfected by political artifice. (The sequence is completed in Callipolis, where one or a very few are perfected by intellectual inquiry.) In the True City, all are naturally united in a shared way of life; in the Virtuous City, the warriors alone share one way of life, and must be taught to care for the flock they guard by means of a duplicitous origin myth, the Noble Lie. The True City is healthy; the Virtuous City, in which the illness induced by poetic excess is treated by a kind of homeopathic medicine—the purposeful stamping, molding, tuning, and dyeing of souls and bodies—is convalescent.[10]

PLATO'S REVERSAL OF HOMER

The difference between the True and Virtuous Cities is illuminated also by Plato's allusions to Homer. The investigation of justice in the soul, Socrates observes in introducing the former, requires sharp vision. Under the circumstances, it would "look like a godsend [*hermaion*]" if one could read the little letters of the soul after having first considered the same letters in the bigger format of the city—"if," he adds, "they do happen to be the same" (368c–d). A *hermaion* is, in particular, a gift of Hermes, the Olympian guide of souls and intermediary between gods and men who gives his name to the circular and oracular modes of interpretation that the Greeks were the first to call "hermeneutical."[11] Letters, for example, must be written before they can be read, and in the first instance it is Socrates who spells out his vision of the basic elements of the True City—a vision that retains its connection with the original religious context of *theōria* inasmuch as it has the ring of prophecy. For if the interpretative circle he has entered is not to be a vicious one, Socrates' story about the True City must be guided by some prior insight into the fundamental nature of the soul.

The most famous tale about a gift of Hermes is told in the tenth book of Homer's *Odyssey*, in which Odysseus narrates his encounter with Circe. When he sends a party to scout the island, Circe uses magical drugs—*pharmaka* can mean "poisons" as well as "medicines"—to turn his men into pigs. Odysseus is saved from the same fate by the intercession of Hermes, who provides him with an antidote to Circe's magic in the form of a plant:

> He drew it from the ground and showed me its nature [*phusis*].
> At the root it was black, but its flower was like milk.
> Moly the gods call it, and it is hard for mortal men to dig;
> But with the gods all things are possible. (*Od.* 10.303–306)

This is the first known occurrence (and the only one in Homer) of the word *phusis*, knowledge of which turns out to be essential to the maintenance of Odysseus's humanity and the restoration of that of his men.[12] Socrates' companions also run the risk of bestialization, but not—at least at this stage—because he treats human beings like domesticated animals. Rather, the arguments of Thrasymachus and Glaucon on behalf of injustice amount to the claim that the parts of the psyche Socrates later likens to a lion and a many-headed monster (588e–89a) should command the human part of the soul. In describing the True City, Socrates tries to save his companions by displaying the well-ordered soul and community as the efflorescence of a nature that is now hidden, like the black roots of the moly, from all but godly human beings.

But there is a crucial twist in Plato's adaptation of Homer: Glaucon's forceful objection that the True City is fit for pigs casts Socrates as Circe and *himself* as Odysseus. His protest reflects not only an appetite for luxuries, but the presence of *thumos*—Homer's word for a warrior's lion heart (cf. 375a–b). What is more, Glaucon gets his way when Socrates abandons the True City; just as in Homer, heroic manliness triumphs over effeminate domesticity.[13] What could this mean?

Glaucon's objection makes it clear that Socrates' preference for the True City amounts to a reversal of Homer and of the classical perspective of Greek heroism. The longing for glory, victory, and power, Plato implies, is a dehumanizing poison for souls and cities. This is consistent with the *Republic* as a whole, which ends with the picture of the soul of Odysseus, having recovered from his soul-sickening love of honor, choosing the quiet life of a private man (620c).[14] The Feverish City effectively reverses this reversal: Socrates' surprising capitulation to Glaucon's cultivated preferences allows manly spiritedness to assert itself in a decisive way, and effects a fateful transition from nature to history, from Loraux's city of anthropologists to that of historians. Socrates seems to regard this capitulation as merely a tactical retreat. A philosophical Circe, he has more medicines at his disposal—charming speeches with which he will appeal to Glaucon's own manly virtues, and so try to treat the sickness he has acquired from living in the Feverish City of Athens. Yet Glaucon's virtues prove to be no more solid and reliable than the Virtuous City itself.

POLITICAL ARTIFICE AND SPURIOUS WHOLENESS

The contradictions of the Virtuous City reflect the contradictions in Glaucon's soul. These contradictions are visible from the moment of the Virtuous City's birth from the Feverish City:

> It is necessary for the city to be bigger not by a little, but by a whole armed camp, which will go out and fight assailants on behalf of all

its wealth [*ousias*], and on behalf of all of the things of which we were just now speaking. (373e–374a)

Socrates' use of *ousia* in this context seems deeply ironic, for the animating principle of the Feverish City is excess—a flood of self-indulgence that repeatedly submerges all existing measures. Socrates refers to the army as a whole (*holon*), but wholeness implies limitation. How can an army that comes into being for the sake of "unlimited acquisition" (373d) be a whole? What is the source of its identity and integrity?

Socrates begins to answer these questions by repeating that those who are fitted by nature for a certain kind of work will do it best if they devote themselves exclusively to that one job (374b–c; cf. 370b). "The contest of war," he observes, is "a matter of art" (*technikē*); "to the extent that the work of the guardians is greater," he adds, "it will require more leisure than the other tasks, and the greatest art and training" (374b, d–e). For these reasons, the army must consist of professional soldiers.

Socrates' emphasis on the technical dimensions of warfare only begins to suggest the extent to which he proposes to undertake a radical refashioning of human beings as they come from the hand of nature. The unity of an army, its *esprit de corps*, derives from something more than just the devotion of individual soldiers to the art of war. Good soldiers must have lean bodies and tough charcaters as well as martial skill; above all, they must have absorbed the warrior ethos of teamwork, pride, and the overriding hope to earn the esteem of their fellows. But the ethos that binds soldiers together in life and death does not spring up spontaneously. Like the military virtues of courage and self-mastery, to say nothing of proficiency in all of the technical elements of warfare (deploying weapons, maneuvering in combat, formulating strategy and tactics, making and breaking camp, hunting and foraging for food and water, etc.), it must be purposefully cultivated. In the best case, as in the Virtuous City, it will be inculcated by a strict educational regimen that governs virtually every dimension of daily life from infancy into adulthood. In the best case, art—not nature—will furnish the necessary beginnings. And the highest art, the political art of molding souls and cities, will be the one exercised by the city's founders.

Socrates' solution to the problem of the wholeness of the army has clear pedagogical advantages and, as we shall see directly, significant historical precedent. A rigorous education will purge the warriors of the Virtuous City of the sicknesses associated with license and luxury. Glaucon, whose own military prowess and aristocratic birth and inclinations predispose him to admire these warriors, may also be moved to emulate their austere excellence, particularly if he develops a pride of ownership by taking a hand in founding the regime.[15] Yet the purged army of the Feverish City can never be more than a spurious whole. An army is subordinate to the city it serves; just so, *thumos* properly serves the soul as a whole. Socrates nevertheless tends to treat the army as the whole of the Virtuous City, while neglecting the Feverish City for whose sake it comes into being (and whose injustice toward its neighbors makes it necessary in the first place). In doing so, he calls our attention to a profound dilemma. If the army exists for the sake of unlimited acquisition, how can it protect itself from the sickness of the Feverish City? But if it ceases to regard itself as a part of the city it was born to serve, where will it derive its purpose? The immodest inflation of a part into a whole—a potentially tragic error to which spirit is no less prone than appetite—is furthermore nothing other than injustice.[16] The Virtuous City, it would seem, cannot escape its vicious origins.

SPARTA AND THE VIRTUOUS CITY

A seemingly offhand remark of Glaucon's indicates the character and anticipates the fate of the Virtuous City. In taking war out of the hands of the citizens and establishing an army of professional soldiers, Socrates contravenes Athenian custom and implicitly supports the practice of the Lacedaemonians, a society of elite hoplites (Spartiates) sustained by agricultural serfs called helots. Socrates defends himself by asking whether a man becomes an adequate combatant simply by taking in hand "a shield or any other of the weapons or tools of war." "Great indeed," Glaucon replies, "would be the worth of those tools!" (374c–d).

Glaucon's reply recalls an anecdote Thucydides tells about the unprecedented surrender of a group of Spartans starved into submission at Sphacteria in 425—the most surprising event of the war, he writes, because the Greeks "thought that neither famine nor any necessity whatsoever would make the Lacedaemonians give up their weapons." Indeed, Thucydides adds,

> they did not believe that the men who had surrendered were the equals [*homoious*] of those who had fallen, and when one of the Athenian allies some time later insultingly asked one of the prisoners from the island whether those who had fallen were noble and good men [*kaloi k'agathoi*], he replied to him that the *atraktos*, meaning the arrow, would be worth a great deal if it could pick out the good men. . . . (4.40.1–2)

The rigors of Spartan education and training were extreme. Those who passed every test of childhood and youth and were elevated to the rank of Spartiates were known as *hoi homoioi*, "the equals"—men sharing an unyielding resolve to fight to the death in battle for their fatherland.[17] The capitulation at Sphacteria, however, indicated that Lacedaemonian system, which had functioned effectively for several centuries, had finally broken down. The captured soldier's reply to the Athenian's jibe is an implicit admission of the failure of his city's acclaimed education: not all Spartiates are *kaloi k'agathoi*.

The similarities between the Spartan regime and the Virtuous City are striking. Both are founded on a program of education that aims to produce warriors who are truly noble and good (cf. 396b–c, 402a): courageous, self-controlled, and animated by the same public-spirited passions and opinions. To this end, both make extensive use of music (including poetry, song, and dance) and gymnastic (physical exercises and contests, hunts, horse races, and the like) while rejecting the traditional standards of heroic excellence introduced by Homer. Both employ a battery of tests throughout childhood, youth, and adulthood that are designed to weed out all but those whose spiritedness, self-restraint, shame before older men, and endurance in the face of pain, fear, and physical hardship render them most fit for service. Both have their soldiers dine in a common mess, and forbid them to engage in commerce, practice mechanical arts, or possess silver and gold. Both are timocratic in spirit: they center on the achievement of esteem (*timē*) through manly virtue, and reserve the greatest honors for the most valorous warriors.[18]

Socrates implicitly begins from the Spartan paradigm in reforming the Feverish City, and in fact takes it to extremes in certain respects; the zone of privacy, for example, is considerably smaller in the Virtuous City than in Sparta.[19] But the most important point of comparison lies in the violence of their origins. Plutarch tells us that the laws proposed by Lycurgus, the founder of the Spartan regime, roused his political opponents to such anger that one of them, a young man, attacked him and put out his eye. Filled with shame at the sight of his bloody face, his countrymen accepted his reforms (*Lyc.* 11.1–2). Similarly, the origins of the Virtuous City also involve a significant aggression: an indispensable, never-to-be-repeated act of political parricide, directed against the founders of the poetico-religious tradition.

Socrates begins by asking how very young children should be "reared . . . and educated" (376c); he has in mind especially the nourishment of their souls with images of virtue so as to make their characters as steady and stable as possible (401b–d; cf. 380d–81a, 388e, 396c–d). His greatest concern is to inculcate reverence for things old and ancestral. To do so, however, he must strike a blow against these very things: he must censor Homer and Hesiod, the oldest of the poets and the traditional educators of Hellas (cf. 606e). For these poets' stories of strife among the gods, and their depictions of insubordinate, immoderate, and cowardly heroes, indirectly encourage the young to rebel against their fathers. The weapon Socrates wields is a general template of political theology that is to guide all poetic productions in the Virtuous City. In particular, all *theologia*, or speech about the gods—a word whose first known occurrence, and the only one in the Platonic corpus, comes at 379a—must conform to two "patterns" (*tupoi*, the impressions left by dies in striking coins). The first is that "the god is not the cause of all things, but [only] of the good"; the second, that the god "remains forever in his own shape," neither transforming himself nor misleading others "by lies in speech or deed" (381c, 382e–83a). Socrates embraces these principles not because they are true—he admits that "we don't know where the truth about ancient things resides"—but because they are of great utility in educating citizens to be as "god-revering and divine" as possible (382d, 383c).

In constructing a virtuous regime on the basis of philosophical axioms, Socrates places politics on a radically new foundation. Through this act, as Stanley Rosen observes, he inaugurates the Western tradition of political philosophy that pursues justice through doctrinal construction.[20] Yet in one crucial respect, Socrates looks to an archaic model. The Virtuous City originates in a rejection of the ancestral authority of the poets, and a correction of their ancestral teachings—deeds over which Socrates proposes to draw a veil of silence by concealing, as far as possible, the violent theology he has suppressed (378a). On the subject of virtue, however, Socrates follows the example of Tyrtaeus, the seventh-century poet whose verses taught generations of Spartans the essential nature of civil courage. Homer praises men like Achilles, who place their own honor above that of the city, and glorifies Odysseus, who uses his cunning to preserve his own life and enrich his family. For his part, Tyrtaeus refuses to sing of any man except the one who places the welfare of the city above all, and deems no excellence worthy of celebration except "prowess in battle."[21] The blow Socrates strikes against the poets is Spartan in spirit.

THE LIMITS OF POLITICAL POETRY

The education Socrates limns in books 2 and 3 aims to produce a soul that is "most courageous and most prudent," and therefore, like the reformed gods, least susceptible to alteration (381a). Among other things, Socrates worries that the poets' depictions of Hades, death, and lamentation will make the guardians "hotter and softer" than they should be (387c). He prefers them to be cool and hard: steadfast in the face of pleasure as well as pain. In addition to courage, they will therefore need *sōphrosunē* (389d–e)—the self-regulation of desire that Socrates elsewhere credits with saving one's wits.[22] But in fact, the warriors of the Virtuous City, like the Spartans, possess only imperfect facsimiles of both of these cardinal virtues.

Moderation is a happy harmony of desire and intelligence, a condition in which all parts of the soul or city sing together (432a). In the *Republic*, it is paradigmatically exhibited in the spontaneous and measured musicality of life in the True City. It involves no forceful overcoming of wayward appetites or special strength of character, and is not to be confused with the resistance to temptation that is the best most human beings can manage. Yet Socrates almost immediately blurs the difference between moderation and self-restraint, speaking of the latter—a kind of endurance in the face of pleasure—as though it were synonymous with the former (cf. 389d with 390b, d). As in Sparta, a virtue the philosophers associate with the enjoyment of peace and leisure is assimilated in the Virtuous City to the painful discipline and fortitude called for in war.[23]

Courage or manliness [*andreia*] is another sort of perseverance: Socrates defines it as "the preservation through everything of right and lawful opinion [*doxēs orthēs*, 'orthodoxy'] about what is and is not to be feared" (430b). But just as self-mastery is inferior to moderation, the courage of politically correct conviction (*dogma*: 412e, 413c) is inferior to true courage (430c). Aristotle illuminates the difference between courage as such and political courage in the *Nicomachean Ethics*. True courage, he writes, "chooses and endures what it does because it is noble, or base not to do so" (3.7.1116a11–12). While true courage involves a moral choice that stands up to fear, political courage resembles cowardice in that it springs from fear: in illustrating its nature, Aristotle quotes passages from Homer's *Iliad* that show heroes facing great danger not because they love what is noble, or even because they long for glory, but because they dread ill repute (3.8.1116a21–26). The Spartans understood this well: the overwhelming pressure to avoid the crushing stigma of cowardice was so fundamental to their polity that they established a temple to *Phobos*, the god of Fear.[24]

While the fortitude of the Lacedaemonians in battle was legendary, they also coveted wealth and were notoriously susceptible to bribes.[25] The Virtuous City, Socrates later confirms, will in the long run succeed no better than Sparta in rooting out the lust for wealth. At the end of book 4, Socrates describes the kingship or aristocracy of the Virtuous City as the one truly good and upright (*orthē*) regime (449a). When he returns to this point in book 8, he distinguishes this city from "the one that is praised by the many, that Cretan and Laconian [Spartan] regime"—the best of four other, defective regimes whose errors he goes on to discuss (544a, c). Yet Glaucon observes in this context that Socrates effectively conflates the Virtuous City and a "still more beautiful" regime, Callipolis (543d–44a); if the Virtuous City really is inferior to Callipolis, it would seem to be identical to the Cretan and Laconian regime.[26] Socrates in any case explains that aristocracy—even one like Callipolis, governed by wise rulers with a mathematically-informed understanding of generation and decay—inevitably devolves into timocracy through insufficient attention to the begetting and education of children, with the result that the regime is pulled toward "money-making and the possession of land and houses and gold and silver" (547b; cf. 548a).

A more immediate problem is that the Virtuous City is likely to corrupt its citizens by means of the very education that is supposed to inculcate virtue. Socrates explains that contests will be established to determine who will cling most doggedly to the opinion that they must in all cases do what is best for the city. In childhood, youth, and adulthood, individuals must be "brought into terrors and in turn passed into pleasures, testing them much more than gold in fire"; "he who comes through undefiled will be appointed ruler of the city and guardian . . . and the one who is not of this sort must be rejected" (413d–14a). Socrates does not observe, however, that these repeated tests must exact a high cost from the many who flunk them. Inculcated with a deep respect for manly courage and self-discipline, yet overwhelmed by extreme fears and intense pleasures, they will have been seriously demoralized by their failure. Such men would have little inclination to put up much of a fight against temptations of any sort.

Nor will these tests suffice to guarantee the virtue of the warriors who pass them. They must also live a life of regimented austerity, and be taught a myth that, among other things, predicts the destruction of the city if a craftsmen or a farmer becomes its ruler—or if the ruling warriors begin to possess private land, houses, and currency (415–c, 417a–b). Socrates calls this myth a noble or well-born (*gennaion*) lie and "a Phoenician thing" (414b–c), partly because it echoes the myth of the Spartoi or Sown Men of Thebes, who began to slaughter one another as soon as they sprang from the ground.[27] The Noble Lie (to which we shall return in Chapter 5) thus implicitly reflects Socrates' worry that the warriors may change from sheepdogs to wolves in relation to the flock they are supposed to guard (416a). Little wonder that he casts doubt on Glaucon's assertion that they "have really been nobly educated" (416b).

A FLOOD OF EXCESS

Adeimantus is Socrates' interlocutor during most of the discussion of education in the Virtuous City (376d–98c), and Socrates associates the city with him in particular: "your city has now been founded, son of Ariston" (427c–d). Yet Glaucon is also a son of The Best, and the inquiry seems to have had a salutary effect on him. He enters the conversation when the subject of song and melody arises, and he quickly agrees that harmonic modes suitable for lamentation and symposia must be forbidden in the Virtuous City.[28] Socrates then observes that "unawares we have again thoroughly purified [*diakathairontes*] the city that a while ago we said a while was luxurious." "We are indeed moderate," Glaucon replies (399e).

In fact, Glaucon does exhibit in this context a modest and prudent awareness of his own limitations. Having just finished defining moderation as "an accord of worse and better according to nature as to which ought to rule both in the city and in each one," Socrates asks Glaucon to help locate justice. "If only I could help," he replies. "But rather, if you use me as a follower, and one capable of seeing the things you point out, you will make very measured use of me" (432a–c). Plato thus quietly indicates that the Virtuous City, second-best in comparison with the True City, is the one most suited to Glaucon's second-best nature: a nature that requires and responds to sensible guidance, and takes pride in the virtues such guidance perfects. It is in this regime that Glaucon would be most able to live a political life that is dignified, morally serious, and productive of something like happiness.[29]

But Glaucon is not destined for political virtue and happiness. Although Socrates' analogy between the city and the soul seems to have convinced him that the just life is preferable to the unjust one (445a–b), his soul contains as many contradictions as the Virtuous City. The fundamental problem is that he has been raised with bad music. He has been "reared on images of vice," and so has not learned to "blame and hate ugly and shameful things in the right way while still young"—the prerequisite, as Socrates makes clear, for becoming genuinely noble and good (401b, 402a). Like a Spartan outside of Sparta, he proves to be unsatisfied—at least when other opportunities present themselves—with the moderate enjoyment of food, drink, and thumotic and erotic satisfactions that Socrates recommends.[30]

Callipolis takes the political poetry of the Virtuous City to the next step: it presumes not just to train warriors and philosophers, but (again following the example of Sparta) to *breed* them.[31] Yet its technical manipulation of the natural process of procreation goes hand in hand with appetitive excess. Indeed, the regime that Socrates later calls "your [Glaucon's] Callipolis" (527c) turns out to be full of opportunities for self-indulgence. Socrates is right to invoke due measure at the beginning of book 5 (450b), for the various forms of appetitive, sexual, and aggressive license he would not allow even in speech in the Virtuous City are realized in deed in Callipolis. Glaucon observes that the Ring of Gyges would make it possible for one "to take without fear whatever he wants from the marketplace, and to go into the houses and have intercourse with anyone he likes, and to kill and free from bonds anyone he wants to, and to do everything else among human beings as the equal of a god" (360b–c). The fact is that in Callipolis, he would have no need of such a ring. As a warrior of outstanding mettle, he would enjoy sexual intercourse (including, with inevitably greater frequently, incest) "as often as possible" with multiple partners, and it would be impermissible for anyone, male or female, to refuse his advances while on campaign (459d, 468b–c).[32] There being "no lawsuits for assault or insult" in Callipolis—the better to encourage physical fitness, and to avoid "bigger divisions"—he would be free at all times violently to discharge his aggression against anyone he chose, including older citizens (464e–65a).[33] He would be feasted on the choicest cuts of beef, enjoying "seats and meats and full cups" (468d–e)—a quotation from the *Iliad* (8.162) that signals the reintroduction of the Homeric immoderation, in verse and deed alike, that Socrates had previously purged from the Virtuous City (see esp. 390a–b). He would be crowned with wreaths, his praises would be sung in poetry, and when he died he would be buried and worshipped as befits "daimonic and divine beings" (468b–69a).

In rewarding a select few with rich and abundant food and drink, inflaming their sexual appetites, removing conventional constraints on aggression, and plying them with honors, Socrates' modifications of the Virtuous City radically undermine the education and training in self-discipline previously provided for the auxiliaries and guardians. These modifications are also certain to generate ill-will and discord within the warrior class. Most important, Socrates asserts that the sharing of women and children (the second wave of paradox, introduced at 457c–d) will produce a "community of pleasure and pain" that will unify the city (462b). In fact, the practice of rewarding the best male and female warriors with frequent intercourse, and severely restricting sex for the worst (459c–60b), will split the citizens into one community of intense sexual pleasure and another of dispirited, painfully frustrated, and envious individuals.

The excesses of book 5 are so blatant that it is difficult not to see them as a deliberate test of Glaucon's character, rather like the pleasures and terrors into which men are deliberately cast in the Virtuous City. If so, Glaucon fails this test: far from raising objections to Socrates' proposals, he is extremely eager to know how to bring into being the regime he has described. His patience gives out at 471c, where he insists that Socrates finally address this pressing question. "For I see that, if it should come into being, all things would be good for the city in which it came to be. . . . So don't talk any more about it [the regime]; rather, let us attempt to persuade ourselves of this very thing: how it is possible and in what way it is possible, bidding farewell to all the rest" (471c–e). Socrates associates the regime with Glaucon as early as 461e, and there can be little doubt about his allegiance to it: when Socrates insists that the regime will never see the light of day unless philosophers become kings, Glaucon metaphorically marshals an army of "not ordinary men"—the very warriors they have just been discussing—who will immediately attack him if he cannot defend this seemingly absurd assertion (473e–74a).[34]

Book 5 exposes contradictions latent not only in Glaucon's soul and the Virtuous City, but also in the ostensible excellence of the Spartans. The Lacedaemonians, too, practiced a rudimentary form of eugenics (including infanticide), and to this end, as Leo Strauss observes, "gave the husband a surprisingly large freedom to indulge in adultery himself and to permit his wife to indulge." This looseness in sexual relations effectively made incest unavoidable in Sparta. In Callipolis, women exercise in the nude alongside the men (457a); Spartan girls and boys also seem to have exercised together, a practice other Greeks regarded as promoting promiscuity. In Callipolis, children are held in common and raised, as in Sparta, in a "herd" (*agelē*: 459e). Spartan fathers had paternal authority over the sons of others, and freely administered whippings to them; men in Callipolis call all children born between six and ten months after "marriage" (state-sanctioned intercourse) "son" or "daughter" (461d). As in Callipolis, the Lacedaemonians encouraged fighting in order to promote physical vigor; they established rival teams of young men who battled whenever they met.[35] As Arlene Saxonhouse observes, book 5, like the comedies of Aristophanes, is replete with animal imagery and "filled with laughter, or the mock fear of it."[36] This resemblance is not coincidental; in producing a *reductio ad absurdum* of Spartan ways and virtues, Plato follows a pattern established as early as Aristophanes' *Clouds*.[37]

But Socrates' interlocutors do not seem to be privy to his implicit criticisms of Sparta or attuned to the political inadequacies of Callipolis. Why would Socrates wish to lend even the appearance of philosophical justification to license and injustice? Why would he choose to cloak vice in a veneer of virtue? Insofar as his intention is to assay Glaucon's character, the results are significant: a soul of nobler or purer metal would not have allowed Callipolis's excesses to stand unchallenged. Socrates furthermore seems to have prepared for this failure. He seems to be betting that Glaucon's enthusiasm for the manly virtues and vices of Callipolis might open him up to the life of philosophy, the necessary condition of the regime's existence.

Pedagogically speaking, everything depends on whether Socrates can channel Glaucon's attachment to the regime into a passion for wisdom that is powerful enough to absorb and redirect his desires, and to eradicate every vestige of his manly hostility toward philosophy. Socrates' attempt to flip Glaucon's psyche in one swift motion, rather than to turn it around gradually, is not unprecedented. It is a version of what this philosophical wrestler tries to do in the *First Alcibiades*, when he presents philosophy as the necessary precondition for the realization of Alcibiades' political ambitions. It is also a long shot that carries significant risks. (At best, it had no positive effect whatsoever on Alcibiades.)[38] But it is a risk that is perhaps justified by the danger Glaucon poses to himself and others owing to the corruption that, as Socrates now knows, he carries in his soul as an Athenian born and bred. For as Socrates observes in book 6, only the best and most vigorous natures are capable of truly great injustice (491b–e).

The Measures of Philosophy: *Erōs*, Wholeness, and Science

In clarifying the measures of nature and virtue, Socrates tells a story about the genesis of the forms of life that exemplify these measures. But there is no story in the *Republic* about the emergence of philosophy. Like Athena springing from the forehead of Zeus, the philosopher, whose inner attunement to the sphere of Being recalls the natural harmonies of the True City, explodes full-blown from the mind of Socrates. This is a literary indication of the unconditioned nature of philosophy—the independence from the corruptions of history and the depredations of Becoming that is in the best case made possible by a philosophical nature. And in the Platonic dialogues, the best case is exemplified by Socrates.

Paradoxically, it is ardor, even more than intellect, through which the philosophical soul comes to possess measure. Socrates defines the philosopher as a certain kind of lover, and he gives three examples that help to clarify the distinctive nature of philosophical *erōs*. A lover of boys loves "all boys in the bloom of youth"; a lover of wine loves "every kind of wine"; a lover of honor desires "honor as a whole" (474d–75a). These lovers not only love different things, but do so in different ways. One who loves all boys—like Glaucon, an "erotic man" who serves as Socrates' example in this case (474d)—loves every individual boy, and so is (to say the least) not very choosy. Those who love every kind of wine are more discriminating; precisely because they take pleasure in the special character of each type of wine, they do not enjoy individual bottles of inferior quality. Finally, one who loves the whole of honor loves honor as such, in the distinctive integrity of its being. Taken together, Socrates' examples represent an erotic progression from fragmentary and partial embodiments of a whole to the richness of the whole itself. As he makes clear in the sequel, the lover who is capable of completing this progression moves from multiplicity to unity, from the intermediacy of generation and decay to the purity of being, or, in Platonic terms, from particular individuals to the Idea that is imaged in them. Just so, true (*alēthinoi*) philosophers, who delight in "tast[ing] every kind of learning," are simply the most dedicated and persistent lovers of wisdom—those few "lovers of the sight of the truth [*tēs alētheias*]" who do not stop short of the whole of wisdom itself (475c–e).[39] Socrates' language in this context reminds us of the penetrating insight with which he uncovers the True City, the concealed core of nature at the heart of human existence.

In Socrates' account, lovers of the whole of a thing are drawn toward the full being of that which they love; their erotic progression toward wholeness is thus the opposite of intellectual abstraction. In abstracting from certain characteristics of a particular existing thing in order to focus on others, one arrives at a concept that necessarily lacks some of the concrete richness of that thing. But in explaining that being appears fragmented and dispersed among particular existing things, Socrates turns upside down our ordinary assumption that existing things are the most real and least abstract entities. Rather, they are very nearly the *most* abstract, because they are distorted images that embody only part of the original that gives them their distinctive character, or embody it only in a partial manner. Conversely, the philosopher's erotic and intellectual progression from (for example) many beautiful existing things to the different kinds of beauty, and finally to the sight of the Beautiful itself, is a process of enrichment that reassembles or reintegrates the whole of Beauty from a multiplicity of fragmentary and deficient instantiations of it. Socrates' inquiry into the question "Who is the philosopher?" itself recapitulates this process. For in taking pains to distinguish the lover of the Beautiful itself from lovers of sight and hearing who delight in beautiful things but "neither acknowledge Beauty itself, nor, if someone should lead [them] to the knowledge of it, [are] able to follow" (476c), he attempts to grasp the erotic inadequacy of the many incomplete and defective likenesses of the philosopher so as to bring to light the distinctive erotic wholeness of the genuine article.

Philosophers sense a reality within the things they love that awaits disclosure through inquiry. The Platonic Ideas are thus more like questions than answers. What is this alluring Beauty that we glimpse in all beautiful things? The mystery of this being calls out to philosophical souls like an imminent revelation, and they answer this call. As Socrates says in book 6,

> it is the nature of one who is really a lover of learning . . . not [to] lose the keenness of his passionate love [*erōs*] or desist from it until he should touch the nature itself of each thing that is. . . . Having drawn near it and coupled with that which truly is, and having begotten intelligence and truth, he would know and live truly and would be nourished and thus cease from labor pains, but not before. (490a–b)

The desires of non-philosophers, by comparison, are incapable of leading them to the innermost nature of the things they love. The non-philosopher is like the eunuch in the riddle Glaucon refers to at 479b–c: a man who was not a man who saw and did not see a bird that was not a bird—that is, a castrated male with bad eyesight who glimpsed a bat. This riddle is meant to express the partial and ambiguous character of all existing things, but its deeper implication is that non-philosophers are no more whole or complete than the many things with which their desires and intellectual vision stop short.

More important, non-philosophers fail to achieve the deep and lasting fulfillment experienced by one who "know[s] and lives truly and thus cease[s] from labor pains." Every soul, as Socrates states in book 6, pursues the good and does everything for its sake, but only the philosophical soul is capable of discerning within the many things that appear to be good the integrity and being of the Good—the divine origin of the Whole whose gifts of life and light Socrates compares to the sun, and whose mysteries we shall explore in Chapter 5. Souls that neither dwell by nature in close proximity to the Good, as do the happy and healthy inhabitants of the True City, nor are capable of entering into its vital warmth and illumination by way of philosophy, fail to derive any advantage from anything else (505d–e). And just as eunuchs can only imagine the pleasures from which they have been excluded by the mutilation of their nature, such souls, stuck in the dark caves of the regimes that have deformed them, must experience the impotence and fruitlessness of their most fundamental desires as a source of profound frustration.

In presenting philosophers as the only human beings who are not erotically defective and therefore erotically unsatisfied, Socrates calls attention to their internal repletion and equanimity. Philosophers remain undisturbed by the powerful agitations of soul that characterize the frenzied competition of non-philosophers for "honors, praises . . . and prizes" described in the Cave Image of book 7 (516c). "For the one who has his intellect truly turned toward the things that are," Socrates tells Adeimantus, "there isn't any leisure to look down toward the affairs of human beings, or, in fighting with them, to be filled with envy and ill-will." Rather, philosophers are absorbed in the contemplation of beings "that neither do injustice, nor suffer injustice at the hands of one another, but remain all in order [*kosmōi*] according to reason" (500b–c). In a cosmos, as in a healthy city, the parts are ordered to the common good of the whole. And because philosophers, like all human beings, imitate and assimilate themselves to the things they admire, their souls inevitably reflect the tranquility and integrity of the ensemble of beings.

Allowed to grow and flourish, Socrates suggests, the passionate love of wisdom may produce the melodious soundness of mind that nature itself furnishes in the True City. But this mysterious salvation, arriving from nowhere at the center of the text—the true gift of Hermes, on which Socrates has been relying all along—is necessarily confined to individuals.[40] For if it is impossible that a multitude be philosophical (494a), and if the feverishness of the cities is rooted in the erotic incapacity and misdirection of the non-philosophical many, then political sickness is both pandemic and ineradicable. Politics, we see once again, is convalescence; the best one could hope for from any political medicine is not to cure our disease, but merely to alleviate its symptoms.

Can Glaucon in particular hope for personal salvation through philosophy? Only, Plato suggests, if he submits to the lifelong guidance of Socrates. But his *erōs* seems indiscriminate and unfocused in comparison with the genuine philosopher Socrates describes in books 5 and 6. He loves victory and is fond of luxuries, and does not object when Socrates furnished multiple examples to establish that he loves all boys "in the bloom of youth" (474d–75a). The desires of true philosophers, however, stream mightily toward wisdom, neglecting all else as they ascend from existing individuals, to Ideas or essential kinds, and finally to the Good that unifies the Whole. Having learned of the "overwhelming beauty" of the Good,

Glaucon echoes the many in wondering if Socrates is speaking of pleasure—a surmise that draws Socrates' quick rebuke: "Don't blaspheme" (509a; cf. 505b). More significantly, in mocking the notion of a Good beyond the beings that are themselves good (509b–c), Glaucon brings to mind the mistake of the mere lover of sights—the man "who acknowledges that there are beautiful things, but doesn't acknowledge that there is beauty itself" (476c).

Glaucon is not unaware of his inadequacy as reckoned by the measures of philosophy, nor does Socrates attempt to conceal his opinion of his limited abilities.[41] Yet given his courage and self-discipline in the work of warfare, his natural deficiencies would not, surprisingly enough, disqualify him from being educated to rule in Callipolis. As we shall see in Chapter 6, the warriors that most exemplify Glaucon's own political virtues are tested one last time by a gymnastic that is the "antistrophe of the bodily gymnastic" (539d). They are subjected to severe intellectual labor in mathematical science and logic, habits of thought that will be honed and tested in philosophical debate, and they cannot cross the threshold of ruling power until they pass through to a battery of examinations. Future philosophers and kings are thus trained to achieve mental agreement with the formal structures of being, structures whose ontological stability may be said to display the nature of lawful order as such. This rigorous schooling is analogous to the training of warriors in the Virtuous City. It is designed to impress on the souls of Callipolis's rulers a specifically intellectual discipline, including a new sort of combat in which they must deploy new tools. In learning the strategies and tactics of high-level philosophical argumentation, they may acquire a specifically dialectical courage and moderation—virtues that will incline them to impress a broader lawfulness on the character of the city. These are, in fact, Socrates' last and somewhat desperate measures in the *Republic*. For to the extent that these intellectual forms of lawfulness are musical and beautiful, they are so only for genuinely philosophical souls. Anyone else must approach this abstract education as a pure grind.

The philosophers of Callipolis are made, not born; an artifice generated by political necessity is called on to supply that which is missing and cannot be acquired by nature.[42] Only in this way can the regime hope to "roll on like a circle in its growth" (424a), for nature cannot be counted on to produce a reliable supply of philosophically erotic souls; the history of Plato's family, from Solon down to Critias, makes this much clear. But the ruling class of Callipolis also runs downward—proving, by its inevitable degeneration, that rearing and education are no substitute for nature.

Why does Socrates choose to blur the erotic nature of philosophy that he had previously made so clear? Why does he speak as if philosophers could be produced and engineered by the regime? Why does he not only fail to correct Glaucon's assertion that the philosopher-kings are "altogether noble and beautiful" (540c), but present them in a way that is virtually guaranteed to elicit this judgment: as "best in philosophy and with respect to war" (543a)? A general answer to these questions is already at hand, for Glaucon's resistance to Socrates' measures of goodness and virtue makes it clear that he will not be satisfied to live in a society in which he cannot aspire to the highest honors and offices. Socrates can do nothing without accommodating himself to Glaucon's aristocratic prejudices and passions, and contending with the particular influences that have molded his unusually vigorous nature. Much of this story, however, remains to be told. If we are to understand Glaucon on the deepest level, we must bring from the shadows a figure that we have so far largely neglected: Critias, whose ideas play a crucial role in the *Republic* even though he is never mentioned by name.

CHAPTER 3

Tyranny, Poetry, and Science

CRITIAS IN THE FRAGMENTS AND THE DIALOGUES

One cannot consider the *Republic* in its historical context without being struck by the resemblance between Callipolis and the oligarchy of the Thirty. Both regimes—one existing only in speech, the other implemented and sustained by increasingly bloody deeds—claim the title of aristocracy, subordinating the many to a cadre of hoplites directed by a small circle of rulers with absolute political power. Both deplore the expansionist, maritime, and commercial ethos of the Athenian democracy, and Sparta is their common denominator.

Critias asserted that "more men are good by practice than by nature" (DK frag. 9), and the training he favored was Spartan. He wrote a *Constitution of the Lacedaemonians* in meter and another in prose; the extant fragments of these writings praise Spartan customs, including those relating to diet, drink, and exercise. Critias and the other Athenian Laconizers who established the Thirty modeled the political structure of the regime on Sparta, and might have imitated other Spartan practices had time permitted.[1] Like Critias's ruling cadre, the Spartan *gerousia* or Council of Elders also consisted of thirty men. Critias compared the leaders of the Thirty to the five Spartan Ephors or Overseers. Like the Spartan kings, the Thirty employed a guard of 300 lash-bearers. The Thirty compiled a list of 3,000 citizens who were to compose the new Athenian Assembly; this was the approximate number of full Spartan peers in 404. Athenians from the lower orders and other outside the Three Thousand were disarmed and ultimately evicted from the city; the regime thus created a subordinate class resembling the *perioikoi* or "dwellers-about" who lived in the villages around Sparta.[2]

The Thirty were backed by a garrison of Spartan hoplites (heavily armed warriors) who occupied the Acropolis. Lysias refers to these men as "auxiliaries" [*epikouroi*] who functioned as "guardians" of the regime [*phulakes*]; these are the exact terms Socrates uses in the *Republic,* where he furthermore recommends that the auxiliaries be stationed in "the most beautiful place in the city for a military encampment, from which they could most of all hold down those within . . . and ward off those without" (415d–e).[3] Aristotle, too, says that Socrates "makes the guardians a kind of garrison, and the farmers and artisans and the rest [he makes] citizens" (*Pol.* 2.5.1264a). The subordination of agricultural laborers and craftsmen in the *Republic,* and especially the expulsion of adults to the countryside, which Socrates recommends as the quickest way to actualize the regime (540e–41a), anticipate the Thirty's disenfranchisement and expulsion of the majority of their fellow Athenians. Finally, the auxiliaries and older guardians of the *Republic*'s regime correspond, respectively, to the Spartiates/3,000 and the Gerousia/Thirty, while the philosopher-kings of Callipolis—a super-aristocracy of exceptional individuals, "best in philosophy and with respect to war" (543a)—are a match for both Sparta's Ephors and kings and Critias's ruling cadre.

The Thirty reflected their preferences even in the new political geography of the city: they remodeled the platform where the Assembly met so that it no longer faced outward toward the sea, the medium of empire under the democracy, but inward toward the land.[4] The oligarchs, Lysias tells us, proposed "to purge [*katharan poiēsai*] the city of unjust men, and to turn the rest of the citizens toward virtue and justice" by restoring what they claimed was the ancestral constitution (Lys. 12.5). Callipolis, too, practices a politics of aristocratic purity. In constructing the Virtuous City, Socrates and his interlocutors "thoroughly purge" the Feverish City of corrupting music (399e); Callipolis augments this cathartic education with eugenics, and employs philosophical education as one last super-aristocratic filter. Designed to exclude from ruling office souls that, in the terms of the Noble Lie, contain anything other than pure gold (cf. 415a–c), this arduous education in mathematical and logical subjects is offered only to courageous and moderate warriors and, in principle, strains out any remaining admixture of base metals.

Callipolis's resemblance to the Athenian oligarchy of 404–03 is a particularly complex instance of Plato's historical irony. Aeschines, a fourth-century Athenian orator, states that the Athenians executed "the sophist Socrates . . . because he was shown to have educated Critias"; Xenophon writes that Socrates' accusers linked him with Critias and Alcibiades, who "became companions of Socrates and did the greatest evils in respect to the city."[5] Does Plato, too, mean to suggest that Socrates' teachings were reflected, if not in Critias's character, at least in his radical political program? Or does this assumption get things backward? Is Socrates echoing Critias's ideas in the *Republic*? If so, why?

In order to reply to these questions, we must consider the evidence pertaining to Critias's thought and character in the surviving fragments of his writings, as well as in Plato's *Timaeus-Critias* and *Charmides*. Only then will we be able to appreciate the extent to which Critias's ideas pervade the *Republic*, entering the conversation through the seminal arguments of Thrasymachus and Glaucon and shaping essential dimensions of Socrates' response to these arguments. The dramatic story of the *Charmides*, in which Socrates enters the scene as a returning war-hero, is illuminating in other ways as well. It concretely foreshadows the tyrannical future of Critias and Charmides, and vividly illuminates Socrates' resistance to the powerful temptations that destroy these men. The dialogue also displays two distinct approaches to the sickness of the human psyche, juxtaposing Socrates' holistic, erotic, and musical medicine for individual souls with Critias's preference for crude and forceful purgations of the body politic.

According to the Eleatic Stranger who visits Athens at the time of Socrates' public indictment on charges of impiety and corrupting the young, the sophist causes the young to mistake the mere appearance of wisdom for its reality, and so leads them away from humanly essential truths (*Soph.* 233a–34e). Plato shows that Critias is himself a sophist in just these respects. He is dangerous to cities and souls alike, for he usurps and transforms Socratic philosophizing in fashioning a dream of scientific tyranny that mistakes itself for the wakefulness of wisdom. Critias the Laconophile projects a distorted image of the apparent excellence of the Spartans; Critias the intellectual confuses mere opinion with scientific knowledge, and science with wisdom; Critias the poet fails to distinguish between his idealized vision and historical actuality. While Socrates proves to be as steadfast in defense of the truth and justice as he is in war, Critias's métier is a deceptive slide of thought that turns even tentative philosophical speculations into instruments of personal aggrandizement.[6]

Invention and Esotericism in Critias's Political Poetry

Names sometimes reveal natures. Socrates son of Sophroniscus—Saving Strength, son of Sound Mind—is a case in point. Critias was the son of Callaeschrus, Noble-Shameful or Beautiful-Ugly. Paradoxical duality ran in his blood.

Critias disparaged the poet Archilochus for besmirching his own reputation by divulging his low birth, poverty, and cowardice (DK frag. 44). He himself was concerned to project resplendent nobility: virtue, poetic creativity, philosophical intelligence, and power. Plato makes clear the pride and rivalry he feels toward his ancestor Solon, a famously wise lawgiver and poet (*Tim.* 21a–d), and his eagerness to earn praise for the aristocratic virtues of his ward and prize pupil Charmides, a youth of marvelous size and beauty whom Jean Ducat describes as "the stereotype of the perfectly educated young boy."[7] When Critias boasts that Charmides is "a lover of wisdom" and "very poetic," Socrates generously replies: "This thing—noble beauty [*to kalon*]—belongs to your family from way back, on account of your kinship with Solon" (*Chrm.* 154e–55a). Socrates' remark is true enough; Critias's intelligence and creativity are typical of the family, and run from Solon right down to Glaucon and Plato.[8] But for all that beauty, Plato portrays Critias as arrogant, impious, and covetous (qualities reflected in his political record), and Charmides as his henchman.

The most important text among Critias's fragments is a speech that comes down to us from Sextus Empiricus, who attributes it to the character of Sisyphus in an unidentified drama. The speech is worth quoting in full.[9]

There was a time when the life of human beings was disordered
And bestial, and subservient to might,
When there was no prize even for the good,
And in turn no chastisement came to be for the wicked.
And then human beings seem to me to establish
Chastising laws, in order that justice might be tyrant
<... words missing> and hold hubris as a slave;
And if someone went thoroughly wrong he was punished.
Thereafter when the laws kept them
From openly doing deeds by violence,
And they did them in secret, then, it seems to me,
<word missing> some man shrewd and skilled in thought
Discovered [*exeurein*] fear <of gods> for mortals, in order that
There might be some terror for the wicked, even if
They do or say or think <something> in secret.
From this motive, then, he introduced the divine,
Saying that it is a deity abounding with unstinting life,
And hearing and seeing by mind, both thinking
And attending to all things, and bearing a divine nature,
Who will hear everything that is said among mortals,
And will be able to see everything that is being done.
"And if you silently plan an evil thing,
This will not escape the notice of the gods, for intelligent thought
Is in <them>." Saying these words,
He introduced the sweetest of teachings,
Concealing the truth with a false speech.
And he asserted that the gods dwelt in that place, where
He would most astonish human beings when he led them to it,[10]
The very source from which he knew that there are fears
And benefits for mortals in their miserable life:
From the revolving vault above, where he observed
Lightning flashes, and fearsome crashes
Of thunder, and the starry-faced frame of heaven,
Beautiful fabric of Time, a skilled builder,
From where the bright hot mass of the star approaches

And the moist rain-shower goes out into the earth.
With such fears he surrounded human beings,
And through them, in speech, he beautifully settled [*katōikisen*]
This deity in a fitting region,
And quenched lawlessness [*anomia*] by means of customs [*nomois*].
<lines missing> Thus for the first time I think someone persuaded
Mortals to believe [*nomidzein*] that there is a race of deities.

The traditional attribution of the Sisyphus fragment to Critias has recently been questioned in the scholarly literature, but not persuasively. One influential article asserts that two authors from later antiquity correctly assigned the fragment to Euripides, but ignores crucial evidence pertaining to Critias's ancient reputation as an atheist.[11] In itself, the fact that the character of Sisyphus embraces atheism proves nothing about Critias's views; Dana Sutton's claim that "no contemporary or near-contemporary writer . . . imputes atheism to Critias or associates him with the sophistic movement in any way" is nevertheless false.[12] Critias is present along with a number of foreign sophists in Plato's *Protagoras*, and seems to be on familiar terms with Prodicus and Hippias (326d–e).[13] Sisyphus's speech engages Hippias's idea of *nomos* as tyrant (*Prot.* 337c–d); more important, the character of Critias in the *Timaeus-Critias* and *Charmides* so lavishly echoes the speech's essential points and emphases that we may be inclined to agree with Laurence Lampert's description of him as "the greatest Athenian sophist."[14]

Sisyphus's skilled or wise (*sophos*) thinker is a mythmaker who fundamentally reshapes beliefs, customs, and laws in fashioning new dogmas about the gods (25, 40–42).[15] Line 38 implicitly compares this poet to *oikistai*, the founders of colonies who were often also lawgivers, evincing what Doyne Dawson identifies as a hallmark of sophistic thought in the fifth century: a "self-conscious view of the state as a human invention and . . . [an] experimental attitude toward politics that were rooted in the colonizing experience."[16] As the leader of a revolution, Critias was necessarily a mythmaker; the founding myth of Athens he tells in the *Timaeus-Critias* (discussed below) displays the richness of his political poetry and the depth of his ambition as a founder and lawgiver. Sisyphus's wise man contemplates the heavens as a physicist or natural scientist, after the fashion of the pre-Socratic cosmologists (31–36); liberated by knowledge, he uses *nomos* to bind the ignorant. Plato's Critias similarly remarks on "the inexperience and extreme ignorance" of human beings regarding the gods (*Criti.* 107b), and invents a demythologizing priest who reveals to Solon the purely meteorological phenomena that underlie Greek myths about the gods (*Tim.* 22b–23b).[17]

Like the myth of human origins told by Plato's Protagoras (*Prt.* 320c–22d), the Sisyphus fragment posits an initial condition of brutality that is resolved by a superior political intelligence.[18] The fragment teaches that political order is founded on physical and emotional mastery rather than rational persuasion: the original chaos and savagery of human life is overcome by the tyranny of justice (*dikē*) in the form of "chastising laws" (6), later augmented by the terror of divine punishment. Elsewhere, in the context of a discussion of the helots, Critias remarks that men are most free and most enslaved at Sparta—suggesting, as Dawson has noted, "that the one condition requires the other."[19] What is more, he nakedly practiced the politics of force and manipulation in the time of the oligarchy. According to Xenophon, Critias explained to Theramanes, one of the Thirty who complained that the leaders were putting too many men to death, that "it is necessary that those changing the government here to an oligarchy have the greatest number of enemies, both because this is the most populous of the Greek cities, and because the people have been nurtured in freedom for the longest time" (*Hell.* 2.3.24). He immediately went on to wield the letter of the new law as a weapon, using executive privilege to remove Theramenes from the Three Thousand—whose members alone were entitled to a vote of the Council on capital offenses—so that he could be summarily executed.[20]

Critias presumably derived support for his conduct from the idea that politics is a productive art of crafting souls and bodies; the cobbler, after all, does not seek the leather's permission to work and shape it into a shoe. This notion, fully articulated in the Sisyphus fragment's conception of human beings as raw material to be fashioned by godlike men using the instruments of law and custom, is probably traceable to Protagoras. In the *Protagoras*, the eponymous sophist teaches that human beings are by nature blank slates: they come into the world "naked, unshod, unbedded, and unarmed," wholly bereft of the natural powers of the non-rational animals, and unable even to "articulate sounds and words" (321c, 322a). However this may be, the lofty perspectives of Protagoras and the poet/law-giver of the Sisyphus fragment have much in common. Protagoras downplays his superiority to the many (cf. *Prt.* 328a–b), but does not entirely conceal it. While "the powerful human beings of the cities" saw through the disguises of the sophists of old, he notes, "the many, so to speak, perceive nothing, but merely sing the tune these men announce" (*Prt.* 317a). In Plato's *Theaetetus*, Socrates describes Protagoras as an "all-wise" esotericist who poses riddles "for us, the vast mob, but for his pupils speaks the truth in secret" (152c; cf. 161c). The wise inventor of the gods in Critias's fragment is of necessity similarly cautious; the verb *exeurein* in line 13, "to discover," suggests the masked creativity of his act. Sisyphus takes no such pains: in his telling, this political poet towers above the ignorant multitude and their "miserable life" (30).

In the poetic tradition, Sisyphus suffers divine punishment for his overt defiance of the gods (Hom. *Od.* 11.593–94); in the fragment, he avenges himself on the gods by declaring that they do not exist. It is a safe bet that the gods get the better of this argument in the drama of which the fragment is a part. But there is good reason to believe that Sisyphus's fate serves as cover for Critias's atheism, deceptively implying that he has no truck with the very notions he wishes cryptically to endorse.

Unmasking the Delphic God

Several scholars have recognized that Critias does indeed embrace esotericism about the gods in the *Charmides*, where Plato presents him as a demanding tutor of his young cousin—a would-be sculptor of souls and poet of everyday life who manipulates others in the presumption of his wisdom.[21] Critias sets the stage for Socrates' examination of Charmides by directing his slave to lie to the youth about Socrates' identity, and (with characteristic impudence) only then asking Socrates to go along with the deception that he is a doctor who can treat headaches (155a–b). Critias's substitution of technical expertise for philosophical understanding is typical of the sophists—Protagoras identifies *politikē sophia* and *politikē technē* (cf.

Prt. 321d with 322b)—and it represents Socrates as both more and less than he actually is. More, because he possesses no such medical art; less, because Critias reduces to a narrow skill whatever sound-mindedness Socrates may possess by nature, or whatever wisdom he may have acquired by philosophy.

Socrates nevertheless plays along. Having just returned from a long campaign in Thracian Potidaea, he claims to have learned a charm for the youth's headaches "from one of the Thracian doctors of Zalmoxis, who are also said to make men immortal" (156d). The Thracians, Herodotus writes, have worshiped Zalmoxis, a former slave, ever since (as some say) he is supposed to have returned from death, having actually disappeared into an underground chamber and then emerged after three years in hiding (4.95). The Greeks of the Hellespont furthermore attribute his success in this ruse to his association with Ionians, including his former master Pythagoras, "not the weakest sophist of the Greeks" (4.95.3). Socrates' story echoes that of Zalmoxis. He has been away from Athens for almost three years, as Critias would be during his exile in Thessaly in 406–04, and he, too, seems to have escaped death: he comes to the wrestling school of Taureas *ex aprosdokētou*, "from an unexpected place"—an unusually violent battle in which many Athenians were slain (153b–c). The *Charmides* thus begins by referencing, in deed and speech alike, a myth about a sophistically-trained man who presents himself as immortal and deceives others about the gods.[22]

Plato frequently locates especially important or questionable material in the middle of his dialogues, as he does in the *Charmides*.[23] This dialogue's central section concerns the Delphic oracle, and the injunction of the Delphic Apollo to "Know Thyself."[24] In a rather cryptic speech, Critias rejects the fundamental teaching of the Greek religious tradition, affirmed by Socrates in the *Apology* (23a–b), about the radical inferiority of mortals to immortals:

> I pretty much assert that this is soundness of mind [*sōphrosunē*]: to know oneself, and I agree with the one who set up the inscription of that sort at Delphi. For this inscription seems to me to be dedicated as a salutation of the god to those entering [the temple] instead of "Rejoice"—as this salutation, "Rejoice," is incorrect, and they should instead exhort one another to "Be of Sound Mind." Thus indeed the

> god addresses those entering into the temple in a manner different from that of human beings, as the one who dedicated the inscription intended, so it seems to me. And he says to each who enters [*ton aei eisionta*] "Be of Sound Mind"—this is what he says. But he says it in a riddling way, like a diviner. For "Know Thyself" and "Be of Sound Mind" are the same, as the inscription asserts, and so do I. But someone might perhaps think that they are different—the mistake, as it seems to me, of the ones who set up the later inscriptions "Nothing to Excess" and "A Pledge, then Perdition." For these supposed that "Know Thyself" was a piece of advice, but not the god's salutation of those who were entering. (164d–65a)

Critias's interpretation of the injunction to seek self-knowledge ironically rests on his presumption of possessing it. According to Critias, who never mentions Apollo by name, the one who inscribed "Know Thyself" on the temple at Delphi spoke for the god in a way that distinguished him from most other men. Far from being a piece of divine instruction addressed to all human beings, he claims that this inscription has an exoteric surface and an esoteric core: what it says to the few who enter into (*eisō*) the temple—the priests and priestesses who administer the oracle and speak for the god, and (in an extended sense) those who share their privileged understanding—is misunderstood by the many who remain outside (*exō*). In the inscription, the god greets those who know the temple from the inside as one hails one's friends and equals. Those who remain outside are not only incapable of solving the riddle of the inscription, but do not even recognize it as a riddle. They take the god to be giving cautionary advice, the authority of which is rooted in the perception of a fundamental difference between gods and human beings, and they do not understand that the god to whom they attribute the inscription is, as Seth Benardete remarks, "nothing other than the man who wrote it down."[25] In his own riddling way, Critias erases this difference for himself, and for others in the know, while maintaining it for the multitude. His phrase *ton aei eisionta*, literally "the one ever entering," hints at the divinity of those on the inside: *hoi aei ontes*, "they who are always," is good Greek for "the immortals."

Socrates claims in the *Protagoras* that "Know Thyself" and "Nothing to Excess" were inscribed on the temple at Delphi by the Seven

Sages; the central figure in his list of these wise men is Solon (343a–b). Critias separates these maxims, and disparages the understanding of those who authored the second one; self-knowledge, he implies, does not entail moderation in the ordinary sense of the word. As W. Thomas Schmid observes, Critias's speech about the Delphic oracle dispenses altogether with "the normative voice of revelation," substituting—in the midst of a discussion of moderation, no less—"the amoral human praise of self-certainty" for the "divine moral counsel of self-restraint."[26] This substitution flies in the face of Socrates' characteristic self-subordination to the obligations of a superior divinity, to say nothing of his knowledge of ignorance, the philosophical core of his sound-mindedness.[27] It also exemplifies Critias's tendency to appropriate both traditional and contemporary ideas, including the thought of Socrates, in ways that efface the distinction between philosophy and poetry, the acquisition of knowledge and the production of fiction.

Plato explores Critias's ways of playing the philosopher in the *Timaeus-Critias* and *Charmides*, dialogues that are thematically and dramatically connected with the *Republic*. Glaucon deliberately engages and rivals Critias's mythmaking in the political archaeology of the Ring Myth, while Socrates' Myth of Er, a philosophical reply to Glaucon that astronomically expands the horizons within which the ultimate beginnings of human existence come into view, echoes the poetic cosmology of Timaeus in form and action alike. The *Charmides*, too, anticipates essential dimensions of the *Republic*. But it also presents a richly concrete picture of Socrates as a man in full: physically rugged, tough-minded, spirited, sexual, and replete with curiosity and intelligence. It thus helps us to see Socrates as the best young Athenians must have seen him, and so to appreciate his magnetic influence on the likes of Alcibiades, Charmides, and the sons of Ariston.

Outperforming Solon: The Fabulous Athenians of the *Timaeus*

The *Timaeus* and *Critias* are connected with the *Republic* both dramatically and substantively. These dialogues, too, take place during a religious festival: the Greater or Lesser Panathenaea (cf. *Tim.* 21a), celebrations of the eponymous patron goddess of Athens. Starting with the *Timaeus*, Socrates is treated to a feast of speeches honoring Athena in exchange for those he served up to "yesterday's feasters" (17a). As in the *Republic*, the conversation of the *Timaeus-Critias* is conspicuously situated within the historical context of the Peloponnesian War. Socrates is hosted by Critias and two foreign visitors, Timaeus and Hermocrates; these two are noblemen from Locri and Syracuse, cities that fought against the Athenians during the war.[28] Both cities were settled by the same people who settled Sparta: Dorians, a tribe that emphasized the rigorous cultivation of manliness. While Plato seems to have invented the character of Timaeus, Hermocrates was a leader of the Syracusan oligarchs who played a crucial role in defeating the Sicilian Expedition.[29]

Critias's contribution to "today's" feast must also be considered in relation to the war. His account in the *Timaeus* of Solon's visit to Egypt prefaces the myth of Atlantis that he tells in the *Critias*. Solon learns in Egypt that the region of Attica was once inhabited by "the noblest and best race among human beings" (*Tim.* 23b)—paleo-Athenians whose aristocratic republic defeated invaders from the now submerged island of Atlantis when they sought to enslave the entire region around the Mediterranean Sea (22c–25d). The story of the defeat of Atlantis has the tragic, timeless quality of an unheeded warning. It implicitly celebrates the young and lean Athenian democracy that led the Greeks in rebuffing another barbarian empire, that of the Persians, and anticipates the sinking of the very same city—now a bloated new Atlantis—in the quagmire of Syracuse almost seventy years later.[30]

Most important for our purposes, Socrates' recapitulation at the beginning of the *Timaeus* of the head part (*to kephalaion*) of the speeches he recounted yesterday about the best regime (*aristē politeia*) reads like an overview of the city discussed at the home of Cephalus in the dialogue called *Politeia*, except that it omits everything after the second wave of book 5, including the entire discussion of philosophical *erōs* and the rule of philosophers. Socrates' reference to "speeches" (17c) may suggest that yesterday he narrated what was originally a dialogue, but if so, it cannot have been the one he relates in the *Republic*: the festival of Bendis was held two months earlier than the Panathenaea. He nevertheless invites Plato's readers to compare his summary with the *Republic* when he wonders whether something might be missing from it (19a).[31]

Socrates observes that one of the four guests who was present yesterday is absent today, and states that "the work of filling the part of the one who is missing" falls to Timaeus and his companions (17a). Conditions are ripe for a test of his interlocutors, who must satisfy his desire to see the city he has described engaged in fighting battles and negotiating with enemies (18b–c).[32] His question about the possible incompleteness of his summary underscores in particular the absence of philosopher-kings from his synopsis of the best regime. Timaeus and Critias proceed to fill this double void, and Socrates gives us a sense of what we can expect from each. Timaeus, he says, hails "from the city in Italy with the best laws, Locris, and being second to none there in substance and birth [*ousiai kai genei*], has taken in hand the greatest offices and honors in the city, and has, in turn, in my opinion arrived at the summit of all philosophy" (20a). Of Critias, he remarks only that "everyone, I suppose, knows that he is a layman in none of the things we are speaking of" (20a). Timaeus goes on to display great theoretical imagination and mathematical sophistication in speaking of the cosmos. But the work of philosophers in the *Republic* is not entirely, or even primarily, theoretical: Socrates introduces them in order to explain how the city in speech might be brought into being. Are we to understand that Critias—who is thumotic, but not philosophically erotic, and who insists on the historical truth of the Atlantis tale—will begin to perform an equivalent task of actualization in the *Timaeus*?[33]

Plato at any rate calls attention to what Critias *does* with Socrates' city in speech. Critias explains how he and his companions plan to satisfy Socrates' request to see his city at war: first, Timaeus will discuss the origins of the cosmos and of human beings; then he himself, identifying some of these human beings with the well-educated citizens Socrates described yesterday, will make them citizens of Athens and narrate their struggle against the men of Atlantis almost a millennium ago (26c–27b).[34] Critias's story about Solon's visit to Egypt is meant to whet Socrates' appetite for the main course to come. Nested within this preface is another story, one that professes, on the good authority of priestly documentation, to preserve the memory of greatly distant events. Yet there are ample grounds for doubt about the narrative he presents in the *Timaeus-Critias*: told, forgotten, and retold over centuries, increasingly garbled or embellished with each iteration, and finally adapted for the present occasion, his tale of the first Athenians must necessarily be woven from a few strands of fact and a hank of fiction. Critias replaces the ruling guardians of Socrates' regime with a cadre of scientific priests; maintains that this reconfigured tripartite regime, founded by Athena from divine seed (*sperma*) that was taken from Earth and Hephaestus, was the original city of Athens; and asserts that its near-image still exists in Saïs (23d–24d). All of this is meant, among other things, to suggest the feasibility of the archaic Athenian regime as a practical political model.

But we are getting ahead of ourselves. Socrates has prompted us to wonder about gaps in what is said or recollected on the present occasion, and to ask how these gaps will be filled. Let us consider the omissions and deficiencies of the *Timaeus* as they arise.

Socrates desires to see his city display its "education and nurture" in the deeds and speeches of war, but deems himself incapable of providing the encomium he envisions. In his opinion, moreover, neither the poets nor the sophists are up to the task, which concerns a life of virtuous political engagement they have not lived and do not know. Poets are rooted in particular times and places and speak local dialects; Socrates calls them an *ethnos* or tribe (19d). But for all their idiomatic fluencies, poets—including "those who came to be long ago and those who are now" (19d)—are incapable of imagining and imitating things outside their upbringing. Their art works on the raw material of inherited tradition, with all of its excesses and vices (cf. *Rep.* 401a). Sophists, on the other hand, are "very experienced in many other beautiful accounts," but their lack of any fixed abode—they dwell within the firmament of scientific discourse, "wandering [*planēton*] over the cities"—makes them unsuited to speak of "men who are at once philosophers and statesmen," and so to do justice to Socrates' theme (19c–e). Because they exist as far as possible in the cosmopolitan sphere of international celebrity, sophists are strangers to their native cities and fellow citizens, and cannot speak meaningfully of the attachments and commitments that root human beings in their communities.

Is there a middle ground between the poets' corrupting saturation in everyday life and the sophists' uncitizenly detachment from the same? Where could one find someone displaying such measure in speech and deed? Socrates asserts that his companions do not share the defects peculiar to the poets and the sophists, although only his description of Timaeus, to whom Critias is clearly a distant second in his estimation, gives one confidence that this might be so. Critias nevertheless claims the lead in planning the speeches that are to satisfy Socrates' desire, revealing a love of preeminence that, judging by Glaucon's behavior in the *Republic*, seems to run in the family. But his plan is riddled with temporal and logical gaps that can be spanned only by artful discourse. The story Critias fabricates for this purpose reveals itself to be a fiction masquerading as a scientific history—a brilliant hybrid of poetry and sophistry that nevertheless reflects the moral and intellectual shortcomings of both.

On the occasion of his initiation as a child into his family's clan at the festival of the Apatouria—a festival at which he competed in reciting epic poetry, thereby learning of poetry's importance and seriousness[35]—Critias heard what he is careful to call an "account" (*logos*: 20d, 21a), of "the greatest and most justly famous of all deeds": the defeat of the invading armies of Atlantis by the Athenians some nine thousand years previously (21d; cf. *Criti.* 108e). He will present this account in the form of a narrative that he performs for his companions as in a poetic competition before a theater audience (*theatron*: *Criti.* 108b, d). This narrative, he nevertheless maintains, differs from a mere story (*muthos*) in that it tells of actual historical events that are attested by authoritative sources, events that can be known with precision because they have been preserved in writing (23c, e).[36] His speech may have "the shape of a story," yet will be (as Socrates generously allows) "not a fabricated story, but a true account [*alēthinon logon*]" about deeds "not spoken of, but genuinely performed" (21a, 22c, 26e). Critias aspires, however, to have his monologue accepted and acknowledged as what a Greek political myth fundamentally *is*: an ancient tale of gods and men, told and retold, that gives a people its foundational identity by revealing its origins.

The paradoxical character of Critias's performance is especially apparent when seen in the light of his obvious desire to be acclaimed by his audience (cf. *Criti.* 108b–c). If he is merely repeating a speech he once heard, he deserves little credit for his performance; if the speech substantially originates with him, its plausibility as a report of actual events is compromised. Critias tries to resolve this particular paradox by representing his account as true and accurate, but incomplete. Considered from an evidentiary perspective, however, his speech is beset with inconsistencies.

Critias states that Solon told his great-grandfather Dropides the tale of Athens' defeat of Atlantis, and Dropides subsequently told the story to his son Critias. Later, however, Critias omits Dropides from the chain of transmission, making it seem as if Solon spoke directly to his namesake (20d–e, 25d–e).[37] He claims to have learned the account by overhearing a conversation between Critias and a man named Amynander; later, he maintains that he questioned Critias at length; still later, that his grandfather had notes written by Solon ("who had it in mind to use the account for his own poetry," but never got around to it), and that these notes are now in his possession (21d, 26c, *Criti.* 113a–b). With multiple qualifications that suggest the abysses he must bridge by poetic invention, Critias tells Socrates that "I was struck with wonder in recollecting the things I am now saying, because I realized how daimonically, from some chance, you weren't far from the mark in agreeing for the most part with what Solon said" (25e). He says he kept quiet at first because "I did not remember adequately owing to the lapse of time. So I thought I ought not to speak in this way until I had recovered everything by myself." Yet he also says that he began to relate what he remembered to Timaeus and Hermocrates as soon as he left Socrates' company, and only later that night went on to recover what he had forgotten (25e–26a).

Perhaps most obvious is the gap that separates Critias's poetic and political turn of soul from Socrates' philosophical one. His suggestion that Socrates is insufficiently concerned with truth radically distorts the difference between the two men:

> [T]he citizens and the city you went through for us yesterday as in a story [*en muthōi*], we, having now transferred them here into the truth [*epi t'alēthes*], shall set down that city as being that very one [of ancient Athens], and we shall assert that those citizens you had in mind are our true [*alēthinous*] ancestors, of whom the priest was speaking. (26c–d)

Critias makes it clear in this passage that he differs fundamentally from Socrates regarding truth and the nature of speech. As Catherine Osborne observes, he associates truth not with the orienting measures of human existence, but with the effective actuality of existence itself—"facts in the world" and "historical events."[38] For Socrates, speech is essentially dialogue, and its character is erotic and philosophical; it is a medium of exploration in which natures reveal themselves, beings come to sight, and souls may be turned around and set in motion toward guiding truths. For Critias, speech is essentially monologue, and its character is thumotic and political; it is an instrument of control, through which facts may be constituted and designs actualized. Critias at one point represents his companions as a panel empowered, like the judges that scrutinized boys proposed for admission to their clan at the Apatouria's ceremony of Coureotis, to certify the Athenian pedigree of Socrates' citizens; in this way, he explains, he will be able "to make [*poieisthai*] my speeches as though they concerned men who are already citizens and Athenians" (27a–b). As this rhetorical device suggests, the truth in which he is interested arises in human life not from an erotic aspiration to Being, but through the impress of an intelligent plan on the dynamic field of Becoming.

Critias's particular designs in the *Timaeus-Critias* are personal and political. His tale of Solon's visit to Egypt aims to aggrandize not only the Athenians, but also his family and, most of all, himself. It is *his* city, a city older even than Egyptian Saïs (23d–e), with which Socrates' spirited and philosophic citizens must be identified—a city "best in war," populated by "the noblest and best race among human beings," and "in all respects exceedingly well-ordered by good laws" (23b–c). It is *his* relative, Solon, who retrieved and preserved the knowledge he will now share with his companions, and in accordance with whose "law and word" Socrates' citizens will become citizens of Athens (27b).[39] It is Critias who makes himself conspicuous as the architect of the speeches that will render appropriate thanks to Socrates and praise to Athena on her feast-day (20e–21a, 25d–26e). And it is Critias who, in finishing the story that his ancestor brought from Egypt, will implicitly show himself not only to be a greater poet than Solon, the "wisest" of men and "most noble" of the poets, but more worthy of esteem than even Homer and Hesiod (21c–d).[40]

But what exactly would it mean for Critias to "complete" or "perfect" Solon's account (21c)? Here we must observe that the Egyptian priest presents the city of Saïs as a historical copy of the original, politically paradigmatic regime of the ancient Athenians. Saïs was founded a thousand years after Athens (which itself endured for a thousand years) by the goddess the Egyptians call Neith and the Greeks Athena, "a lover of war and a lover of wisdom" (cf. *Rep.* 543a); its residents furthermore "assert that they are very fond of the Athenians, and in some manner relatives" of them (21e, 23d–e, 24c–d). The priest tells Solon that he may get a sense of the laws and customs of the first Athenians by looking at the only slightly inferior ones of Saïs, "for you will discover here and now many examples of the things that existed then among you [Athenians]" (24a; cf. 24d)—things preserved for millennia only because Egypt is not susceptible to the floods that periodically destroy the dwelling of human beings elsewhere on the earth, including the flood of history (22e). He mentions in particular the separation of the classes of priests, craftsmen ("of which each sort does its crafting by itself, without mixing with another"), shepherds, hunters, farmers, and especially warriors—men "kept apart from all the other classes, who have been ordered by the law to care for nothing other than the things concerned with war" (24a–b; cf. 17c). The archaic regimes of which the greatly aged priest speaks resemble fossilized animals. While the *Republic*'s cities in speech are living polities that come into being and pass away, the rigidly separated hereditary castes of Saïs and proto-Athens reflect the dream of a political *archē* that is both essentially reproducible and unsusceptible to historical decay.[41]

The city of Saïs is governed by a practical and technical understanding of human affairs that is rooted in physical science. The priest gives us a glimpse of this foundational science when he chastises Solon for relating childish tales about the most ancient things, thus confusing myth with truth (*to alēthes*). He illustrates this point with reference to the fanciful legend that Phaethon burned the earth when he lost control of the chariot of the sun, the truth of which resides in the necessities of celestial mechanics (22c–d). A later statement explicitly connects the scientific study of the physical cosmos with practical expertise:

> And again, concerning practical wisdom [*phronēseōs*]: you see, I suppose, how much attention the law here has devoted right from the beginning to the cosmos, having discovered all that accrues to human things from these divine beings, even as far as divination and the medical art that aims at health, and by having acquired all the others studies that follow these. (24b–c)

The priest clearly identifies *phronēsis* or practical wisdom—the knowledge of how to live that reflects moral intelligence and sound judgment about the human good—with an applied science derived from the study, not of the human things *per se*, but of the natural world.[42]

In sum, the *Timaeus* begins to reveal the ideological shape and scope of Critias's ambition. To bring Solon's account to completion, as Critias sets out to do in the *Timaeus-Critias*, would be to surpass him as a poet in the ordinary sense. To do so in deed would be to best Solon as a founder and lawgiver by reproducing the ostensibly uncorrupted regime of the first Athenians among their distant descendants. Critias aims to outdo his ancestor (as well as his companions in the *Timaeus-Critias*) on every front. If he can be believed, the feasibility of Socrates' city as a political program has already been historically demonstrated among barbarians as well as Greeks. The bold fiat whereby he settles Socrates' citizens in ancient Athens foreshadows what he and his fellow oligarchs would attempt to accomplish in deed through the revolution of 404–03. Saïs and proto-Athens are ruled by a scientific elite that cloaks its knowledge in the garb of religion, and that has at its disposal an army of well-equipped professional land warriors (24b). His tale of these two cities anticipates both what Munn calls "the hyper-archism of the Thirty"—their "radical vision of ancestral essence, sought in a distant and ill-documented past"—and their strange conceit of restoring the ancestral Athenian regime through a combination of scientific rule and quasi-Spartan militarism.[43]

Because Critias's myth is ultimately intended to authorize his revolutionary deed, he must present it as something other than a fanciful yarn, or even the sort of "likely story" (*eikos muthos*) that Timaeus, with all due measure and caution, tells about the origins of the cosmos (29d). Critias claims to offer a verified account of the foundations of Athenian life—one that argues for their reproducibility among people of identical or similar stock. His deed in the *Timaeus-Critias* is hardly less audacious than the one Sisyphus praises in his famous fragment; he, too, authors a religious myth, one that is intended to be, in every sense, a political *archē*. In doing so, he arguably furnishes *the* prototype for an activity in which all totalitarian regimes have specialized: that of rewriting the past to suit the purposes of the present.

Twin Cities: History and Character in the *Critias*

In the *Timaeus,* Critias displays poetic brilliance, rhetorical and political cleverness, and great personal ambition in reweaving a Socratic discourse into an ideological myth. The *Critias,* however, brings into focus his surprisingly tragic understanding of the overall shape of human history.

In the *Critias,* the son of Callaeschrus fills in the story he told in outline at the beginning of the *Timaeus.* Sandwiched in between his Egyptian story and the *Critias* is Timaeus's account of the origin and structure of the cosmos, a magnificent philosophical tale about the greatest of all subjects (and one with an extraordinarily influential afterlife in the Western intellectual tradition) which Critias, with a partisan rancor that even he recognizes is "very honor-loving and more harsh than it ought to be," absurdly begs his audience to regard as but a prelude to his more difficult exposition (107a–08a).[44] Timaeus's description of the paradigmatic work of the Demiurge, the divine craftsman of the cosmos who looks toward the model of Being in imposing order on a recalcitrant field of disorderly motion, anticipates Critias's top-down, technical conception of politics.[45] It also paves the way for Critias's sense that the historical rhythms of human existence reflect tragic cosmic necessities.

In the *Critias,* the city of Athens—gloriously victorious in the Persian Wars, ignominiously vanquished in the Peloponnesian War—is presented from two different points of view.[46] The city Critias describes at 110d–12e is the Athens whose victory over Atlantis was, according to his eponymous grandfather, "the greatest and most justly renowned of all actions this city ever enacted" (*Tim.* 21c).

That city was vibrantly healthy in every respect. Almost ten thousand years ago, the region of Athens was covered with rich soil that yielded ample lumber, abundant fruits, and fodder for grazing animals, "and over the land the seasons mixed most temperately"; today, stripped of soil by floods and earthquakes, the land resembles "the bones of a body wasted by disease" (*Criti.* 111b, e). Along with the class of priests, the male and female warriors of Athens inhabited a high and vast plateau over what is now the bare stone of a much smaller Acropolis; the artisans and farmers lived below them (112a–c). Yet although they were "guardians [*phulakes*] of their own citizens and leaders of the rest of the Greeks, who followed them willingly" (112d), these ruling Athenians were in no way corrupted by their power. Sharing a life lived "in the middle ground between luxurious display and illiberality," they and their children's children grew old in common dwellings "ever handed down unchanged to others like themselves" (112c). The ancient Athens of the *Critias* recalls Socrates' description of the inhabitants of the *Republic*'s True City, "living their life in peace and with health . . . and hand[ing] down another, similar life to their offspring" (372d). Although Critias's original Athenians combine martial prowess with technical development, they remain somehow immune to historical transformation. Theirs is truly, in Pierre Vidal-Naquet's words, "a republic of the land: a republic united and unchanging."[47]

Timaeus teaches in his cosmic myth that the universe is compounded of the Same, the Other, and Being (*Tim.* 35a–b). If Critias's prehistoric Athens is, as Vidal-Naquet has observed, "the political manifestation of the Same," swollen Atlantis, the mythical analogue of democratic, imperial Athens, is its metaphysical, spatial, and temporal antipode. An island belonging to Poseidon, god of earth and sea, and divided by an intricate series of waterways filled with ships (117e), Atlantis is Athens subjected to the influence of history: the Same interlaced with, and ultimately destabilized by, the Other.[48]

Athena and Poseidon, the contending gods whose fight over Attica was depicted on the Parthenon, are at first peaceably separated in Critias's myth. Athena's allotted city lies in the east, on solid ground; Poseidon's in the far west, in the open ocean beyond the pillars of Heracles. Athens and Atlantis are the same city with two different births—Athens originates in peaceful autochthony, while Atlantis is conceived in Poseidon's rape of a mortal female (113d–e)—and living two different lives, one sealed within an inviolable morning and the other tracing an all-too-human collapse into old age, infirmity, and decadence. Atlantis is Athens adrift on the seas of history, forsaking—as it did in the period between the Persian and Peloponnesian Wars—the modest decorum of Athena for the thumoerotic explosiveness of Poseidon.

Numerous clues connect Atlantis on the verge of its invasion of the eastern Mediterranean with Athens around the time of the Sicilian Expedition, a massive naval venture that Alcibiades envisioned as the first step of a plan to conquer the western Mediterranean (including Italy and Carthage), recruit barbarians from Iberia and elsewhere, invade the Peloponnesus, and ultimately "rule the whole of the Hellenic world" (Thuc. 6.90.2–4). Cleisthenes fathers the democracy in the last years of the sixth century, and divides the Athenians into ten tribes; Poseidon sires ten kings (five sets of twin sons) and divides the land into ten parts (113e). The nine subordinate kings of Atlantis are called *archontes*; Athens had nine Archons. The two cities have very similar temples adorned with chryselephantine statues of their gods (the one of Athena in the Parthenon having been financed by Athens' imperial revenues), and fortified harbors teeming with ships and full of tumult. Finally, the presence in the *Critias* of Hermocrates—who is supposed to have compared the invading Athenians to the Persians, and whose foresight and cunning in defending his city are reminiscent of the Athenian leader Themistocles—leaves no doubt that the mythical antithesis of Athens and Atlantis is meant to suggest the ineluctable arc of history as it sweeps, like the heavenly bodies themselves, round the posts of east and west, and yesterday's fresh and virtuous army of Davids becomes today's sclerotic imperial Goliath.[49]

Critias nevertheless sees room for human agency in the orbit of history. His mythical evocation of the eternal renewal of the past dovetails with a strange but significant detail of his story: the regular reenactment of a ritual in which the kings of Atlantis purify themselves by pouring bull's blood over their heads, and seal oaths by drinking it from goblets (119d–20b). In spilling the blood of their political opponents, the Thirty themselves would engage in what was supposed to be a purification of the Athenian body politic, and specifically a purgation of injustice.[50] The end of the *Critias* endows such recourse to cleansing violence with the mythical authority of Zeus, "the god of gods, who rules by laws" (121b). Seeing that the people of Atlantis have over time become "filled with unjust lust for possessions [*pleonexias*] and power," Zeus moves "to impose justice on them, in order that, having been recalled to sound-mindedness [*sōphronisthentes*], they might come to be more harmonious" (121b–c). The agent of this divine chastisement will be Athens, the moderate city Atlantis once was—and might, through forceful reattunement, become again.[51] In proposing to complete the Spartan scourge of the new Atlantis, the Thirty similarly hope to restore their own city to its ancestral purity.

Just as Callipolis is in a sense Glaucon writ large, Critias's description of Atlantis implicitly reveals his mind and character. It can hardly be coincidental that Atlantis is founded by a notably rivalrous and resentful Olympian who contends for honor against men no less than gods. In the *Iliad,* Poseidon fears that the wall and trench built by the Achaeans to protect their ships will win them a measure of fame (*kleos*) that will eclipse his own (7.446–53). In the *Odyssey,* Homer notes that his rancor against Odysseus is pitiless and unforgiving (1.19–21). The very end of the *Critias,* which breaks off as Zeus is about to pass sentence on Atlantis, recalls the sudden interruption of Homer's narration of the fate of the Phaeacians—a dramatic indication of the severe punishment that Poseidon, fearful that he "will no longer be esteemed among the immortal gods," metes out to a people that honors him above all other deities (*Od.* 13.128–29, 187).[52]

The story of Atlantis begins with Poseidon's rape of a woman whose name, Cleito, suggests both isolation and renown: *kleiō* means both "I shut, enclose" and "I celebrate." Having impregnated Cleito, the god sequesters her within multiple rings of land and seawater that he crafts expertly and precisely—they are "perfectly equidistant from one another"—so that the hill on which she lives becomes "inaccessible to human beings" (113e). Poseidon's conduct establishes a paradigm for the behavior of the kings he fathers. In secluding Cleito, he also exhibits traits that are associated with Critias and reappear in Callipolis: an obsession with hereditary purity, and a preference for artful compulsion rather than persuasion in the arrangement of human life.

The descendants of Poseidon are highly skilled craftsmen, and Critias's fascination with the political application of technical knowledge is reflected in the extraordinary development of their applied sciences, the vastness and geometrical precision of Atlantis's physical plan, the enormity of its buildings, and the immensity of its armament on land and sea (114d–19b).[53] But the double character of the son of Callaeschrus becomes most apparent in the last lines of the dialogue, where he describes the condition of the people of Atlantis when they are eventually corrupted by wealth and power:

> To the one capable of seeing, they appeared ugly and shameful, as they were losing the most noble and beautiful parts [*ta kallista*] of their most precious possessions, but to those incapable of seeing the true life of happiness, they were then opined to be most beautiful in every respect and blessed. (121b)

The *Critias* implies that the idealized Athens the Thirty proposed to reconstitute, a community of courageous and moderate warriors, cannot in fact be separated from its equally idealized twin, the swollen city it sets out to purge with strong political medicine. History confirms the truth of what Critias himself seems dimly to have sensed. For all of his indignation at the excesses of Athens' imperial democracy, Critias ends up leading a regime that imitates the tyrannical injustice and immoderation he condemns.

Looking back over the *Timaeus* and *Critias*, one may be inclined to find fault with Socrates. Why does he let Critias's slippery and self-serving notion of truth pass unchallenged? Why doesn't he question his technocratic assumptions? Is he insensitive to the serious errors Critias would be inclined to make if some chance of rule were to fall to him? Two replies suggest themselves.

First, the *Timaeus-Critias* involves a formal exchange of gifts: rich and pleasurable banquets of words, prepared and enjoyed in celebration of the goddess on her feast-day (*Tim.* 17a, 20e–21a). For Socrates to call Critias to account on this occasion would be inauspicious and indecorous: it would mar his praise of the goddess, and spoil his attempt to repay Socrates for his speeches. Socrates himself concisely lays out the protocol of the day, beginning with an invocation: "With good fortune [*agathēi tuchēi*], you must speak; and I, in exchange for my speeches of yesterday, must keep quiet and listen in turn" (*Tim.* 26e–27a). More important, Socrates has *already* conducted a probing examination of Critias. The *Charmides* records a conversation that occurs prior to the *Timaeus* in dramatic time, but which Socrates narrates many years later. In the *Charmides*, Socrates publicly, and at times vehemently, exposes the emptiness of Critias's abstract and self-serving intellectualism. At the same time, he quietly displays his own modest and sound-minded nature, and he does so in the face of temptations that would destroy all but the most steady and self-possessed souls. He is thus seen to stand poles apart from Critias with respect to the very virtue under discussion, a core element of aristocratic excellence that Critias claims both for himself and for Charmides, whom he is busy trying to mold in his own image: *sōphrosunē*.[54]

Socrates at the Crossroads: The Temptation of Charmides

In Aristophanes' *Clouds*, the character of Socrates worships vaporous beings given evanescent form by speech—Clouds, Chaos, Vortex, Aether, Respiration, and Air, shaped by Tongue. The Clouds, Socrates explains at one point, manifest the nature of those to whom they appear; seeing a coward, for example, they take on the shape of a deer (346–55). By the same token, Socrates' perception of the Clouds' mimetic elasticity must spring from their reflection of his *own* imitative powers. Put another way, Aristophanes—who in the parabasis of the *Clouds* speaks in his own name in the guise of the lead Cloud (518–626)—uses his imitative art to reveal Socrates' nature in much the way Socrates himself does in the Platonic dialogues, where his ironic imitation of interlocutors is meant to illuminate their dispositions.

For his part, Critias does not so much imitate the thought of others as appropriate it. Socrates is erotic and uncertain, and opens himself to others in philosophical dialogue; Critias is spirited and dogmatic, and impresses himself on others through rhetorical and political craft. Nowhere is this contrast clearer than in the *Charmides*, a dialogue that begins with Socrates playing a role dictated by Critias. Whereas the *Timaeus* is a performance of prepared speeches that stand at several removes from the dialogue that inspired them, the *Charmides* is Socrates' narration of a philosophical conversation. Because indirect discourse allows for editorial comment, the narrative form of the *Charmides* makes it possible for Socrates fully to display the inner difference between himself and Critias.

The opening scene of the *Charmides* allows us to glimpse Socrates' disciplined and dignified bearing as a soldier. A poor man who nevertheless chose to serve as a hoplite, Socrates somehow acquired the panoply he needed to elevate himself into the Athenian warrior-caste. He spent years on campaign over the course of the Peloponnesian War, acquiring a reputation for bravery that recommended him to the generals even in his late forties—and also to courageous and spirited young men like Alcibiades and Glaucon.[55] The *Charmides* begins just after he concludes almost three years of service in Thrace. On returning to Athens from the army camp at Potidaea, Socrates tells us in the first lines of the dialogue, he goes directly to the wrestling-school, where he can engage young men in philosophical dialogue. He is greeted by a throng of people eager for news about the bloody battle from which he has just come, and in which he showed exemplary courage in saving the life of a wounded Alcibiades (*Symp.* 220d–e). While almost anyone in a similar position would hold forth with pleasure, he seems to regard it merely as a duty to answer their questions. A willing and distinguished warrior, Socrates is nevertheless not a lover of honor.[56]

At the first opportunity, Socrates asks "about philosophy, how it stands now, and about the young, whether some among them had come to be distinguished either in wisdom or in beauty or both" (153d). Critias tells him that the one held to be most beautiful at the present time is about to arrive: his ward Charmides, son of Glaucon (the grandfather after whom Plato's brother was named), who would then have been about seventeen years old.[57] Socrates' description of Charmides' entrance is worth quoting in full:

> Now I, companion, am no measure. For I am simply [*atechnōs*] a white line in relation to the beautiful: pretty much all those of that age seem beautiful [to me]. Even so, that one then seemed to me to be amazing in size and beauty, and indeed all the others seemed to me, at any rate, to be in love with him: they were that knocked out and bewildered when he came in. And many other lovers followed

> in train behind. Now the reaction of the men was less to wonder at. But I also paid attention to the boys, how not one of them looked anywhere else, not even the smallest, but all beheld him just like a statue. And Chaerephon called me and said "What do you think of the youngster, Socrates? Is he not fair of face [*euprosōpos*]?"
>
> "Preternaturally," I said.
>
> "But," he said, "if this one were willing to strip, he would seem to you to be without a face [*aprosōpos*]; so entirely beautiful is his form [*eidos*]." (154b–d)

The scholiast explains that a builder's line drawn on white stone is invisible if it is itself white. Said to have been a stonemason (Diog. Laert. 2.19), Socrates here denies any connection between that trade and his relationship with young men. As he makes clear in the *Theaetetus* (148e–51e), his pedagogy follows the example of the midwife; he does not regard the young as merely so much uncut marble, to be shaped and fitted by technical means according to a preexisting plan. That description applies rather to Critias, who wishes to stamp his young cousin with conventional notions of resplendent nobility. In comparing Charmides to a statue, Socrates subtly indicates the human cost of such forceful instruction. As a sculptor of men, Critias is concerned with shaping and polishing visible surfaces; he is uninterested in what Charmides may think or feel in his own right. To possess the apparent perfection of a statue is furthermore to lose one's individuality in the eyes of others: Charmides' many lovers do not even notice his face.[58] All of these implications are reflected in Socrates' later observation that Critias "seemed to me to be angry with him [Charmides], just like a poet with an actor who recites his verses badly" (162d): actors play parts and utter speeches assigned by others, and their faces are obscured by masks with generic features and expressions.

Charmides' face is virtually invisible to others not simply because of his physical perfection, but also because they invest him with a shared, socially-produced image of aristocratic excellence (*kalokagathia*). Socrates makes it clear, however, that he is exempt from the almost universal mimetic desire inspired by Charmides' entrance.[59] His subsequent erotic arousal when he looks inside the youth's cloak (155d) is therefore all the more striking. What is the meaning of this arousal, and of his successful resistance to it? These questions take us to the heart of Socrates' nature as a philosophical educator.

Socrates opines that Charmides would be "an unbeatable man . . . if he happens to have only one small thing in addition," namely, "if in respect to his soul he happens to be naturally well-formed" (154d).[60] Having been assured by Critias that Charmides is noble and good in soul, he proposes to "strip this very part of him, and contemplate it before his form [*eidos*]" (154e). The form to which he refers is double: he expresses the wish that Charmides' soul could be considered not only apart from the distraction of his splendid body, a relatively easy task, but also apart from the social expectations and demands that have obscured his individual nature—a more difficult one. Socrates will try to strip and contemplate his soul by engaging him in dialogue.

As it turns out, Charmides recognizes Socrates and is not deceived by Critias's ruse that he is a doctor who can treat his headaches (156a). He nevertheless comes to sit in between the two men, a position that reflects their implicit struggle over the education of this fatherless adolescent.[61] It is at this point that Socrates is almost derailed by temptation:

> But then, my friend, I started to feel perplexed, and my previous boldness in thinking that I would very easily engage in dialogue with him was thoroughly knocked out of me. And when Critias said that I was the one who knew the cure [*ho to pharmakon epistamenos*], and he looked into me with something like an irresistible [*amēchanon*] expression, and was just about to ask a question, and everyone in the wrestling-school was surging all around us in a circle—then indeed, you noble fellow, I saw what was inside his cloak and became inflamed and was no longer in myself, and I believed that the wisest in respect to the erotic things was Cydias, who in speaking about a beautiful boy advises another to "beware lest coming as a fawn before a lion you are seized as his portion of flesh"; for I seemed to myself to have been captured by some such creature. Nevertheless, when he asked me if I knew the medicine for his head, I somehow managed to answer that I did know it. (155c–e)

It is too much to believe that Socrates, who a few minutes previously had coolly observed everyone else's erotic attraction to Charmides, is carried away by the sight of his genitals. Why, then, is he aroused?

Socrates gives us all the clues we need to answer this question. To begin with, he is about to utter his first lines in a role that Critias scripts in accordance with his presumption of knowledge in doctoring the city and crafting its citizens. That Socrates is now at the center of attention along with Charmides—surrounded, as in the theater, by a large, excited, and expectant audience of Athenians of various ages—suggests that he might be tempted by the power and influence made possible by this pretense of technical expertise. That he *is* so tempted is confirmed by his description of the look in Charmides' eyes, in which he sees, in the deepest sense, what is beneath his cloak of quiet self-possession (cf. 159b): *amēchanon*, "irresistible," can also mean "helpless." Charmides' look is doubtless filled with emulation and longing, much like the gaze directed at *him* by the men and boys who now surround the bench on which he sits. For Socrates is the heroic warrior he himself aspires to be, and his name is on everyone's lips.[62] Charmides' longing to be like Socrates makes him deeply vulnerable to manipulation and exploitation, and it is precisely this vulnerability that tempts Socrates to play his role in earnest. Were he to make the fraudulent and sophistical persona of Critias his own, this beautiful youth, and many other young Athenians as well, would be so much putty in his hands. It is this enormously seductive prospect—the aphrodisiac of extreme power over the souls and bodies of others—that causes him briefly to take leave of his senses.[63] The lion that threatens Socrates' fawn-like innocence is, in other words, inside him (cf. *Rep.* 588d): it is the surge and roar of thumoerotic domination, the force that ultimately destroys both Critias and Charmides because they unleash it and feed it, finally with the blood of their fellow citizens.[64]

In sum, Socrates' sudden sexual arousal indicates that he has arrived at what is surely one of the most definitive moral crossroads of his life: he can become Critias or return to himself. He finds himself in actuality in roughly the same place Glaucon stands in imagination as he contemplates himself as cock of the walk in Callipolis. If any moment calls for *sōphrosunē*, it is this one.

In the end, Socrates finds salvation as well as temptation in Charmides' expression, and in the deeper *erōs* it solicits. Of all those present, he alone really sees Charmides' face—sees who he *is*, and not just what others have made of him. It is his respect for the sacred boundary of the other that saves him. This feeling of respect is not a concern for how he appears in the eyes of others; it is not socially-induced shame (*aischunē*), but something like religious awe (*aidōs*).[65] The ancestor of Gyges—a mythical representation of actual tyrants, including the future one Socrates addresses as "dear son of Glaucon" (*Chrm.* 158b)—commits rape and murder in the face of his victims' terror and helplessness; Socrates could never do such things. His saving moderation is in this decisive instance rooted in his sense that our intrinsic humanity has nothing in common with the sheer exteriority of a statue, and in his desire to preserve the guttering flame of divinity in himself and others. Rekindled by this desire, Socrates warms to the musical and erotic activity of philosophical conversation.

Thracian Music and Greek Science

Just before introducing him to Charmides, Critias tells Socrates that the youth is "a lover of wisdom [*philosophos*], and, as he seems to others and to himself, very poetic" (154e–55a). If Socrates' aim in the dialogue that ensues is to bring his interlocutors to reflect critically on their basic assumptions about philosophy and poetry, he fails. Neither Charmides nor Critias gives any indication of receptivity to Socrates' moral intuitions and commitments. In fact, neither acknowledges that character—the condition of the soul as a whole, as opposed to the epistemic content of thought—is at all relevant to their activities. Critias has taught Charmides that the knowledge he needs is what we now call "value-free," and Socrates hardly puts a dent in either one's conviction.

When Charmides asks about the medicine (*pharmakon*) he possesses to treat his headaches, Socrates replies as follows:

> I said that it was itself some leaf, and that there was some incantation over the medicine, which if one sang at the same time one was using it, the medicine would produce health in every respect. But without the incantation there was no benefit in the leaf.
>
> And he said "Then I'll copy the incantation from you in writing."
>
> "If you persuade me," I said, "or even if you don't?"
>
> Then he laughed and said "If I persuade you, Socrates."

"Well," I said. "And do you know my name precisely [*akribois*]?"
"If I do not do injustice," he said . . . (155e–56a)

Socrates' use of a philosophical incantation to treat Charmides anticipates the "*logos* mixed with music" he applies in the *Republic* to Glaucon and his companions, declaring it to be the savior of virtue (549b). But Charmides supposes that the music of Socratic discourse is *reducible* to a *logos*, one that is furthermore neither a dialogue nor even an argument, but a magic spell—a series of words that need not even be understood in order to be effective. At best, this would be like saying that reading the lyrics of a song has the same effect on the soul as hearing it performed by a dedicated musician.[66] The youth with no face acts as though he were a head without a heart, and that in a political as well as an intellectual sense: he imperiously proposes to appropriate the content of Socrates' knowledge even before he has obtained his permission.

Charmides does do injustice to Socrates, and cannot do otherwise. His knowledge is exact but superficial: he knows the philosopher's name, but not who he is.[67] He is unaware that Saving Strength will not get pushed around, because he is ignorant of what the soul's saving strength is or does. For *sōphrosunē* is not the mind, the organ of calculation and precision, but that which makes it good and useful; it is the "savior [*sōdzousan*] of prudent intelligence [*tēn phronēsin*]" (Arist. *Eth. Nic.* 1140b11–12). By this point in the *Charmides*, we are already on notice: the injustice of Critias's science of politics is connected with its inability to know individual human beings. Socrates certainly has his work cut out for him. He sees an opening for the face-to-face justice of dialogue and begins to "rekindle to life" (156d) when Charmides agrees that good doctors are right to treat the body as a whole in attempting to heal a part of it. The immediate sequel, it seems, will display Socrates' vital, essential activity in an especially lucid fashion.

The Thracian doctor who taught him the incantation, Socrates explains to Charmides, told him that "Zalmoxis, our king, who is a god, says that just as one must not attempt to heal eyes without head, nor head without body, so also not body without soul"; most illnesses therefore elude the Greek doctors, "because they are careless of the whole." Before medicine is applied to the head, the soul must be treated by means of "certain incantations"; these incantations "are speeches, beautiful ones, and from such speeches moderation comes to be in our souls, and when it has been engendered and is present, it is easy to furnish health both for the head and for the rest of the body."[68] While some doctors attempt to cure the body with medicine apart from the incantations that treat the soul, Socrates is determined to avoid this "error [*hamartēma*] concerning human beings": he swore an oath to the Thracian doctor that "no one, however wealthy, or well-born, or beautiful, will persuade me to do otherwise" (156d–57c).

In telling the story of the Thracian doctor, Socrates engages in a brilliant act of dramatic improvisation that effectively takes the role Critias has assigned him and makes it his own. His only slightly misleading talk of beautiful speeches and charming music puts an attractive face on the difficult but noble practice of elenchus or refutation that constitutes the negative core of his pedagogical activity. If he can indeed engender moderation in an individual's soul, it is by showing him that he is ignorant of what he thought he knew.[69] His conversation with Theaetetus, one of his most promising interlocutors in the Platonic dialogues, is a case in point. Socrates has prepared Theaetetus to become pregnant with better ideas than the ones he has refuted; if he remains barren, he will at any rate be "less harsh on your associates and tamer, moderately [*sophronōs*] believing you don't know what you don't know." "Of only so much is my art capable," he declares, "and nothing more" (*Tht.* 210c).

Socrates' Thracian story is noteworthy in several other respects. Critias suggests in the *Timaeus* that the scientific politics of the Egyptians, including "the medical art that aims at health" (24c), is derivative: just as Saïs is an inferior image of ancient Athens, its priests have learned only what the Greeks already knew. Herodotus's story of Zalmoxis, who learned how to dupe ignorant Thracians by associating with the mathematician and preeminent sophist Pythagoras, might similarly be taken to indicate that Greeks surpass barbarians in practical intelligence. But these examples are political illustrations of the very deficiencies to which Socrates' description of Zalmoxian medicine calls our attention in relation to the individual. Critias champions a spuriously precise political science, one that errs fundamentally in mistaking a part for the whole. The Egyptian and Thracian students of the Greeks attend almost exclusively to the head of the body politic, at best equipping only a few with the special knowledge of rule. Heads of state (like the Thirty) who justify the use of physical force by claiming to purge the city or body of vice, much as doctors do with emetics, excisions, and amputations, furthermore pay insufficient attention to the charms of music, which exercises an inner, erotic compulsion. These rulers compel bodies and souls, but do not lead them; they are adept in techniques of force and deception, but ignorant of the erotic attractions of genuine beauty and goodness. Socrates' dialogical catharsis of false opinion from individual souls is occasionally harsh; in comparison with the crude violence of a political purge, however, it looks like a supremely modest, gentle, and thoughtful means of improving the city.

Socrates' story also tellingly reverses Critias's insistence on the primacy of Greek wisdom in relation to the barbarians: the Thracian understanding of the soul provides just the antidote for what ails Greek medicine. As Socrates makes clear when he states that he must converse with Charmides so as not to "turn to doctoring in an unexamined way" (158e), Thracian soul-medicine must be applied directly to the individual, and cannot be used to doctor the city as a whole. Socrates himself seems to have undergone this Zalmoxian treatment; his having sworn an oath to the Thracian doctor implies that he has been initiated into the sacred mysteries of this distinctly philosophical medicine. Seen in connection with his criticism of Greek medicine, Socrates' remark that the Thracian physicians are "said to make men immortal" (156d) challenges the cryptic notion of self-divinization Critias propounds later in the dialogue. His account of their psychic medicine also helps to explain why the *Republic* is limned by the festival of a Thracian goddess, and by rites reenacting the immortality of the soul: Socrates will apply the therapeutic music of Zalmoxis to exponents of Greek cleverness like Thrasymachus and Glaucon.

The Tyranny of the Head: Critias's Ruling Science

Critias's response to Socrates' proposal to apply the incantations to Charmides—but only if he is willing (157c)—shows that he has not understood him at all:

> Having heard me saying these things, Critias said "The weakness of the head would be a godsend [*hermaion*] for the young man, Socrates, if on account of his head he will be compelled to become better in intellectual capacity [*dianoia*] as well." (157c–d)

Critias is evidently so used to making others do what he wants that he fails to observe that Socrates' musical treatment will not involve external compulsion. His surmise that Socrates aims to improve Charmides' *dianoia*, the faculty of discursive intelligence that is paradigmatically exhibited in "the disposition of geometers and such" in relation to mathematical objects (*Rep.* 511d), indicates that he is insensitive to Socrates' main point—the irreducibility of the human soul to the head, let alone to any specific kind of cognition. His characterization of Socrates' philosophical music as a *hermaion* is thus an ironic echo of the godsend according to which Socrates recovers the wholesome inner harmony of genuine moderation in the *Republic*'s True City.

Critias assures Socrates that Charmides "seems to be very much the most moderate [*sōphronestatos*] person of the present generation" (157d). Socrates asks the youth to look quietly into himself in order to see what sort of thing moderation or sound-mindedness might be (158e–59a), but Charmides is unable to produce a satisfactory definition of his supposedly preeminent virtue.[70] After two false starts and some gentle chastisement (159b, 160d–e), Charmides remarks: "I remembered just now what I once heard someone say, that moderation is doing one's own things" (161b). Socrates' response is extraordinarily harsh: "You pollution [*miare*]!—you heard it from Critias here, or from some other wise man" (161b). What explains this outburst?

Critias denies that he is the source of the definition Charmides proposes, but Socrates does not believe him (162c). Perhaps he is ashamed to have been caught plagiarizing Socrates, who in the *Republic* describes justice as a man's doing one's own things "with respect to what is within, what truly concerns himself and the things that belong to him, not allowing each part in him to do the work of another, nor allowing the classes in the soul to meddle with one another [*polupragmonein*, lit. 'to do many things']" (443d). Thus understood, justice is virtually indistinguishable from *sōphrosunē*, which

Socrates characterizes as the internal harmony of the parts of the soul (431e–32a).[71] Critias's fraud is especially despicable because he brazenly pawns off as his own another's idea of doing one's own things; in his mouth, even the truth turns into a lie. But in fact, appropriating and distorting the thought and work of others *is* Critias's thing. Rivaling Greeks and barbarians, Spartans and Athenians; claiming for himself the distant past as well as the future of his city; asserting the identity of human cleverness and divine wisdom—in all of this, Critias is the Platonic archetype of intellectual and political *polupragmosunē*: quasi-philosophical meddling and posturing in every fundamental sphere of human endeavor.[72]

It is now reasonably clear why Charmides merits the epithet *miare*. Charmides is intellectually lazy: his instinct on encountering philosophical criticism is to reach for the opinion of another who has also failed to think for himself—an opinion to which he can only be indifferent, as he has not troubled to reflect on it. If Charmides has no personal stake in the conversation, he cannot be refuted, and therefore will remain unpurified of falsehood and uncharmed by Socratic music. He is, and chooses to remain, polluted with unnecessary ignorance only because he is following the example of Critias; the moral and intellectual deficiencies of the teacher are mirrored in the student.[73] And if Socrates' language is unusually harsh, it is perhaps because their errors, as he immediately goes on to suggest, will be multiplied ten thousandfold if they should ever put their hands to governing the city.

Socrates seems to anticipate Charmides' self-destruction in tyranny when he exposes a problem with his secondhand definition of moderation as doing one's own things. Having gotten Charmides to agree that the grammarian does something (*prattein*) when he writes and reads, he asks him another question:

> "Does the grammarian seem to you to write and read his own name only, or teach you boys [as well], or did you [pl.] write the names of your enemies no less than your own names and those of your friends?"
>
> "No less."
>
> "Then were you meddlesome and immoderate in doing this?"
>
> "In no way."

> "And surely you were not doing your own things, if indeed to write and to read is to do something." (161d–e)

Even as boys, Charmides and his cohort divided themselves into hostile groups, and it is the actions of these groups, the childish forerunners of adult political factions, with which Socrates is concerned. To write and read as the schoolteacher instructs one is neither meddlesome nor immoderate; to write a list of friends and enemies of the regime—as the Thirty, setting an example for future ideological tyrannies, were perhaps the first to do—and to use this list as a medicinal leaf that will purge the city of vice, is both. The political medicine of the Thirty is indistinguishable from poison; because they presume to possess expertise in rule without having learned the difference between good and evil, they befoul the city with violence.

Pressed by Socrates to explain the apparent riddle of the definition they are examining, Charmides opines that its author may not have known what he was talking about (162b). For Critias, whom Socrates also provokes by suggesting that the man in question might be "some fool," this is the last straw. Socrates tells us that Critias "had clearly been anxious for a long time, and was eager to win honor in the eyes of Charmides and those present"; having "previously restrained himself with difficulty, [he] was then no longer able to do so" (162b–c).[74] Vehemently rebuking Charmides for his ignorance, Critias bursts into the dialogue in much the way Thrasymachus does in the *Republic* (336b–c, discussed in Chapter Four); like Thrasymachus, he is angry at Socrates, eager to appear knowledgable, and incapable of restraining himself.

Critias goes on to defend his thesis by interpreting a statement of Hesiod's. According to Xenophon, Socrates understood Hesiod's remark that "work is no disgrace, but idleness is a disgrace" to mean that "those who make or do [*poiountas*] anything good do work and are workers, while those who gamble or do any other base and harmful thing he denounced as idle."[75] Critias is silent on the subject of idleness (he quotes only the first half of Hesiod's assertion), but he rejects the notion that the poet would have considered such lowly activities as cobbling anything other than a disgrace. Rather, Hesiod "called 'works' things made or done beautifully and beneficially"; only such things should be considered our own things—the very things with which *sōphrosunē* is concerned—while "all harmful ones belong to others" (163b–c). Critias is disdainful of the everyday work that makes human existence possible. His understanding of good and bad manifests a similar aristocratic detachment and intellectual abstraction—together with his calculating egoism, a fatal combination for his fellow Athenians. It will suffice to highlight only certain details of his long discussion with Socrates in order to appreciate these points.

Although Critias interprets the Delphic inscription "Know Thyself" (*gnōthi seauton*) to mean "Be of Sound Mind," he understands sound-mindedness not as the introspective recognition (*gnōsis*) of one's own particular nature, but as a science (*epistēmē*)—what is more, a science not of concretely existing individuals, but "of itself and the other sciences" (165c, 166e).[76] Critias imagines a ruling metascience that would be able to distinguish what is scientific from what is not, and so certify the authenticity of the sciences. This epistemic gatekeeper would dramatically improve the human lot by admitting no lowly imitators into human life, but only genuine forms of knowledge (cf. 171d–73d). In theory as in politics, Critias aims for a purity that is inconsistent with the humble activity of philosophy.[77] But the second-order science of sciences he envisions is perhaps *too* pure, inasmuch as it abstracts from the content of every first-order science. In its ignorance of all that is actually known by any particular science, it has for its own content only the form of science as such (170b–d). What that form might be—or whether it is anything at all, or at least anything that could be known—is left unsaid. Pressed to address these difficulties, Critias "was ashamed before those present . . . and said nothing clear, concealing his perplexity" (169c–d). His talk of a master science of sciences seems to be nothing more than a particularly self-assertive kind of intellectual poetry.[78]

Socrates' self-knowledge prevents him from supposing that he is competent to determine whether such a science of sciences is possible, or whether *sōphrosunē* is this kind of science (169a–b). As he will do in discussing the community of women and children in book 5 of the *Republic*, Socrates sets aside the question of possibility in order to focus on that of goodness: he provisionally grants the theoretical coherence of Critias's meta-science in order to consider how it might benefit human beings in practice (cf. Rep. 457e–58a). His searching examination of Critias's technocratic faith seems designed to model the possibility of rethinking one's basic presuppositions.

Socrates begins by articulating the political implications and potential benefits of Critias's line of thought. He opines that the science Critias has described would allow us "to live out our life without error, both we ourselves who possess soundness of mind and all the rest who are ruled by us." Equipped with this science, we would allow those we rule "to do nothing other than what, in doing, they would do correctly; and this would be that of which they possessed a science." "With error [*hamartias*] rooted out," Socrates adds, "and correctness leading us, it would be necessary for those thus disposed to do and fare nobly and well in every action, and for those who do and fare well to be happy" (171d–72a). Critias strongly agrees with these statements, and later asserts that Socrates had spoken "beautifully" (172a, e).

After all this talk of avoiding life-spoiling error, however, Socrates reveals his fear "that we did not inquire correctly" in assuming that scientific correctness is a sufficient condition for happiness. He communicates his concern in the form of a dream that he claims to be unable to evaluate. In this dream, he envisions that everything in human life is done "according to the sciences," so that we would have "more bodily health than now, and be saved from dangers in the sea and war, and our implements and all clothing and shoes would be skillfully [*technikōs*] made for us." The problem, he says, is that we are not able to determine whether "in acting scientifically we would do and fare well and be happy" (173a–d). Here as elsewhere, Socrates equates *technē*—art, skill, or craft—with science; the unifying conception of knowledge in the context of politics is one of practical, technical expertise.[79]

Critias does not share Socrates' uncertainty. Indeed, he seems to view Socrates' second thoughts as a personal insult: "You will not easily discover some other fulfillment of acting and doing well," he asserts, "if you do not esteem acting scientifically" (173d). Critias's umbrage is not entirely misplaced, for Socrates easily proceeds to show that his technocratic self-confidence is groundless. Exploiting

Critias's disdain for lowly but necessary occupations, Socrates gets him to agree that acting scientifically does not suffice to make shoemakers or brass-workers happy; what makes one happy, it seems, is "living scientifically concerning certain things," not all things (173d–e). When pressed to say what science *does* make us happy, Critias replies "that of the good and the bad" (174b). Socrates responds to this statement with the same epithet he had earlier applied to Charmides:

> "You pollution!" I said, "for a long time you have been dragging me around in circle, concealing that it was not living scientifically that makes one do well and be happy, not even with all the other sciences put together, but with this one alone, the one concerning good and bad." (174b–c)

Far from engaging in some noble work, Critias has wasted Socrates' time with idle chatter. But Socrates goes so far as to imply that his talk has been downright pernicious. How so?

Critias's response helps to answer this question: "If *sōphrosunē* is above all a science of the sciences, and presides over the other sciences, surely it would benefit us also by ruling this science concerning the good" (174d–e). Eva Brann has written that Critias "prefigures the modern totalitarian ruler, a creature who rules by abstractions."[80] In the face of Socrates' criticism, Critias's instinct is to retreat still further into the combination of theoretical and bureaucratic abstraction that is the hallmark of ideological tyranny. He embraces a ruling science that departmentalizes all tasks while knowing nothing of the matters under its authority; it is neither medicine nor politics, and is ignorant of health and justice; it is "nothing other than science" (170b). His supreme intellectual and political hubris is to imagine that the Good itself—which according to Socrates cannot be known scientifically, because it stands beyond being and essence as their very source (*Rep.* 507e–11b)—can be cut, dried, and made into the special object of a subordinate branch of technical expertise.

The conclusion of the *Charmides* dramatically anticipates the political extremism of both Critias and Charmides. Critias tells his ward that "this will be a proof for me that you are moderate: if you present yourself to Socrates to be charmed," and Charmides agrees to do his bidding. Catching wind of their agreement, Socrates calls them out:

> "You there," I said, "what are you two plotting to do?"[81]
>
> "Nothing," said Charmides, "we've finished plotting."
>
> "So you'll use force," I said, "and not even grant me a preliminary hearing?'
>
> "I will indeed use force," he said, "since this one commands me; you take counsel, then, as to what you are going to do."
>
> "But that leaves no room for any counsel at all," I said. "For if you undertake to do whatever you like by force, no human being will be able to oppose you."
>
> "Well then," he said, "don't you oppose me."
>
> "Then," I said, "I won't oppose you." (176c–d)

Socrates' refutation of Critias seems in no way to have diminished Charmides' respect for his guardian's authority. Earlier, Charmides relented when Socrates pushed back against the notion that he could write down the incantation without his permission. Now, however, he commands as he is commanded, and his only superficially playful decision to press himself on Socrates demonstrates a willful deafness to reasonable appeal that places him beyond the reach of philosophical persuasion. Contrary to Critias's assertion, Charmides is incorrigibly immoderate. In this he resembles the man he now reveals to be his absolute master, whose self-certainty is so great that he does not bother to answer Socrates' question, even though it was addressed to him as well.

The Riddle of the *Republic*

The Platonic dialogues demonstrate the duplexity of the son of Callaeschrus. Critias's founding myth of Athens is a *tour de force*: a poetically brilliant and rhetorically stunning projection of nobility and beauty. Warman Welliver nevertheless justly remarks that Plato depicts Critias in the *Timaeus-Critias* as "an ingrate, a transgressor of the laws of hospitality, a blasphemer (at least in Socrates' opinion), a boor, a cheat, a perfidious partner, and a liar." The *Charmides*, in which Socrates is somewhat less constrained by the norms of hospitality, more bluntly portrays Critias as a calculating, narrow egoist, a self-aggrandizing liar, and a harsh and domineering guardian.[82] Perhaps most important, Plato follows the utopian ideal Critias would attempt to implement in Athens from its abstract theoretical beginnings in the *Charmides* to its schematic articulation in the *Timaeus-Critias*, revealing it to be what Schmid has aptly described as a "strangely decadent, quasi-fascistic synthesis of aristocratic/Laconophilic and epistemic/sophistic presumption."[83]

Socrates' encounters with Critias in the Platonic dialogues bring to light fundamental differences between these two men. For Socrates, philosophy springs from a concrete knowledge of ignorance and is characterized by erotic, dialogical openness to others; for Critias, philosophical speech is rooted in abstract certainties and consists in a personal display of sophistication and cleverness. Socrates' philosophizing is guided by the imperatives of moderation, justice, and care for individual souls; Critias's intellectual productions are guided by the imperative of self-aggrandizement. Perhaps it is not surprising that Critias's technical and sophistical understanding of politics is echoed in Thrasymachus's account of the science of rule, or that his atheistic esotericism is reflected in both the form and substance of Glaucon's mythical defense of injustice. But anyone who comes to the *Republic* after reading the *Charmides* must be astonished that Socrates builds Callipolis on the foundations laid by Thrasymachus and Glaucon, combining political technicism and poetic esotericism in an ostensibly philosophical tyranny. What is the meaning of this riddle? This question will guide our return to the *Republic*.

CHAPTER 4

Channeling Critias

THE ROAD TO CALLIPOLIS

One of the most dramatic moments in the *Republic* is Thrasymachus's explosive entry into the dialogue about a third of the way through book 1. Socrates has just finished refuting Polemarchus's assertion that justice is helping friends and harming enemies, and Polemarchus has agreed to join him in battle against those who say that it is just to harm anyone at all (335e).[1] This proves to be a timely alliance, for they are immediately attacked by Thrasymachus:

> But when we paused . . . he could no longer keep quiet, but gathered himself together just like a wild beast and threw himself upon us as if he wanted to tear us to pieces. And Polemarchus and I took fright and fluttered away. And into our midst [*to meson*] he bellowed: "What is this nonsense that has long possessed you, Socrates? And why do you play the fool and bow down to one another? But if you truly want to know what the just is, don't just ask questions and contend for honor by refuting whenever someone makes some reply—for you know that it is easier to ask than to answer—but you yourself answer, and say what you assert the just to be!" (336b–c)

While Thrasymachus's rude interruption recalls Critias's angry intrusion into Socrates' discussion with Charmides, he has good reason to be upset with Socrates and Polemarchus. Their respectful dialogue has been a model of democratic equality, but they act as if they are utterly oblivious to the reality of Athenian power politics—a reality that has made the arms-dealer who hosts them a rich man. As if to emphasize the insubstantiality of their understanding of justice, Thrasymachus's shout flushes them like birds from the public space that the Greeks called *to meson*, the middle ground of political debate about the advantageous and the just.[2]

Thrasymachus has no doubt that the Athenians are a gang of thieves. He is a citizen of Chalcedon, a subject-city of Athens that defected to the Peloponnesians, was besieged by the Athenians (who seized the Chalcedonians' property), and was ultimately spared from destruction by the intervention of the Persians.[3] Well acquainted with the lot of both the nominal friends and real enemies of Athens, he knows firsthand the truth of the assertion, attributed by Thucydides to the Athenians prior to their annihilation of the Melians, that "right, as the world goes, is only in question between equals in power, while the strong do what they can and the weak suffer what they must."[4] He must be particularly incensed to hear Socrates attributing the view that justice involves harming enemies not to the Athenians, but to foreign tyrants, despots, and rich men like Periander, Perdiccas, Xerxes, and Ismenias (336a).

Thrasymachus's angry outburst injects a measure of reality into the conversation of the *Republic*. He compels Socrates to consider the (almost) universal political behavior of individuals as well as groups, and to begin to acknowledge the widespread political phenomena of indignation and cynicism—attitudes promoted in no small part by Athenian policies and practices. In motivating Glaucon to reframe and deepen his argument (358b), he also sets in motion the exploration of city and soul that constitutes the main work of the dialogue. That exploration bears the impress of Thrasymachus's orienting assumptions about knowledge and power, assumptions that hark back to the *Charmides* and *Timaeus-Critias*.

Like Critias, Thrasymachus advocates a conception of politics as a master science (and science of mastery) that is capable of supplying its practitioners with benefits sufficient to produce happiness. Like Critias, he supposes that political knowledge can be stated—as can the knowledge of *ta mathēmata*, "the learnable things," that is paradigmatic of both theoretical and applied science—with clarity and precision (336d).[5] And he, too, mixes knowledge and coercion, for he supposes that one licenses the other. Thrasymachus's bravura performance in the *Republic* gives dramatic expression to his conviction that possession of the science of rule in itself warrants the exercise of political authority, including the use of compulsion and violence to suppress intellectual challenges to the rulers' knowledge claims. At what he calls "the banquet of the festival of Bendis," he serves up to Socrates a would-be force-feeding of the illiberal sophistry Critias offers elsewhere in the dialogues (354a; cf. 345b).

Thrasymachus and Critias are linked in other respects as well. Their political inclinations are anti-democratic, they both have practical experience in political agitation, and their intellectual backgrounds are similar. Thrasymachus's association with Cleitophon (cf. 340a–b with *Cleit.* 406a, 410c), his characterization of Socrates as a sycophant (more on which below), and his mention of aristocracy but not of oligarchy among the various forms of government (338d–e)—as though oligarchy simply *is* rule by the best—suggest that his opposition to democracy is not mere anti-Athenianism. Critias actively supported revolution in Thessaly; Thrasymachus did the same in Cyme. Cicero names Thrasymachus along with Prodicus and Protagoras as one who "spoke and wrote much . . . about the nature of the physical world" (*de Orat.* 3.128); Critias associated with, and seems to have been influenced by, both of these sophists.[6]

A central claim of this book is that Critias's thought takes root in the *Republic* through the speeches of Thrasymachus and Glaucon, and comes to fruition in Callipolis. We shall see that while Callipolis's strange synthesis of personal immoderation and social control echoes Thrasymachus's conceptions of happiness and the science of rule, its totalitarianism springs more directly from Glaucon's profound evocation of Critias's turn of mind in the Ring Myth. In adopting the poetic idiom Critias favors—the archaic language of *muthos*, replete with hidden meanings (cf. 378d)—Glaucon transforms Critias's atheistic esotericism and Thrasymachus's praise of tyranny into foundational political principles. But these principles come to be reflected in the city of philosopher-kings only because Socrates takes his cues from his interlocutors, and ultimately bends over backward in accommodating his understanding to their characters and prejudices.

The Tyranny of Ideology

Having demanded that Socrates state "clearly and precisely [*saphōs . . . kai akribōs*]" what justice is, Thrasymachus forbids him to claim that it is "the needful, the beneficial, the profitable, the gainful, [or] the advantageous."[7] Socrates responds that this is like forbidding a man to say that twelve is "two times six, or three times four, or six times two, or four times three"; Thrasymachus's rejection of this particular analogy—"How very like this case is to that," he jeers—suggests that the terms he prohibits are in his view insufficiently lucid and exact. Of course, quasi-mathematical precision may be unavailable with respect to the question of justice (cf. Arist. *Eth. Nic.* 1094b11–27). Nor does policing speech alter the truth: Thrasymachus may forbid Socrates to assert that justice is the needful or the advantageous, but as Socrates observes, "nothing prevents it" from being so. Socrates will in any case say what he believes to be true, and because Thrasymachus lacks the power to silence him by force, he cannot, like the Thirty, shut him out of the middle ground (336d–37c).

Thrasymachus will nevertheless use all of the rhetorical tools at his disposal. As if he were speaking before a jury (this section of the *Republic* is laden with anticipations of Socrates' public trial), he wonders what punishment Socrates would deserve "if I show you another answer about justice besides all these that is better than they are" (337c–d). Why would Socrates merit punishment in that case? The two men are evidently already familiar with each other: Socrates watches to see how Thrasymachus will be affected by his argument with Polemarchus, and Thrasymachus remarks on Socrates' "habitual irony" and "accustomed behavior" (336d; 337a, e). It is likely that Thrasymachus has previously made public the accusations he enumerates on this occasion, and so proceeds as if with a preliminary indictment in hand.

Socrates does wrong, Thrasymachus alleges, because (1) he acts in bad faith, and (2) he cheats others by taking their teachings without recompense. Specifically: (1) Although Socrates knows very well what knowledge is, he tries to harm others in argument, including those who in fact have knowledge (337e, 338d, 341a). He does this because it is the easiest way to gratify his love of honor (336c). (2)

Socrates is unwilling to teach others, and does not even thank them for what they teach him (338a–b). In Thrasymachus's view, it would seem, Socrates not only knows what knowledge is, but has some himself.

Thrasymachus's insistence that Socrates is a slanderer or "sycophant in arguments"—a point important enough to be repeated four times (340d, 341a–c)—gives an aristocratic slant to his indictment. In democratic Athens, sycophants were professional informers who targeted men of wealth and standing and earned a reputation as blackmailers.[8] Because they were particularly "burdensome to the nobles" (Xen. *Hell.* 2.3.12), sycophants were also the first target of the Thirty. In denouncing Socrates as a sycophant, Thrasymachus suggests that he is himself an intellectual aristocrat, one who will not allow his rightful claim to knowledge to be besmirched by a plebian upstart whose vulgar speech is comparable to the breaking of wind. (At 338d he says that Socrates is *bdeluros*; *bdein* means "to fart.") He thus makes explicit the political undertone of the charge, dramatized by Aristophanes (*Clouds* 887–1103) and repeated in the *Apology* (18b–c), that Socrates makes the "weaker" speech "stronger"; *hēttōn* and *kreittōn* can also mean "worse" and "better" in social rank. Thrasymachus need now only establish his philosophical and political *bona fides* by indisputably besting Socrates in argument (cf. 341b).

Thrasymachus's judicial rhetoric anticipates the way the Athenians, oligarchs and democrats alike, ultimately used the lawcourts to resolve the problem of Socrates. An intellectual bully, Thrasymachus would have been at home among the fist-pounding radical elites of the twentieth century, including theoreticians of communism and fascism, except for one thing: his perspective is not limited to any particular -ism. Rather, he articulates and defends the concept of ideology as such, and he does so ideologically: with recourse, in other words, not merely to logical acumen and argumentative cogency, but to socially-constituted power. Thrasymachus's confrontation with Socrates—who genuinely wants to learn, and will not be pushed around—dramatically underscores the point that ideology is a kind of ersatz philosophy; it is not erotic dialogue, but dogmatic monologue, and it requires political protection because it cannot sustain probing criticism. The derivative nature of ideology is visible also in Thrasymachus's exemplification of the very behavior with which he charges Socrates: public exposure and denunciation, fueled by the love of honor (cf. 338a). His characterization of Socrates is a projection of his own frustrations, and this is no surprise; the conceit of wisdom, political or otherwise, resounds with the echo of offense when it encounters the humble ignorance of philosophy (cf. 337d).[9]

Politics as Pseudo-Science

Thrasymachus states that "for one who calculates correctly"—here again, his language is mathematical—"the just is everywhere the same: the advantage of the stronger." "Each ruling group," he explains, "sets down its laws with an eye to its own advantage; a democracy establishes democratic laws, a tyranny tyrannic ones, and the others in the same way." Justice is therefore nothing other than "the advantage of the established ruling body" as articulated in positive law (338e–39a). As Thrasymachus describes it, justice is a political simulacrum of the internal obligations of logical necessity and moral calling experienced by the likes of Socrates. It is what one is obliged to do, not by a thoughtful consideration of foundational truth or goodness, but by the external compulsion of another sort of *archē*: that of ruling power. This is the frank teaching of a hard-boiled observer of political realities, a truth that is neither good nor bad, but is simply the way things are.[10]

Thrasymachus's account of justice is nevertheless deeply questionable. We may doubt that legal coercion suffices to achieve all of a ruler's aims. Law may be too blunt an instrument for certain purposes.[11] A more serious problem is that the use of coercion and violence may itself be disadvantageous. While Thrasymachus tries to structure his interaction with Socrates in a quasi-legal fashion that gives him freedom to say what he wishes while denying it to his opponent—an echo of Critias's zero-sum concept of freedom as inseparable from slavery—this asymmetric use of law seems only to impede the acquisition of truth, the peculiar advantage sought by philosophical dialogue. More generally, the assimilation of rule to the exercise of technical expertise turns the ruled into passive objects, like the Athenian seedlings the "good farmer" Meletus hopes to protect from the corruption of weeds like Socrates (*Euthphr.* 2c–3a).

The resulting relationships will be disadvantageous in all instances where the good that is sought can be secured only by a community of equals. This includes the goodness of political community itself, which rests, Aristotle teaches, on the public exercise of intelligent speech (*logos*).[12]

Another problem with Thrasymachus's definition of justice arises as soon as Socrates gets him to agree that rulers sometimes mistakenly establish laws and issue commands that are detrimental to their interests. In such cases, it would be legally obligatory—that is, just—to do what is actually disadvantageous for those who rule and are stronger (339c–e). Polemarchus is very impressed with this line of argument: "By Zeus, Socrates . . . this is extremely clear [*saphestata*]" (340a). This expression of support provokes a response from Cleitophon that is loaded with historical irony: "If you are to witness for him, Polemarchus." Cleitophon's remark implicitly questions the metic's right to be heard in what he frames as a quasi-judicial proceeding, and so is of a piece with Thrasymachus's earlier attempt to impose extrinsic restrictions on Socrates' speech. Metics could bear witness in Athenian courts under the democracy, but they were specially targeted by the Thirty, whose decision to rob and execute wealthy men like Polemarchus was denounced by Thermanes as "doing greater injustice than the sycophants" (Xen. *Hell.* 2.3.22). Seen in hindsight, Cleitophon's insistence that "to do what is ordered by the rulers is just, Polemarchus" is chilling; it is genuinely tragic if Cleitophon himself was put to death by the Thirty.[13]

Cleitophon attempts to eliminate the contradiction Socrates observes by asserting that Thrasymachus identifies "the advantage of the stronger . . . [with] what the stronger believes to be his advantage" (340b). Thrasymachus denies that this is what he meant, and in fact takes the opposite tack. We say that the doctor, calculator, or grammarian "made a mistake," he tells Socrates, but "according to the precise speech—since you, too, speak precisely—none of the craftsmen makes mistakes. For the one who is mistaken errs because of a deficiency of science [*epistēmēs*], in which respect he is no craftsman; so no craftsman, wise man, or ruler makes a mistake at the time he is ruling." Stated "most precisely," "the ruler, insofar as he is a ruler, does not make mistakes; and not making mistakes, he sets down what is best for himself, and this the one ruled must do"

(340d–41a). Thrasymachus's exposition is strangely ambiguous for a man who values exact speech: medicine is a stochastic art, writing is a productive art, and calculation is neither. Still, it is clear that he regards ruling as a craft that secures the advantage of its practitioners with scientific precision.

Socrates responds with an internal refutation of Thrasymachus's argument that is itself a model of logical precision. He gets Thrasymachus to agree that, whereas the arts repair the natural deficiencies of their particular objects—so that medicine, for example, makes up the defect of a body with regard to its distinctive advantage, health—the arts themselves, considered precisely, are in no way defective. Thrasymachus does not dispute that nature furnishes the proper measures of art. He furthermore concedes that an art, "in being correct, is itself free from impairment and pure" (and so in need of no other art) "as long as it is precisely and wholly what it is" (342b). It follows that the arts—and therefore their practitioners, precisely insofar as they merit the name of craftsmen—do not provide for their own advantage.

Except for his explicit distinction between the advantage of the rulers and that of the ruled, Thrasymachus's conception of an inerrant ruling science is similar to the one Critias endorses in the *Charmides*. Socrates' refutation of this conception points toward the limitations of technical knowledge in a way that is also reminiscent of the *Charmides*. By assimilating the practitioners of the arts into the arts themselves, Socrates deprives Thrasymachus's notions of stronger/better and weaker/worse of any independent social and political meaning. But if he abstracts from the real context of human relations in which the arts are employed, and in particular from the widely observable disparities of power that give rise to Thrasymachus's definition of justice, he is able to do so only because he follows his interlocutor's lead. For Thrasymachus's insistence on scientific precision and clarity paradoxically obscures the very features of human existence his definition of justice is meant to capture.

In asking whether the arts are somehow themselves defective (342a–b), Socrates also leads one to wonder about the adequacy of a purely technical approach to the problem of advantage. In remedying the particular defects of its specific object, each art provides a peculiar benefit (346a). Is advantage as such therefore merely an aggregate of peculiar benefits? Are all human imperfections specific ones that can be addressed by particular arts, or are we deficient also in some comprehensive manner? And even if we are not comprehensively deficient, what understanding of advantage as a whole guides the actual employment of any particular art? It may be true that there is "for each of the arts . . . [no] advantage other than to be as perfect as possible" (341d), but the specificity of every sort of technical expertise would seem to imply that the arts can neither individually nor collectively instruct us on whether and when to use them, how to prioritize their use, or whether to develop new arts.[14] On a societal level, these questions tend to be decided by the market; Socrates will later observe that the benefit that accrues to craftsmen from the employment of their arts is provided by the additional art of wage-earning (346c). But what understanding of advantage determines how individuals or governments should employ the arts of making, investing, and spending money? To ignore this question is to accede to the rule of money: *ploutokratia,* whose very name suggests rule over souls that are as passive and thoughtless as the dead.[15]

A Deluge of Desire

In Socrates' view, the sorts of questions we have just raised ultimately draw the soul toward the contemplation of the Good. Thrasymachus finds it possible to reply to them only by abandoning the previously established foundations of his notion of the ruler or craftsman in the precise sense. When it becomes apparent that "his account of the just had turned in the opposite direction" with Socrates' demonstration that the arts do not provide for their own advantage (343a), Thrasymachus responds with an abrupt argumentative twist of his own. Forsaking talk of the ideal art of rule, he speaks of the actual disposition of rulers. In delivering a spirited defense of comprehensive injustice, he shifts his attention from natural deficiencies to social ones, and from the criteria of advantage supplied by nature to the tokens of success furnished by convention.

Thrasymachus's argumentative pivot once again brings to light the nature of ideology as a claim to knowledge protected by, and in the service of, social power. Within the context of the *Republic,* it is he who first articulates the fundamental perspective of the Cave:

that politics is a zero-sum competition for relative advantage as denominated in the fungible social currencies of power, money, and honor—a competition, moreover, in which the ignorant many are duped by a knowing few. This, too, is reminiscent of Critias. Seen from the perspective of the Cave Image's distinction between clever puppeteers and blinkered prisoners, poets of justice and their captive audience, Socrates appears to be a simpleton rather than a sycophant. In Thrasymachus's blunt estimation, his childish attachment to justice makes him a sheep bound to be fleeced and eaten by those who merely pretend to care for the flocks (343a–d).

The conception of advantage Thrasymachus so candidly articulates is rooted not in natural necessity, but in the forceful assertion of inflamed desire—*pleonexia* (344a), the desire to "have more" (*pleon echein*) that is the hallmark of the Feverish City. This desire is not private and absolute, but social and relative; it is by allowing those who "truly rule" not only to have more than others, but to be conspicuous in their possessive superiority, that the "truly simple [*euēthikōn*, lit. 'of good character'] and just" make rulers "happy" (343b–d).[16] And while the desire to have more seems to spring from the innate human tendency to imitate others and to want what they want, it bears no necessary relationship to the natural deficiencies and structures of being that came to light in the previous discussion of the arts and their objects, and that are further illuminated in Socrates' description of the True City. The object of the competition Thrasymachus describes is always the same, but the rules and game pieces differ from place to place and change over time. This is why the shift in Thrasymachus's argument is so abrupt: his turn from theoretical ideality to practical actuality, and from art and nature to desire and convention, plunges us into the almost hermetically-sealed human construction that Socrates will later represent as a great dark cavern.

Despite the detachment of any particular cultural cave from the stable measures of nature, Thrasymachus's notion of advantage is immediately accessible: when in Rome, one does as the Romans do. But in limiting the scope of human desire to the political competition for purely conventional goods, Thrasymachus threatens to reduce moral judgments to social facts. What in particular people do or refrain from doing in the quest for power, money, and honor—

what is, in other words, commonly acknowledged to be permissible and forbidden, profitable and unprofitable—is just what has been and is now done, a measure so fluid as to allow for virtually any content. Cleitophon's relativistic reduction of advantage to beliefs about advantage may not work in the face of ineluctable natural realities, but it captures the way in which the conventions and rewards of public competition depend entirely on social agreement.

In lecturing Socrates on the dispositions of justice and injustice, Thrasymachus nevertheless persists in employing the language of truth, knowledge, and perfection that he used in connection with the arts. He distinguishes those who "truly" (*hōs alēthōs*) rule from the "truly" simple and just (343b–c), and he asserts that Socrates will learn most easily if he takes his bearings by the "most perfect" (*telēōtatēn*) injustice—injustice in its most comprehensive, least defective, and purest form:

> And this is tyranny, which by stealth and force takes away what belongs to others, both what is sacred and holy, private and public, not bit by bit, but all at once. (344a)

Tyranny alone does "the whole of injustice" (344c), laying claim to the entirety of human existence and respecting no boundaries. Thrasymachus is said to have remarked that "the gods do not observe human affairs, for they would not have disregarded justice, the greatest of goods for human beings, which we see human beings violating" (DK frag. 8). "What is sacred and holy" may refer specifically to sanctified property associated with religious rites,[17] but this phrase has a more general connotation as well: unchecked by religious awe, tyrants appropriate the traditional authority of the gods in seeking their private advantage through what they officially present as justice.

Thrasymachus's association of perfect injustice with the most extreme covetousness and grasping is not coincidental. If detected, partial injustice results in punishment and reproach; tyrants, however, are called "happy and blessed" just insofar as they are known to commit total injustice (344b–c). The same is true of what Thrasymachus calls the "best" and "most perfectly unjust" city—the tyrannical city that "attempts to enslave other cities unjustly and to subjugate them, and to keep many enslaved to itself" (351b). He is surely thinking of Athens.[18]

In what is supposed to be its comprehensive achievement of advantage, the overreaching boldness of the tyrannical disposition takes the place of the ruling art that both Critias and Thrasymachus had posited but failed to clarify. Tyranny's orientation to what it mistakenly understands to be the whole of human existence, and its promise of liberation from the shackles of custom, makes it a political anticipation of philosophy. In its strange combination of religious antinomianism and conventional desire, extreme self-inflation and radically truncated eroticism, the tyrannical injustice Thrasymachus defends is a decayed image, in the mold of Critias, of Socratic or philosophical justice. Socrates compares Thrasymachus's harangue to the ear-flooding water poured by a bathman (344d). His speech is cleansing, because it allows the fundamental issue of the dialogue—the question of the best life—to stand forth clearly (344e); but it is also deafening, because the roar of appetite and ambition it evokes muffles the quiet voice of philosophical intelligence.

Socrates must find a way to make himself heard, and his solution is to accommodate his speech to the dispositions of his companions. This attempt to maintain the middle ground of considered reflection and public debate about what is good and just proves in the long run to be a costly moral concession.

Defining Goodness Down

In replying to Thrasymachus, Socrates does not directly address the matter of the best life. Instead, he paints a picture of "the best," "the good," and "the decent" (*hoi beltistoi, hoi agathoi, hoi epieikeis*: 347a–c) that is designed to appeal to various elements of his companions' self-conceptions: their sense of noble dignity on the one hand, and their anti-democratic prejudices and insecurities on the other. This picture is not entirely satisfactory, however. For in their relative indifference to the well-being of others and their excessive concern with dishonor, the good men Socrates describes are inferior to his own moral example. His distorted characterization of the good and the just in this context is a first, small step toward Callipolis's extremism in the suppression of injustice.

When Thrasymachus attempts to leave immediately after his diatribe, Socrates complains that he seems "to have no care for us at all, and not to have any concern whether we shall live worse or better in our ignorance of what you claim to know" (344e). Care for others and concern with their lives are the hallmarks of Socrates' public philosophizing (cf. *Ap.* 29d–30b), yet he later asserts that "any man of understanding would choose to be benefited by another rather than to take the trouble of benefiting another" (344e, 347d). It seems that Socrates does injustice here to generous souls like himself because he wants to make ruling look less attractive than Thrasymachus has made it out to be—less attractive, that is, to men more selfish than he, as he evidently judges his companions to be.[19] "No one willingly chooses to rule and to have a hand in straightening out the troubles of others," he asserts (although *he* does so, at the cost of considerable grief); rather, like all craftsmen—who derive no benefit just from the practice of their arts—"he asks for wages" in return (346e–47a).

Athenian laborers, craftsmen, and all but wealthy farmers and tradesmen would have been unable to serve in public office without remuneration, which they duly received under the democracy. As an artisan, moreover, Socrates cannot have objected to being paid for honest work. Yet he echoes Critias's disdain for the skilled labor of craftsmen (*Chrm.* 163b–c) in proceeding to depict the good as too self-respecting, or perhaps too eager to distinguish themselves from their social inferiors, to be seen accepting remuneration of any sort for exercising the art of rule. While the good will not rule for the sake of honor, "for they are not honor-lovers" (Socrates is just now speaking to the honor-loving Glaucon), they are evidently more sensitive to dishonor than Socrates, who will not stop philosophizing in spite of the reputation for criminal impiety and corruption his inquiries produce (cf. *Ap.* 29d–30b). In Socrates' telling, the best men in fact care deeply about their reputations: "they don't wish, in openly practicing rule for the sake of wages, to be called wage-earners, nor on their own to take pay by stealth from their office and be called thieves" (347b). Considered in the context of Athenian history, this sentiment has an anti-democratic undertone: those who served as magistrates or on the Council were paid from public funds prior to the oligarchy of 411, which eliminated compensation for most officials.[20] Once again, Socrates accommodates his case for justice not only to the limitations of his companions, but to their political prejudices as well.

Because the best men don't love honor and won't take pay for public service, Socrates asserts that they will rule only "because they have no one better than or like themselves to whom to turn it over," and because they want to avoid "the greatest penalty: being ruled by an inferior [*ponēroterou*, lit. 'more base'] man" (347c). But how, exactly, is one penalized by the rule of lesser men? While Socrates does not directly answer this question, he gives us some hints about it in the immediate sequel. The unjust man, he gets Thrasymachus to agree, desires to have more than everyone—the just and the unjust alike; the just man, however, neither thinks it fit nor wishes to get the better of the just, but only of the unjust (349b–c). (Yet we have already seen that the good father of the timocratic man, far from striving to get the better of the unjust, "is willing to have less so as not to be bothered" [549c].)[21] The just do not want to be taken advantage of by the unjust, in no small part because it is offensive to their pride; they will not put up with "being called simpletons and held in small account," like those who "mind their own business" (550a). Decent as they may be, the just as Socrates portrays them here are nevertheless deformed by their attachment to the manly business of the Cave.

In sum, Socrates implies that good, decent, and just men—self-respecting *kaloi k'agathoi—will* rule, if at all possible. The "necessity" that compels them (347c) is internal: they cannot brook the injustice of the inferior individuals who will inevitably hold office in their stead. What is more, the argument by which Socrates goes on to refute Thrasymachus one last time implies that the claim of good and just men to rule is supported by their superior knowledge. The unjust seek to get the better of everyone, but those who possess scientific knowledge (*epistēmē*) seek to get the better only of the ignorant, not of other knowers: musicians agree about tuning a lyre, and doctors about food and drink (350a). (Knowers, it would seem, resist being taken advantage of by the ignorant no less than the just by the unjust.) Those who know are wise, and the wise are good; the just man and the unjust man are each furthermore "such as the one he is like." The just, being like those who have knowledge, are therefore good and wise, while the unjust are ignorant and bad (350b–c).

We have seen that Thrasymachus identifies perfect injustice with total, tyrannical control of the city. If the perfection of injustice involves comprehensively getting the better of everyone, would not the perfect justice that Socrates, following Thrasymachus, posits as its exact antithesis (348b) involve comprehensively getting the better of the unjust and ignorant with the aid of precise knowledge?[22] And would not the best sort of people, at least as Socrates has described them, wish for just such political perfection? Socrates asserts that perfect or total injustice is impossible, because the unjust must refrain from doing injustice to one another while they seek to do it to others (352c). But this does not really change matters, for Glaucon will later observe that the unjust must refrain only from the *appearance* of injustice. Especially given Socrates' characterization of good, decent, and just men, Glaucon's assertion that "the extreme of injustice is to seem to be just while not being so" (361a) justifies extreme counter-measures in the war against injustice. It thus sets the stage for the political arms race that unfolds in books 2 through 7—a race that culminates in Callipolis, in which justice and injustice ultimately converge.

Glaucon's Anti-Myth: The Fellowship of the Ring

In debating Thrasymachus, Socrates accommodates his defense of justice to his cultivated but less than well-educated interlocutors—men whose better instincts have been distorted by powerful social pressures, and whose opinions reflect the influence of fashionable theories. If Thrasymachus lays out a version of the main sophistical teachings advanced by Critias—that rule is an exact science of comprehensive advantage, and that the wise manipulate the ignorant in achieving what they define as justice—Glaucon's restatement of Thrasymachus's argument more clearly and directly reflects the influence of Critias himself.

Glaucon proves to be just as imaginatively gifted as Critias, and similarly inclined to rival the poets. In the *Timaeus-Critias*, Critias uses the historical fiction of a demythologizing Egyptian priest to attack the authority of the Greek poetic tradition, even as he furnishes a new myth of the Athenians' divine origins. In the *Republic*, Glaucon produces his own ostensibly archaic and genuinely radical anti-myth. He, too, uses a barbarian to teach the implicit truth of atheism, as well as the political utility of the theodicy embraced (if only half-heartedly) by the poetic tradition—a theodicy grounded in the lie that human beings cannot hide from the gods. The Ring Myth is in these fundamental respects a token of his intellectual kinship with Critias.[23]

But Glaucon is not content simply to reproduce Critias's insights. Rather, he thinks them through to their logical conclusion. In particular, his myth exposes the inadequacy of the solution to the problem of justice set forth in the speech of Sisyphus. The Ring Myth is thus an anti-myth in two senses. As a veiled confirmation of atheism, it is an attack on traditional belief that is intended to be understood as such by the likes of Critias: men in the know and intellectuals. But it also exposes a fundamental flaw in the assumption that religious myth is an adequate instrument of social control. For if even an ignorant shepherd on the bottom rung of a rigidly hierarchical empire can fully enjoy the extreme political power made available through esoteric knowledge, political and intellectual elites in the Greek cities must discover some other means to enforce their conception of justice and protect the fellowship of the ring.

Glaucon's argument also anticipates the moral drama of the rest of the dialogue. He supposes that even the just—those who are habitually law-abiding, both by disposition and because of their understanding of the ills of anarchy—would be corrupted by the ring of invisibility. Similar tests of character are institutionalized in the Virtuous City, where the warriors' ability to withstand pleasures and fears is repeatedly examined, and are applied to Glaucon over the course of his conversation with Socrates. His failure to live up to the measures of virtue, particularly as indicated by the eagerness he displays in the face of the Gygean temptations of Callipolis, bodes ill for his final, decisive test, which comes in the form of Critias and the Thirty.

At the beginning of book 2, Glaucon explains that he has not yet learned from Socrates what he wants to know about justice and injustice, namely, "what each of them is, and what power [*dunamis*] each has all by itself when it is in the soul" (358a). What makes a soul capable of performing just or unjust deeds, and what do these capabilities or capacities do to the soul that possesses them? Glaucon asks these questions because he is genuinely perplexed. While others claim that "the life of the unjust man is much better than that of the just man," he tells Socrates, "it does not at all seem to me so"; indeed, he had earlier voiced his opinion that the life of the just man is "more profitable" than that of the unjust man (347e). "But I am at a loss," he confesses, "having been talked deaf by Thrasymachus and countless others" (358b–c). Glaucon's uncertainty will be resolved only if he can come to know what it is to *be* just and what it is to *be* unjust. This knowledge cannot be conveyed by a philosophical definition. As Socrates says in in book 9, the proper judge of the misery or happiness of the tyrant is "he who is able in thought to enter into a man's character and to see through it" (577a). Vision of the sort that could adequately compare the inner experiences of justice and injustice is necessarily imaginative and sympathetic. It accessible only by way of a story, such as the myth Glaucon proceeds to tell about the Gygean ring.

Glaucon nevertheless resists the internal moral understanding that his myth makes available. He attributes his entire speech to the "they," repeatedly bringing forward as evidence for his assertions what "they" say or what "every man" supposes (358c, 358e, 360b–d, 361e). His embrace of anonymity in defending injustice imitates the invisibility of the nameless shepherd of the myth. Similarly revealing is his invitation to envision a just man who has been given "license to do . . . whatever he wishes," to "follow and watch" him in thought, and to "catch him in the act of going the same way as the unjust man on account of *pleonexia*, which every nature naturally pursues as good" (359c). To see what another does is *not* the same thing as to imagine doing it oneself. Just as Glaucon refuses to be accountable for the argument he advances, he puts himself in the story he tells only as an external observer with a view from nowhere—the view of a god, or perhaps an anonymous spectator in a dark theater. Little wonder that Socrates later says Glaucon has "thoroughly scrubbed [*ekkathaireis*] each of the two men [the just and the unjust] for their judgment, just like a statue" (361d). Like Critias, Glaucon prides himself on exposing the hidden core of things; like Critias, he is nevertheless inclined to measure human existence only by its visible surfaces.

Glaucon's superficial approach to the problem of justice puts him at moral risk, even though there is reason to believe that he would not, at least in his present condition, deliberately choose a life he knows to be unjust. He argues, after all, that justice in the form of restraining laws "has grown naturally" from the painful experience of anarchy, and he never contradicts the opinion of "the many" that justice, like exercise and medical treatment, belongs in the class of goods toilsome in themselves but choiceworthy for their wages and consequences (357c–d, 359b). Socrates is furthermore "exceedingly pleased" and finds it "altogether divine" that he and Adeimantus seem not to have been persuaded that injustice is superior to justice.[24] Finally, Glaucon could be counted on to support Athenian law and custom just to the extent that he is disgusted, as he must be, by the possibility that an obscure and unlettered agricultural laborer like Gyges' ancestor could rise to tyrannize men of high birth and noble refinement like himself.

A greater danger is that, not having grasped the inner moral reality of justice and injustice, Glaucon could put himself in a position that would make resisting injustice difficult if not impossible. He might well be inclined to do so in the name of justice, and because he fails to appreciate the corrupting influence of the extreme power that would seem to be necessary to eradicate injustice. This would be an ironic outcome, given the teaching of the Ring Myth about the demoralizing effect of godlike power on the souls of the just. But the myth underscores a fundamental problem for all who embrace legal order and the social hierarchy it protects: that of the brutal but clever person who does not fear the gods, and is sufficiently bold and cunning to get away with secret injustice on a massive scale. This is a problem the poetic theology praised by Critias's Sisyphus fails to envision. Short of changing the character of human beings, it could be solved only if a just regime were to acquire the omniscience that Sisyphus's wise poet falsely attributes to the gods. Practically speaking, however, such omniscience entails totalitarian rule.

Glaucon's Esoteric Critique of Critias's Sisyphean Wisdom

The first part of Glaucon's speech at the beginning of book 2 (358e–59b) explains "what sort of thing justice is, and where it came from." The second part (359b–62c) is a thought experiment. Glaucon states that we might best perceive the power of injustice in the soul if we should produce a kind of demonstration of it "in the medium of thought"; the Ring Myth opens up an imaginative space within which certain truths may become perceptible to the mind. Glaucon invites us to envision what would happen if two men, one just and one unjust, should each put on a ring of the sort he has just described. The just man, he maintains, would then act no differently from the unjust one. Finally, he asks us to compare the lives of a perfectly unjust man and a perfectly just man. This comparison leads him to conclude that "from gods and human beings, the life that is provided for the unjust man is better than the one for the just man" (362c).

"They say," Glaucon asserts, "that doing injustice is by nature good, and suffering injustice is by nature bad." Injustice is naturally good, we may infer, because human beings by nature desire to get the better of one another (359c). But because the bad in suffering injustice outweighs the good in doing it,

> it seems profitable—to those who do not have the power to escape the one and choose the other—to establish an agreement among themselves neither to do injustice nor to submit to it. And from there, they began to set down laws and covenants among themselves, and to name the commandment of the law "lawful" and "just." (358e–59a)

Justice is a mean between "the best," doing injustice without paying the penalty, and "the worst," suffering injustice without being able to avenge oneself (359a). Law creates powerful disincentives against fulfilling natural desires, but it also establishes recompense for all who are otherwise too weak to punish those who have harmed and dishonored them.[25] *Nomos* thus springs from *phusis*: while laws and covenants are human constructions, they have "grown naturally" from the widespread suffering inherent in the original human condition (359b).

Glaucon's account of the origin and nature of justice is essentially identical with that of the Sisyphus fragment. Sisyphus describes an initial state of anarchy in which the wicked go unpunished, the good unrewarded, and human life is "disordered and bestial"; in response to this situation, human beings establish justice in the form of "chastising laws" that make punishment for wrongdoing inevitable. Like Sisyphus, Glaucon locates the fundamental limitation of law in the possibility of doing injustice in secret. But while Sisyphus's wise poet quenches secret lawlessness by inventing "fear of gods for mortals," Glaucon makes it clear that this solution is incapable of restraining those vigorous or intelligent enough to remain unmoved by this fear.

The Ring Myth illustrates the sort of "license" (*exousia*: that which exceeds the measure of being) capable of establishing that those who practice justice "do it unwillingly, from an incapacity to do injustice" (359b). The myth begins as follows:

> The license I'm speaking of would be most nearly such as would result if they [the just man and the unjust] had the sort of power they say once came to the ancestor of Gyges the Lydian. For he was laboring as a shepherd for the ruler of Lydia at that time, and when a great rainstorm and earthquake occurred, the earth broke open and a chasm appeared at the place he was pasturing. He saw it, wondered at it, and went down. And besides other wonderful things about which they tell myths, he saw a hollow bronze horse, with windows. Peering through them, he saw a corpse inside, as it seemed, of greater than human size. There was nothing but a gold ring on its hand; he took it off and went out.

As in the *Timaeus-Critias,* deluge and earthquake here signify an epochal transformation: a fracturing of cultural foundations (symbolically reflected in the opening of an abyss) and a radical break with the past. Such catastrophes, like actual floods and earthquakes, recur periodically; this one involves a *coup d'état* from a most unexpected quarter. And here is another echo of Critias: the events Glaucon describes are located in remote antiquity. The shepherd is an ancestor of Gyges, who overthrew the Heraclid dynasty and ruled Lydia four generations before Croesus, the sixth-century monarch who was the last of Gyges' line. Like his mythical ancestor, Gyges came to power through regicide; Herodotus informs us that, although he was filled with the shame before *nomos* that his ancestor conspicuously lacks, he nevertheless egregiously violated the law (Hdt. 1.8–13). The past repeats itself because it is forgotten, and especially, Glaucon implies, because its truth is deliberately concealed. Socrates describes Glaucon as "most courageous [*andreiotatos*] in everything" (357a); his myth reveals the genuinely archaic or foundational truth that lies hidden beneath the veneer of tradition, but can always be rediscovered by a doer or thinker who is "truly a man" (*hōs alēthōs andra*: 359b).

The shepherd has the courageous inquisitiveness, if not the education, of a natural philosopher. "He saw it, wondered at it, and went down"; wonder, Socrates tells Theaetetus, is "the beginning [*archē*] of philosophy" (*Tht.* 155d). The domain he enters, and fearlessly violates, is the underworld of the poets: a place of mythological wonders. But the only thing we know for certain that he sees there is a corpse—not gods or spirits, but a dead body, entombed in a structure that brings to mind the great hollow horse the Achaeans passed off as an offering to Athena (359d–e). This is the central point of the myth. To say it plainly, Glaucon implies that *inside the reverent constructions of the poets, one finds only mortals of heroic proportions.* This is an essential truth accessible only to those who are free from religious awe: men like Gyges' corpse-robbing ancestor, or the few whom Critias supposes understand the hidden meaning of the inscriptions at Delphi.

The ring is rich with symbolic meaning. Its theft looks like a rite of initiation for membership in a gang of criminals. Such rites are meant to prove that one has a gangster's nature, and the shepherd's imperturbability in the underworld leaves no doubt that he already possesses the vigor or manliness for which the ring substitutes in the case of more timorous souls. But the closed gold circle of the ring is a symbol of knowledge as well as daring, the knowledge of the insider who is sworn to secrecy. In this it anticipates Callipolis, where those of gold soul, the philosopher-kings, are also the bearers of secrets—including the truth of political violence that is veiled, but not completely concealed, by ostensibly noble but certainly false religious myths.[26] Finally, the ring is the sign of the corpse, and in slipping it on the shepherd takes the place of the corpse. His subsequent actions show that he is morally and emotionally dead to other human beings, or that his being is sheer exteriority—all beautiful surface and no interior, like the statue into which Critias wishes to mold Charmides.[27]

In the sequel, the shepherd attends a monthly meeting at which herdsmen report to the king about their flocks. He discovers by chance that turning the collet of the ring "toward himself, to the inside of his hand" makes him invisible to those seated alongside him, who "discussed him as though he had departed" (359e–60a). Evidently, he is not invisible to himself; the visibility in question is socially mediated. This, too, induces wonder and reflection, and he confirms by experimentation that rotating the ring allows him to appear and disappear at will. This knowledge leads him to embrace the inward turn of total self-enclosure. "He straightaway contrived to become one of the messengers to the king. When he arrived, he committed adultery with the queen; with her he set upon the king and killed him, and seized the rule" (360a–b).

In relation to the corpse, the shepherd possesses the power of invisibility even before he steals the ring: he sees the corpse, but knows that it cannot see him. Starting with the queen—before whom he suddenly materializes, like a god—he treats all of his victims like corpses, and in doing so becomes like one himself. Here again, Glaucon's curious resistance to inner experience proves to be significant. Glaucon supposes, for example, that committing rape with the aid of the ring would be one of its most attractive uses (360c). But if we consider the matter from the inside, as Socrates indicates we should (cf. 577a), it becomes clear that raping is not like robbing a grave. The ring makes you invisible to your victims, but it does not make your victims invisible to you, and whereas the face of a violated corpse remains impassive, the face of the living victim does not. The victim cannot see you, but in her eyes you can see her terror and pain; unlike a corpse, the victim also has a voice, with which she pleads for mercy. How can you see the victim's face and hear her words without seeing through her eyes? Most of us cannot answer this question, because this is the point at which imagination fails us. Yet this very failure tells us something about the condition of radical injustice. In order to commit rape with the aid of the ring, you must *already* be unable, in some fundamental way, to see through the eyes of another existing individual. Because you remain untouched by the profound suffering that you have caused your victim to feel, her terror is for you a surface without depth.

To those capable of looking beneath the surfaces of things, Glaucon's thought experiment shows that men like Gyges' ancestor, who is predisposed to seize any opportunity to commit secret crimes, would be morally unchanged by the ring. It is also doubtful that possessing the ring would without exception transform previously law-abiding individuals into criminals. It is simply not the case, as Glaucon asserts, that "no one is just willingly, but only under compulsion . . . since whenever each thinks he will be able to do injustice, he does it" (360c); were this so, no atheist could be trusted in public libraries or near coat racks. What is more, Glaucon himself implies that at least some individuals will not behave unjustly even when they can get away with it: if someone with the license to commit injustice were unwilling to do so, he opines, "he would seem most wretched and foolish to all who were aware of it" (360d).

Glaucon nevertheless concludes that the opportunity conferred by the ring would suffice to reveal that all human beings are internally disposed to get the better of others whenever they can:

> Now if there were a pair of such rings, and the just man were to put one on, and the unjust the other, there would be no one so adamant as to stand fast in justice and endure to keep away from the possessions of others and not to touch them, although it would be possible for him to take whatever he wanted from the marketplace without fear, and to go into the houses and have intercourse with whomever he wished, and to kill and release from bonds anyone he liked, and to do all other things among human beings as the equal of a god. (360b–c)

Glaucon's language is noteworthy. His mention of standing fast (*menein*) and enduring (*tolman*) suggests the struggle of a warrior in the face of an enemy. Even the man whose natural strength of soul has been toughened by training and discipline, he implies, would be unable to resist doing injustice if he should happen to acquire the power the poets attribute to the gods. In that case, however, injustice springs as much from moral weakness and incontinence as from manliness and vigor. Perhaps this is why he speaks of a pair of rings (he uses the dual grammatical form): the just and the unjust man confront one another as mirror-images, in which virtue and vice are reversed from each perspective. This reversal is possible, however, only because the gods as traditionally conceived are deeply ambivalent figures. The fear induced by the teaching that the gods punish wrongdoers goes hand in hand with the desire aroused by the fantasy of their unconstrained sexuality and aggression.

In the end, Glaucon goes only so far in his rejection of the mythological tradition: neither the moral stamina of the just man nor the courage of the unjust man suffices to free either one from the corrupting influence of the gods of the poets. Critias's Sisyphus, a criminal who is eternally punished by the gods, gets his revenge on them by declaring that they do not exist. According to him, the wise inventor of the gods is audacious, ingeniously deceptive, and unafraid of divine retribution. But in these respects, Sisyphus's wise man resembles Gyges' ancestor, and if Glaucon is correct, he, too, would be unable to refrain from secretly pursuing injustice while publicly supporting justice.

In thinking through the implications of Critias's esotericism, Glaucon indirectly raises a still more serious problem. Even if a regime were to use the political equivalent of the power of the ring strictly to combat injustice, it could eliminate the secret pursuit of injustice only by reducing to zero the sphere of privacy in human life. The comprehensive surveillance necessary to achieve this end—to say nothing of the radical transformation of the family, childrearing, and other private associations the regime would have to undertake, together with the indoctrination necessary to support this transformation—would effectively prohibit the cultivation and meaningful expression of interiority, or of the individual soul. The Ring Myth helps us to see that the dream of Callipolis is an inhuman nightmare.

Herodotus's Naked Queen

The conclusion Glaucon draws from his thought experiment outlines a story that is told or alluded to throughout the *Republic*: that of a man who is by all appearances virtuous—Amphiaraus, the future timocrat, the soul that chooses the greatest tyranny in the Myth of Er (619b–c)—but who finds himself in a situation that overwhelms his moral resources. This is also the story Herodotus tells about Gyges, a law-abiding man whom Socrates nevertheless later identifies with his criminal ancestor (612b). Herodotus's story supports Glaucon's argument because it concerns the corruption of men who are not, like Gyges' ancestor, obviously predisposed to injustice. Considered in connection with the question of what extreme power does to the soul, Herodotus's story of a king and his bodyguard—a ruler and his armed auxiliary—has the ring of prophecy.

In Herodotus's tale, Candaules, the ruler of Lydia, compels Gyges to violate the law by seeing his wife naked. He hides Gyges in a closet, and assures him that he will be able to see the queen without being seen himself. Unbeknownst to both men, the queen catches sight of Gyges and perceives what Candaules has done. She secretly confronts Gyges and gives him a choice between killing her husband and marrying her or paying for his injustice with his life. Gyges chooses his own survival, and becomes the ruler of Lydia after murdering the king.

The first part of the story reads as follows:

> This Candaules fell in love with his own wife; and being so in love, he believed that he had in her by far the most beautiful of all women. So he believed. Now, he had among his bodyguard Gyges, the son of Dascylus, who was his special favorite. To this Gyges, Candaules used to confide even very serious affairs, and in particular he used to praise his wife's looks [*to eidos tēs gunaikos*] excessively. After a little while—for it was fated to turn out badly for Candaules—he spoke thus to Gyges: "Gyges, since I do not think that you believe me when I tell you about my wife's looks—for human beings happen to trust their ears less than their eyes—contrive to see her naked." But Gyges cried out and said: "Master, what an unhealthy speech you are speaking, in ordering me to look upon my mistress naked! For when she takes her clothes off, a woman strips off the sacred awe [*aidōs*] that envelops her. One must learn from the noble and beautiful things that human beings discovered long ago. And among these, this is one: that each should look upon his own things. I do believe that your wife is the most beautiful of all, and I beg you not to demand of me anything unlawful." (Hdt. 1.8)

What Candaules overpraises, and what he wants Gyges to see, is not his wife; it is rather her *eidos*—the visible look of her body. Candaules places the highest value on what meets the eye, and he accordingly denigrates speech, the medium in which law and tradition are constituted and transmitted. His report of his wife's superlative beauty is in his own view inadequate, for speech is indirect and therefore incapable of conveying certain truths. Gyges protests that he does believe Candaules' wife is most beautiful, even though he can only imagine what her naked body must look like on the basis of her clothed form. But in this case, Candaules wants to leave nothing whatsoever to his imagination.

Why does Candaules want Gyges to see his wife naked? In telling us that Candaules believed his wife was by far the most beautiful of all women, Herodotus twice uses the term *nomidzein*, belief that accords with law, custom, or convention. *Nomos* is in this case divided, for Candaules' desire brings him into conflict with ancestral law. He wants to see the look in Gyges' eyes when Gyges sees his wife's naked body. He may be sexually excited by this prospect, but the voyeuristic pleasure he seeks in showing off his most prized erotic possession is largely thumotic. Candaules seeks the pleasure of receiving genuine esteem from a trustworthy judge; without actually seeing the queen's body, however, Gyges' affirmation of her beauty would be *pro forma* and therefore worthless. But one suspects that this is not all, and that Candaules is also motivated by the stirrings of a higher *erōs*: that he wishes to share with another—a confidant if not a friend, with whom he discusses very important matters—an intimate experience of beauty. Neither of these purposes could be imputed to Gyges' ancestor, whom Glaucon portrays as completely and fundamentally alone.

Both the queen and Gyges are nevertheless essentially invisible to Candaules, just as he is essentially invisible to himself. Candaules' failure to imagine what it would be like to be his wife or his bodyguard causes him fatally to misjudge both of them. He treats his wife, who remains anonymous throughout, as though she were a beautiful statue rather than a human being. Insofar as he regards her only as an object to be seen, he cannot see his inner ugliness through her eyes. In fact, there is a point beyond which he cannot imagine her seeing anything at all. This becomes clear when he tries to reassure Gyges by explaining that he has a plan whereby he can gaze upon her without being detected (1.9). Candaules' narcissistic imagination radically limits his understanding: he is able to envision only how he himself will appear to Gyges after the sight of his wife's beautiful yet unavailable body has awakened Gyges' longing. Insofar as the boundaries of his self-knowledge are fixed by his imagination of what he looks like to other men, he also treats himself as though he were an outside with no inside—something whose entire being consists in its visibility.

For his part, Gyges resists the role that Candaules has prepared for him. Like Candaules, he has already undressed the queen in his mind, but he sees her nakedness from the inside, so to speak. Perhaps because he is himself a subservient and relatively defenseless being, he takes pains to imagine what a woman's lot would be in a world in which men have lost respect for law.[28] In any case, Gyges recognizes that a woman would be nothing but a naked body—and, as such, could potentially be possessed by any man with eyes to see—were it not for the sacred awe that surrounds and protects her from the male gaze.[29] Yet while he sees more than Candaules does, there is more to the queen than even he suspects.

Gyges respects the law that each should look upon his own in part because he understands it. In resisting the opportunity to gaze upon a beautiful body, he is guided by the beautiful or noble things that were discovered by his Lydian ancestors (among whom, however, Glaucon includes the shepherd). But Gyges would not have perceived the beauty of the law had he not been able to penetrate the surfaces of things by an act of sympathetic imagination, and to take note of what he sees. Candaules does not understand this, for he supposes that Gyges is hesitant only because he fears being detected by the queen. Yet Gyges is strongly reluctant to kill the king even with the crucial support of the queen, a point Herodotus mentions three times (1.11–12).

It would be a mistake, however, to regard Gyges as the hero of Herodotus's tale. Gyges is first compelled to take a role alongside the unsuspecting queen in what amounts to a puppet-play that is authored by the king. But the queen secretly rewrites the play, and compels Gyges, on pain of death, to attack the unsuspecting king. Herodotus tells us that "among the Lydians, and pretty much among the rest of the barbarians, for even a man to be seen naked brings him into great shame" (1.10). Because the queen keeps her shame hidden, however, neither Gyges nor Candaules is aware that their scheme has been discovered. Indeed, Gyges comes to the queen "thinking that she knew nothing of what had been done," and he is "filled with wonder" when she forces him to choose between being killed or killing Candaules. "Take me, and the kingship of the Lydians," she tells him, "or you must yourself die straightaway" (1.11). One suspects that Gyges' wonder stems not just from this dramatic reversal of Candaules' plot, but from the very fact that the queen has hatched a plot of her own: he simply did not imagine that she had it in her.

Although his vision is keener than the king's, Gyges, too, is unable to see beyond the surface of this barbarian queen. Deceptive, vengeful, and distinguished by cunning intelligence, she is very like a tragic female from the Greek stage. The queen instructs Gyges to attack Candaules "from the very same place from which he showed me to you naked" (1.11), as though Candaules' death were nothing but the extension and completion of his original injustice. By hiding Gyges in a closet, the queen in effect gives him a ring of invisibility, just as the king had done. But in this story, unlike that of Glaucon, the purely unjust use of the ring is punished: it is in the service of the law that the queen demands Gyges break the law. She emerges from the shadows just long enough to repair the fabric of *nomos* that is her greatest protection.

Gyges and Candaules in Callipolis

Herodotus's tale of Candaules and Gyges underscores the broad applicability of Glaucon's case for the irresistible attraction of injustice. While Gyges' ancestor starts out at the very bottom of the social hierarchy, Candaules stands at its pinnacle; one is a poor slave, the other a wealthy potentate. Yet Candaules, too, longs for more than he has, and resorts to injustice in order to satisfy his desires. His judgment is corrupted by erotic passion, which causes him to overestimate his wife's beauty, but even more by his status as an absolute master (*despotēs*), which warps his understanding of human intimacy and inflates his self-perception to the point where he loses the reverence for the law that safeguards him as well as others.

Candaules' fate proves that neither the royal person, nor the legal order on which political authority is founded, can be protected in the absence of a sacred awe that is shared by ruler and ruled alike. This is an ominous lesson, for the founders and philosopher-kings of Callipolis are utterly shameless in their attempts to maintain such awe among the ruled. But a still more disturbing lesson is contained in the behavior of Gyges. How is it that a man with a healthy respect for the law, whom Glaucon would certainly regard as just, comes to commit the extreme injustice of regicide? The queen did not have to order Gyges to slay her husband, and Gyges did not have to comply; she is driven by a desire for revenge, and he, at least in part, by the attractions of power, honor, and wealth—unjust gains that nevertheless seem preferable to dying in the cause of justice. Gyges' corruption is progressive; his second and greater injustice is prepared by the first one, his illicit observation of the naked queen—a vision of what is concealed by law and custom, like the naked corpse his ancestor sees inside the hollow horse.

Even for Gyges, who far exceeds Candaules in sympathy and respect for others, the sight of what is by nature, and of the power and license available to him beneath the covering of law, is ultimately incompatible with justice. One could certainly not expect better of the spirited and erotic warriors of Callipolis, a city where men and women exercise naked, and no one can look only upon his own things because all is held in common. But what of Callipolis's kings, who, like Candaules, prefer what they take to be the direct vision of form to the hearsay of tradition?

At some point in book 6, Socrates wonders "in what manner a city, taking philosophy in hand, will not be destroyed" (497d). This is a strange question, for it implies that philosophy runs the risk, in becoming explicitly and decisively political, of destroying the very community it is trying to save. While Socrates does not explain what he means here, one problem seems to be how to avoid letting ailing patients usurp the authority that properly belongs to their doctor. If a city were simply and directly to "manage" or "use" philosophy—these being the relevant senses of the participle *metaxeiridzomenē*, "taking in hand"—philosophy would be compelled to conform to the political sickness that it is supposed to treat. It would then only feed the fever that it seeks to starve.

As we shall see in the following chapters, philosophy in Callipolis is made to conform to notions of theoretical and practical utility. It comes to be conceived as a conceptual and political tool, one that steers the city through its scientific grasp of the highest objects of contemplation. Laboriously learned, the unerotic and unmusical philosophy of Callipolis's kings—philosophy as technical expertise—is out of tune with the Whole, the harmonious ensemble of beings that show forth in the light of the Good. It is thus incapable of saving the city from the injustice of rulers and auxiliaries alike.

CHAPTER 5

Disgracing the Song

THE MYTHS OF CALLIPOLIS

In the *Republic,* Socrates bends to the prejudices and passions of his interlocutors. While such flexibility is integral to his assessment of Glaucon's mind and character, it also serves a more general strategy of inclusion that aims to build a community of dialogue within which he can pursue his essential work of caring for souls. Socrates' ability to generate and sustain (however briefly) a genuine community of speech underscores the failure of Callipolis, the city *in* speech, to do the same.

But Socrates also seems to envision a special public role for Glaucon. In book 1, he succeeds in recruiting a philosophical ally: with regard to future arguments about justice, Polemarchus declares, "I am ready to be your partner in battle" (335e). Socrates seems to regard Glaucon as another potential ally—an informal auxiliary to his guardianship of the philosophical pursuit of truth, who will battle at his side within the Athenian intellectual context. This relationship would potentially benefit Glaucon at least as much as Socrates. If winning him over requires initially blurring the truth, Socrates may later be able to lead him to a clearer and deeper understanding of essential matters, and to the moderation that comes with a recognition of ignorance. As unlikely as this consummation may be, it is devoutly to be wished, for Glaucon has shown from the very beginning of the *Republic* that he *will* lead others.

Socrates' attempt at community-building appears to be successful. Most notably, he befriends Thrasymachus, who was at one point prepared to storm off (497c–d). But his strategy of accommodation has hidden costs and unforeseen consequences. When he begins to purge the Feverish City, Socrates states that he and his interlocutors will proceed "like men mythologizing in a myth" (376d). This remark emphasizes the fundamentally poetic character of the cities and souls he goes on to discuss. More particularly, however, Socrates' word-doubling calls attention to a specifically political kind of tragic *muthos* or plot that is reproduced in each of the nested narrative and interpretative frames of the *Republic.*

First, there is the story of the city in speech, whose life increasingly attracts Glaucon as the Virtuous City's unity gives way to the decadence and fragmentation of Callipolis. Socrates produces a regime that conceives of governance primarily as the treatment of sick souls, but whose political medicine exacerbates the problems it is supposed to address. Like Atlantis, Callipolis fatefully confuses wisdom with science; its laws furthermore encourage personal immoderation and violence and promote civic rivalry and discord. A rise in power coincides with a fall into vice: all ancient histories reflect this tragic archetype. The unhappy destiny of Callipolis may be read even in the founding myth it shares with the Virtuous City. The Noble Lie teaches that the first citizens are formed and reared by the gods; as we shall see, it also implies that later generations are doomed to descend into civil strife.

Second, there is the arc of the conversation Socrates narrates, which tracks that of the city in speech. The precious patrimony of character and intelligence is apt to slip when handed off, like the torch of Bendis, between galloping, jostling generations. Just as Socrates fears at the beginning of book 5, he falls from truth and virtue and drags his friends down with him in the very process of generating the city of philosopher-kings. He and Glaucon slacken in soul as their political imagination is given its head, and their immoderation is reflected in the regime they are constructing. In particular, Socrates equips Callipolis's rulers with a spurious knowledge that seems brighter and harder than his own tentative insights and explorations—a comprehensive science characterized by technical rigor and precision, both in cognizing the totality of the beings and in producing laws and citizens.

The race of soul that runs through the *Republic* comes to a fork in its central books. One road leads down to Callipolis, the other up to the Good. A divided and fragmented community, Callipolis is infected with immoderation and ruled by technicians supported by a rhetoric of expertise, the practical but philosophically spurious side of the formal ontology in which the city's kings are trained. At the same time, Socrates offers prophetic images of the Good, the unifying origin of the Whole, that allow us to glimpse the truest and deepest mysteries of philosophy. For genuinely erotic souls, the light of the Good, more brilliant than any flame, points the way toward virtue and happiness. This fundamental ambiguity in the drama and argument of the *Republic* brings to mind Sophocles' *Oedipus Tyrannus*. Steering clear of Corinth so as to escape the dire fate prophesied by the priestess of Apollo, and with nothing to boast of but his wits, Oedipus opens a path to the throne of Thebes by unwittingly killing his father, King Laius, at a place where the road from Delphi splits. Oedipus tells this story at the center of Sophocles' tragedy, just as it dawns on him that he may be both a bastard prince of Corinth (a rumor he had hoped to exterminate with the oracle's help) and a well-born orphan of Thebes.[1] In the *Republic*, the philosopher, born at the center of the dialogue to rule in Callipolis, stands at the crossroads of a similarly inverted duality of nobility and baseness. The path of natural erotic development leads to the perfection of the genuine philosopher, "be he ne'er so vile" (as Shakespeare's Henry V puts it); that of thumotic political production, to Callipolis's purebred but philosophically illegitimate rulers.

Like Sophocles' tragedy, Socrates' discussion of Callipolis focuses on the problem of filiation: the production and reproduction of kings of pure philosophical nature and political pedigree. This problem is highlighted by references to lameness, bastardy, and blindness, particularly in the mythical line of Thebans that runs from Cadmus through Labdacus, Laius, and Oedipus to Polynices and Eteocles. Socrates also alludes at a crucial point to the political degeneration of Corinth under the rule of the Cypselids, culminating in the notorious tyranny of Periander. The historical Cypselids and mythical Labdacids violate the sacred bonds of family and norms of human sexuality, and their lineages end with the sons of Oedipus and Periander, who die in civil strife.[2] The *muthos* of Callipolis runs along similar lines. Speaking "tragically" like the Muses of the *Iliad*, Socrates explains in book 8 that Callipolis, whose wavelike birth-pangs and sexual inbreeding feature prominently in his account, will fall when later generations of rulers are torn apart by internecine conflict (545e–47a). In the course of his discussion of the Good, Socrates also alludes to the myth Critias mentions in the *Timaeus*. Wishing to prove that he is a child of King Helios, Phaethon insists on driving, and then crashes, the chariot of the sun. In the *Republic*, as in the Honecker joke from *The Lives of Others*, control of the source of light and life becomes a potent symbol of the blind ambition of ideological tyranny.[3]

The final interpretative frame of the *Republic* is the actual, historical world in which Plato produces the written text of the dialogue. Seen from this vantage point, historical deed and philosophical *muthos*—the intellectual presumption and moral disgrace of the Thirty, and the philosophical totalitarianism of Callipolis—display an essential kinship with one another. Perhaps this is all that can be confidently said about their relationship, because even if Critias's deed imitates Socrates' speech, Callipolis seems to imitate Critias's own political mythologizing. What is original in all this, and what image?

The *Republic*'s multiple levels of perspective, and the dramatic analogies that connect them, in any case allow for a progressive ascent of critical comprehension. They give us access to Socrates' judgment of himself and his companions, as well as to Plato's appraisal and correction of his teacher—responses Socrates invites in worrying that he may prove to be more culpable than an unwilling murderer (451a). But before we can consider these dimensions of the *Republic*, we must chart the fateful course of Socrates' speeches and deeds in the dialogue's central books. We shall once again follow the music, taking our bearings by the myth of Arion, a well-known tale about a famous singer whose primary patron was Periander of Corinth. For it is to Arion's desperate plight that Socrates compares the situation in which he and Glaucon find themselves as they begin their construction of Callipolis, and it is the musician's disgrace at the hands of a paradigmatically tyrannical ruler that illuminates the central, tragic story of the *Republic*: the drama of Glaucon's fate.

Rough Passage: Arion's Plunge

Like its citizens, Callipolis is a child with many fathers, including Thrasymachus and Glaucon and, at one remove, Critias—a small irony, since the regime is ultimately unable to reproduce itself. The problem of cultural transmission is implicit in the remarkable poetic analogy with which, in one stroke, Socrates frames the whole of the political mythologizing of books 5 through 7. In defending the first wave of book 5—the proposal to educate and employ women as warriors—Socrates must contend with the accusation that educating women as warriors contradicts the principle that each must do his own things (453b). If the first wave does contradict this principle, it violates his own understanding of justice and moderation. Faced with the difficult case he must make, he observes:

> Whether one falls into a little reservoir, or into the middle of the greatest sea, he nevertheless swims all the same. So we, too, must swim, and attempt to save ourselves from the argument, hoping either that some dolphin might take us up, or for some other desperate [*aporon*] salvation. (453d)

Socrates alludes here to Herodotus's myth of Arion, a poet and citharist who was forced by larcenous sailors to jump from a ship and then miraculously saved by a dolphin. When he returns to Periander filthy with sea-scum, the tyrant arrests him and makes him play a part in the drama of interrogation and confession he arranges for the sailors. Socrates and his companions find themselves in a comparable situation, and whatever argumentative salvation they may achieve will be mixed with moral stain. In Socrates' hands, Herodotus's tale of the impotence and humiliation of soul-ordering song under tyranny serves as a prophetic allegory of the debasement that the music of philosophy will suffer in Callipolis.

Like Arion as he walks the plank, Socrates faces a situation of great perplexity at the beginning of book 5. He poses an alternative of slender hopes. The first is miraculous rescue by a dolphin, and there is one small clue, propitious at least for Socrates, as to what this might mean. Herodotus relates the myth of Arion in the context of a larger story about how the Lydian king Alyattes was cured of illness after he consulted the oracle at Delphi, and the *delphis* that rescues Arion may be an avatar of the Delphic god that buoys Socrates, too, in the sea of existence.[4] The second is some other rescue that is *a-poros*: offering no passage, no way out—at least none through which intelligent persons could see their way clear. What is more, the argument that threatens to overwhelm him and Glaucon is their own. Indeed, it is not the accusation of self-contradiction that most particularly resembles a sea, but their response to this accusation—an argument that builds on itself, with each new wave drawing energy and form from the backflow of the preceding one. It is the surge of *this* argument, and of the deep forces of the soul that it both mimics and unleashes, that ultimately threatens to overpower the two of them.

Herodotus tells us that Arion of Methymna was a world-famous poet and performer, "a cithara player second to none at that time, and the first of human beings who made and named the dithyramb, and produced it at Corinth" (Hdt. 1.23). Arion was supported by the tyrant Periander, with whom he spent most of his time; but he once traveled from Corinth to Italy and Sicily, where he earned a great deal of money practicing his art. He hired Corinthian merchantmen to sail him back to his adoptive home and patron, but they plotted to take his money and throw him into the sea. Arion pleaded with them to spare his life, but to no avail; they ordered him either to kill himself if he wanted to be buried on land, or immediately to leap overboard. Having entered such doubtful, dire straits (*es aporiēn*: 1.24.4), he decided to go out in style:

> Arion entreated them, since they were so determined, to behold him standing and singing in full dress on the raised benches at the stern; and having sung, he promised to kill himself. They were pleased that they were about to hear the best singer of human beings, and they retreated from the stern to the middle of the ship. And he put on his full apparel and took his cithara, and standing on the raised benches he went all the way through the Orthian Song [*nomon ton orthion*], and when he had finished the song, he hurled himself into the sea as he was, in full dress. So they sailed away to Corinth, but they say that a dolphin took him up and carried him to Tainaron. And he disembarked from it and journeyed to Corinth in dress, and when he arrived he related all that had happened. But Periander, in disbelief,

> kept Arion under guard and would not let him leave, while watching attentively for the sailors. When they arrived, he summoned them and asked if they could tell him anything about Arion. And while those men were saying that he was safe in Italy, and that they had left him prospering in Tarentum, Arion appeared before them, just as he was when he jumped overboard; and they were astonished, and when cross-examined [*elenchomenous*] were no longer able to deny what had happened. (1.24.4–7)

Socrates resembles Arion in several respects. Like Arion, he is arrested—detained on his way home from the Piraeus, and again in book 5. He begs to be released, but his entreaties fall on deaf ears, and he, too, responds by making a display of political music. Arion is a poet whose song is a *nomos,* a localized melodic idiom that seems to have been meant to inculcate fondness for the traditional ways of a particular community.[5] Socrates is also a poet whose song is a *nomos,* one that starts with the beautiful harmony of the True City and continues through the musical measures of the Virtuous City, the philosophical soul, and the Good. Arion's law/song is *orthios,* "upright" (and perhaps "high-pitched"); Socrates' law/song is *orthos,* "correct." Both *nomoi* are associated with Sparta and the customs of the Lacedaemonians: Timothy Power points out that Arion sings "*the* famous citharodic *nomos* called the *Orthios,* which was traditionally attributed to Terpander," a seventh-century poet who is said to have quelled civil discord among the Lacedaemonians with his song.[6] Arion is "the best singer of human beings": the best singer *about* human beings as well as among them. Socrates, too, is a preeminent singer in both senses, and his performance in the central books of the *Republic,* like Arion's, involves a leap into perilous waters.

What might all this mean? To begin with, the myth of Arion concerns the limited power of political music to straighten warped characters. Arion fails where Terpander succeeds; he is incapable of communicating cultural legacy through song to the corrupt men for whom he performs. The Corinthian sailors are entertained and even captivated by his music, but not gripped and uplifted. It does not set in order their mercenary souls: souls gone to seed in a city grown rich from the land and sea trade that passes, by necessity as well as convenience, through its narrow, centrally-located isthmus.[7]

The sailors' behavior is echoed in Socrates' image in book 6 of the Athenians democracy as a vessel commandeered by a crew intent on pilfering the ship's hold (488a–89a).[8] Indeed, both he and Arion bear some resemblance to the "true pilot" of this image, who risks being killed by his ignorant and greedy rivals. (The word "governor" captures both the sound and the meaning of *kubernētēs*, a pilot or helmsman.) Yet the sailors who rob Arion get their comeuppance at the hands of a tyrant whom nothing and no one escapes—including Arion himself, whom Periander detains while he checks his story. In Herodotus's tale, souls that cannot be erotically attuned to the beautiful song of upright *nomos* are forcefully corrected, perhaps with the help of a god (whether *delphis* or Delphic), but ultimately by a human ruler of godlike power and omniscience. This alternative recalls the distinction between prehistoric Athens and Atlantis, and is more precisely reflected in the difference between the True City and Callipolis.

Arion's plunge is the most striking detail of his story—far more so than his miraculous rescue, to which Herodotus devotes only a few words. Herodotus places special emphasis on the elaborate costume the singer is wearing when he leaps into the sea. The *skeuē* or apparel of a citharist was impressive: we must picture Arion decked out in a sumptuous and colorful ceremonial outfit (including a richly-embroidered robe, mantle, and soft boots), wearing a crown, and holding an ornamented instrument, perhaps inlaid with gems.[9] His splendid regalia are ruined in his jump from the ship; his beautiful clothes must be salt-streaked and soiled with mud and flotsam when he arrives at Periander's court. This detail nicely anticipates the ambiguity of Socrates' performance in the *Republic*'s central books: while the measures of the philosophical soul are beautiful and noble, the erotic activities of poetry and philosophy are besmirched or debased in the construction of Callipolis.

Arion's relationship to Periander, whom Socrates mentions in book 1 along with other rich men who think they have great power (336a), helps to flesh out the nature of this debasement. While Arion fails to order souls with music, Periander simply lays down the law. The Corinthian tyrant had a reputation for wisdom in the Greek tradition: Diogenes Laertius includes him in his *Lives of Eminent Philosophers*, and even identifies him as one of the Seven Sages (1.13,

94–100).[10] In Herodotus's story, Periander uses his power to uncover the truth, much as the riddle-solving Oedipus does when he doggedly tracks down the murderer who is polluting his city. The scene of judgment at his court is remarkable: the greatest living performer of political music stands aside in silence, clothed in his ruined finery, while the tyrant exposes the sailors' wrongdoing by means of *elenchos* or cross-examination, Socrates' trademark mode of philosophical inquiry. Seen in the light of the *Republic*, the two men—one a disgraced lover of song, the other a thumotic and triumphant ruler—present two very different versions of the philosopher.

At the moment he jumps from the ship, Arion is doomed and the robbers are saved; in the end, however, their fates are reversed. Like Zalmoxis and Er, Arion seemingly returns from death. His story is in important ways reminiscent of poetic tales about the expulsion, homecoming, and revenge of historical or wholly mythical men of royal blood—men like Oedipus, crippled and abandoned on a hillside by the king whose life, marriage, and office he later takes; Cypselus, the son of a lame woman and a low-born father who nevertheless topples the Corinthian aristocracy; and Odysseus, the beggar who reclaims his home, wife, and throne from nobles who despise and abuse him. But crucially, Arion is not an actual ruler. Regal in soul and attire, he nevertheless sings at the pleasure of the tyrant, as Herodotus emphasizes when he reports that Periander kept him under guard (*en phulakēi*). While Periander exacts justice, Arion stands apart and looks on, a figure not of triumph but of weakness and shame.

Given the connection between clothing and *nomos* in Herodotus and Plato (consider especially the Eleatic Stranger's analogy of statesmanship and weaving in the *Statesman*), it is noteworthy that even the criminal mob of sailors does not compel Arion to strip. Like the lovers of beautiful sights and sounds whom Socrates later distinguishes from philosophers (476a–c), the sailors delight in seeing and hearing Arion, and they furthermore allow him to keep his valuable clothing and equipment; although they are lawbreakers, they are not entirely insensitive to what Gyges calls *ta kala*, "the noble and beautiful things that human beings discovered long ago." Periander is something else. His penetration of appearances in uncovering the truth resembles rape more than love, and he engages in nothing less than a wholesale destruction of the beautiful fabric of law and custom.

In Herodotus's *History,* the genealogy and actions of Periander are related by a Corinthian named Socles at a meeting of Spartans and their allies in 504. Fearing the growing power of the new Athenian democracy, the Spartans propose to restore the Peisistratid tyranny at Athens by reinstating Hippias, whom they themselves had helped to depose in 510. Socles speaks against the proposal, arguing that "there is nothing more unjust or bloodstained among human beings" than tyranny. He explains that Corinth was once ruled by an oligarchy, the Bacchiads, "who used to give and take from one another" in marriage. Labda, one of the daughters of the Bacchiads, was lame; as no one wanted to wed her, she was taken as a wife by a man outside of the ruling family. Labda—her name is the archaic spelling of the Greek letter *lambda,* a hobbled stick figure (λ)—gave birth to Cypselus, who "drove out many of the Corinthians, robbed many of their property, and deprived by far the most of their lives" (5.92.α–ε).[11]

The violence of Cypselus was but a prelude to the comprehensive tyranny of his son. "All that Cypselus left undone in murdering and banishing," Socles asserts, "Periander brought to completion," thereby displaying "the sort of thing tyranny is . . . and the sort of deeds it involves" (5.92.η).[12] Periander began to slay "the prominent among the citizens," Corinthians whose status or virtue might impede his consolidation of power, after he received cryptic advice to this effect from Thrasybulus, the tyrant of Miletus.[13] He was a thief and a pervert as well as a murderer. Eager to learn from the ghost of his wife Melissa (whom he had beaten to death) the location of a deposit of money belonging to a guest-friend, he proceeded to make amends for having had intercourse with her corpse. He lured the women of Corinth to the sanctuary of Hera, where they arrived in festive attire. "But he, having posted his bodyguards in ambush, stripped them all alike, the free and their handmaids, and having collected the clothes in a pit, he prayed to Melissa and burned them completely" (5.92.η). Socles' assessment of Periander seems wholly justified. He epitomizes tyranny as Thrasymachus describes it—he "takes away what belongs to others, both what is sacred and holy, private and public, not bit by bit, but all at once"—and his behavior confirms Socrates' assertion in book 9 that the tyrant "will refrain from no terrible murder, or food, or deed" (344a, 574e).[14]

Socles' story, however, has a disturbingly familiar ring. Like the ruling regime of Callipolis, the Bacchiads were an aristocracy of *andres mounarchia* (5.92.β), "monarchic men" united by blood, who preserved their power by exchanging their daughters as wives. Like the fall of Callipolis, the collapse of the Bacchaid regime was foretold in oracles, and occurred when one of their women took her mate from the lower orders, giving birth to a man of lion-like spirit.[15] As in Callipolis, where "the women guardians must strip, since they will clothe themselves in virtue instead of garments" (457a), Periander compels the women of Corinth to go naked in public. And like Periander, the philosopher-kings of Callipolis show little respect for the boundaries of what is sacred and private.

The full implications of the myth of Arion for our understanding of the *Republic*'s argument and action will become clear in due course. For now we may note two things. First, Socrates becomes angry toward the end of book 7 at the spectacle of his beloved Philosophia being "undeservedly spattered with mud" when "lame men and bastards" court her (536a–c). This remark links Arion's story with the fate of philosophy in Callipolis, with Socrates' own conduct in the *Republic*, and, most broadly, with his relationship to Critias. In all of these matters, the contrast between Arion and Periander is instructive: we shall see that the peculiar lameness of Callipolis's philosopher-kings results directly from a deficiency in music. Second, Socrates' leap into a heaving sea of argument anticipates the fateful plunge of the sea Glaucos of book 10, who is unable to escape from the simultaneously sub- and super-human existence into which he leaps. Might Glaucon, too, be trapped by the undertow of the argument? Socrates rightly feared that he and Alcibiades would be overcome by the strength of the city of Athens (*Alc. 1* 135e); in the *Republic*, he and Glaucon are endangered by the Beautiful City he reveals in speech. While Alcibiades' encounter with Socrates splits him in two inwardly and emotionally, the vision of Callipolis may help to draw Glaucon closer to a still more terrible brokenness of soul. In pursuing the oxymoronic doubleness of the philosopher king, he may trade his humanity for the monstrous combination of bestiality and godhood exemplified by Gyges, Periander, and Oedipus.

Of all those who make the passage from Italy, Arion alone survives—Periander undoubtedly executes the sailors—and he does so with divine assistance. Socrates' situation is comparable. He states in book 6 that the philosophical soul will come to grief "unless some god should happen to help it," and that the guidance of his *daimonion* or divine sign has enabled him to join a "very small group" that has been saved from corruption and injustice (492a, 496c). Socrates later laments that the lawlessness of the cities makes it impossible for the philosopher to "save the common things along with the private" (497a). He may be thinking particularly of the community of philosophical discourse that has formed around him in the *Republic*, for he implies in more than one way that his music—a philosophical song of well-ordered souls and cities, and of "the *nomos* that dialectic performs" (532a)—will fail to reform the pleasure-loving men who have detained him in the port of Athens. In any event, one fears for his companions.

Political Medicine and the Noble Lie

In book 2, the attractions of the Feverish City eclipse the health and goodness of the True City. A similar problem arises in the transition from the Virtuous City to Callipolis, a transition that blurs the measures of virtue and reverses Socrates' purification of the luxuries and inflamed desires of Feverish City. Socrates nevertheless makes it clear that Callipolis's harvest of sickness is sown at the inception of the Virtuous City. Much of this story is already known to us, but we have yet to examine the primal myth of these regimes.

Socrates' first order of business in constructing the Virtuous City is to correct the foundational tales of the poetico-religious tradition, not because they are false but because they are base: the poets lie *ou kalōs*, "ignobly" (377d). His approach to this matter is distinctly Sisyphean: he explicitly endorses esotericism concerning the first and "greatest things," the myths about the gods. In particular, he advocates the paternalistic deception of the ignorant many, especially including those who are "senseless and young" (378a), by a wise few. Even if the stories about the vicious strife between Uranus, Cronos, and Zeus were true, he maintains, it would be best "to remain silent, and if there were some necessity to speak, for as few as possible to hear them as secrets [*di'aporrētōn*]" (378a); the word *aporrēta* may refer to closely-guarded philosophical doctrines and religious mysteries as well as state secrets.[16]

Socrates is initially content to set forth general theological principles to which the myths of the Virtuous City must adhere, but he goes further down the path of poetic duplicity in the sequel. In book 2, he explains to Adeimantus that "you and I are not poets at present, but founders of a city. And it is fitting for founders to know the models according to which it is necessary for the poets to tell their tales [*mythologein*], and beyond which they must not be permitted to go, but they must not themselves compose tales" (379a). It is a sign of the increasing immoderation of these founders that they have forgotten this restriction by the end of book 3, where Socrates, with the encouragement of Glaucon (cf. 414c), dares to fashion a political myth of origins that he knows to be a lie.

Socrates introduces the Noble Lie only after he has finished discussing music and gymnastic in the Virtuous City. He is evidently concerned that the education he has described will not suffice to prevent the ruling warriors from preying on the citizens they are supposed to protect (cf. 416a–c). At 414b–c, Socrates asks Glaucon whether they might employ "one of the lies that come into being in the case of need, of which we were just now speaking—some one well-born lie to persuade, if possible, even the rulers themselves, but if not, the rest of the city." A little earlier, he had reminded Adeimantus that lies are useful to human beings only as a kind of medicine. "Such a thing," he warned, "must be assigned to doctors, but private men must not touch it"; only the rulers must be allowed to lie, and that for the benefit of the sick among the ruled (389b; cf. 382c). Here again, the argument quickly erodes: in proposing that the rulers themselves be subjected to a medicinal lie, Socrates implies that he considers even the best citizens of the Virtuous City—the guardians—to be less than healthy. Later, in book 5, we find ourselves even further down the slippery slope: this one noble lie is no longer sufficient, and "many medicines" and "extensive lying and deception" will be needed for the benefit of the auxiliaries (459c). The citizens of Callipolis must be sick indeed.

In book 1, Socrates observes that a man who deposits weapons with a friend when of sound mind should not be told the whole truth if he goes mad and demands them back (331c). If it is just to lie to a madman in order to prevent him from becoming armed, would it not also be just to lie to armed men in order to prevent them from becoming mad? The political medicine of Callipolis is clearly not the Thracian sort Socrates uses on Charmides, which must be applied to particular individuals and requires their consent to be treated (*Chrm.* 157c). Although the Noble Lie has barbarian antecedents, the broad political medicine of Callipolis is the Greek sort favored by Critias.

With conspicuous hesitation, Socrates introduces the Noble Lie as a "device" that is "nothing new . . . but a Phoenician thing," a poetic fiction that has proved persuasive in many places, but might not be possible "among us" (414c). The lie requires unusual daring, because it is quite unbelievable: Socrates will tell the citizens that they were dreaming when, for many years, they thought they were awake. "With respect to the rearing and education we gave them," he will say, "all these things seemed, just like dreams, to happen to them and to come to be, but at that time they were in truth under the earth within, being molded and reared themselves, and their weapons and the rest of their equipment were being crafted." When this process was complete, "the earth, being their mother, sent them up" (414d–e).

This myth, Socrates admits, will not persuade the first generation of citizens, but is likely to be believed by their descendants (415c–d). For later generations will be asked to believe not that *they* came from the earth, but that their ancestors did so, and the passage of time will give the lie the patina of truth. The city's first rulers (to say nothing of its founders) are thus in the position of doctors whose own sickness has not been, and cannot be, treated by the medicinal lie they transmit to others. This ineradicable trace of illness in the city's ancestral bedrock proves consequential. Autochthony, which Froma Zeitlin describes as the "political myth of collective solidarity,"[17] is meant to prevent the doglike auxiliaries from savaging the sheep they are supposed to guard (416a). But in calling the citizens "earth-born" (415d), Socrates inauspiciously links them with the first Thebans, the Sown Men (*Spartoi*) who sprouted from seeds of dragon-teeth spilled by the sword of the Phoenician Cadmus, "rose armed from the earth," and began to kill one another (Apollod. *Bibl.* 3.4). Athens' major Boeotian rival is the setting of many Athenian tragedies, and Socrates specifically picks up the theme of warring siblings announced in Glaucon's earlier allusions to Aeschylus's *Seven Against Thebes*.[18]

Promoting civic unity, however, is not the only function of the myth Socrates proposes to tell. He seems to model the Noble Lie on a particular Phoenician fiction proposed in Euripides' *Bacchae*, a tragedy in which the ruling family of Cadmus reaps the seemingly inexhaustible harvest of internecine strife sown at Thebes' founding. When Cadmus's grandson Pentheus, the city's headstrong young king, refuses to acknowledge the divinity of his cousin Dionysus, Cadmus offers this advice: "even if this is not a god, as you assert, call him one, and lie nobly [*kalōs*], in order that Semele [Pentheus's aunt] may seem to have given birth to a god, and esteem may accrue to our whole family [*genei*]" (Eur. *Bacch.* 333–36).

Cadmus's counsel alerts us to the specific tyrannical hubris of the Noble Lie. Thrasymachus and Glaucon, we recall, associate total injustice with the appropriation of the power and authority of the gods. While the claim of autochthony confers dignity on the future citizens of Callipolis by making them children of the sacred earth, Socrates' myth particularly exalts the ruling tribe (which the practice of eugenics will increasingly turn into a single family of blood relatives), for it lends divine authority to the subordination of supposedly bronze- and iron-souled citizens by the gold- and silver-souled classes. Socrates even asserts that "the god" commands the rulers above all to maintain this hierarchy in succeeding generations, and he invents an oracle predicting the destruction of the city if they fail to do so (415b–c). He thus goes far beyond the general principles of moral theology articulated in book 2, which make no divisions of human beings and favor no single class of citizens.

The Noble Lie also incorporates central elements of the Ring Myth. Gold, the material of the ring, is now represented as being inside the souls of the guardians, who are in turn identified with shepherds (416a). The claim that various metals have been mixed into the citizens' souls, an image borrowed from Hesiod's *Works and Days* (106–201; cf. 546e), suggests that Socrates envisions their rearing and education as a kind of human smithing—a matter of technical production, like minting coins. Since the Noble Lie is essential to the formation of future citizens, poetry in the ordinary sense is central to this political production.

Critias would find nothing strange in Socrates' technical and political *poiēsis*. But what guarantees the purity and integrity of its final product? The city's first citizens are supposed to have been fashioned by the gods; in imitating this divine work, later generations of guardians must pitilessly assay, sort, and assign value to souls according to the gold standard of their own natures (415b–c). Errors creep into texts as scribes copy them over the centuries; just so, if each new generation of rulers is the measure of the next, gradual dilution and inflation of the human currency would seem to be inevitable—as Socrates later confirms it is.[19] This is a mimetic evocation of features of Socrates' exposition that we noted earlier: the transgression of limits and proliferation of lies as he takes the political poetry of the Virtuous City to a new extreme. The Virtuous City contented itself with establishing a regimen designed to mold the souls and bodies generated by nature; Callipolis will use eugenics and euthanasia to control the process of sexual reproduction itself. The scientific politics of Callipolis stands at a great remove from the natural measures of the True City.

Falling from the Truth

Pressed by Glaucon and the others to discuss women and children, Socrates turns from the "manly drama" to "the effeminate" (451c). It soon becomes clear that these adjectives describe the unfolding drama of the discussion as well as its new subject. They reflect Socrates' increasing intellectual slackness, as well as the unmanly immoderation of the best warriors of the city in speech.

Socrates begins by returning to the question of what may be learned about warriors from the example of dogs (cf. 375a). Female dogs, he observes, are expected to do the same work of guarding and hunting as male ones, and so must be trained in the same way and taught the same things. Similarly, females in the city in speech should be expected to do the work of war, and should be educated in music and gymnastic alongside the male ones (451d–52a; this is the first of book 5's three waves of paradox). The canine analogy is well-chosen, both rhetorically and substantively. Glaucon and his companions have chased game. They have firsthand experience of the matters discussed in Xenophon's *On Hunting*, the Greek title of which, *Cynegeticus*, refers to the art of commanding hounds. They are familiar with the noble dignity of well-trained dogs of good natural attributes, and with the virtues such dogs demand of their masters, including trustworthiness, clarity, consistency, attentiveness, and good judgment.[20] Ethically and politically, moreover, training dogs to track, chase, and retrieve is much like training children to be warriors. In both cases, previously undisciplined individuals learn to obey, and to command themselves as well as others. They learn the virtues and pleasures of teamwork and companionship, and develop a sense of themselves as capable and self-controlled agents—responsible selves that can be counted on by their peers and superiors. If anything, the comparison between hunting dogs and warriors flatters human beings: well-trained dogs set a standard for uncomplicated loyalty and dependability that few people can hope to achieve.

But we are not accustomed to treating men and women *exactly* like dogs. Dogs don't wear clothes, nor will females in Callipolis. The spectacle of ugly old women exercising naked in public alongside men would look ridiculous "as things now stand," and elicits an exclamation of shock from Glaucon (452b). In his defense, Socrates notes that the custom of naked exercise seemed "shameful and laughable" to the Greeks when it was introduced by the Cretans and the Lacedaemonians, as it does even now to most of the barbarians (452c–d)—a point Herodotus, too, makes in connection with Gyges (1.10.3). Socrates encourages Glaucon not to fear "the jests of witty men"; rather, they should beg these men—certainly including Aristophanes, whose *Assemblywomen* ridicules a society in which women and property are held in common[21]—"not to mind their own business, but to be serious" (452c). The comic poets use laughter to defend Greek ways; for them, as for Gyges, it is neither healthy nor pious to look upon or practice anything other than one's own things. In proposing shamelessly to expose what is modestly concealed by received laws and customs, Socrates finds himself in the position of Candaules.

Socrates differs from Candaules, however, both in motive and in understanding. While the king commands Gyges to behold a beautiful naked body, Socrates undresses ugly ones in speech; and while Candaules trusts his eyes more than his ears, the philosopher insists that "what is best as revealed in speeches" is more creditable than what is "ridiculous to the eyes." Socrates alleges that the proper standard of beauty is the good, and only "the sight of what is foolish and bad" is laughable (452d–e). But *why* is it good to give women the same education as men?

Socrates does not address this question directly. Instead, he suggests that they first determine "whether these things are possible or not" (452e). He reminds Glaucon of their agreement, in founding the True City, that each must "do his own things" according to nature (453b; cf. 370a–c). At stake is the aptitude of women for waging war and ruling, jobs that have always been assigned to men. While the poets argue from *nomos*, Socrates and Glaucon must make their case according to *phusis*. They must show that a woman does not "differ very much from a man in nature," for otherwise the work to which she is by nature suited—her *ergon*, or proper activity—will differ as well (453b–c). Yet the range of things Socrates considers to be possible is not identical, at least in this context, with the range of things that can actually be done; asserting that it is "possible" to assign women the same tasks as men means simply that doing so does not conflict with their natural capabilities. By the same token, practices that do so conflict are not impossible in the ordinary sense, for such practices can, and do, exist (cf. 456b–c).

That said, Socrates overstates the implications of the proof of possibility. As he makes clear, the kinds of work that individual women are capable of performing well are many and varied (455d–56a). Someone might make an equally good nursemaid, weaver, and soldier; to which of these jobs should she be assigned? That it is not against nature for women to serve as soldiers and rulers does not in itself establish, as Socrates immediately goes on to assert, that the particular law that assigns women the same common training, life, and work as the male warriors is "according to nature," or that the way things now stand is against it (456b–c). Such claims could be justified only with reference to the one truly relevant standard for which Socrates has so far vouched in the *Republic*: the natural measures of human being and community that came to light in the True City.

The argument Socrates offers for the goodness of the first wave is no less careless than his discussion of its possibility. We saw earlier that the existence of a class of dedicated warrior-rulers becomes necessary only when the measures of nature are eclipsed in the transition from the True City to the Feverish City. Socrates seems to forget this crucial point when he makes the case that it is best for women to receive the same education in music and gymnastic as men. "In the city we were founding," he asks Glaucon, "which do you think will work out to be better men [*andras*] for us: the guardians, who happen to have the education we went through, or the shoemakers, who have been educated in shoemaking?" "You are asking a ridiculous question," Glaucon replies. If the guardians are the best of the citizens, and what is best for a city is "for the best possible women and men to come to be in it" (both premises to which Glaucon agrees), it follows that the law they have proposed is "not only possible but also best for a city" (456d–57a). Earlier, however, Socrates had used the phrase "the city you were founding" to refer to the True City (453b)—the one organized according to the principle on which he rests his argument: that each must mind his own business according to nature. In *that* city, the original and authoritative measure of a community's unity, wholeness, and health, there are shoemakers but no guardians, much less politicized males. In asserting that it is ridiculous even to ask whether guardians are better than shoemakers, Glaucon repeats the very mistake Socrates attributes to the comic poets, that of ignoring what is best as revealed in speeches. Yet Socrates does not object.

Could Socrates nevertheless be attempting to extend his previous effort to reproduce, in the context of a historical (military and political) regime, the prehistorical or mythical goodness and happiness of the True City? That city's relatively effeminate life is characterized by the public nakedness of both sexes; perhaps imitating it in this respect would help to temper the Virtuous City's hyper-masculine spiritedness by fostering the bonds of erotic love and familial intimacy. This suggestion, however, does not withstand scrutiny. Socrates does claim that citizens united by the bonds of kinship would be less prone to faction—the "greatest evil for a city," and one about which he has long been worried (462a–64b). But in destroying marriage and the family, the community of women and children militates against natural affection and intimacy. Aristotle argues that affection is diluted when women and children are held in common (*Pol.* 2.4.1262b). The experience of Sparta—where *esprit de corps* was built by weakening, but not eliminating, marriage and the family—confirms this point: Plutarch writes that the Lacedaemonian husband had "a strong and unadulterated lack of passion [*apatheia*] with regard to his wife."[22] In doing away with the family, Socrates destroys the original human context in which children and parents naturally learn how to live and work together in community. This bodes ill for the city as a whole.

The Fantasy of a Slack Soul

Although Glaucon asserts that the second wave of paradox—the law that women and children will be held in common—is "much bigger" than the first "as regards doubt concerning its possibility and benefit," Socrates supposes no one would dispute that such an arrangement would be "the greatest good." When Glaucon reiterates his opposition, Socrates acts like a coward caught in a lie: he confesses that he wanted to run away from the argument, and he agrees that he must "submit to justice" (457d–e). But he begs Glaucon's indulgence:

> Let me take a holiday, just like idle men who are accustomed to feast their minds by themselves whenever they journey alone. And I suppose that such men, before they discover in what way something they desire can exist, set this aside, in order that they should not become weary deliberating about what is possible or not. They set down what they want as already existing, and immediately arrange and enjoy the rest, and go through the sorts of things they will do when it comes into being, making a soul that is otherwise idle more idle still. Now I myself am already soft, and I desire to toss aside and examine later in what way those things are possible, and now, having set them down as possible, to consider—if you allow me—how the rulers will arrange those things as they come into being, and whether, having been put into practice, they would be of all things most advantageous for the city and its guardians. (458a–b)

In this remarkable passage, Socrates compares what he is about to say to the daydream of a self-indulgent slacker. Having admitted to cowardice and dishonesty, he presents himself as the very opposite of the sort of man the Virtuous City aims to produce. Socrates says that the private fantasies of an idle soul cause it to become still more idle, yet he shares his pleasurable daydream with his companions; his speech therefore runs the risk of corrupting them as well as himself. In gratifying his appetite for laziness and inflaming Glaucon's imagination, he debases the serious work of city and soul that he has elucidated in speech and displayed in deed. His vices are reflected in the regime that he will eventually consider how to bring into being—for only the problem of actualization, and not agreement with nature, is all that remains of the question of possibility once he and Glaucon come back around to it (cf. 471c).

Socrates has offered a fitting preamble to the second wave of paradox in book 5. This new and bigger wave pushes the city in speech into a swift moral and political decline, characterized by an eruption of erotic and aggressive license and a fragmentation of the body politic—ills that stem from tyrannical overreach on the part of the rulers.

Socrates first remarks that the rulers will be above the laws to which their fellow citizens are subject: at their own discretion, they will obey some and "imitate" others (458c). One wonders whether they will abide by the laws regulating sex that he immediately goes on to establish. Living and working together, the male and female warriors will be drawn by "inborn necessity" to sexual intercourse—"not geometrical but erotic necessities," Glaucon observes, adding that the latter are "more piercing" (458d). The rulers will nevertheless attempt to exercise something like geometrical control over sex in the city, using religion as a pretext for their arrangements. "We'll make marriages sacred to the greatest extent possible," Socrates proposes, "and the most beneficial marriages would be sacred" (458e).[23] But what makes a marriage beneficial?

On this matter, the judgment of Callipolis's founders and rulers is distorted by a combination of technocratically-inflected spiritedness and political opportunity. Socrates observes that Glaucon owns "hunting dogs and a great throng of well-born birds," among whom some are "best"—most capable, that is, in the aggressive physical activities of chasing game and cock-fighting.[24] Glaucon agrees that he is "eager [*prothumēi*: lit. 'with spirit to the fore'] to breed from the best as much as possible," believing that "the stock [*genos*] of birds and that of dogs" would otherwise "be much worse," and that the same holds true of the human race (459a–c). But this is the first we have heard about any fundamental deficiency in the class of warriors. In fact, Socrates had argued in book 4 that the army—which at that time did not enjoy the benefit of competent female soldiers, much less a dedicated program of selective mating—would easily be capable of defeating forces even three times as large (422c). Why employ eugenics in order to produce a "flock" of "tip-top" quality (459d–e) if there is no need to do so? Glaucon loves victory, and he attends to the breeding of dogs and cocks because he wants to best other Athenian gentlemen in blood-sports. Just so, the practice of eugenics in Callipolis seems to be driven more by a kind of hyper-aristocratic zeal than by military or political necessity.

The language of the immediate sequel confirms this impression. Socrates asserts that, of the men and women, the best (*hoi aristoi*) must have the most frequent intercourse, and the worst (*hoi phaulotatoi*) the least frequent; that only the offspring of the best are to be reared; and that only the rulers are to know of these arrangements. In the same passage, he refers to the warriors, whom he had previously compared to sheepdogs, as a flock or herd (459d–e). The manipulation of this flock by a "most courageous doctor" employing "many medicines," including "extensive lying and deception" (459c), brings to mind the bold rulers praised by Thrasymachus and Glaucon who defraud sheep-like simpletons. Socrates' rulers, of course, act for the advantage of the city; yet like those other shepherds, they appropriate the authority of the gods to achieve their ends. The "marriages" of citizens—a euphemism for isolated acts of insemination—are ostensibly determined by cleromancy (the drawing of lots to divine the will of the gods) that has in fact secretly been rigged to produce desired outcomes; they are sanctified by festivals and sacrifices, and celebrated in propagandistic odes composed for the occasion by a cadre of poets (459e–60a). Glaucon does not object to these arrangements. Indeed, his response to the segregation of the offspring of the best in a "pen" or "fold," and the euthanization of the offspring of the worst, reveals a strong aristocratic prejudice: such measures are necessary, he avers, "if the tribe of guardians is to remain pure" (460c).

Callipolis's radical sexual inequality will inevitably produce political divisions, as Socrates indirectly acknowledges when he insists that the rulers' management of intercourse be disguised in order to avoid faction (459e). In effect, only inferior warriors will be held to the standard of moderation established in the Virtuous City; the best and strongest will live like Homeric heroes. Socrates' later assertions that the warriors are united by a common experience of pleasure and pain, and that they will be free from faction because "they possess nothing private but the body" (462b, 464d), are ludicrous. Particularly given the ubiquity of naked females in the city, the ineliminable privacy of the body *guarantees* that the intense pleasure of the sexual haves (to say nothing of their other rewards and honors) will be matched by the strong envy and displeasure of the have-nots.[25] More than in most regimes, sex in Callipolis is inseparable from aggression.

The danger that erotic desire will fuel political animosity helps to explain the absence of laws against assault and insult in Callipolis. If, as Socrates asserts, allowing citizens to dissipate their anger by fighting will help to forestall "bigger divisions [*staseis*]" (465a), it does so in part by providing a safety-valve for the release of sexual frustration and envy. Socrates nevertheless seems to anticipate faction (*stasis*) among the ruling warriors. Although Callipolis will follow the Spartan custom of empowering an older person to rule and punish younger ones (465a), there is reason to doubt that the regime succeeds in inculcating Spartan respect for the aged. The children of Callipolis are taught that "no citizen was ever angry with another, and to be so is not holy" (378c); yet Socrates implicitly admits that such anger exists in the city, for he counts on shame and fear to restrain young citizens from attacking older ones (465a–b).[26] Nor is it reassuring to hear that "a younger man, unless rulers issue a command, will not, as is likely, attempt to assault or strike an older one" (465a). Any form of legally permissible behavior is bound to occur with some frequency; beyond this, high-spirited men and women are prone to lose their tempers, often disrespecting, when they do so, the boundaries of age and sex that traditionally restrain physical violence.

One also wonders under what circumstances rulers might actually command the young to assault their elders. To consider this question in the context of Athenian history is to be reminded of the Thirty's use of armed young men in the arrest and execution of Theramanes, whom they regarded as a serious threat to the oligarchy. Socrates states that guardians' freedom from faction will eliminate the danger that "the rest of the city will split into factions against these rulers or one another" (465b); for one thing, they will be able to present a united front against any sort of rebellion. Critias similarly underscores the need for unity within the oligarchy if it is to protect the established order from violent dissolution at the hands of the many.[27] But Socrates has perhaps not reckoned with a fact observed by Aristotle: that "spirited and warlike men" would be inclined to rebel against a ruling class they are never allowed to enter, and whose privileges they are never allowed to enjoy (*Pol.* 2.5.1264b).

In sum, Callipolis's elimination of the family, its practice of eugenic selection, and its discriminatory distribution of sexual rewards leads inevitably to the Oedipal crimes of incest and parricide, both literal and political—violations of sacred order that are closely associated with the tyrant (cf. 571c–d with 574d–e).[28] This was evident to readers as early as Aristotle, who places special emphasis on these points in his critique of Callipolis. Having argued that Socrates weakens the bonds of affection in holding women and children in common, Aristotle anticipates civic fragmentation. The warriors, he asserts, will not easily avoid "outrages and homicides, involuntary and voluntary, and fights and verbal abuse," both among themselves and between them and the farmers and artisans they rule. "None of these things," he adds, "is holy when it involves fathers and mothers and those not distant in kinship . . . yet they must happen more frequently among those who are ignorant [of their relatives] than among those who are familiar [with them], and when they do occur, only those who are familiar can perform the lawful expiations, but the others cannot." Aristotle also notes that Socrates prohibits sexual intercourse between parents and children, but not erotic love itself, which is "most unfitting" when it involves fathers, sons, and brothers (*Pol.* 2.4.1262a–b).

The Net of Hephaestus

Callipolis's rulers attempt to control erotic longing and aggression—forces, to paraphrase Freud, that rule the world[29]—by deploying the political equivalent of the invisible metal web in which Hephaestus ensnares Ares and his sister Aphrodite, the gods of war and love, after their incestuous adultery is spied by all-seeing Helios. The smith-god is a master of technical production; it is he who in book 18 of the *Iliad* crafts the shield of Achilles, a magnificent microcosm of the whole of human existence. Hephaestus, rejected by his mother Hera because he was lame (Hom. *Il.* 18.396–97), can in compensation for his immobility fashion automata that move at his command. Yet for all his productive and prosthetic power, he cannot change the character of the gods. Seeing Ares helplessly entwined with Aphrodite, Hermes tells Apollo that he would gladly change places with him, even though all the gods could see him. Similarly, the political arts of Callipolis's kings not only fail to control, but even promote, sexual and aggressive excess.[30]

In a passage in book 8 whose mathematical density seems to mock Callipolis's attempt to achieve technical mastery over erotic necessities, Socrates states that ignorance of the "geometrical number" governing reproduction will result in the admixture of base metals in the souls of the rulers (546a–47a). Sexual disorder and violence go hand in hand; such impurities, he remarks, "always spawn war and hatred." Quoting *Iliad* 6.211, he adds that "it is necessary always to assert that faction is 'of this ancestry' wherever it comes to be" (547a). These words are spoken by the Trojan warrior Glaucos, who utters them shortly before he foolishly trades his gold armor for Diomedes' bronze (*Il.* 6.232–36). Hesiod, whom Socrates mentions at 546e, associates bronze with violence and the "lamentable works of Ares" (*WD* 146). Immediately before quoting Glaucos, Socrates specifically warns of mixing bronze with gold in the souls of the rulers (547a); the first stage in the decline of the best regime is the genesis of the timocrat—the lover of "deeds of war and the things concerned with war" to whom Adeimantus compares Glaucon (548d, 549a).

Hermes admits that he would happily be shackled many times over if only he could sleep with "golden Aphrodite." For his part, Glaucon seems too dazzled by the pleasures of life in Callipolis (at least for highly courageous and erotic men like him) to notice the chains of necessity that bind its citizens. Socrates emphasizes that the warriors will be free of the ills associated with maintaining a family and a household, including rearing children, making money, and paying debts (465b–c). He does not mention that the price of the irresponsible liberty exemplified in the casual sexual unions of the gods is the loss of domestic love and joy, the great happiness of the True City.

The best of Callipolis's warriors may not be Olympian gods, but Socrates insists that "they will live a life more blessed than the most blessed one the Olympic victors live": their victory—"the salvation of the entire city"—is greater, and their public support is more extensive (465d).[31] In the True City, the whole community, crowned with wreaths, feasts on vegetables and sings of the gods; in Callipolis, the warriors alone are "crowned" with "everything necessary to life," and receive "prizes" and "a worthy burial" from the rest of the city (465d–e). In fact, the rewards of valor in Callipolis far exceed what is necessary for life. They include captives taken as slaves, erotic delights and liberties, choice cuts of meat like those with which Ajax was honored at Troy, poetic encomia, promotion to "the golden tribe" at death, and worship "for the rest of time" as a *daimōn* or minor divinity (468b–69b).[32]

In listing the prizes of manly virtue in Callipolis, Socrates rehabilitates Homer and Hesiod, poets he roundly criticized in establishing the music of the Virtuous City (377e–91e). He had earlier censured Odysseus's praise of banquets where tables are laden with bread and meat and cups brim with wine on the ground that even hearing such speeches—let alone actually feasting in the manner of the epic heroes—will be detrimental to a young man's self-mastery (390a–b; *Od.* 9.8–10). Now, however, he asserts that "we will be persuaded" by Homer's recommendation of "seats and meats and full cups" for the warriors (468d–e; *Il.* 8.162). He also resurrects the Sisyphean theodicy of divine omniscience. Having previously attacked Homer for claiming that the gods visit the cities in disguise, he now asks Glaucon to trust Hesiod's assertion that those of golden soul became hallowed divinities who wander the earth (381d, 469a–b). In the passages immediately following the ones Socrates quotes, Homer explains that the gods "keep watch over the hubris and lawful order of human beings," and Hesiod that the gold-souled *daimones*, shrouded in mist, take note of "justice and cruel deeds" (*Od.* 17.485–87; *WD* 122–25).

Socrates' restoration of the poetry and heroic ethos of Olympianism is a clear sign that the regime he is now describing suffers from a relapse of the sickness of the Feverish City. Ajax, after all, is a profoundly tragic character. In Sophocles' *Ajax*, his public humiliation when he is passed over by the Greek leaders at Troy for the prize of outstanding valor drives him to homicidal madness; in the Myth of Er, his soul—still misanthropic a thousand years after his death—chooses reincarnation as a lion (620b). Glaucon nevertheless much prefers the pleasures of Callipolis, a city in which human beings really are bred and manipulated like animals, to those of the True City, in which they only apparently live like pigs. He pointedly agrees that the life of the auxiliaries, which "seems much more beautiful and better than that of Olympic victors" (he neglects the lot of second-class auxiliaries), is incomparably superior to that of shoemakers, farmers, or any other craftsmen (465d–66b).[33]

The Dream of a Wakeful Philosopher

Socrates proceeds to deal with the conduct of Callipolis's soldiers in warfare, but Glaucon soon has enough of this subject. "Don't say anything more about it," he urges, "but let us now attempt to persuade ourselves of this alone: that it [the regime] is possible, and in what way it is possible" (471e). Socrates reluctantly agrees to do so, but not before he provides some context for what he is about to say. If the care with which he prefaces the third, "greatest and most difficult" wave (472a) is any indication, the philosopher enters the *Republic* under circumstances that are likely to produce misunderstanding.

Socrates begins by observing that it was for the sake of a pattern (*paradeigma*) that they were seeking "what justice by itself is like, and the perfectly just man," and well as "injustice and the most unjust man." Their intention was to determine what share of happiness and its opposite each one has, on the assumption that "he who is most similar to them would have a lot most like theirs." "We were not seeking them," he emphasizes, "in order that we might demonstrate that it is possible for these things to come to be." A painter, he adds, who draws a pattern of the most beautiful human being is no less good if he cannot prove that such a man can come into being. The same applies to "the pattern in speech of a good city" that they have produced; they will have spoken no less well even if they cannot prove that it is possible to found such a city (472c–e).

A *paradeigma* can be either an exemplar or a model—a paradigmatic instance of something, or a design according to which something is to be molded.[34] Socrates makes it clear that the patterns of soul and city under discussion are exemplary, and are not to be understood as blueprints for political production. (The image of the city, we recall, was initially introduced to shed light on the soul.) Here as elsewhere, however, he emphasizes that he and his companions have themselves constructed these patterns, and that they stand at a certain remove from the realities they image. Socrates compares to statues the perfectly just and unjust men Glaucon describes at the beginning of book 2 (361d); later, he compares the Virtuous City to the statue of a human being onto which he and his companions are painting features (420c–d). When Socrates has finished describing the philosopher-kings at the end of book 7, Glaucon remarks that "just like a sculptor, you have fashioned rulers who are wholly beautiful and noble" (540c). While the attempt to articulate what one sees is always to some extent poetic or productive—a thought can be expressed in many different ways and languages—such passages alert us to the excessive artificiality of the images of soul and city these men have crafted.

Moral exemplars are necessarily ideal: in giving us something to aim at, they help to lift us above the baseline of everyday human behavior. The situation is otherwise with models, in constructing which one must pay close attention (as any architect knows) to the constraints of reality. To treat as a political model what was intended as a moral exemplar is therefore a dangerous business, especially if the exemplar is intrinsically flawed. But this is precisely what Glaucon insists on doing when he urges Socrates to explain how the city in speech can be brought into being.

This is not the only problem Socrates must face "if it is necessary," as he tells Glaucon, "to strive spiritedly, for your gratification, to prove in what way, and under what condition, it [the city] would be most possible" (472e). Socrates hints here that bringing the city into being, even if only in speech, will require him to use force in the face of an intransigent reality. Callipolis is a construction of the spirit more than the intellect, and this is especially so because action necessarily falls short of speech. "Can anything be done as it is said," Socrates asks Glaucon, "or does action touch on truth less than speech, even if it does not seem so to someone?" (473a). Socrates may be thinking of Critias, who identifies truth with historical actuality and associates philosophical speech with myth.

There would at any rate be good reason for Socrates to recall the designs of Critias at this juncture. Things have gotten quite turned around since book 2, when he introduced the True City in order to clarify the exemplary soul; now, he is compelled to introduce an exemplary soul—the philosopher—in order to complete a model city. Even so, his statement of the third wave does not immediately entail any attempt at political engineering. There will be no rest from ills for the cities or for humankind, Socrates asserts,

> unless the philosophers rule as kings in the cities, or those now called kings and rulers philosophize legitimately [*gnēsiōs*] and adequately, and political power and philosophy fall together in the same place, and the many natures now making their way to each apart from the other are by necessity excluded. (473c–d)

The word *gnēsiōs* is related to *genos*, "kind" or "tribe," and *gennaios*, "well-born"; if a king happens to belong by nature to the family of philosophers, or a natural philosopher happens to acquire political power, the best regime might be realized. Because this outcome depends on chance, the third wave is not really a model or plan of action at all. But once a philosopher-king comes into existence, the requirement that the many unsuitable natures be excluded from philosophy and from rule could certainly be taken as an invitation to establish political institutions for maintaining the purity of the governing tribe.

When Socrates introduces the third wave, he fears that he will be deluged by laughter and ill-repute (473c). The union of philosophers and kings is indeed incongruous. Philosophers are supremely erotic, kings supremely thumotic; philosophers love truth and being, kings love power and honor; philosophers transcend the Cave, kings glory in it. How could one person combine these traits without being seriously unbalanced—like Periander, lame in soul, and Oedipus, lame in body as well? And if a true philosopher-king came to be, how could he or she find suitable successors—other well-balanced souls to receive the staff of rule, so that the regime would not stumble and fall from having passed into illegitimate hands? These questions are much on Socrates' mind, not least because he finds his passage blocked, and trips up in speech when he attempts to transmit the meaning of his Arion-like song—the legacy of philosophy—to Glaucon and his companions.[35]

Glaucon's inclinations are in any case mixed in a way that at least points toward the desired combination. In warning Socrates that he will be attacked by a large band of elite warriors eager to exact due retribution in mockery if he cannot defend his proposal, he reminds us that he is as spirited in the cause of justice as any member of the political tribe. Yet in pledging to offer Socrates what support he can—"good will and encouragement, and perhaps to answer you in a more well-proportioned way than another" (473e–74b)—he displays just the sort of modest self-knowledge a philosophical ruler would wish for in an auxiliary. Socrates receives Glaucon's pledge with gratitude for "so great an alliance." He subsequently points to him as an example of an erotic man, and he supposes that he will be more able than others to understand the distinction he draws between genuine philosophers and those who resemble them (473e–74b; 475a, d). He seems to believe that Glaucon has the makings at least of a loyal friend and ally of philosophy.

Socrates tries to clarify the erotic nature of the philosopher by distinguishing between the many lovers of hearing and sights, who delight in beautiful things, and the few "lovers of the sight of the truth," who alone are "able to approach the beautiful itself and to see it by itself." Concerning "justice and injustice and good and bad and all the forms [*tōn eidōn*]," he says, "each itself is one, but by community with practices and bodies and one another, each shows forth everywhere in multiple phantasms." Lovers of sights, together (Socrates now adds) with "lovers of arts [*philotechnoi*] and practical men," are strongly attracted by these apparitions, but are not drawn—and do not look—beyond them. He has in mind a small-time lover who "acknowledges [*nomidzōn*] that there are beautiful things [or 'noble deeds'], but neither acknowledges that there is beauty itself, nor, if someone should lead him to the knowledge [*gnōsin*] of it, is able to follow" (476a–c).

Socrates' language indicates two important things. First, non-philosophers are occupied with phantasms: insubstantial and distorted images of what is that arise from multiple causes. Socrates alludes to *nomos*; for most people, justice, goodness, beauty, and nobility are seen through the dense atmosphere of local custom, which refracts and filters their light. But the more universal practices of the arts and sciences also generate phantasms. Expert knowledge, including theoretical and productive science, proceeds by specialized or technical means and considers only a part of what is seen. Yet practical and technically-minded people are likely to regard the scientific expert as paradigmatic of the knower *per se*. This mistake is elucidated by the Eleatic Stranger of Plato's *Sophist*, who explains that a *phantasma* is an image that does not reflect the proportions (*summetria*) of the exemplar or model it imitates. The Stranger observes that sculptors are inclined to distort the harmonious measures of the original when they fashion large images of beautiful things; seen from below, an "unbeautiful" perspective, the big, beautiful whole would otherwise appear disproportionate, with the upper parts looking smaller than they should and the lower larger (235d–36b). We are given to understand that a similar problem arises with respect to representations of philosophers, the paradigmatic originals of human wisdom who "appear in all sorts of phantasms," as Socrates says, "looking down from on high at the life below" (*Soph.* 216c). The exalted image of scientific knowers in the popular consciousness today, and in the minds of the educated Athenians of yesterday, is an example of just the sort of poetic distortion the Stranger describes: they are taken to be wise, but only because their heads are too large for their feet—an asymmetry that is bound to manifest itself in an ugly gait.

Second, philosophers—whose souls, to recall a remark of Theaetetus, stretch toward being (*Tht.* 186a)—transcend the phantasms of custom and art in attempting to acquaint themselves with what is. *Gnōsis* is recognition; like the German *kennen* and the French *connaître*, *gignōskein* is the verb used to say that one "knows" an acquaintance (cf. 476d). It is also the verb the god at Delphi uses when he enjoins human beings to "Know Thyself."

It is at this point that distortions begin to enter into Socrates' picture of the philosopher. Glaucon agrees that the people Socrates has described are dreamers, for dreaming consists in "believing that the likeness of something is not a likeness, but is the very thing to which it is like." But philosophers, who can distinguish between original and images, the form and the many things that participate in it, are awake. The thought of non-philosophers is opinion; that of philosophers, knowledge—if only knowledge of their ignorance of the originals, or of the difference between seeming and being (476c–d). The harshness of the many men who Glaucon imagined would attack Socrates proves to be a taste of things to come: supposing they are awake, dreamers claim to have knowledge, and are hostile to those who say otherwise. "What then," Socrates asks, "if this man should be angry with us—the one who we say opines but does not know—and should dispute that we are speaking the truth? Do we have any way to soothe him [*paramutheisthai*] and gently to persuade him, while hiding that he is not healthy?" (476d–e).

Socrates' question is strange. If the contradictor is unhealthy, it is because he confuses phantasms and beings, opinion and knowledge, and his self-esteem impedes correction. Why should these facts be concealed from him? After all, Socrates habitually forces his interlocutors to confront their ignorance, and he is used to harsh reactions.[36] In this instance, he seems to be thinking politically: an angry multitude would never acknowledge the authority or accept the rule of a philosopher. But how could the contradictor be persuaded of the superiority of the philosopher without acknowledging his own condition? Because he cannot be awakened, the only solution is to give him another kind of dream: to bring to bear (*para-*) a calming *muthos* that will make him see the philosopher in a more favorable light. He will still be sick—his disease is chronic and incurable—but he will at least become tractable enough to allow others to manage his illness.

Socrates goes on to articulate the necessary medical myth in a staged dialogue in which he assigns to Glaucon the role of the dreamer. "Come on," he says to him, "consider what we'll say to him. . . . You answer me on behalf of that man" (476e; cf. 478e–79a).

Here we must proceed cautiously. Socrates' conduct in the only public office he held in his lifetime provides evidence that *this* philosopher, at least, is prepared to exercise political power justly and thoughtfully. When the generals who commanded the sea battle at Arginusae in 406 were charged with neglecting their duty to retrieve shipwrecked men and corpses after the engagement, they blamed Theramenes and Thrasyboulos, ship captains who were assigned the job but failed to complete it because of a storm.[37] The Assembly met to decide the fate of the generals immediately after the city-wide festival of the Apatouria, and the Council, on which Socrates happened to be serving (he had been selected by lot), had say over how they would proceed. The Athenians were angry, for they had been stirred up at the Apatouria by the presence of a great many people with the shaved heads and somber clothes of mourners. On top of this, Theramenes, seeking to shift the blame, bribed one man to accuse the commanders in the Council, and others to appear in the Assembly in the guise of mourners and kinsmen of those who had perished at Arginusae. Appearing at a joint meeting of the Council and the Assembly, Socrates alone objected to the trial of the generals as a group on the ground that it was unlawful, and he met with severe public opposition. As he tells the Athenians at his trial, "the orators were prepared to indict me and arrest me, and you were ordering and shouting" (*Ap.* 32b). Socrates' argument failed, and six of the generals were tried and executed—a deed of which the citizens soon repented (Xen. *Hell.* 1.6.34–7.35).

Guided by his good character and sound moral intuitions, Socrates behaved justly and courageously in the Arginusae affair, and fought for the spirit of the law if not its letter.[38] But the account he proceeds to give Glaucon of the superiority of the philosopher makes no mention of character or moral intuition. His misrepresentation of the philosopher is easy to see if we attend to his language. Starting at 477b, he characterizes the philosopher's knowledge as *epistēmē* rather than *gnōsis*; this new term appears at least a dozen times in the next two Stephanus pages.[39] But he had previously given no indication that the philosopher possesses scientific knowledge of justice and injustice, nobility and baseness, the good and the bad. Philosophical wakefulness was said to consist not in the achievement of a body of science, but in the ability to "look upon" each thing itself as well as what participates in it, together with the belief that these things—original and images—are distinct (476d).

Socrates is evidently playing to the prejudices of his interlocutor. Glaucon remarks that knowledge differs from opinion as "that which is inerrant" differs from "that which is not without error [*tōi mē anamartētōi*]" (477e). Science, he implies, is a sure means to avoid error, including serious moral error regarding justice and the rest. Like Critias, Glaucon embraces a phantasm of the philosopher as a scientific knower, and Socrates does not correct him. Socrates thus obscures the nature of the genuine philosopher, the sort he himself is: an erotic lover of wisdom who in dialogue catches sight of, and gives voice to, what is. Why does he do so?

In making the idea of a philosopher-king palatable to the multitude of non-philosophers, Socrates succeeds in securing his interlocutor's allegiance to the regime. When he asks if the lovers of opinion "will be very irate" to be spoken of as dreamers, Glaucon replies "No, if at any rate they are persuaded by me, for it is not sanctioned [*ou themis*] to be angry at the truth" (480a). *Themistes* are sacred ordinances; like a loyal auxiliary, Glaucon is prepared to meet objections to the rule of philosophers by invoking the authority of divine law. He cannot, however, be considered a spirited defender of reason. It would be more accurate to observe that, because he is ready to defend the rule of philosophers with rhetorical and political force, his allegiance to the philosopher-kings is essential to the constitution of reason as ideology. Just how reason decays into ideology in Callipolis, and philosophy into a science of wisdom, is the guiding question of the following chapter.

CHAPTER 6

Philosophy in Eclipse

SOCRATES AND THE KINGS OF CALLIPOLIS

In the *Republic*, the philosopher Stanley Rosen has argued, Socrates "founds the radical Western tradition according to which justice must be pursued by doctrinal construction"—a tradition, we may add, in which the work of political construction comes to be construed as the domain of experts and specialists, organized in bureaucracies of power.[1] Books 6 and 7 offer ample evidence for Rosen's contention, while also presenting two very different versions of the philosopher and of the kind of political poetry a philosophical ruler would undertake. Through most of book 6, Socrates describes a philosopher whose erotic nature resembles his own, and whose political work in crafting laws and virtues reflects his manner of educating individuals in dialogue. The radical tradition of which Rosen speaks is truly inaugurated only when Socrates finally declares that "the matters having to do with women and children have been brought to completion, but it is necessary to pursue what concerns the rulers [*tōn archontōn*] from the beginning [*ex archēs*], as it were" (502e).

Socrates' new beginning mixes two modes of knowing and speaking that sit uneasily together: philosophical prophecy and political science. He starts with an image that likens the generative and unifying work of the Good, the origin and ruling principle of the Whole, to the sun's governance of the visible sphere. He then establishes a formal education designed to train selected individuals to assume the job of philosopher-king in Callipolis—a job that requires knowledge of the Good. Yet while his own speech about the Good is erotic and poetic, the curriculum is rigorously scientific: mathematical, abstract, and systematic. In fact, those who emerge from this education as certified philosophers are not necessarily erotic lovers of wisdom. But they are indeed a new breed of rulers, for they are *themselves* the product of doctrinal construction.

Let us consider these developments in order.

Socratic Philosopher-Kings

Socrates begins book 6 by speaking of those far enough advanced in the quest for wisdom to rule a city. While philosophers are "able to touch upon that which remains always the same in the same respects," the rulers Socrates envisions are more than just intellectually capable: they "know each thing that is, and neither lack experience nor fall short . . . in any other part of virtue" (484b, d). If Socrates elevates philosophers by quietly endowing them with comprehensive knowledge of being, it is because the souls he is describing are exemplary. Having followed the love of wisdom to its consummation, they "partake adequately and perfectly in what is" (486e; cf. 490a–b). In them, moreover, cognitive perfection is inseparable from goodness of character.

Socrates illuminates the connection between moral and intellectual excellence in these perfected philosophers when he asks Glaucon to consider their political craftsmanship:

> Well, then, do they seem to differ at all from blind men—those, that is, who really lack the knowledge [*tēs gnōseōs*] of the being of each thing, and neither have a clear pattern [*paradeigma*] in the soul, nor are able, just like a painter, to look away toward what is truest [*to alēthestaton*], and always referring to it and contemplating it as precisely as possible, to set down laws here about what is noble and just and good, if any need to be given, and as guardians to preserve those that have already been established? (484c–d)

This passage reminds us that philosophical vision requires a correct orientation of one's whole being. Philosophers can see what is most true only because they have a clear pattern of being in their souls; they recognize what is noble, just, and good through their kinship with these measures. This observation harks back to book 3, where Socrates observes that decent individuals, at least when they are young, are easily deceived by unjust men "because they have in themselves no patterns of affections like those of base men." The unjust man, he remarks in that context, seems clever when he deals with other criminals, for he "looks toward the pattern in himself"; but "when he associates with good men who are older, he seems stupid—being unsuitably distrustful and ignorant of a healthy character—because he does not have a pattern for this sort" (409b–d).

In book 3, Socrates explains that good patterns are established in the soul by the love of what is beautiful and noble, aroused and nourished by good music (cf. 401b–d with 403c). If they are fortunate enough to live in a regime with good laws and good music, nonphilosophers with some spark of *erōs* in their souls may become attuned to passable images of nobility, justice, and goodness. For philosophers, however, the love of learning, perfected through intellectual inquiry, produces an erotic and self-conscious attunement not just to images, but to the things themselves—reduplicating, insofar as possible, the natural, instinctive, and supremely musical soul-formation of the True City. Of all human beings, philosophers are therefore most suited to produce and preserve good laws: *nomoi* that attempt to stabilize "the many beliefs [*ta nomima*] of the many" (479d) by imaging the order of Being within the fluid realm of Becoming.

Once again, however, a problem arises from the ambiguity of Socrates' *paradeigma*: philosophical exemplars are inevitably distorted when they are used as models for political production. The Form or Idea of justice is for the philosopher an object of inquiry and aspiration: something to be approached in the stepwise give-and-take of reflection and dialogue, of hypothesis and criticism, and to live up to just insofar as it is understood.[2] But one does not reach out to an Idea that is a model; as the foundation of a construction rather than the end of an inquiry, it is presumed to be already in hand. Both the process and the product of understanding must be reconceived accordingly. This is why the epistemic language of precision slips into the previously quoted passage in connection with the image of the philosophical legislator as a painter.

Later passages bring these problems into sharper focus. Socrates first imagines guardians who are genuinely erotic lovers of wisdom: they not only know what each being is, but share fully in every part of virtue. True philosophers love all kinds of learning; hate falsehood and embrace truth; forsake the pleasures of the body (except presumably the glow of health and fitness, as in the True City); care little for money; are liberal and courageous in speech and deed; are just and gentle; learn easily; have good memories; and are musical, graceful, charming, and measured (484d–86d). The root of their comprehensive excellence is *erōs*: powerfully drawn to the sight of being and truth, they admire, and therefore imitate, "things that neither do nor suffer injustice from one another." Ignoring the rancorous pettiness of human affairs, and keeping company with that which is divine and decorously ordered (*kosmion*, after the fashion of the cosmos), they themselves become as divine and orderly as is humanly possible (500b–d).

Socrates' description of the erotic philosopher's soundness of mind and perfection of soul is one of the most beautiful parts of his *nomos*: meant to elicit a healthy longing, his philosophical music recalls the happy harmonies of the True City. Socrates can be faulted only for implying that the path by which philosophers come into the presence of truth and being is straight and smooth, like the movement of the mathematical mind of young Theaetetus, which his teacher Theodorus compares to flowing olive oil (*Tht.* 144b). The course of the inquiry in the *Republic* suggests rather that philosophy's gait is limping and unsteady: halted repeatedly by perplexity and by the objections and interruptions of his companions, Socrates time and again stumbles, begins anew, and circles back to ground already covered. Similarly, his practice of philosophical cross-examination and refutation causes others to lose their balance, and sometimes to come up lame.[3] Hesitancy, doubt, and indecisiveness do not, of course, inspire widespread confidence in one's understanding and judgment, which is why politicians, aiming for smoothness, often seem unctuous. Nor is the oblique movement of Socratic inquiry as it shuttles between Being and Becoming, truth and existence, appropriate to a regime that aims "to roll on like a circle" (424a).

After Socrates explains that philosophers order their own souls by imitating the beings, he considers the case of a philosopher whom "some necessity" compels "to practice putting what he sees there [in the realm of the beings] into the characters of human beings, both in private and in public, and not only to mold himself." Such a person, he suggests, would not be "a base craftsman [*dēmiourgon*] of moderation and justice and ordinary virtue as a whole" (500d). The craftsman Socrates goes on to describe resembles him in working not just publicly, but privately and with particular individuals, and in training himself as an educator through what the immediate sequel makes clear is a kind of experimentation. What he strives to produce in the souls of others, however, is not the excellence he himself acquires through direct contact with truth and being, but virtue that is suitable for the people as a whole (*aretē dēmotikē*: 500d).

The Eleatic Stranger at one point describes a Socratic educator who scours the souls of his interlocutors by refutation, believing that they cannot learn until free of the opinion that they know what they do not know.[4] Philosophical craftsmen would similarly first wipe clean, "just like a writing-tablet," the human materials on which they propose to work, "and would be willing to touch neither private man nor city, nor to draw laws, until they should either receive it clean [*katharan*] or make it so themselves." Only then would they begin to fill in the virtues, "looking back and forth between what is just by nature, noble, and moderate and all such things, and what they are fashioning in human beings"; "they would erase one thing and again draw in another, until they made human characters as dear to the gods as they admit of being" (501a–c). This process resembles the tentative and dialectical movement of Socratic dialogue, which continually advances, withdraws, and reformulates hypotheses as it weaves its way between concrete experience and the timeless structures of reality. The public work of philosophical craftsmen, however, consists in "mixing and compounding the image of man from the [virtuous] practices, judging by the very thing Homer, too, called both god-formed and the image of god [*theoeides te kai theoeikelon*] when it comes to be in human beings" (501b). But what thing is that? The only individuals to whom Homer applies both of the adjectives Socrates mentions are King Alcinous (Mighty-Mind) of the Phaeacians, Odysseus's son Telemachus (Far-Fighter), and Priam's son Deiphobus (God-Fearer). Socrates thus seems subtly to imply that Callipolis's philosophical craftsmen learn by trial and error how to fashion citizens who are distinguished by demotic versions of their own comprehensive philosophical excellence: ruling intelligence, courage and self-control, and sacred awe.[5]

What this political experimentation would look like is not clear. But a regime of the sort Socrates describes would be at least temporarily unfinished, and its philosophical legislator would be free to modify or rescind the laws and practices that have already been established, starting with those of the Virtuous City. This flexibility, however—the flexibility of Socratic philosophizing, which in its knowledge of ignorance turns hither and thither, exploring, reformulating, discarding, and generating a multitude of hypotheses on its way toward wisdom—is politically untenable, not least because it must often fail to find a soul in which it can reproduce itself. What is needed is a reliable procedure for producing rulers whose competence and confidence inspire the obedience, if not dedication, of non-philosophers. Callipolis's kings, having started out looking like Socratic philosophers, must become dogmatic ones. The vehicle of this transformation is the curriculum for future philosopher-kings that Socrates lays out in book 7.

When he announces the need for a new beginning regarding Callipolis's rulers, Socrates indicates that he is returning to a part of the argument that previously passed by "with its face covered, for fear of setting in motion what is now before us" (502e–03b). This curious detail recalls the *Phaedrus*, where he covers his face out of shame when delivering a speech that slanders the god Eros (237a, 242b–43b). What is shameful and ugly in the education Socrates goes on to describe will become clear if we first consider his noble and beautiful teaching about the Good.

A Reluctant Mystagogue

In turning to the Good, Socrates explicitly calls attention to the difficulty of transmitting philosophical teachings. Adeimantus (who had taken over the conversation at 487b) has heard Socrates speak about the subject many times, but is either unable or unwilling to recall that "even if we had as much knowledge as possible [*epistaimetha*] of the rest . . . it would be of no profit to us" in our ignorance of this "greatest study" (504e–05a). Socrates's discussion of the Good starts where an earlier conversation with Critias ends: by recognizing the uselessness of living scientifically in the absence of the knowledge of good and bad (*Chrm.* 174b–c). He proceeds to approach the Good in the mode of philosophical prophecy, and to clarify it through images—ways of knowing that, when it comes to the soul's erotic quest for ultimate reality and meaning, are less exact but more accurate than science.

If anything can draw souls toward philosophy, it is the problem of determining what is good. For only in this instance do human beings, many of whom are satisfied with the mere appearance of justice and nobility, universally despise opinion and reputation and "seek the things that are." Indeed, the fullest being of goodness, Socrates says, is "the very thing that every soul pursues, and for the sake of which it does everything"—a statement whose metaphysical breadth suggests a truly cosmic teleology.[6] But for human beings, at least, this pursuit is inconstant and beset by obstacles, like walking in the pitch of night; "the soul divines that it [the Good] is something, but is perplexed, and is neither able sufficiently to grasp just what it is, nor is guided by a stable trust [*pistei chrēsasthai*] of the sort that is has concerning other things." These words have a religious ring: one of the primary meanings of *chrēsasthai* is "to consult an oracle," and *pistis* would later become the favorite New Testament word for "faith." Much as when he availed himself of the godsend of Hermes in conceiving the True City, Socrates divines that no one will know the just and noble things before knowing in what way they are good. "You divine beautifully," Adeimantus replies (505d–06a).

The knowledge of which Socrates has been speaking is nonepistemic recognition or familiarity (*gnōsis*). Strikingly, however, he suggests—and Adeimantus agrees—that "our regime will have been perfectly ordered [*kekosmēsetai*]" if its guardian is "a scientific knower" of just and noble things (506a–b). He himself nevertheless claims to have only an opinion about the Good, one that he is hesitant to share when pressed. Opinions apart from *epistēmē*, he declares, are ugly; does Adeimantus want to see ugly, blind, and scoliotic things (506c–d)—things like a blind and limping Oedipus, bent over his staff and tapping his way?

The ensuing scene follows much the same script as the beginning of book 5. Socrates fears misleading his interlocutors and paying the penalty in ridicule, and Glaucon, taking over from Adeimantus, forcefully insists that he speak: "By Zeus, Socrates . . . you are just at the end and you stop short!" Socrates declines to share his opinion of the Good, which he claims is beyond "the present charge [*hormē*, a military term]" of the argument. But he responds with a counter-offer: he will speak of "what appears to be a child of the Good and most similar to it" (506b–e). Glaucon's encouragement, and Socrates' reply, are highly significant:

> "Just speak," he said; "in the future you will pay what is owed on the father's narrative."
>
> "I could wish," I said, "that I were able to pay it and you to receive it, and not just the interest [*tokos*], as is now the case. But receive this interest and child of the Good itself. Take good care, however, that I do not in some way unwillingly deceive you in giving you a fraudulent account [*kibdēlon logon*] of the interest."
>
> "We'll be as careful as we can," he said. "But just speak." (507a)

Socrates' caution recalls his earlier fear that he might involuntarily deceive his companions about noble, good, and just things in laws. In that context, Glaucon granted him legal indemnity (451b). Here, he accepts a dividend—*tokos* literally means "offspring," because money generates interest—and allows him an indefinite extension on returning the capital he has borrowed. Yet Socrates, who had earlier (with tongue in cheek) directed Adeimantus to "observe how stingily I make images" (488a), warns that he may unintentionally pay his companions in false coin. *Kibdēlon* refers to gold or silver that has been adulterated with base metals, as if to suggest that the risk of impurity seems to extend beyond his account of the Good to the souls of the rulers who are to take their bearings by it. What might this mean?

Socrates' language is both erotic and technical, and his image refers to a form of political production—coined currency (*nomisma*)—that is essential enough to appear in the True City. In his account, as we shall see directly, the Good is more abundantly alive and generative, more fundamentally and purely an origin, than any beginning outside of the creative God of the Hebrew Bible. The image of the Good as the potent father of what is and the begetter of the sun underscores its fecundity as the source of Being and Becoming alike.

Socrates' talk of capital and interest, however, emphasizes its useful effects: payoffs in the coin of custom.[7] More generally, there is a tension in his discussion of the Good between prophetic images of the natural, living Whole and mathematical or formal reasoning, suitable for practical calculations as well as the articulation of metaphysical structure. But there can be no question of which of these modes of thinking is primary. While Socrates clarifies the soul's relationship to the Good in the images of Sun, Line, and Cave (507c–17a), mathematics is explicit only in the Line. What is more, the ratios of the Divided Line reflect the analogical structure of the Whole, which Socrates conceives as a hierarchy of imaging relationships: a ladder to the Good that can be traversed by poetry and prophecy as well as mathematics. Most important, the Good is "beyond being [*tēs ousias*]" (509b) and so does not appear in the Line, the highest quadrant of which represents the cognition of Ideas by means of philosophical dialectic (511b–c).

The Divine Magnanimity of Being

The Sun Image concerns the mystery of the first things, and is the most splendid and exalted passage of Socratic music in the *Republic*. Socrates delivers the image in good humor, but with a solemn reverence that tolerates no blasphemy (cf. his rebuke of Glaucon at 509a). While the sun's light and life figure in the rituals of Bendis that limn the *Republic*, the Good occupies a realm beyond the heavenly deities. The image presents the Good as an absolute *archē*: the superabundant beginning, progenitor, and ruler of the Whole. The Good transcends all that is, yet brings forth beings in a manner analogous to its cosmic child—the "lord," "god," and "king" that causes the earth to sprout with life (508a, 509d).

In the Sun Image, Socrates conveys knowledge in the modes of philosophical prophecy and poetic analogy: the Good stands to the intelligible realm as the sun, "which the Good generated in due proportion [*analogon*] to itself," stands to the visible realm (508b). The powers "yoked" or adequately fitted together by the sun are seeing and being seen: the manifestation and perception of bodies that come into and pass out of existence. These powers overflow from the sun as from a treasury (508b); the sun's light and warmth are the precondition of all life, and so of the eye that sees and the good green earth in which it delights. The sun "supplies the seasons and years" (516b), dispensing its vital wealth in good order and with due measure.

The Good presides over the realm of Being just as the sun, "the steward of all things in the visible region" (516b–c), presides over the realm of Becoming. The source of cognition and of the perspicuity of what is, the Good endows the mind's eye with vision and allows beings to show forth in the intrinsic intelligibility they already possess. Its illumination makes possible the unity of soul and being at which all human beings knowingly or unknowingly aim in all they do (500d–e). For it is abidingly and fundamentally good to come into the presence of what is, and so to be fructified by its powers and teem, like Socrates, with images of goodness in speech and deed.[8]

The Good orients and orders human souls to the extent that they feel its vital power and see in its light. Its measures, erotically and intellectually accessed in the philosophical life, are displayed in the ordered ensemble of the beings (500c). They are also reflected in the natural wholesomeness and unity of the True City, and may be politically imitated in good laws. But the soul can be sundered or unyoked from the order of being by the intellectual equivalent of blindness. Socrates' remark that the powers of seeing and being seen bestowed by the sun are fitted together by a yoke (light) that is "more honorable than the yokes uniting other teams" (508a) recalls the chariot of Helios and the disaster of Phaethon, who drove the sun into the earth when he could not control his father's divine horses. (At 509c, Glaucon invokes Helios under another name, Apollo.) In implicitly acknowledging the human potential to interfere with the unifying and ordering work of the Good, Socrates offers a mythical analogue of the intellectual inadequacy of the class of philosopher-kings.[9]

Phaethon's Lesson

The priest of Saïs in the *Timaeus* regarded the myth of Phaethon as childish folklore provoked by the movement of fiery bodies through the atmosphere (22c–d). His view has recently been supported by astronautical engineers, who argue that the myth was inspired by the distant memory of a particular event—the massive asteroid, reported by a Sumerian astronomer in 3123 BCE, that passed "over Sodom and Gomorrah . . . [and] would have broiled those below at temperatures reaching seven hundred and fifty degrees."[10] This fascinating explanation is entirely plausible, but nevertheless ignores the profound human meaning of the myth.

Paternity and inheritance are favorite themes of the Greek poets. Homer's *Odyssey* is on one level a coming-of-age story, in which Telemachus proves that he has inherited his father's mind and spirit. Less fortunately, a vexed Oedipus rushes to Delphi to stamp out the rumor that he was adopted by King Polybus of Corinth. Phaethon similarly seeks to put to rest doubts about *his* paternity by proving that he can master Helios's divine steeds and drive the chariot of the sun, even though Helios strongly discourages him. It is unclear whether he fails to maintain the uninterrupted motion of the sun—a model of the smooth operation to which all regimes aspire—because he cannot handle the horses, or because he cannot see where he is going.[11] In any case, his failure offers yet another image of the political lameness produced when some blindness or incapacity of the soul, bred in the bone, is matched with the ungoverned spirit of an aristocrat dispossessed of rule.[12] Critias fits this bill perfectly; one can hardly fail to notice the irony of his mention of Phaethon in the context of Saïs, a regime whose eight thousand years of continuous political reproduction he implicitly offers as a kind of promissory note (worthless, in the event) for his future political plans.

As its father's unalloyed child—Socrates does not mention its mother—the sun perfectly reproduces within the visible realm the work of the Good in the intelligible realm, and so could never fall short of the Good in the way that Phaethon falls short of his father. The Good's pure generativity is *the* paradigm of legitimate filiation in the *Republic*. This generativity is directly evident in Socrates, a legitimate son of the Good whose overflowing humanity fertilizes open souls and nourishes their spiritual offspring. It also furnishes an ideal analogue of the desired spiritual transmission or asexual reproduction of philosophy through generations of kingly teachers and learners in Callipolis.

The Sun Image helps to underscore the stark contrast between Socrates and Phaethon. At Potidaea, Athenian troops and their allies observe Socrates standing in thought from dawn to dawn and concluding his meditations by praying to the sun (*Symp.* 220c–d). On the day of his execution, Socrates likens his exploration of being through the medium of speeches to observing the sun in its reflection in water: just as those who look at the sun directly during an eclipse damage their eyes, natural scientists, who make use only of material and efficient causes in speaking of what is, risk blinding their souls (*Phdo.* 99d–e). For Phaethon, however, the sun is not something to be revered and contemplated from a respectful distance, but to be taken in hand and controlled; goodness consists not in ordering and assimilating oneself to what is, but in subordinating it to one's own purposes. Surprisingly, however, Socrates lays the groundwork for the very misunderstanding Phaethon exemplifies, one that is reflected in the way Callipolis's rulers approach the Good.

Socrates indicates that the Good links *nous* or intelligence with what is intellected (508c). A little later, he makes it clear that when intelligence cognizes being in the light of the Good, it achieves knowledge in the form of *gnōsis* (508d). But in responding to Adeimantus's complaint that he is willing to tell the opinions (*dogmata*) of others about the Good but not his own (506b), he goes on to employ the terminology of correct belief, including opinion ordered by law:

> As the cause of science [*epistēmēs*] and truth, you can understand it [the Good] as a thing known, but as beautiful as both of these things are—knowledge [*gnōseōs*] and truth—you will believe correctly in believing that it is other and still more beautiful than these things. With respect to science and truth, just as there it is correct to believe [*nomidzein*] that light and sight are sunlike, but it is not correct to believe that they are the sun, here, too, it is correct to believe them both to be like the Good, but to believe that either one of them is the Good is not correct. (508d–09a)

Socrates here instructs his companions in the fundamental dogma, so to speak, of the church of the Good. This philosophical catechism plainly indicates that the Good, in its lofty uniqueness, cannot be adequately cognized by a purely formal ontology or with scientific precision. Yet it makes no clear distinction between scientific and non-scientific forms of knowledge.

If the Good makes possible knowing as a whole, it is in a fundamental sense the cause of every particular sort of knowledge, including *gnōsis* as well as *epistēmē*. An insufficiently attentive auditor might nevertheless take Socrates to mean that intellectual vision is essentially, or in its highest instance, *identical* to *epistēmē*. To make this mistake is to eclipse the philosophical prophecy by which Socrates brings the Good into view, and the specific divinations that guide him and Glaucon in discerning the soul-turning usefulness of mathematical studies (523a, 531d). Yet it is this very misunderstanding on which the education of the philosopher-kings is based. Indeed, the unwarranted exaltation of scientific knowledge in Callipolis is nothing other than the false coin against which Socrates warns his companions when he begins to speak about the Good.

Dogmatic Philosopher-Kings

In taking up the education of the philosopher-kings near the end of book 6, Socrates recalls the previous discussion in book 3 of the need to test warriors so as to select those who are "lovers of the city" and will not abandon their conviction under the influence of pleasure or pain. Only the one who "comes out altogether undefiled, tested like gold in fire" must be installed as ruler, while the others must be rejected (503a). Socrates reminds Adeimantus of these things because he is about to establish new labors and tests, over and above the earlier ones, for another, specifically intellectual kind of love or dogma that the rulers must also possess.

Socrates now "dares" to say that philosophers must be established as "the most precise guardians" and share in "the most precise education" (503b, d). Recalling his remark in book 4 that the methods or roads of inquiry (*methodoi*) they were currently employing would not allow them "precisely" to grasp the forms of the soul (435c–d), he reminds his companions that their earlier discussion was "deficient in precision"; a longer way will be needed if "the greatest things" are to be seen with "the greatest precision" (504b–e). In particular, the city's guardians must "go the longer way around and labor no less in studying than in gymnastic" (504c–d). The longer way of inquiry turns out to be the royal road of philosophical education Callipolis establishes for its kings.

If Socrates' language recalls Thrasymachus's technically precise art of rule, his equally Thrasymachean daring or boldness in speech is our first hint that philosophy in Callipolis is largely a thumotic enterprise. Socrates observes that "vigorous and magnificent" natures that are quick and good at learning are easily carried away and do not choose quiet and orderly lives, while dispositions that are steadfast in war and trustworthy in the face of fears are "hard to move and hard to teach" (503c–d). Ideally, philosopher-kings would combine exquisite philosophical responsiveness with the utmost political steadiness; they would cling to the orthodoxy they absorb in their training as auxiliaries even as their souls catch fire with intellectual excitement. But while these two natures could in principle grow together in one individual, Socrates makes it clear that the education of the philosopher-kings would favor the kind of character for which the previous education has already selected. Those chosen to embark on the royal road are to be drawn from the pool of young warriors with the most stable and courageous dispositions. Their education will be every bit as laborious as their previous training, for it involves a toilsome kind of intellectual struggle that resembles the grind of battle. The soul that has proved itself in labors, fears, and pleasures, Socrates says, must now "also undergo gymnastic in many studies, to see whether it will be able to bear the greatest studies, or whether it will play the coward, just like those who are cowardly in other pursuits" (503e–04a).

Socrates' strong language, replete with Spartan harshness, indicates that each new test will produce a sharp distinction between winners and losers. However the regime may present the matter, some few will be promoted and given special honors; the rest will be passed over, and barred from the highest political offices. Just as the rewards that flow exclusively to the best of the warriors divide the class of auxiliaries, these selections will increase the likelihood of discord between souls mixed of silver and gold—especially because all discontented parties in Callipolis, with the exception of the classes of craftsmen and farmers, are spirited and warlike. Indeed, all those who prove cowardly in studies will already have demonstrated courage and self-discipline in the pursuits associated with war.

Socrates gives us a clearer picture of the royal road to rule in book 7. Like the Spartan education, this road runs from childhood well into adulthood, and involves multiple levels of scrutiny. To begin with, children will be introduced to the rudiments of calculation, geometry, and the rest of the studies preparatory to philosophical dialectic. They will approach these studies as play, and without compulsion—both because "no forced study abides in a soul," and because this will allow them to reveal their natural aptitudes (536d–37a). Those who show intellectual promise *and* who prove to be capable in bodily gymnastic will be selected for greater honors and promoted to more synoptic studies at age twenty (537b)—roughly the age at which young Lacedaemonian men were considered for membership in a common mess and entry into the ranks of the Spartan peers.[13] This group of potential philosopher-kings is not identical with the group of auxiliaries selected for frequent intercourse in book 5 (although there may be some overlap between them), for the latter includes "those among the young who are good in war or elsewhere" (460b). Callipolis will evidently place young men and women on multiple tracks, honoring and mating some because they are outstanding soldiers, others because they show promise as rulers. Socrates says in book 8 that the philosopher-kings are "best in philosophy and with respect to war" (543a); they surpass others by demonstrating excellence in both pursuits, but are not necessarily the very best in each. From the first, philosophy in Callipolis involves compromises with politics.

The curriculum leading up to philosophy is designed to attune souls to the most authoritative measures of lawful order: the ensemble of beings "that neither do injustice nor suffer injustice from one another, but remain all in decorous order according to reason" (500c). In preparation for the song of dialectic, which Socrates presents as the purely intellectual, discursive understanding of the community and relationship of the beings, students will learn number theory and calculation, then plane and solid geometry, and finally pure astronomy and harmonics—the study of mathematical consonances that are only imperfectly instantiated in the motion of visible bodies and audible sounds (524d–33c). This gymnastic involves leaps and rolls solely on the top two sections of the Divided Line, which images the soul's relation to purely intelligible, imperceptible entities (511a–e).

The abstract disciplines that pave the royal road are designed to cultivate order in the soul while revealing it to the mind. They tame wayward eroticism by helping to detach souls from Becoming and turning them toward the unchanging ratios or symmetries of Being (530a–b). They also prepare students to give and receive philosophically disciplined arguments about the community of beings within a community of teachers and learners (531e–32a)—a social activity that involves rules of engagement and structures of authority, and therefore requires a kind of moral and political habituation. As Socrates and Glaucon repeatedly emphasize, moreover, these studies are far from useless for "polemical men," for military tactics require a knowledge of calculation and geometry (521d, 522d–e, 526c–d). Nor are they useless for the mathematical science of eugenics—a kind of polemic against nature that restricts and channels sexual eroticism, much as pure mathematics does with intellectual eroticism. In fact, these studies seem to provide a theoretical foundation for the applied science of politics as a whole, which reflects the structures of Being in impressing form and order on the city.

Another selection will occur at age thirty; "the preferred from among the preferred"—the best of the all-round best—will be assigned still greater honors and introduced to dialectical inquiry (*dialektikē*) in the medium of philosophical argumentation (*dialegesthai*), which will occupy them for the next five years (537d, 539d–e). Those passed over in this case will have completed all studies preparatory to philosophy. They will evidently assume military leadership and secondary political offices, using their mathematical knowledge strictly for practical and political ends; we may infer this from Socrates' remark that those who complete the education in philosophy must return to the Cave and do the same from age thirty-five to fifty, "so that they will not lag behind the others in experience" (539e). More esteemed than those unable to advance beyond the rank of auxiliary, but forever barred from the highest power and honor, these royal and philosophical bridesmaids will constitute yet another envied and envious class.

Socrates emphasizes that children who do not take to mathematics will not be placed on the path of philosophical education. But this does not in itself ensure that all philosopher-kings will be erotic lovers of wisdom. It could do so only if the disciplines mastered along the royal road comprised the whole of wisdom, and only if aptitude in these studies were equivalent to love of them. But neither of these things is the case.

Although Socrates speaks of dialectic as a song (*nomos*), it is a far cry from Arion's alluring music, and bears little resemblance to the richly pleasurable fabric of history, myth, imagery, and prophecy that constitutes Socratic conversation and Platonic writing. While Socrates later says that the best guardian of virtue and savior throughout life is argument mixed with music (549b), Callipolis's guardians and "saviors" (502d) are trained in a regimen consisting exclusively of heavy intellectual lifting. Music is omitted in the rulers' education because, as Glaucon notes, it does not produce scientific knowledge—an observation Socrates calls "most precise" (522a). In the education of the auxiliaries, Socrates observes, music "was the antistrophe to gymnastic"; it complemented strenuous physical exercise and athletic competition by softening and taming a soul that would otherwise be savage and graceless (522a; cf. 411c–e). The education of the philosopher-kings, however, is amusic and therefore unbalanced: it is the "gymnastic antistrophe of the bodily gymnastic" (539d).[14]

The thumotic character of this philosophical gymnastic is most explicit at 534b–c, where Socrates briefly describes the final examination future rulers must pass. "Whoever is unable to distinguish in argument the Idea of the Good, having separated it off from all other things, and going through all trials [or 'refutations': *elenchōn*] just as in battle, spiritedly exerting himself to refute not according to opinion, but according to being, comes through all this with the argument still standing"—whoever cannot do these things, he suggests, cannot be said to know the Good. Socrates himself, however, claims to have been thrashed in argument by "thousands of Heracleses and Theseuses" (*Tht.* 169b). What sort of victory, one wonders, is achieved by the thinker who repeatedly does battle in ontological argument without ever falling?

Socrates describes dialectic as a methodical inquiry (*methodos*) that grasps what each thing is by means of discursive intelligence or *dianoia*, applied to the philosophical study of the beings themselves (533b–d). After remarking that he won't quibble about names, he proceeds to make a mistake that is too revealing to be unintentional. In listing the four cognitive functions of the soul "just as before"—that is, when he enumerated them in connection with the image of the Divided Line—he substitutes *epistēmē* in the top quadrant for what he previously called *noēsis,* direct intellectual perception (533d–34a; cf. 511d–e). By implication, he also promotes *dianoia,* the faculty employed in mathematical inquiry (and productive of mathematical science) that occupies the second quadrant in the Divided Line, to the top rank of cognitive functions. What is the significance of these questionable substitutions?

Dialectical science, the culmination and coping-stone of the edifice of philosophy in Callipolis (534e), evidently completes the original noetic perception of the beings and the Good: what was previously "seen" by the intellect (*nous*) in its erotic receptivity is ultimately "grasped" (*lambanein*: 533b) through the instrument of conceptually precise speech. Dialectic, in other words, is the fulfillment of the philosophical ambition for a systematic understanding of reality. But like the prehensile hand, conceptual comprehension to some extent inevitably conceals the things in its grip. The purely formal perspective of dialectic reveals the internal ontological structure of the Good in its relationship with what is: its *idea* or *eidos.* Insofar as the Good is beyond being, however, it is not identical to the Idea of the Good. To fail to make this distinction is to mistake the living nature of the Good for an artifact of philosophical methodology.

In sum, Callipolis's philosopher-kings answer to the demands of *thumos,* including the demand for intelligibility. They are conceived in the context of political necessity, and formed by a rigorous program of drilling and testing that calls for unusual intellectual hardihood. As Roslyn Weiss has observed, Socrates' description of their education in book 7 includes no mention of intellectual *erōs;* while those who are by nature philosophers (and who spring up spontaneously in actual cities) love learning and strive passionately to live up to truth and being, Callipolis's philosopher-kings are compelled to leave the Cave, compelled to reenter it so as to rule in war and hold the political offices suitable for young men, compelled to contemplate the Good, and compelled to order the city and their own souls in the light of what they see.[15] Yet the philosopher who enters into the sunlight in the Cave Image explores the outer world on his own, willingly contemplates the Good, and spontaneously reenters the Cave (516a–e).

While there are surely some lovers of learning among the philosopher-kings, Socrates makes it clear that philosophical *erōs* in Callipolis is narrowly channeled and guided. In particular, the education-by-compulsion of Callipolis's rulers bears only a superficial resemblance to the free play of Socratic dialogue. Although students on the royal road learn to formulate and respond to philosophical arguments, they are taught only the most precise sort of knowledge pertaining to the most perfect things (cf. 530e–31a). The curriculum is not designed to encourage non-mathematical modes of imagination, and selects specifically for those who are quick in dealing with formal systems and intellectual abstractions. More generally, it gives preference to those who are "steadfast [*monimoi*] in studies and steadfast in war and the rest of what is established by law [*tois allois nomimois*]" (537d). Socrates' wordplay underscores the intellectual conformism of these thinkers, monologically devoted as they are to intellectual as well as political convention—specifically, to what the regime certifies as authoritative knowledge.

Perhaps most important, the education of the philosopher-kings is a process of deliberate rationalization. It operates on souls in a manner akin to mathematical procedures for dealing with incommensurable magnitudes, and its success is gauged by political efficacy, not truth or intellectual fruitfulness. "For I don't suppose," Socrates remarks to Glaucon, "that while they are as irrational [*alogous*] as lines, you would allow them to be rulers in the city and sovereigns over the greatest things" (534d). Socrates refers here to the Pythagorean discovery that the lengths of the side of a square and its diagonal stand to one another in the proportion $\sqrt{2}$, an irrational number. The side and the diagonal share no common measure: no line segment, be it ever so small, will fit without remainder into both. Similarly, the education and training of the auxiliaries had attempted to establish a common measure, but apparently without complete success; their souls retain some politically decisive remainder of particular individuality that resists the *logos* of the city. Those would-be kings who are not naturally drawn toward order and harmony by erotic means must therefore be corrected or *made* rational by thumotic ones.[16] This is the most fundamental sense in which, in Callipolis, the beautiful *nomos* of Arion gives way to the onerous law of Periander.

The Limits of Compulsion

This is by no means to say that the studies that comprise the royal road would not benefit genuinely philosophical natures. To the contrary, lovers of wisdom could not be considered philosophically well-educated without them: while these studies are not the soul of philosophy, they are certainly its backbone. Pressing upward toward the transcendent Good, their *erōs* would be disciplined by dialectical science, and they would acquire powerful conceptual tools. But because they are aware of what Sherwood Belangia refers to as the "erotic remainder" in philosophy, "the gap between attainment and desire" in relation to the Good that dwells beyond all beings, they will not mistake this epistemic and systematic part of philosophy for the whole.[17] Nor will they confuse their theoretical understanding of the community of beings and its reflection in the political structure of the city with the community or being-together (*sunousia*) of human beings in a shared life.

Erotic philosophers, however, need no state-sponsored education, for Socrates explains that they spontaneously pursue wisdom until they beget intelligence and truth, and perhaps also thereafter (490a–b). If institutionalized philosophical training is necessary in Callipolis, it is because nature does not generate a reliable supply of genuinely philosophical souls. The regime presupposes, in other words, that at least some who possess intellectual aptitude but lack philosophical *erōs* can nevertheless be turned into kings of adequate political competence and properly sovereign character. This, Plato indicates, is precisely what it means to embrace doctrinal construction in politics. Indeed, Socrates' claim that no forced study abides in a soul is highly questionable. The piano student who unwillingly submits to years of instruction from a strict taskmaster may never be an inspired musician, but she *will* become a competent pianist; constant repetition and drilling, coupled with penalties for mistakes, are effective means of teaching everything from the multiplication table to the conjugation of Greek verbs.[18]

But can one who does not love the highest things truly know them? Is erotically-detached proficiency in systematic metaphysics sufficient when it comes to the Good? Mustn't the Good be distorted and diminished when those who are merely competent approach it in the spirit of mathematics independently of music? Socrates' prophetic speech about philosophical *erōs* and the Good leaves no doubt about the answer to these questions.[19] We furthermore learn in book 8 that Callipolis's education-by-compulsion fails in the long run. Mathematical studies and philosophical dialectic prove to be no more successful than eugenic science in disciplining and directing human nature.

To be clear, all philosopher-kings in Callipolis must be presumed to be erotic in some fundamental way. No one could successfully complete the rigorous curriculum Socrates describes without combining intellectual acuity and agility with either a strong love of learning, a passionate devotion to the city, or a great lust for political power and esteem. The highly theoretical education provided to future philosopher-kings, however, seems to offer no basis for determining the specific erotic inflection of given individuals—the fundamental aim around which their souls revolve, and from which they are determined not to stray. If any *genuine* philosopher came to the end of the royal road, he or she would rule intelligently in the light of the Good. Those non-philosophers who are driven by their love of the city to become kings will perhaps be competent in discharging the responsibilities of their office, but no more; they will resemble schoolmen, intellectual sectarians rather than lovers of wisdom erotically attuned to the Whole. But anyone who endured all trials and tests for the sake of the rewards Socrates dangles before Glaucon in book 5—and this possibility cannot be definitely ruled out—would come to power with all the eagerness of a future tyrant.

This last point must be kept in mind when we reflect on Socrates' assertion that philosopher-kings resemble those who are said to have gone "from Hades up to the gods" (521c)—an echo of the journey of Gyges' ancestor—and that their happiness is akin to that of those who dwell on the Isles of the Blessed (519c, 540b). Having won Glaucon's loyalty to the rule of philosophers by the end of book 5, Socrates thereafter encourages him to see himself as more than just an ideological auxiliary to a philosophical ruler. By the end of book 7, he has convinced him that Callipolis's philosopher-kings are *pankaloi*, "altogether noble and beautiful" (540c). Their combination of surpassing virtue and supreme power, to say nothing of the signal honors they would receive—including, even while alive, memorials and sacrifices either as daimons or as "happy and divine men" (540b–c)—speaks to the deepest longings of this son of Ariston, not least his desire to prove that his is worthy of his father's famous name (cf. 368a). Socrates' insistence on the courage required to complete the royal training, and the curriculum's heavy emphasis on mathematical studies, must furthermore raise Glaucon's hopes of being recognized as The Best.[20]

Socrates has finally sung a song that is fully in tune with Glaucon's peculiar combination of virtue and decadence, noble longing and wayward appetite. The measures of the royal road, demanding measures that he embraces with passion and energy, are in fact a reverie of the intellect, designed to impart a sense of philosophical wakefulness to those who sleep. But the sleeping mind is also morally lax, as any dreamer knows. In imagining himself as King of Callipolis, as Socrates deliberately invites him to do,[21] Glaucon forgets that the Noble and Beautiful City originates as an idle and self-indulgent fantasy.

Socrates' Unphilosophical Ire

If Socrates argues for a regime and a curriculum that he knows to be philosophically and politically deficient, he does so not simply to test Glaucon's nature, but also in the hope of keeping him at his side. Callipolis is in this sense an individually-tailored advertisement for Socratic philosophizing, designed to make Glaucon invest more deeply in their relationship. As always, however, this relationship must be seen in the context of Socrates' rivalry with Critias—a rivalry that, in the *Republic,* seems to bring out the worst in him.

In book 6, Adeimantus complains that most of those who spend much time in philosophy are "very twisted, not to say completely vicious," while the rest—those considered "most decent"—are "useless to the cities" (487d). (*Allokotous,* "twisted," literally means "different in rancor or ill-will"; the vicious philosophers are characterized by an atypical kind of small-minded spiritedness.) Socrates doubtless surprises Adeimantus by agreeing with him. He asserts that genuine philosophers, the ones Adeimantus calls useless, are in fact the few among the few. Few human beings possess philosophical natures, and most of those who do are unable to resist the relentless social pressure to conform to the ways and opinions of the nonphilosophical many. For whatever private philosophical education a young man may have had, Socrates explains, is likely to be carried away by the resounding flood of praise and blame that rushes in from all sides when men "sit down in large numbers together in assemblies or courts or army camps or any other common meeting of the multitude," so that, in the end, "he'll assert that the same things are noble and shameful as these men do, practice what they practice, and be such as they are" (492b–c). The existence of only a very few genuine philosophers furthermore leaves the field largely free for their imitators. Some clever men among the many who are by nature incapable of philosophizing nevertheless presume to be able to do so. These constitute the majority of those who are known as philosophers, and they are the ones Adeimantus calls twisted and vicious.

Socrates goes on to speak with unusual vehemence about the shameful condition of philosophy as things now stand. He likens *philosophia* to a noble but humiliated woman (in Greek, abstract nouns ending with *–ia* are grammatically feminine). Philosophia has been abandoned by those for whom she is most suited, and "other unworthy men come in afterwards and shame her and drape her in disgrace, as though she were an orphan bereft of relatives." Socrates' language in this context is replete with harsh diminutives: he calls these unworthy men *anthrōpiskoi*, "piddling little men," and describes them as "most clever in their little art." These manikins leap into philosophy "just like those who run away from prisons to take sanctuary in temples." They resemble, Socrates says, a little bald worker in bronze who has acquired some silver, bought his way out of slavery, and proposes to marry the daughter of his impoverished and destitute master. The offspring of such men, whose "stunted" and "broken" souls make them "unworthy of education," will be naturally be "things bastard and foul" (495b–96a).

Socrates' comparison of these sham philosophers to slavish and vulgar bronze-workers who use silver to improve their station sounds like a criticism of the social fluidity of democratic Athens, where class is no measure of intrinsic nobility. Socrates himself, after all, is a bald stonemason, while others of high birth—including

Critias—are ignoble in soul. The rulers of Callipolis, by comparison, take great pains to ensure that souls of base metal do not enter into their ranks. They do so by deeming worthy of philosophical education only those natures the regime has already certified as silver, and then using additional training as a means of sifting for nuggets of psychic gold.

In sum, the professionalization of philosophy in Callipolis offers Socrates a solution to the problem of vicious philosophers. We have seen that this solution, the establishment of an institutional mechanism that excludes from philosophy all who shrink before the considerable labors of abstract studies, fails to select exclusively for the most erotic and philosophical natures. But it does bar the way to the *least* erotic or intellectually capable ones. It does bar the way to Critias, whose great longing for power is backed up by poetic creativity, but not by the capacity for rigorous philosophical thought.

To the extent that Socrates is influenced by animus toward Critias, however, he comes to resemble the very men he deplores: would-be philosophers whose souls are twisted with rancor. He seems to have forgotten the lesson he taught Polemarchus: that the just man doesn't harm enemies (*echthroi*, those who are hateful), because he is simply not the sort of person to act out of hatred. In spite of his observation that the philosopher has no leisure to fight with human beings "and be filled with envy and ill-will" (500b–c), he allows his hostility toward people he acknowledges to be of no account whatsoever to obscure the truth about the highest and most important things: the erotic remainder of the Good, and above all, the beauty and pleasure of philosophizing. He thereby decisively distorts philosophy, the ruling principle of the regime he is founding.

To be sure, philosophers hate *falsehood* (485c), and it is only natural that they do so; this is the flip side of their love of truth. But in succumbing to the temptation to suppress counterfeit and vicious philosophers, Socrates himself lapses into falsehood and ignobility concerning the most important matters. In so doing, he clouds the erotic purity of his soul with the unphilosophical spiritedness of an ideologue. This is an instance of the worst sort of lie, a lie in the soul about "the most sovereign things" (382a), and it is one of which he soon repents.[22]

Lame Men and Bastards

We know that Socrates has gotten unduly worked up over the pusillanimity of those who now pursue philosophy, for he says so explicitly.

As soon as he finishes laying out the curriculum of the philosopher-kings, Socrates revisits the question of who should be selected to undertake the studies he has prescribed. Preference must be given, he states, to the steadiest and most courageous natures, "and insofar as possible, the best looking"—a remark that flatters Glaucon, and reminds us that higher education in Callipolis is formulated with a view primarily to political considerations. Beyond this, he notes, the severity of the philosophical gymnastic requires that students exhibit "keenness in studies"; in particular, care must be taken to avoid "the error [*hamartēma*] and dishonor that has befallen philosophy on account of the things we spoke of previously . . . for legitimate natures, not bastards, should put their hands to it" (535a–c).

Philosophical bastardy, Socrates explains, may consist in an imbalance in the soul's loves. Lame is "he who loves gymnastic and the hunt, and loves toil in all things accomplished through the body, but is not a lover of learning, and neither loves listening nor is an inquirer." Lame, too, is "he who has turned his love of toil to the opposite of this man's." But souls may also be disfigured with respect to truth. "Won't we set down as maimed," Socrates asks Glaucon, "whatever soul hates the voluntary lie, and finds it hard to endure in itself, and becomes exceedingly angry when others lie, but is content to receive the involuntary lie"—the lie in the soul about what is, which one least ought to accept (cf. 382b)? Finally, souls may be bastard in relation to "moderation, and courage, and magnificence, and all the parts of virtue"; the city and private individual that are incapable of guarding against such illegitimacy will unwittingly make use of "lame men and bastards, some as friends, others as rulers." We must therefore bring to "so great a study, and so great a training" only those who are "sound of limb and sound of mind." If we do so, Socrates concludes, "justice herself will find no fault with us, and we will save the city and the regime, but in leading to it those of another sort, we shall do exactly the opposite, and shall pour still more ridicule over philosophy" (535d–36b).

It is at this point that Socrates confesses he has gotten carried away:

> I seem to have been somewhat ridiculously affected just now. . . . I forgot that we were playing, and I spoke rather vehemently. For in speaking I looked toward philosophy, and having seen her undeservedly spattered with mud, I seem to myself to have become incensed, and to have said what I said too seriously, just like one who has been stirred to anger against those who are responsible. (536c)

To what particular speech is Socrates referring here? Not, it would seem, to his just and cautionary remarks about lameness and bastardy. Indeed, these remarks prove to be prophetic. Socrates' Athenian accusers would later blame him for Critias; Socrates says lame learners yawn when confronted with difficult studies (503d), and in the *Charmides* he compares Critias's intellectual exhaustion to yawning (169c).

But there is another side to this matter. In the *Republic,* Socrates designs a philosophical aristocracy from which Critias would be excluded. He thus exacts a kind of poetic revenge against a man he could not, after all, prevent from ruling in actuality. It is a lame revenge, and that in more than one way. In asserting that he was ridiculously affected when he forgot they were playing and became angry at those who bring ridicule upon philosophy, Socrates indicates that he has imitated those he sought to punish. The bespattering of philosophy by worthless men is reminiscent of the crime that forces Arion into the sea and soils his beautiful clothes. Arrested and forced to appear in filthy finery, Arion is disgraced and humiliated as much by Periander's justice as by his shipmates' injustice. Just so, Socrates' indignation blemishes the play of philosophy in the light of the Good. Standing in this light, the philosopher of the Cave Image would pity those below (516c). Socrates mixes pity for some with anger at others, and indulging this anger in a serious way gives rise to still more anger.

Roslyn Weiss rightly observes that Socrates is angry more at himself than at the paltry, vicious souls that have brought philosophy into disrepute.[23] In constructing Callipolis, he has come to resemble the very men he despises—mean, small-souled men who pollute

Philosophia with their indecent association. He brought no credit to his beloved in book 5, when he spoke of women and children after the manner of a lazy coward who is disposed to run from truth and justice alike (457d–58b). And now, in gratifying his desire to avenge philosophy, he has managed only to shame her once again.

Gambling with Glaucon

Socrates seems particularly concerned about how his bad behavior might influence Glaucon. Shortly after his confession, he speaks of the lawlessness that philosophical dialogue produces in the souls of the young. He compares this to the case of a young man whose story echoes the myths of bastardy that frame the story of Callipolis: "a changeling, reared in much wealth, in a numerous and great family and among many flatterers; when he becomes a man, he perceives that he does not belong to these so-called parents, and is not able to discover those who really gave birth to him." Socrates asks Glaucon whether he can divine what this young man would experience, but Glaucon prefers that Socrates do the divining (537e–38a).

Socrates' divination looks like this. While the young man is still unaware of the truth, he would honor his parents and those he assumes to be his kin more than the flatterers. But when he becomes aware of "that which is" (*to on*), he would turn his soul over to the flatterers, ceasing to care for his adoptive kin, unless he happened to be "very decent by nature." Just so, we are nourished as children by convictions (*dogmata*) about just and noble things, as by our parents. Opposed to these are "pleasurable practices, which flatter our soul and draw it toward them"—practices that "do not persuade men who are at all measured, who rather honor those ancestral ways and obey them as rulers." Yet even a measured and sensible man will cease to honor ancestral ways and convictions when the arguments of the lawgiver are repeatedly refuted, and when he is unable to find the truth from which he is in fact descended (538a–39a).

With all of this in mind, Socrates recommends not allowing those under the age of thirty to participate in philosophical arguments. He had earlier compared children just starting out in studies, or watching war for the first time from the safety of horseback, to puppies getting their first taste of blood (536e–37a). Now he warns that allowing the young to "taste arguments" encourages them to refute others as they are refuted. Pulling and tearing like puppies at the fabric of *nomos* "as though it were play," "they profoundly and quickly fall into not believing what they previously believed; as a result, they themselves and the whole of philosophy are slandered by the rest of men." An older man would be more measured than these combative youths; moreover, "the natures with which one shares arguments are to be well-ordered and stable, and not, as is the case nowadays, any chance and entirely unsuitable person who comes to it" (539a–d).

Socrates contradicts his recommendations even in the course of articulating them. He took no comparable precautions with Alcibiades—whom he approached before he was twenty, and who was notoriously unstable even as a child—and he has taken none with Glaucon.[24] Nor could he have, if he hoped to sound out their souls and attune them to philosophy while they were still pliable. Philosophy is necessarily a dangerous endeavor. Alcibiades knows this well, having suffered a wasting spiritual paralysis in listening to what, for him, was Socrates' Siren-song (*Symp.* 216a).

In constructing Callipolis, however, Socrates exposes Glaucon to extreme and perhaps unnecessary risks. When he admits to speaking too seriously about those who disgrace philosophy, Glaucon vehemently objects. "No, by Zeus," he avers, "not in the least, as it seems to me, the listener." "But to me, the speaker," Socrates replies (536c). Glaucon's reply can only confirm Socrates' fears. He cannot see that thumotic score-settling, be it ever so justified, spoils erotic, philosophical play. He is not tuned in to the essential difference between Socrates and Critias, and Socrates is partly to blame. For his aggressive pursuit of justice has temporarily eclipsed the love of wisdom, and his political seriousness has made philosophizing look heavier and smaller than the light, airy, and wholesome activity it should be. The Beautiful City appeals not just to Glaucon's strong instincts for pleasure and self-aggrandizement, but more dangerously, to his noble indignation. When the time comes, the tumult of desire and spirit in his soul will form an alliance to convince him that Critias's crude version of Callipolis, which is itself a distorted image of a truly just and philosophical community, is authentically Socratic. In muddling these things and muddying his beautiful and noble beloved, Socrates inadvertently pushes Glaucon away from philosophy.

Like any human being, Socrates is prone to errors. But he is also unusually self-critical, and quickly detects when he has gone astray. In the *Phaedrus*, he immediately atones for slandering the god Eros—an activity he associates with blindness—by delivering a purifying palinode, or song of recantation, in praise of the divine madness of love (244a–57b; cf. 243a–b). It will not be so easy, however, for him to cleanse himself of the pollution he incurs in the *Republic*. If his distortion and degradation of philosophy contribute to Glaucon's fall, he will require a salvation every bit as extraordinary as Arion's dolphin.

When Socrates proposes to speak of a child of the Good, Glaucon urges him to go ahead; "in the future," he says, "you will pay what is owed on the father's narrative" (507a). But it is Glaucon who ends up footing the hefty bill Socrates runs up in the construction of Callipolis. And it is Plato who, in finding a way to make good on the moral and intellectual debts of the father, proves to be Socrates' legitimate philosophical son—as well as, in a literary and pedagogical sense, his savior.

CHAPTER 7

Socrates Reborn

MYTH, MEMORY, AND THE SALVATION OF PHILOSOPHY

"One, two, three," Socrates asks at the beginning of the *Timaeus*, "but where is our fourth . . . of yesterday's feasters and today's hosts?" (17a). His question introduces a problem of cosmic proportions that is central to the *Republic* as well: the recovery of the decayed beginnings and fragmented foundations of human life. The lines along which Critias and Timaeus approach this problem exemplify two fundamental modes of engagement with the Whole. Crossing millennia to connect with a specific historical origin, or moving up toward the eternity of Being and back, their philosophical myths follow something like the celestial axes of right ascension and declination in traversing the space of human existence. A still more expansive perspective is reflected in the *Republic*, in which Socrates prophetically ascends to the Good, the origin of the Whole. What is more, the concluding Myth of Er maps the *Republic*'s action and argument onto the broadest of backdrops: the endless cycle of souls through the universe, and across the vast moral and metaphysical plains of human existence.

In more ways than one, the *Republic* ends by returning to the beginning. The circular motion of Socratic, philosophical archaeology, which repeatedly begins anew in seeking the foundations of a good life, is particularly evident in the Myth of Er. Like the great myth of the erotic soul Socrates tells in the *Phaedrus*, the Myth of Er is a microcosm of the Whole and its mimetic double, the dialogue, which an anonymous commentator from late antiquity describes as "a kind of cosmos."[1] It is in this myth that Plato settles accounts with Socrates and Glaucon, enlarging their powers of teaching and learning while diminishing the ultimate significance of their concrete historical identities. Considered in connection with Glaucon's fate, this philosophical expansion and contraction—a recapitulation of the literary achievement of the *Republic* as a whole—exemplifies the extraordinary generosity of Plato's Socratic writing.

The Geometry of Human Existence

Timaeus and Critias proceed along different tracks in attempting to unearth the *archai* of human life. Critias's mythopoetic history stretches through millennia, positing a particular political beginning—the thousand-year regime of the first Athenians, short-lived only by the standards of mummified Egypt—and connecting it with himself, the heir and savior of this precious ancestral legacy. Timaeus's mythopoetic philosophy moves perpendicular to the flow of events, up toward the Demiurge's construction of the heavens, the stars, and time itself (all images of Being), and back down from this universal beginning to the formation of human beings by divine intelligence. Critias offers an ostensibly hoary myth of origins, one that presents him as the unique bearer of divinely-revealed political knowledge and the brilliant consummation of a noble and illustrious heritage. Timaeus is, more modestly, a conservative in the usual sense: he embraces Spartan austerity and discipline, and takes pains to clarify the crucial role of good laws and hard training in imposing order on the soul's disorderly motion.[2] Yet his intellectual perspective is in one essential respect democratic: he teaches that the Demiurge reveals essential truths to every human intellect prior to its incarnation, together with instruction in the human vocation of mastering and harmonizing the motions of soul and body (41e–42d). Knowledge of the paradigmatic order of the cosmos and the mathematical music of the spheres is furthermore in principle recoverable by anyone whose life and soul are sufficiently well-ordered to allow for philosophical contemplation.[3]

Socrates calls Timaeus's philosophical tale about the origin and nature of the cosmos a *nomos* (29d). While his lawgiving song is shaped by erotic receptivity to the beauty and harmony of what is (cf. 28a–31a), the only superficially musical and beauty-loving Critias absorbs Timaeus's divine or natural history within his own myth of Athens. He cannot help himself: his lust for personal preeminence and victory causes him to move at right angles to his philosophical guest. With a characteristically Athenian sense of entitlement, he assumes the quasi-legal authority to claim the work of his companions on behalf of his city, his clan, and himself:

> I am to come after this man [Timaeus], as though receiving from him human beings who have come to be in speech, and from you [Socrates] some of them educated in the highest degree. Then, according to the word and law of Solon, I am to lead them in before you as before judges and make them citizens of this city, on the ground that they are indeed the Athenians of that time whom, being hidden, the oracular voice of the writings of the priests revealed. As for the rest, I am to make my speeches as though concerning citizens and men who are already Athenians. (27a–b)

As this passage reminds us, Critias's performance in the *Timaeus-Critias* is a dress-rehearsal for the part he was to play as leader of the Thirty, when his word alone sufficed to determine who was, and was not, a citizen. The passage reads like an intellectual genealogy of his political radicalism: Critias took only what he could use from the philosophizing of Socrates and others, reducing their multidimensional speeches about man and world to discrete points along the vector of his ambition.

I have recalled *Timaeus*'s juxtaposition of speeches and deeds that move along the *z*-axis of intellectual *erōs* and ontological stability with others that remain on the *x-y* plane of *thumos*, war, and historical perturbation because the *Republic* unfolds in a similarly delineated space, and exhibits a still richer psychological and political geometry in its quest to recover the authoritative beginnings of human life. This geometry is implicit in Socrates' comparison of human souls to irrational lines (534d), like the diagonal of a square—a line segment that is incommensurable with the sides. Stretched as we are between the orthogonal trajectories of eternity and history, ideality and actuality, thought and action, erotic longing and thumotic drive, the universality of intelligible being and the particular urgencies of the body, even the best of us cannot perfectly square our individual existence with its fundamental constituents. This is the human condition *per se*, the condition of existing individuals. Under the circumstances, it is tempting to unstring the paradoxical bow of a human life by abandoning one of its two legs: retreating, perhaps, into ethereal philosophical contemplation, or plunging headlong into political competition. But it is the unceasing and generally limping attempt to walk sturdily on both of these legs that produces the soul's creative tension and energy. Human perfection is necessarily imperfect.[4]

Philosophy and the Problem of the Good

In the *Republic*, Socrates subtly but radically extends the line of philosophical *erōs* traced in the *Timaeus*. In spite of his demurral when asked for his opinion of the Good, he goes further in the direction of the ultimate beginnings than Timaeus does, for his thought thrusts beyond the cosmos, and even beyond Being, in reaching for the absolute *archē* of the Whole (509b).

The Good, Socrates divines, is what "every soul pursues, and for the sake of which it does everything," but the soul, perplexed about what it is, wanders and cannot collect itself (505d–e). Working to locate or supply the gravitational focus of the psyche, philosophy succeeds in practice even as it falls short in theory. "Uneducated and without experience of truth," Socrates says, non-philosophers "have no single target in life, in aiming at which they must do all that they do in private or in public" (519c). His understanding of this goal further distinguishes him from Timaeus. For while the Locrian visitor seeks to cognize a stable and trustworthy beginning from which the intelligent soul can move down and forward to the pressing tasks of life (cf. *Tim.* 17b), Socrates prophesies that the philosophical soul achieves unity, stability, and focus by organizing itself erotically around the Good *as a problem*.

Yet Socrates' account of the Good emerges only when his own

mythopoetic history of souls and cities is well under way. Philosophy is a latecomer in the *Republic*, because goodness is initially unproblematic. *Erōs* in its natural simplicity is paradigmatically present in the True City, where no part has as yet asserted itself in separation from the whole, individuals reflect a felicitous marriage of body and soul, and desire answers naturally and instinctively to the Good. In this happy community, erotic innocence is the living ground of human goodness. It is not easy to say whether philosophical dialogue occurs in the True City, for while the essential conditions of speech, leisure, and friendship are all present, existential perplexity is absent. But if philosophy does exist there, it is pure pleasure or play, untainted by aggression and neediness.[5]

The natural rectitude of the True City, its instinctive orientation toward the Good, is lost with the fall into history. Desire oversteps the bounds of being in the Feverish City, and ceases to function as an adequate compass of the soul. *Erōs* can recover its guiding power only on the basis of forcefully imposed order, provided that the political and psychological foundations laid by compulsion leave space for erotic development. This is why philosophy is absent in the Virtuous City, where the foundations of justice are thumotic rather than erotic.

Looking back on the Virtuous City in book 4, Socrates asserts that souls and cities consist of intellectual, spirited, and appetitive elements, each with its corresponding virtue: wisdom, courage, and moderation. But what unifies these parts? The answer would seem to be justice—an unarticulated remainder, left over after the other three virtues have been identified (433b–c). The work of justice anticipates that of the Good, and of the *erōs* that responds to its call: Socrates asserts that justice provides "the power of coming into being to all those other [virtues], and once they have come into being, it provides their preservation" (433b). Yet at this stage of the argument, Socrates treats erotic longing as a mere appetite, like hunger or thirst, and locates it in the lowest of the soul's three parts (cf. 439d). *Erōs* as the foundation of justice in souls and communities—as a healer, mending broken wholes, filling in gaps, and doing the productive work of deep moral integrity that Socrates identifies with philosophy—is a missing fourth in the Virtuous City.

Callipolis and the Socratic Community of the *Republic*

One might have expected that the explosion of philosophy into the dialogue at the end of book 5 would supply Callipolis with the erotic fourth. The integrative work of philosophical politics, however, is absent in Callipolis: shared passions unify its parts, but divide the whole. The community of the best warriors is united by sexual desire, among other things; that of the philosophers, by intellectual desire. Yet the sharply-drawn borders of these communities exclude men and women within the classes of warriors and rulers alike, who are consequently bound together by envy, frustration, and anger.

Callipolis's fragmentation reflects the absence of a common language, built around a shared emotional, moral, and intellectual vocabulary. The language of the Virtuous City translates the playful and celebratory idiom of the True City into one of discipline, courage, and pious respect for ancestral ways. In Callipolis, however, the orderly language of virtue is replaced by a babble of dialects—four of them, grouped in two pairs: those of superior and inferior warriors and superior and inferior rulers.

The best of Callipolis's warriors are raised in the vernacular of virtue, but later adopt an incoherent corruption of the mother tongue. In this decayed idiom, the life of victorious excellence is luxuriously spiced with the pleasures of food, sex, and violence, and swollen with honor and power. What is more, this overrich life of Homeric rewards belongs exclusively to superior soldiers, and so effectively deprives all merely good ones of the essential terms of their austere native language: courage, self-control, and shared esteem. The syntax of *their* lives is necessarily disrupted and distorted by resentment.

Callipolis's rulers are similarly divided. The philosopher-kings, the few among the few, stand apart from the invidiously-twinned communities of warriors, but their privileged language produces its own discontented sibling. United in the practice of a well-defined intellectual discourse, the philosophers translate the rigor and discipline of the Virtuous City into a community constituted by theoretical speech. In shared inquiry and discussion, they might achieve something like the healthy erotic unanimity of the True City. But while these thinkers cognize the community of beings, they do not translate their knowledge of this eternal *sunousia* into the lived reality of the city as a whole. Finally, the operative language of those who are forced to leave the royal road of philosophy at thirty—bridesmaids who are fit only to govern—is political and technical. It is the idiom of military strategy and social manipulation, and it, too, must be colored by resentment at being excluded from the sovereign discourse of philosophy.

Callipolis is a community of brothers that cannot avoid coming to blows, like the Achaeans of the *Iliad*. It is no cure for the ills of the cities. Rather, the precautions it takes to avoid these ills guarantee that its inheritance is the violence that has always sickened the Greek cities. But the unity that is lacking in Callipolis is present in the ephemeral community that Socrates elicits in deed in the *Republic*. Socrates' loving care for individual souls, which hums along behind and around the *Republic*'s explicit argument, is a dramatic counterweight to Callipolis's political and spiritual deficiencies. The Good and the sun illuminate all things, allowing them to stand forth in the particularity of their being and existence. Just so, Socrates' response to the Good, a passion for truth that takes the form of attentiveness to others, produces a community of dialogue within which his interlocutors may display their intrinsic natures, each attempting to share what perhaps only he has seen or felt. The emergence of this dialogical community in the *Republic* is a powerful rebuke to the regulation and policing of speech in Callipolis, and more particularly to the censorious Thrasymachus, who tries early on to prohibit Socrates from using certain terms.

In opening themselves to one another, Socrates and his new and old friends participate in an activity of fundamental ethical significance. Just as the sun is responsible for the generation and growth of what comes to be, Socratic dialogue develops, nourishes, and corrects individual natures and habits of thought and action, doing justice to each by involving all in the formation of a distinctively human whole. Perhaps most important, it teaches that communion with others in philosophical inquiry and discussion is fundamentally good and pleasurable. Authentically philosophical justice, the justice of Socrates' erotic politics, is good in itself, independently of its consequences; in implicitly establishing this point, Socrates convincingly honors Glaucon's request that he defend his unequivocal condemnation of injustice. In the *Republic,* the natural justice and erotic unanimity of individuals that is mythically depicted in the True City is most fully realized, not by Callipolis's philosophers, but in Socratic conversation at the home of Polemarchus.

Socrates' Culpability

But Socrates' brief success in the Piraeus, the scene of the decisive battle of the Athenian civil war, is only half of the story. Unlike the True City, the community of the *Republic* stands within the tide of history, which threatens to overwhelm its meaning. For Glaucon and many of his friends and fellow citizens, Socrates' philosophical care was fatally compromised when Critias's revolutionary oligarchy translated into action the essential idea of Callipolis: the imposition of justice by a cadre of intellectuals supported by a body of warriors.

The *Charmides* and *Timaeus-Critias* prove that it is Critias, not Socrates, who uncritically embraces totalitarianism. Yet Socrates makes significant concessions to Glaucon's corrupted natural excellence—necessary ones, if his experimental method of investigating and treating souls is to succeed, but also desirable with a view toward recruiting Glaucon as a philosophical auxiliary. From whom will Glaucon learn the difference between erotic philosophy and thumotic politics? Critias conflates these things, and Socrates himself confuses them in trying to provide a focus for Glaucon's life-path that is not beyond his intellectual reach and psychic momentum. More significantly, Socrates allows himself to be carried away by hostility to those who disgrace philosophy, thereby inadvertently encouraging Glaucon to find warrant for Critias's political seriousness in his own ostensibly playful philosophizing. At a crucial point, Socrates falls short of the moral responsibilities he incurs when he takes Glaucon under his wing.

Xenophon clarifies Socrates' error in a passage in the *Memorabilia* that concerns whether he can reasonably be blamed for the behavior of Critias and Alcibiades:

> Perhaps then someone might say . . . that Socrates should not have taught his companions the political things before he taught them

> to be sound-minded [*sōphronein*]. And I will not argue against this claim. But I see that all the teachers show themselves to their students, indicating in what way they themselves practice the things they teach, and relating them to their argument. And I know that Socrates, too, showed his companions that he himself was noble and good, and spoke most nobly about virtue and the rest of the human things. I know also that even those two [Critias and Alcibiades] were of sound mind when they were with Socrates, not because they feared they would be fined or struck by Socrates, but because they thought at that time that it was best [*kratiston*] to do this. (1.2.17–18)

Xenophon crucially admits here that Socrates erred in presenting arguments about politics to men who lacked moderation. We are left to infer that the arguments themselves were immoderate, much like the revolutionary utopianism he promotes in the *Republic*. Xenophon maintains that Socrates tried to supply the necessary corrective in his life of virtue and philosophy, or in the Doric harmony of speech and deed that the Athenian general Laches perceives in him (*Lach.* 188c–89b), but that this strategy ultimately failed. The strength or *kratos* of his personal example—his exemplary courage and self-discipline, coupled with his near-absolute fidelity to the highest truths—sufficed to keep Critias and Alcibiades in line while they were in his company. But it did not prevent them from behaving badly otherwise, like Spartans outside of Sparta, and eventually leaving him altogether.

Xenophon's remarks help to make sense of what we have observed in studying the *Republic*. Socrates speaks immoderately about politics in Glaucon's presence, even though he knows the young man lacks *sōphrosunē*. He speaks Glaucon's language, that of the pleasures and social rewards of real men: brave, intelligent, and creative souls, graced by strong and beautiful bodies, and brimming with vigorous appetites and ambitions. But he also talks passionately of *erōs* and the Good, of great, transcendent longing and fulfillment. He speaks Critias's language of rule and precise political science, including the art of deception. But he denigrates these demotic, technical affairs in favor of theoretical wisdom, understood as the formal analysis of the structure of being.

Socrates' paradoxical combination of familiar and exotic modes of discourse, including rich, erotic images of the Whole, is designed to keep Glaucon's interest, perhaps long enough to solicit an enduring commitment to the life of philosophizing. Socrates says repeatedly that philosophy is, and must be, a lifelong pursuit if it is to be "a savior of virtue" (549b). "One who has intelligence," he declares at the end of book 9, "will live straining all that is in him toward this"—the acquisition of moderation, justice, and practical wisdom—"first honoring those studies that will make his soul of such a sort, and despising all the rest" (591b–c).[6] He hopes that Glaucon, honoring him as another man in full, and succumbing to the allure of his strange speeches and admirable deeds, will heed these words and become his devoted and steadfast ally. As a fisher of men like the sophist (but one who is not in it for money), Socrates tries to lure the young with the intellectual equivalent of an artificial fly, tied of political arguments that stand in need of moral and intellectual correction.[7] But he is not always able to reel in the youths he has hooked, and as every angler knows, the biggest, most energetic ones are the hardest to land.

Socrates says in the *Theaetetus* that many of those he associated with "went away earlier than they should have," leaving "either on their own, or persuaded by others" (150e). Alcibiades is a notorious example, and a whole dialogue, the *Cleitophon*, is devoted to explaining why its eponymous speaker is defecting to Thrasymachus. Glaucon, too, left Socrates before he should have—that is, before his death. For Socratic dialogue is not a short-course medicine; the psychic and political illnesses it treats are chronic and incurable. Philosophia repays each in kind, and saves only her most constant companions.

A New and Noble Socrates

In his *Second Letter,* Plato presents his authorship in the form of a riddle: "there are no writings of Plato, nor will there ever be, but those now said to be his are of a Socrates grown beautiful and young" (*Epist.* 314c). The dialogues, in other words, are *by* a young and beautiful Socrates (made so through association with the old one) as well as *about* him. Plato speaks of an organic, developing whole, a dynamic and reciprocal relationship. The old Socrates' beauty of soul—his paradigmatic, powerfully fructifying *erōs,* and the harmonious excellence of his virtues of character and intellect—was nevertheless marred by ugliness, as Plato and Xenophon indicate. In what sense, then, does Plato return Socrates' gift of philosophy by ennobling and rejuvenating him in the dialogues?

I have already suggested that Plato's literary art furnishes essential assistance to Socrates' philosophical pedagogy. The meaning of Socrates' speeches and deeds become more intelligible when mediated by writing that is capable of registering their nuances and complexities. The *Republic* allows readers to reflect at leisure on every detail of the conversation at Polemarchus's home, and to see it not only from the narrative perspective of Socrates, but also within the context of history and of the literary cosmos of the Platonic dialogues. Careful reading allows Socrates, like a scoured Glaucos cleansed of salt and barnacles, to stand forth in his intrinsic goodness. This noble and new Socrates, however, is not easily accessible to his interlocutors. Glaucon enjoys none of the advantages of Platonic writing. He must rely solely on his powers of observation and memory in trying to understand what Socrates is attempting to teach him. These tools would suffice, were he strongly inclined to use them in the quest for wisdom. But in that case, he would probably have already embraced the life of Socratic inquiry.

It is perhaps not always true that, as the proverb has it, *tout comprendre, c'est tout pardonner*: to understand all is to forgive all. Yet had Socrates been understood, he would not need to be forgiven. His mistakes could furthermore be said to stem from trying too hard to make Glaucon *want* to understand him. Like his indignation at lame and bastard philosophers, this is a thumotic excess that he knows to be least forgivable in a genuinely erotic soul like his own. Such excessive seriousness and zeal for things that are by nature noble and good, Aristotle suggests, lies at the heart of tragic error.[8] In the *Republic,* Plato does justice to Socrates by making him intelligible in his flawed wholeness. This philosophical justice, an erotic soul's poetic attempt to reveal the whole truth in a broadly human perspective, ennobles Plato while honoring his friend and teacher.

Plato's justice is not limited to Socrates, for he also brings his brother Glaucon to life in all his splendid virtue and decadence. Indeed, Socrates notes in book 9 that the proper judge of the misery or happiness of the tyrant is "he who is able in thought to enter into a man's character and to see through it" (577a), and Plato invites readers to enter into and judge all of his *dramatis personae*. In doing so, we may perhaps see ourselves more clearly, and discern the sources of our own misery and potential happiness. Equipped with this critical self-knowledge, we may even hope to make a new beginning in our lives. Plato's philanthropic writing displays Socratic justice toward his readers.

The *Republic* is, in fact, all about second chances, and their use in manifesting, and perhaps redeeming, an individual's deepest nature. This is clear as early as book 1. In bringing the murdered Polemarchus back to life, Plato puts in his mouth the very opinion one would expect of him if he could speak from beyond the grave: justice is harming enemies as well as helping friends. By the end of his conversation with Socrates, however, he has become an eager advocate of the principle that a just man would not harm anyone (335e). Having hailed Glaucon from below at the beginning of the *Republic*, Polemarchus seems quickly to have overtaken him.[9]

At the end of the *Republic*, Plato gives Socrates one last opportunity to help Glaucon, and if not to avert, then at least to atone for, the ramifying injustice of his construction of Callipolis. The *Republic* is limned by the mysteries of the ultimate things, observed in ritual and contemplated in myth. It begins with a religious ceremony honoring a goddess associated with the promise of continuing life, and ends with a tale of death, judgment, and reincarnation. The former is meant to attune Glaucon to Socratic philosophizing, the latter to encourage him to devote his life to the pursuit of wisdom. The Thracians, a notably spirited people (cf. 435e), compete on horseback in the background of the *Republic*; at the end of the dialogue, the relay race of Bendis comes to symbolize the struggle of the philosophical soul for victory and prizes in the afterlife (cf. 613b–c). Socrates and Polemarchus affirm that the rites of Bendis are worth seeing (*theasasthai*: 327a, 328a); Er is told he must observe (*theasthai*) all things in the afterworld, and he speaks of the sight of souls, including in the first place those of Thracian musicians, choosing new lives (614d, 619e). Building on the themes of descent, ascent, and return from death that run from the *Charmides* through the *Republic*, the Myth of Er bookends the dialogue in another way as well: it replies to the poetic tales of the afterlife that haunt Cephalus. The multiple judgments and tests of souls it describes sort out the philosophers by nature, offering an authentically Socratic alternative to Callipolis's ideological education, purification, and production of philosophers by design. A foundational myth of the erotic activity of Socratic dialogue as a path of salvation, the Myth of Er seals a decisive chapter of Plato's life and the lives of his friends and relatives.[10]

Settling Accounts: The Myth of Er

Socrates introduces the Myth of Er in order to clarify the rewards and punishments just and unjust people may expect to receive in the afterlife. The myth's theodicy explicitly rejects Glaucon's teaching in the Ring Myth: with regard to rewards and punishments, Socrates tells him, he will say about the just "the very things you said about the unjust" (613c–d). While the perfectly just and unjust men of the Ring Myth looked to Socrates like polished statues (361d), he will speak of human beings as they really are—fallible, but in the best case, well-intentioned and capable of learning. The essential thing is moral seriousness: Socrates now redefines the just man as "anyone who is eagerly willing to *become* just, and who, in practicing virtue, likens himself to a god as far as is possible for a human being" (613a–b, emphasis added). The Myth of Er shows that he himself is of such a sort, for it attempts to settle the moral debts he has run up over the course of the conversation—debts quite unlike Cephalus's, but to him just as worrisome. Instead of sacrifices, he offers speeches to the just and the unjust alike, who "must hear" the wages that await them in the afterlife, "in order that, in hearing, each of them might get back in full what they are owed by the argument" (614a). But the just and the unjust as such are present only figuratively. The myth's actual auditors are existing individuals—creditors in good faith, whose life choices may ultimately depend on whether Socrates gives them their due.

The Myth of Er is a cosmic recapitulation of the story of the *Republic*: the round trip to the Piraeus in which Socrates attempts to pass on the torch of philosophy, so that it might continue to illuminate the voyage of souls through the dark night of existence. Socrates informs Glaucon that "I will not tell you a story of Alcinous [*Alki-*

nou], but of a strong [*alkimou*] man" (614b). He refers here to Odysseus's visit to the Phaeacians, and his narration for King Alcinous of his adventures (including his descent to Hades) in books 9 through 12 of the *Odyssey*. The *Republic* as a whole is framed by allusions to Odysseus's journey to the underworld. Socrates' very first words, "I went down yesterday to the Piraeus," echo the beginning of Odysseus's narration for Penelope of his heroic descent—"I went down into the house of Hades" (*Od.* 23.252)—while his last words describe the choice of a new life by Odysseus's chastened soul (620c–d).[11] Socrates has, moreover, *already* told a story of Alcinous and Arete in his tale of Callipolis, a doomed philosophical utopia to which he is carried by three waves of argument, just as Odysseus is swept by three waves onto the ill-fated island of the Phaeacians.[12]

Er, whose *apologon* or story (614b) is implicitly a defense (*apologia*) of Socrates' life, appears to be an avatar of the *Republic*'s protagonist. Er's name appears only once in the *Republic*, in the genitive case, as *Ēros* (614b)—an echo both of *erōs* and *hērōs*, words Socrates connects elsewhere with *erōtan*, his own activity of questioning (*Crat.* 398d). Er's heroism, like Socrates', is not of the ordinary sort. It has to do with listening, remembering, and transmitting divine knowledge—in short, with prophecy. Er is a man of the mythical race of Pamphylon or Everytribe; Pamphylia is also the name of a region in Asia Minor settled by migrating Greeks. This ancient Everyman has no special education or distinction in life, yet he receives saving knowledge. Communicated in the form of a quasi-historical myth about Er's experience of our universal, ultimate fate, this Socratic knowledge becomes available, in principle, to all human beings.[13]

Er is killed in battle, but through Plato's art he, too, gets a second chance at life. He returns from death while lying on his funeral pyre, and tells what he saw in the afterlife. Er says that his soul accompanied many others to "some daimonic place," a kind of cosmic railroad station where transitory souls make their connections, arriving and departing through two openings in the earth and two in the heavens. Newly dead human beings are judged in this place for their deeds in life; those souls deemed just are sent up and to the right, into the heavens, while the unjust are dispatched down and to the left, into the earth. This is the first of several decisive tests to which all human beings must submit in the afterlife—all, that is, with the exception (for now) of Er. The Myth of Er describes a more fundamental sorting or purification of souls and lives than those of Callipolis, with its political equivalents of heaven and earth in the classes of rulers and soldiers, craftsmen and farmers. Standing before the divine judges, Er is told that he must "become a messenger [*angelon*] for human beings of the things there, and they bid him to listen and to observe all things in that place." This, too, is a divine judgment: of all human beings, Er is deemed uniquely suited to the role of witness and prophet of the first and last things (614b–d).

Having been separated from the souls with which he arrived in the afterworld, Er continues his journey with other souls arriving from under the earth "full of dirt and dust" through the opening on the lower right, and still others streaming "pure from the heaven" through the opening on the upper left (614d). We learn later that souls cycle endlessly through death and reincarnation, always choosing their next lives before they are born. Most exchange just lives for unjust ones, and vice-versa; curiously, souls fresh from heaven are generally lured by the deceptive beauty of injustice, while those from the earth most often choose more carefully (619d). Er sees souls speaking with one another, some "lamenting and weeping as they remembered how much and what sorts of things they suffered in their journey below the earth—the journey lasts a thousand years—and others, in turn, from the heaven recounting the beauty of the delights and amazing sights there" (615a). Yet those from heaven tend not to register what the others are telling them; having once been certifiably clean and pure, they seem to have been corrupted by the ease and splendor of their heavenly experience, and want more of the same in their next lives. The superficially blemished souls who come from beneath the earth, however, have for the most part been morally scourged by a millennium of painful punishment. This is, among other things, an otherworldly echo of the corruption associated with the splendid liberties of ruling aristocrats—the political equivalent of heavenly purity—and the decency of those who live simple lives close to the land. But in inviting us to imagine a great stream of souls tracing a ghostly figure eight (or sideways infinity symbol) as they pass counter-clockwise through heaven and hell, with brief detours through earthly existence, Er also recalls Critias's evocation of the tragic pendulum of political history.

Socrates devotes much more attention to the punishment of unjust souls than to their "antistrophes," the rewards of the just (616b)—language that compares both groups to choruses competing in dance and song, as at the dramatic festivals of Athens. Addressing Glaucon by name, he tells him that the unjust were punished ten times over, once every one hundred years, for every injustice they had committed; "for example, if some were responsible for the deaths of many, either by betraying cities or armies, and had thrown men into slavery or were jointly responsible for some other wrongdoing" (615a–b). This list of injustices brings to mind the Thirty, whose crimes included the enslavement by trickery and subsequent execution of the men of the neighboring city of Eleusis (Xen. *Hell.* 2.4.8–10). Given this touch of historical prophecy, the tenfold punishment of injustice may be meant to remind us of the ten named characters in the *Republic* besides Socrates, or perhaps besides Glaucon. For both men bear some responsibility for the sufferings of their companions.

This part of the myth also contains a grim warning: exceedingly evil souls are never able to get free of the underworld and its punishments (615c–16a). These souls, the perpetrators of the greatest and most widespread injustices, get no second chances; like abortions in Callipolis, they are forever cast out of the community. Thus the Pamphylian tyrant Ardiaeus the Great (cf. *ardēn*, "lifted up, exalted" and "taken away utterly"), a figure of celestial proportions during the brief span of his life, vanishes untraceably into the black hole of cosmic justice. (There is further, poetic justice in the fact that, because Socrates has evidently invented this figure, none of his companions have ever heard of him.) Socrates furthermore punctuates his imaginative theodicy with a grotesque and impossible notion. At last sight, fiery beings are stripping Ardiaeus's skin from his soul prior to throwing it into Tartarus beneath Hades, the mythical underworld where the Titans were imprisoned by the Olympians, and from which the so-called Tatars—the Mongol armies of the Khans, invading from the east—were said by certain medieval Europeans to have emerged.[14] Socrates seems here to be hedging his bets: perhaps Glaucon, like Cephalus, needs a more demotic kind of poetry than he has previously provided.

Socratic Dialogue and the Choice of Lives

Er next travels to the center of the cosmos, where the souls he accompanies will choose new lives. His description of this place (616b–17c) is extremely complicated, but several things are nevertheless clear. He observes "a straight light, like a column, stretched from above through all of the heaven and earth, most of all resembling a rainbow, but brighter and purer." This light "binds together the heaven," the revolutions of which are turned by the "spindle of Necessity." Er proceeds to describe the adamant stem and hook of this spindle, as well as its eight hollow concentric whorls, moving at different speeds, whose rims, differing in color and brightness, correspond to the hemispheres in which are situated the fixed stars, sun, moon, and each of the five planets visible to the naked eye. The gist of this image is that light—no longer the visible emanation of the sun, but suspended, like a plumb line, from eternity—is spun like raw wool into the cosmic threads from which we weave our lives. For the movement of the cosmos, as Socrates goes on to explain, is mysteriously connected with human fate.[15]

Er explains that a Siren is perched on each of the eight circles of the spindle as it turns in the lap of Necessity. This detail seems at first to pulse with warning. In the *Odyssey,* the Sirens lure passing sailors to death by starvation with a song of knowledge so beautiful that men who hear it neglect all bodily needs. "For indeed we know all things that in wide Troy the Trojans and Argives endured by the will of the gods," they sing, "and we know all things that come to pass on the all-nourishing earth" (12.189–91). Of more particular interest to us, Alcibiades compares Socrates to a Siren, as if he had wasted his vitality in becoming enchanted by his song of philosophy (*Symp.* 216a), and Aristophanes' *Frogs* picks up on this point. At the end of the *Frogs*, a comedy set in Hades, Dionysus decides to bring Aeschylus back to life so that he might rejuvenate the war-weary Athenians with his fructifying poetry. The chorus (composed of initiates into the Eleusinian Mysteries, which were said to secure blessings in the afterlife) then declares that "it is graceful not to sit with Socrates and babble [*lalein*], throwing aside music, and the greatest legacies of the tragic art" (1491–94). Alcibiades and Aristophanes agree: Socratic conversation is psychologically and politically sterile.

It is unmusical—among other things, it lacks the meter, rhythm, and pitch of poetic verse—and it is insignificant: the Greeks sometimes use *lalein* to describe the vocalizations of animals.

The Myth of Er implicitly responds to these criticisms of Socrates by transforming the song of Homer's Sirens. Each Siren no longer speaks, but "utters a single sound, one tone," and these tones produce "a single harmony." This, the music of the spheres, is the true Siren-song of philosophy: the deep, divine harmony of nature that sets the tune (as in the True City) for a good human life. In Socrates' telling, the three Fates, each a daughter of Necessity, accompany this celestial music with something like epic lyrics: "Lachesis [sings] of what has been, Clotho of what is, and Atropos of what is going to be." Clotho, the Spinner, puts her right hand from time to time to the outer revolutions of the spindle, and Atropos, the Unbending, does the same with her left hand to the inner revolutions, but Lachesis, Giver of Lots, "puts one hand to one, and the other to the other, each in turn" (617b–c). Socrates' meaning is unmistakable: some incalculable proportion of the present and the future is spun, willy-nilly, by the past—which not even a god can change, as the tragedian Agathon observes.[16] One furthermore suspects that the Fates touch the spheres not simply to power their rotation, but to sense, and then sing, their meaning. Intuitively translating motion into intelligible speech, they bring to mind the priestesses at Delphi, who uttered prophecies in a meditative trance induced by the occasional inhalation of hallucinogenic gases.[17] Like tragedy, Socrates' depiction of the work of the Fates raises deep questions about the extent of human freedom and responsibility.

The problem of human agency pervades the next part of the myth, which resonates with allusions to drama. The souls are required to go straight to Lachesis, from whose lap a divine *prophētēs* or interpreter takes "lots [*klērous*, also 'legacies' or 'inheritances'] and patterns of lives"; our present and future choices spring almost literally from the womb of the past. The prophet then arranges the souls in order, as one might position the members of a chorus, and addresses them from a raised platform (*bēma*), like a poet announcing the plot of his plays in the ceremony at the Athenian festival of Dionysus known as the Proagon (cf. *Symp.* 194b). His observation that they are about to embark on another "death-bringing circuit" further recalls the choral rotation of strophe and antistrophe.

For all of these hints that souls must act out roles scripted by great and mysterious powers, the prophet of Lachesis emphasizes that they alone are responsible for the lives they will lead:

> The speech of Lachesis, maiden daughter of Necessity: Ephemeral souls, this is the beginning of another death-bringing cycle for the race of mortals. A *daimōn* will not select you, but you will choose a *daimōn*. And first, let him to whom the lot fell first choose a life to which he will be bound by necessity. Virtue is without a master; honoring and dishonoring her, each will have more or less of her. Responsibility belongs to the one who has chosen; god is blameless. (617d–e)

Souls are obliged to choose a life, and so to bind themselves to a kindly or demonic power that will determine their happiness (*eudaimonia*) or misery (*kakodaimonia*). Virtue, the prophet warns, is the only relevant criterion in making this choice, and she cannot be forced: like philosophy, she favors only those who freely favor her. The prophet's message is unambiguously anti-tragic: character is destiny.

The prophet distributes his lots more or less randomly, unlike the rigged mating-lottery in Callipolis: he casts them out among the souls, and each picks up the nearest one. He then lays out the patterns of lives, of which there are "many more than souls present." That souls choose among patterns (*paradeigmata*) is significant, for it implies that particular lives are not unique in their essentials; they come in distinct kinds, and the same basic variety of stories—"lives of all animals, and moreover all the kinds of human lives"—seems to be available at all times and places. (This juxtaposition suggests that the kinds of human lives tend to reproduce themselves, more or less like the species of animals.) Er observes in these patterns many things besides virtue: tyrannies, some ruined midway and ending badly; lives of men and women of notable beauty, strength, competitive excellence, or high birth and virtuous ancestors; and lives of others without repute in these things. All of these conditions are furthermore mixed with various degrees of wealth and poverty, sickness and health. Finally, Socrates notes that the patterns do not contain an ordering of the soul, because the soul "necessarily becomes different, having chosen a different kind of life" (617e–18b). Choice individuates: although the patterns of lives are general, the character of any particular soul is uniquely formed, like the infinite series of digits in an irrational number, by the specific sequence of all of its past life-choices.

Socrates pauses at this point to make sure that the man for whom his tale is particularly intended grasps its essential implications:

> Now here, as it seems, my dear Glaucon, is the whole risk for a human being. And on account of these things, each of us, neglecting all other studies, must take care especially to be a seeker and a student of that study by which he might be able to learn and discover who will give him the ability and the knowledge to distinguish the good life from the bad, so as always and everywhere to be able to choose the better from among those possible. (618b–c)

The study (*mathēma*) Socrates so strongly recommends is not mathematics, or any of those included in the curriculum of the philosopher-kings. While these branches of knowledge concern immutable structures, the inquiry he speaks of aims above all at living justly, and equips us to judge human lives (cf. 618d–e). This has a familiar ring, for the search for a study that will make us capable of living a good life is nothing other than Socratic dialogue. How to live well becomes the central question of the *Republic* as early as book 1 (cf. 344d–e), and if any activity involves both "making analogies of" and "reckoning up" (*analogidzesthai*) "all the things we have just spoken of [office, birth, beauty, strength, wealth, poverty, etc.] and how they stand, both in combination with one another and separately, with respect to the life of virtue" (618c), it is the image-rich, critically reflective conversation of Socrates.[18]

But how distant is the goal Socrates sets before Glaucon, and how focused the life that leads to it! If he is not to be ill-starred and miserable, he must exclusively seek that study capable of determining who can teach him what he most needs to know. Unlike the education of Callipolis's kings, philosophical dialogue is interminable; while a body of science may be grasped in whole or part, human wisdom is never more than a regulative ideal. Because this is so, however—because philosophy knows no perfect tense—and because philosophical dialogue is any case good and pleasurable, the life of dialogue effectively becomes the *answer* to the question of how to live. Dialogue, which begins as an ethical practice, comes to have metaphysical significance as a vessel of transcendent truth and light. If only he could see through Er's heroic/erotic eyes, Glaucon might understand that Socrates—the one human being who has taken the trouble to learn and declare who he truly is—is precisely the man he should be looking for.

The Promise of Healthy Philosophizing

In the Virtuous City, guardians are selected based on their tenacity in clinging to political orthodoxy without being distracted by pleasures and fears. In the Myth of Er, Socrates replaces political dogmas with a guiding opinion of a different sort, directing Glaucon to look beyond the horizons of the city in steering his course. The better life is always the one that leads the soul to become more just; a human being, Socrates insists, "must go to Hades adamantly holding this opinion, in order that he should be undaunted there by wealth and other such ills, and not fall into tyrannies and other such practices, and work many incurable ills, and himself undergo still greater suffering" (618e–19a). This remark is ambiguous: the action of the *Republic* itself seems to take place in Hades, and Socrates at one point explicitly compares the Cave of the city to the underworld (516d).[19] For Glaucon, who right now faces "the mightiest choice in life and death" (618e), Hades is the city of Athens, where souls as mindless as Homer's gibbering shades are moved by monstrous phantasms of happiness.

The inadequacy of a merely civic education, even in a well-ordered regime, emerges forcefully in the sequel. The prophet of Lachesis encourages the souls as follows: "Even for the one who comes forward last, if he chooses with intelligence and lives earnestly, a desirable life is laid down, not a bad one. Let the one who begins not be careless in his choice, nor the one who is last be disheartened" (619b). This advice fails to reach those who need it most: souls grown lazy and foolish in heaven because they are *agumnastoi*, lacking in the naked exercise of spiritual labor (619d). Because the one who chooses first is of this sort, his luck in the lottery of lives becomes a curse. Although he previously lived a life of virtue in an orderly regime, he participated in virtue "by habit, without philosophy"—like the workers, warriors, and perhaps even the rulers of Callipolis, who do not engage in Socratic inquiry about the best life. Driven by "folly and gluttony," simmering vices now brought to a boil, he immediately selects "the greatest tyranny" without noticing the horrors listed in this terrible life's fine print (619b–d). His experience—joy, succeeded by recognition and lamentation—follows a common path; human beings are generally oblivious to the undesirable consequences of their choices, and tend to learn only by suffering. But had he pursued virtue philosophically, studying the combinations of human conditions and circumstances in relation to the acquisition of virtue, he would not have needed to read the fine print. For he would have been able to infer the relevant consequences simply from the life's general description: tyranny. Stripped of mythical adornment, this is the saving promise of philosophy.

Er observes that most of those who made hasty and foolish choices came from heaven, "but most of those from the earth, because they had labored and had seen others labor, did not make their choices on the spur of the moment. On account of which, and due to the chance of the lot, there was an exchange of ills and goods for most of the souls" (619d). Er reports that most chose new lives "according to the shared habituation [*sunētheian*] of their previous life" (620a). These observations radically qualify the prophet's insistence that each soul is fully responsible for its choices: character is destiny, but, with few exceptions, only in a purely formal sense. The horrifying truth is that character, the sedimentation in the soul of acquired habits, is for most souls basically extrinsic and unessential. Like the shells and rocks that disfigure the body of Glaucos, it is an adventitious encrustation from the sea of human existence—one that most are furthermore eager to shed as quickly and completely as possible. For the many non-philosophical souls, destiny proves to be character after all, inasmuch as their habits and capacities of thought and action are not fundamentally their own. The soul that chooses the greatest tyranny, and then blames "all things rather than himself" (619c), is not an unsympathetic figure.

But we have not yet reached the last level of analysis. In calling the assembled souls *ephēmeroi*, "creatures of a day" (617d), the prophet of Lachesis echoes the ridiculous grandiloquence of the character of Socrates in Aristophanes' *Clouds*, who addresses Strepsiades from on high as "you ephemeral one" (223). Like the *Clouds*' protagonist, the prophet seems to be a comic image of the philosopher; for most human beings, his assertion that "responsibility belongs to the one who has chosen" must strike the disinterested observer as laughable. Yet in advancing his own prophecy about the meaning of what Er has witnessed, Socrates explains the serious truth at the heart of this claim. While nothing is guaranteed—contingency plays too great a role in human life to suppose otherwise—there *is* a way in which we can become responsible for our own lives:

> If someone, whenever he arrives at the life here, always philosophizes in a healthy way, and the lot for his choice does not fall among the last, then it is likely, from the things reported from that place, that he will not only be happy here, but also that he will journey from this place to that one and back again not by the rough road beneath the earth, but by the smooth and heavenly one. (619d–e)

Socrates' mention of healthy philosophizing helps us to see that his pedagogy has come full circle. For the salutary myth that concludes the *Republic* matches the edifying ritual with which it began, when he accompanied Glaucon to the festival of Bendis hoping that this fresh moment of civic unity might attune him to the sacred goodness of genuine community. These harmonious measures of deed and speech suggest that unhealthy philosophizing is essentially the sort that undermines or violates such goodness: the sort practiced by Critias and reflected in Callipolis. This thought must weigh heavily on Socrates' mind as he speaks to Glaucon.

The Problem of Saving Music

Socrates' remark about healthy philosophizing shades into a reflection on unhealthy music, and the misanthropy and misology it may promote. Er witnesses souls choosing new lives "for the most part according to the habituation of their former life," a sight that was "pitiable to see, and laughable, and wonderful [*thaumasian*]" (619e–20a). These responses are associated with tragedy, comedy, and philosophy—for philosophy, as Socrates asserts in the *Theaetetus*, begins in wondering (*to thaumadzein*: 155d)—and they are sequentially elicited by the choices of eight individual souls, belonging to men and women known from poetry and myth.

Seen in the context of their previous lives, the choices of the first four souls—the celebrated musicians Orpheus and Thamyras, and the Homeric heroes Ajax and Agamemnon—are tragic: all four draw early lots, but decide to be reincarnated as animals out of hatred for human life. Those of the next three souls reveal their natures in a comic way. The female Atalanta, who hunted the Calydonian boar alongside Amphiaraus, selects the life of an athletic male; Epeius, who built the Trojan horse, and whose art of boxing is said in the *Laws* to be "useless in the partnership of war," chooses reincarnation as technically-skilled woman; and the buffoon Thersites, whose beating at the hands of Odysseus in the *Iliad* provokes laughter, elects to become an ape.[20] The very last choice belongs to the soul of the great Odysseus, King of Ithaca and leader of warriors, who elicits wonder both in selecting the life of "a private man who takes no part in public affairs," and in declaring that he would have done the same even if he had drawn the first lot (620a–d). Having situated philosophy in this way within the framework of music, Socrates provokes reflection on the philosophical music of the *Republic* itself.

The choices of the first two souls and the last one are of special interest, because their former activities and identities connect them in various ways with Socrates and Plato. Plato's *Laws* mentions "the sweet hymns of Thamyras and Orpheus," and a character in Sophocles' lost drama *Thamyras* speaks of arriving at "the place of assembly" under the compulsion of a "music-mania . . . [arising] from the lyre and from songs [*nomōn*], with which Thamyras produces outstanding music."[21] Thamyras may have been the king of the Thracians in Sophocles' play, which would further underscore the political character of his performances. Thamyras's art did not, however, prevent him from boasting that he could win a contest against the Muses, an act of hubris for which the Muses made him lame or blind (*pēros*) and deprived him of his power to sing and play the cithara (Hom. *Il.* 2.594–600). His decision to become a nightingale, whose song the Greeks associated with mourning, is a reflection of his profound sorrow at being crippled by his own immoderation.[22]

Socrates relates that Er saw the soul of Orpheus "choosing the life of a swan, from hatred for the female kind; on account of his death at their hands, he was unwilling to be born having been generated inside a woman" (620a). Orpheus was a singer so gifted that he could enchant even stones and trees; he went into Hades to retrieve Eurydice, but failed when he turned around too early; and he was torn to pieces by Thracian maenads (Apollod. 1.3). The religious movement of Orphism included teachings about metempsychosis and reincarnation that are echoed in the Myth of Er,[23] and Adeimantus criticizes the "noisy throng of books by Musaeus and Orpheus" prescribing rites of purification and mystery initiations that promise to "deliver us from the ills" in the afterlife, "but for those who do not sacrifice, terrible things await" (364e–65a). According to the *Bassarids*, a lost tragedy by Aeschylus, Dionysus set his maenads on Orpheus because he ceased to honor him after his journey to the underworld; instead, Orpheus would rise before dawn to worship the sun, which he identified with Apollo.[24]

Thamyras and Orpheus were both Thracians; Socrates is a practitioner of Thracian music. Thamyras was maimed by the Muses for his hubris; Alcibiades compares Socrates to the satyr Marsyas, a superb player of the *aulos* (a double-barreled reed instrument) who challenged Apollo to a musical contest and was skinned alive when he lost (*Symp.* 215b–c; Apollod. 1.4). The resemblances between Orpheus and Socrates are still more obvious. While in Thrace, Socrates was known to worship the sun in a manner similar to Orpheus (*Symp.* 220c–d). Orpheus chooses reincarnation as a swan, a musical and supposedly prophetic bird that belongs to Apollo; Socrates considers himself to be "a fellow servant of the swans, and consecrated to the same god" (*Phdo.* 84e–85b). All of these connections are significant, for the tragic fates of Orpheus and Thamyras in the Myth of Er spring from deficiencies of character and music. These things go together: music cannot reconcile human beings with their lot if does not promote virtue, particularly *sōphrosunē*—the moderation and self-knowledge exhibited by every truly healthy soul. Does the music of Socrates pass this test, either as he performed it in his own voice at the home of Polemarchus, or in the richer and more durable form of the written text of the *Republic*?

Er reports that the soul of Odysseus chose his new life having "recovered by memory of its former labors from its love of honor" (620c). While it is not immediately clear whether Er is referring to Odysseus's epic labors, or to others imposed on him in the afterlife, his observation that souls coming down from heaven were "without exercise in labors" (619d) suggests that the hero's soul has come up from the underworld. Odysseus certainly *deserves* punishment: the *Cypria, Little Iliad,* and *Sack of Troy,* non-Homeric parts of the so-called Epic Cycle that were nevertheless well-known to the Greeks, record his numerous crimes. These include his murder (with Diomedes) of Palamades; his attempted murder of Diomedes, so that he alone would have the honor of stealing the Palladium (a talismanic image of Athena) from Troy; and the slaughter of Hector's toddler Astyanax during the sack of Troy.[25] It also seems significant that Er mentions Epeius, the builder of the hollow horse; the sins for which Ulysses and Diomedes are punished in Dante's underworld include the "ambush of the horse" (*Inferno* 26.59–63). He furthermore alludes to the notorious "judgment of the arms," when Agamemnon and Menelaus suborned the judges to give Odysseus Achilles' armor, the prize of valor that should have gone to Ajax (620b). In Sophocles' *Ajax,* this humiliating injustice provokes the hero to demonic rage and then suicide; in the *Republic,* the bitter flight of Ajax's soul's from human existence is itself a kind of suicide.

Odysseus's choice of a quiet, private life harmonizes with the wisdom the shade of Achilles offers him when he visits the underworld: it is better to be a poor serf in the land of the living than a king in Hades (Hom. *Od.* 9.489–91). While Socrates uses this remark to illustrate the perspective of the philosopher who reflects on life in the Cave (516d), only Odysseus's *next* life-choice can determine whether his soul has in fact forsaken the tragic pendulum and truly become philosophical. But what can this episode tell us about Socrates, whom the *Republic* portrays as a kind of philosophical Odysseus? In granting that "Socrates should not have taught his companions the political things before he taught them to be sound-minded," Xenophon makes it clear that his life was not that of an *apragmōn,* a man who steers clear of public affairs and minds his own business. Does the choice of Odysseus's soul reflect lessons implicit in Socrates' own unfortunate involvement in politics?

Memory and Forgetting, Myth and History: The *Republic*'s Salvation

Er reports that after all the souls had chosen new lives, they went to Lachesis, who "sent with each the *daimōn* he had chosen, as a guardian of his life and fulfiller of his choices." Each *daimōn* then led its soul to Clotho, the Spinner, who "ratified the destiny [*moiran*] it had been allotted"—language that again reflects a tragic tension between choice and fate—and finally to Atropos, who "made the threads irreversible." The souls then passed under the throne of Necessity "without turning around." In recalling Orpheus's failure to retrieve Eurydice from the underworld, this detail reminds us that many of the soon-to-be-incarnate souls have condemned themselves to a ghoulish existence of injustice and suffering.[26] But beyond this, the souls are just *now* entering what could rightly be called Hell: a hot, dusty, utterly barren region, where yet one more test and purification awaits. In the smothering plain of Lethe or Oblivion, they camp by the river Ameles, No-Care (620d–21a).

Here we encounter a paradox at the heart of human existence. On one hand, the plain of Lethe is a place of danger for souls, a region where the memory of truth (*alētheia*) is threatened by forgetting and heedlessness. On the other, the "terrific, stifling heat" of the dusty plain, so oppressed by the blazing sun that it is "bereft of trees, and all that the earth brings forth" (621a), suggests that it is impossible for these souls to live in the full light of the truth—a harsh and unfructifying light, unlike that of the Good, because the truth in question is that of their own diseased natures. Socrates expresses the tension between memory and oblivion in a fittingly paradoxical manner. The river Ameles, he remarks, flows with "water [that] no vessel can contain"; as though it had spilled its banks and flooded the entire plain, the river itself is later called Lethe (621a, c). Carelessness heeds no measure, and so, it would seem, is itself intrinsically unlimited. All souls must nevertheless partake of its waters, but wise ones will do so in a restrained and careful way:

> It was necessary for everyone to drink some measure of the water, but those who were not saved [*sōidzomenous*] by prudence [*phronēsei*]

> drank more than the measure. And each one as he drank forgot all things. (621a–b)

Socrates' language makes it clear that *the* saving virtue for a soul that is about to embark on a human life is *sōphrosunē*, the adherence to measure that is capable of controlling even the most powerful desires. Parched and overheated, souls are obliged to drink from the river, and all of them forget what transpired before their birth. But those who surrender entirely to their thirst, Socrates suggests, lose something deeper. Just as actual floods are said periodically to destroy the cultural memory of the Greeks, a deluge of oblivion permanently eradicates any knowledge of essential human truth these souls may have acquired in the afterlife.

Souls cannot literally be thirsty, so how are we to understand the necessity that they drink waters that induce forgetting? In the Myth of Er, the memory of the past is also a prophecy of the future; a soul born with autobiographical foreknowledge might well find its life humanly unlivable. What is more, souls that *do* "turn around" and look back, repenting of their past choices or future incarnations, will be inclined to drink deeply—too deeply—from the river of Lethe. But this point can be understood independently of the myth as well. Individuals and communities that have suffered trauma often have recourse to amnesia, instinctively or intentionally suppressing memory (*mnēmē*) when the burden of the past overwhelms the present and threatens the future. Such was the case after the restoration of the democracy in 403, when the Athenians swore to embrace political *amnēstia* and civic amnesia in the Oath of Amnesty: "I will not recall past wrongs against any of the citizens, except the Thirty and the Ten and the Eleven, and not even against whoever among these is willing to submit to an accounting of his office."[27] Although this oath was understood specifically to forbid prosecution for crimes against the public,[28] it helps to explain the absence in the *Republic* of direct evidence for Glaucon's involvement with the Thirty: Plato could not have explicitly recalled the involvement of anyone in the oligarchy, including Critias and Charmides, without violating at least the spirit of his solemn promise to forget.

The philosophical craftsmen of the virtues Socrates describes in book 6 begin by wiping souls like a whiteboard, because they are unwilling to work on individuals or communities that have not been cleaned or purified (501a). Forgetting the past is one way of cleaning the slate of the psyche or city in preparation for a new beginning. Coming at the end of the *Republic* and the dawn of a new day, Socrates' myth of death and reincarnation suggest that he, too, stands at the threshold of another life—a new and beautiful life in literature, produced by a young and noble version of himself. For it is Plato's attention to Socrates' message of memory and care—a message preserved in the myth by Er's thirsty soul—that allows him to receive the torch Socrates failed to pass on to Glaucon.

The *Republic* begins with a descent to the Piraeus, and ends with souls being carried "up to their birth, shooting like stars" (621b). Among these shooting stars are the souls of Socrates son of Sophroniscus and Glaucon son of Ariston, historical individuals whose capacities of teaching and learning are radically expanded when they are reborn as characters in the *Republic*. While this literary reincarnation inevitably blurs their particular identities, Plato's historical fiction certainly aims to preserve the essential truth of the deeds and speeches of his brother and his mentor. The "thunder and earthquake" that accompany the event of reincarnation in the Myth of Er bring to mind Gyges' emergence from the underworld as a tyrant, while the image of Er awakening on his funeral pyre may (as Munn speculates) have been inspired by Plato's "memory of the last sight of the corpse of his beloved brother."[29] Socrates' final exhortation—"And thus, Glaucon, a myth was saved and not lost, and it could save us, if we were persuaded by it, and we will make a good crossing of the river of Lethe, and not pollute our soul" (621b–c)—furthermore applies not just to the tale saved by Er, but to the *muthos* of the *Republic* itself. For in exemplifying the moral and intellectual pollution to which human beings are subject, the personal and political tragedy of the *Republic* underscores the necessity, and highlights the particular nature, of philosophical purification.

The saving power of the *Republic* depends, however, on its being understood. It is a grotesque irony that Plato's philosophical medicine continues to be confused with the political and spiritual disease it is intended to treat, but no thoughtful reader can find it a surprising one. For this is the very confusion with which Critias and Glaucon were affected, and from which even Socrates was in a certain sense not entirely free. Like all great books, the *Republic* reads us as much as we read it. Its historical reception reminds us yet again that Philosophia, like virtue, is her own master. She favors those who approach her with magnanimous erotic openness, and gives only grudgingly to those of small mind. But those crude souls that would enslave and disgrace her succeed in winning only her old and ugly sister, whose name is now known far and wide: Ideology.[30]

It would be unjust, however, to end on this discordant note. The *Republic* concludes with the thought that Glaucon might yet be rescued by Plato's saving myth, even if he fails to heed Socrates' words in this life.[31] Souls are reincarnated, and Glaucon's soul, looking back on his life and death in Athens and its otherworldly consequences, will once again have an opportunity to choose the saving path of philosophy. The *Republic* has been with us for millennia, and it stretches indefinitely into the future in a way that could in principle save any of its readers—including, in Plato's beautiful and consoling fantasy, a revenant Glaucon. In the *Republic,* Plato's faith in the redemptive power of philosophical music thus becomes a ground of hope for all of us.

Notes

Introduction: Saving the Myth

1. František Novotný, *The Posthumous Life of Plato,* trans. Jana Fábriová (Prague: Academia Prague, 1977), 393–94. Novotný quotes from Copernicus's *On the Revolutions of the Heavenly Spheres,* 1.10.

2. Florian Henckel von Donnersmarck, *Das Leben der anderen: Filmbuch von Florian Henckel von Donnersmarck* (Franfurt: Suhrkamp Verlag, 2007), 61. Cf. Yevgeny Zamyatin, *We,* trans. Mirra Ginsburg (New York: Avon Books, 1987). George Orwell, who reviewed *We* in 1946 for the *Tribune* of London, drew heavily on the novel in *Nineteen Eighty-Four,* which was published three years later.

3. Karl Popper, *The Open Society and Its Enemies,* 5th ed., vol. 1, *The Spell of Plato* (Princeton: Princeton University Press, 1966).

4. Plato behind the Iron Curtain: see Tomasz Mróz, "On the Reception of Plato's Political Ideas in Polish Philosophy of the First Half of the Twentieth Century," *Problemos* 81 (2012), 124–30. On Pol Pot, see Philip Short, *Pol Pot: Anatomy of a Nightmare* (New York: Henry Holt and Company, 2004); see also *The Killing Fields,* directed by Roland Joffé. Khomeini's debt to Plato is documented in Vanessa Martin, *Creating an Islamic State: Khomeini and the Making of a New Iran* (London and New York: I.B. Tauris, 2007). On Al-Farabi's Islamic adaptation of Plato, see the excerpts from "The Political Regime" in *Medieval Political Philosophy: A Sourcebook,* 2nd ed., ed. Joshua Parens and Joseph Macfarland (Ithaca: Cornell University Press, 2011), 36–55.

5. Friedrich Nietzsche, *Thus Spake Zarathustra* 1.11 ("Of New Idols"); William Butler Yeats, "The Second Coming."

6. The main lines of scholarly response to the *Republic* are charted in Gerald A. Press, "Continuities and Discontinuities in the History of *Republic* Interpretation," *International Studies in Philosophy* 28.4 (1996): 61–78.

7. He certainly seems to have done so: see 612a–14a. My first book was *The Republic: The Odyssey of Philosophy* (New York: Twayne Publishers, 1993), reprinted by Paul Dry Books, 2004.

8. Ruby Blondell calls this Plato's "historical irony." See *The Play of Character in Plato's Dialogues* (Cambridge: Cambridge University Press, 2002), 32.

9. 1500 dead is the figure given in Xen. *Hell.* 2.4.21 and Arist. *Ath. Pol.* 35.4. Peter Krentz, *The Thirty at Athens* (Ithaca: Cornell University Press, 1982), cites other ancient sources that put the total as high as 2,500 and as low as 1,200 (79 n. 30). On the murder of Niceratus, see Xen. *Hell.* 2.3.39 with Krentz, 79–80; on Cleitophon, see Paul A. Rahe, *Lysander and the Spartan Settlement, 407–403 B.C.*, Ph.D. diss., Yale (1977), 198. Lysias's courtroom speech *Against Eratosthenes* (= Lys. 12) describes the murder of Polemarchus and the confiscation of his family's considerable wealth. On Lysias's support of the exiled democrats, see Krentz, 73 (n. 11) with 81 and 83. Socrates' association with Critias and Charmides was well known; see Xen. *Mem.* 1.2.12 with 3.7. On the location of the *Republic*'s opening scene in Munychia, along the road that leads to the shrine of Bendis in the Piraeus (Xen. *Hell.* 2.4.11), see Mark Munn, *The School of History: Athens in the Age of Socrates* (Berkeley: University of California Press, 2000), 239.

10. Munn, *School of History*, 239. To my knowledge, only Blondell (*Play of Character*, 212 n. 159) and Catherine H. Zuckert (*Plato's Philosophers: The Coherence of the Dialogues* [Chicago and London: University of Chicago Press, 2009], 150 n. 5) have taken note of Munn's hypothesis.

11. Glaucon's ambition is documented at Xen. *Mem.* 3.6.1–18. Socrates quotes the poem at *Rep.* 368a; following Schleiermacher, Debra Nails identifies Critias as its author. See *The People of Plato: A Prosopography of Plato and Other Socratics* (Indianapolis and Cambridge: Hackett Publishing Company, 2002), 155.

12. Stanley Rosen is a notable exception. Socrates, he writes, observes that "potential philosophers who are spoiled by political ambition in their youth turn out extremely badly. . . . Adeimantus and Polemarchus will soon forget what they have heard [in the *Republic*], or relegate it to the memory of a stimulating conversation. But Glaucon is likely to remember, and with bad consequences both for himself and the city." See *Plato's Republic: A Study* (New Haven: Yale University Press, 2005), 165.

13. On the New Historicism, see *The New Historicism*, ed. H. Aram Veeser (London: Routledge, 1989). Blondell discusses the relevance of history to the interpretation of Plato (*Play of Character*, esp. 31–37), and Nails's *People of Plato* has helped to promote interest in the same; both books appeared in 2002.

14. Blondell notes that Glaucon and Adeimantus are "young men from the governing class, whose own futures hang in the balance"; the fact that they "are members of a socially and politically empowered aristocracy . . . gives extra urgency to the matter of their beliefs and proper education. It also means that they may be expected to be open to the elitist program that Sokrates will put

forward" (*Play of Character*, 193, 203). She also observes that "Glaukon's possible status as both *erastēs* and *erōmenos* [lover and beloved] . . . would place him at a liminal moment in the process of maturation to manhood" (214 n. 166; cf. 368a with 402e).

15. David Roochnik makes essentially the same point in *Beautiful City: The Dialectical Character of Plato's Republic* (Ithaca and London: Cornell University Press, 2003).

16. Cf. *Chrm.* 156d–57a, discussed in ch. 3, herein. The Athenian Stranger practices a similar kind of therapy in Plato's *Laws.* See Randall Baldwin Clark, *The Law Most Beautiful and Best: Medical Argument and Magical Rhetoric in Plato's Laws* (Lanham, MD: Lexington Books, 2003).

17. A recent example is Donald R. Morrison, "The Utopian Character of Plato's Ideal City," in *The Cambridge Companion to Plato's Republic,* ed. G.R.F. Ferrari (Cambridge: Cambridge University Press, 2007), 232–54.

18. On Critias and Alcibiades, see Xen. *Mem.* 1.2.12, and cf. 1.2.24–25 with 1.2.39.

19. DK frags. 25, 20–21, 26.

20. Aristotle remarks that the virtue of a citizen consists in the capacity to rule and be ruled (*Pol.* 1277a26–27); by this criterion, Rosen suggests, there are in Callipolis "no citizens . . . in the full sense of the word" (*Plato's Republic,* 124; cf. 183: "In order to guarantee the rule of the best, the city is transformed from a city of pigs into a city of slaves").

21. Particularly when considered in the context of the regime's extreme control and manipulation of its citizens, the existence of this measure contradicts Ferrari's assertion that in Callipolis there are "no resident informers reporting on their neighbors in each state-owned block of apartments" (G.R.F. Ferrari, *City and Soul in Plato's Republic* [Sankt Augustin: Academia Verlag, 2003; reprint, University of Chicago Press, 2005], 47).

22. Some Romanian philosophers I know were forced to do just this during the time of Ceaușescu. For example, an inconspicuous (and forbidden) reference to the work of Karl Popper, hidden from the censors in the middle of a book, would signal the author's solidarity with the regime's opponents.

23. The Athenian oath of amnesty, in which citizens swore after the restoration of the democracy that they would not "recall past wrongs" committed by their fellows in the time of the Thirty (Andoc. 1.90), offers an additional, political reason for Plato's reticence. I return to this point in ch. 7, herein. Plato's first readers in any case already knew the facts, and he would have wished to protect both Glaucon and Socrates from the hasty judgments of later ones.

24. Stanley Crouch, Introduction to Saul Bellow, *Mr. Sammler's Planet* (New York: Penguin Books, 2004), xvii.

25. Oaths of amnesty: Hom. *Od.* 24.482–85. Three waves: cf. *Rep.* 457b–c and 473c–e with Hom. *Od.* 5.366, 393, 425. The philosopher-kings resemble those who are said to have gone "from Hades up to the gods" (521c); Alcinous is descended from Poseidon and the Giants, and is said to have been made "wise

in counsel from the gods" (*Od.* 6.12, 7.54–6). On the *Republic* as a philosophical version of the *Odyssey*, see my *Odyssey of Philosophy* as well as "The Mythology of Philosophy: Plato's *Republic* and the Odyssey of the Soul," *Interpretation* 33.3 (2006): 219–41.

26. Eva Brann, "The Music of the *Republic*," in *The Music of the Republic: Essays on Socrates' Conversations and Plato's Writings* (Philadelphia: Paul Dry Books, 2004), 108–245, at 116; cf. Rachel Barney, "Platonic Ring-Composition and *Republic* 10," in *Plato's Republic: A Critical Guide*, ed. Mark L. McPherran (Cambridge: Cambridge University Press, 2010), 32–51.

27. Bruce Rosenstock, "Rereading the *Republic*," *Arethusa* 16.1&2 (1983): 219–46, at 221. On death and rebirth in Thracian religion, see *Chrm.* 156d.

28. Rosenstock, "Rereading the *Republic*," finds it "quite likely" that the dialogue ends at dawn (220). On the linguistic roots of *nostos* and *nous*, see Douglas Frame in *The Myth of Return in Early Greek Epic* (New Haven: Yale University Press, 1978).

29. The center of the text is 473b; the third wave breaks at 473c–e. See Jacob Howland, "The *Republic*'s Third Wave and the Paradox of Political Philosophy," *Review of Metaphysics* 51.3 (1998): 633–57.

30. Munn, *School of History*, 239. The image of a revenant Er, Munn suggests, may have been inspired by Plato's "memory of the last sight of the corpse of his beloved brother."

31. Jean-Pierre Vernant and Pierre Vidal-Naquet, *Myth and Tragedy in Ancient Greece*, trans. Janet Lloyd (New York: Zone Books, 1990), 37.

Chapter 1: Glaucon's Fate

1. "Ephors": Lys. 12.43; cf. Krentz, *The Thirty*, 45–46 with David Whitehead, "Sparta and the Thirty Tyrants," *Ancient Society* 13/14 (1982/83): 106–30 (at 114–17). At Xen. *Hell.* 2.3.34, Critias declares "the most noble and beautiful regime" (*kallistē politeia*) to be that of the Lacedaemonians; cf. 2.3.47, where Theramenes categorizes the regime as *aristokratia*. Ancestral laws (*patrioi nomoi*): Krentz, *The Thirty*, 48–50; Munn, *School of History*, 219–20. Council (*boulē*) and magistracies: Xen. *Hell.* 2.3.11; Arist. *Ath. Pol.* 35.1.

2. Sycophants: Xen. *Hell.* 2.3.12. Cf. Arist. *Ath. Pol.* 35.3, where it is asserted that "the city was delighted at these measures, believing that they did them for the sake of the best"; Xenophon more cautiously reports that "the Council gladly condemned these men, and the rest [of the Athenians]—as many, at any rate, as were conscious that they were not like them—were not displeased" (*Hell.* 2.3.12). Xenophon affirms the earlier date for the Spartan garrison (*Hell.* 2.3.13), Aristotle the later (*Ath. Pol.* 37.2); for a discussion of the issues see Krentz, *The Thirty*, 131–47. Arrests and executions: Xen. *Hell.* 2.3.14; Arist. *Ath. Pol.* 35.4.

3. Reign of terror: Xen. *Hell.* 2.3.15–4.8; Arist. *Ath. Pol.* 35.4–37.2. Brann describes this period as "an early, perhaps the earliest, example of ideological purification" ("The Tyrant's Temperance: *Charmides*," in *Music of the Republic*,

66–87, at 69). On the Thirty as the realization of the tyrannical ideal see my "Plato's Reply to Lysias: *Republic* 1 and 2 and *Against Eratosthenes*," *American Journal of Philology* 125.2 (2004): 179–208.

4. On Socrates' opinion of the Spartans, see *Hipp. Maj.* 283e–84d and *Alc. 1* 122c with Xen. *Mem.* 3.5.15–16 and Xen. *Ap.* 15. See also Ar. *Av.* 1281–82, where the "Laconian-mad" men of Athens are described as "Socratified." On the Thirty's attempts to restrict Socrates, see Xen. *Mem.* 1.2.31, 35. The Thirty selected the 3,000 from among the *kaloi k'agathoi* and "the best" (*hoi beltistoi*): Xen. *Hell.* 2.4.1; Krentz, *The Thirty*, 65–66. On Socrates' membership in the 3,000 see Ellen Meiksins Wood and Neal Wood, "Socrates and Democracy: A Reply to Gregory Vlastos," *Political Theory* 14.1 (1986): 55–82 (at 73–74) with Krentz, 82–83.

5. Cf. Rosen, *Plato's Republic*, 14–15 with Leo Strauss, *The City and Man* (Chicago: University of Chicago Press, 1964), 63. Glaucon utters not a word of protest when Socrates makes it clear that he regards the many as insatiable and peevish cattle bent on feeding and copulating (586a–b).

6. Compare Arist. *Poet.*1453a7–17 with the discussion at Arist. *Eth. Nic.* 7.4 of moral weakness and *hamartia* in the pursuit of things that are "noble and good by nature" (1148a29–30). Socrates speaks in a similarly tragic vein in warning Alcibiades that one who does not know will miss the mark (*hamartēsetai*), and that "in thoroughly erring [*exhamartanōn*] he will do and fare ill both in private and in public" (*Alc. 1.* 134a; cf. 117d).

7. The approximate dramatic date of the dialogue is 432 (cf. Nails, *People of Plato*, 310–11).

8. Plut. *Alc.* 16.1–2. At 2.1 and 6.3, Plutarch emphasizes Alcibiades' love of rivalry (*philoneikon*), love of preeminence (*philoprōton*), love of distinction (*philotimia*), and love of honor (*philodoxia*).

9. Plato's *Alc. II* (whose authenticity has been questioned by modern scholars) picks up where *Alc. I* leaves off, for it is replete with tragic imagery and presentiment. See my "Socrates and Alcibiades: Eros, Piety, and Politics," *Interpretation* 18.1 (1990): 63–90.

10. Cf. *Symp.* 216a and Hom. *Od.* 12.190 with Patrick Deneen, *The Odyssey of Political Theory: The Politics of Departure and Return* (Lanham, MD: Rowman & Littlefield, 2000), 221–24.

11. Nails, *People of Plato*, 309.

12. Zuckert, *Plato's Philosophers*, 150–51. Plato may also have wished to remind readers that the scientific, materialistic cosmology of the Ionians (and in particular of Anaxagoras, the most famous of the Clazomenaean philosophers) stands at a significant remove from the living teaching of Socrates. Cf. *Phdo.* 97b–99d.

13. Allan Bloom supposes that Apollodorus's narrative took place in 404 (*Love and Friendship* [New York: Simon & Schuster, 1993], 447); an earlier date is ruled out by 172c–73a. Agathon left Athens in approximately 408; see *Aristophanes: Frogs*, ed. Alan H. Sommerstein (Oxford: Aris & Phillips, 1997), 164,

ad loc. 83. On the dramatic date of the *Republic* see Nails, *People of Plato,* 324–26. In the *Symposium,* Aristophanes and Pausanias, speaking in the presence of Socrates, mention events that occurred years after his death in 399. Aristophanes refers to the Spartan dispersion of the Mantineans in 385 (cf. 193a with Xen. *Hell.* 5.2.5–7), and Pausanias to the terms of the King's Peace, which the Greeks accepted in 387 (cf. 182b with *Hell.* 5.1.31). The *Parmenides* is also apparently anachronistic: Socrates and Parmenides are supposed to have met at the Great Panathenaea in 450, at which time Parmenides would seem to have been too old, and Aristotle of Thorae (a future member of the Thirty) too young. See Reginald E. Allen, *Plato's Parmenides* (New Haven: Yale University Press, 1998), 72–73.

14. Bruce Rosenstock, "Socrates as Revenant: A Reading of the *Menexenus,*" *Phoenix* 48.4 (1994): 331–47; Brann, "Music of the *Republic,*" 116–18. At *Menex.* 245e, Socrates refers to the Peace of Antalcidas of 387–86. The attempt to determine the authorial chronology of Plato's dialogues (which I have critiqued at length in "Re-reading Plato: The Problem of Platonic Chronology," *Phoenix* 45.3 [1991]: 189–214) is a separate matter, and is irrelevant to the problem of assigning historical dates to the dialogues in which Glaucon appears.

15. "Decree of the Thracian *oregōnes* of Bendis" (*IG* II^2 1283), in *Greco-Roman Associations: Texts, Translations, and Commentary,* vol. 1, ed. John S. Kloppenborg and Richard S. Ascough (Berlin: Walter de Gruyter, 2011), 125–27.

16. Thus Oedipus sends Creon to Delphi as a *theōros* (Soph. *OT* 114).

17. See esp. the debate about the best form of government at Hdt. 3.80–82, and cf. Thuc. 2.37, 4.126.2, and 6.39.1.

18. See the note on *ei dokei* (*ad loc.* 328b) in Allan Bloom, trans., *The Republic of Plato,* 2nd Edition (New York: Basic Books, 1991).

19. Cleitophon assisted in preparations for the oligarchic constitution of 411, but was a moderate among "respectable" Athenians (Munn, *School of History,* 137, 209–10). Aristotle names him along with Theramenes as one who sought the ancestral constitution and did not belong to any political association (*Ath. Pol.* 34.3). Thrasymachus had practical political experience: he assisted in overthrowing the democracy at Cyme, an act that directly opposed Athenian interests in Ionia in the last decade of the war (Stephen A. White, "Thrasymachus the Diplomat," *Classical Philology* 90.4 [1995]: 307–27, at 319 and 326–27). White argues that Thrasymachus also served in Athens as an ambassador for Chalcedon; this is contested by Harvey Yunis, "Thrasymachus B1: Discord, not Diplomacy," *Classical Philology* 92.1 (1997): 58–66. The other characters Socrates identifies by name in the *Republic* are Charmantides, an Athenian, and the metic Cephalus, Polemarchus's aged father.

20. On Glaucon's musical knowledge and ability, see 398e–403c with 548d, and cf. Leon Craig, *The War Lover* (Toronto: University of Toronto Press, 1994), 115, 122. Glaucon displays mathematical knowledge at 528a–d. See also Blondell, *Play of Character,* 203–06, who describes Glaucon's qualities as "possible harbingers of philosophical success."

21. *Sōphrosunē*, whose range of meanings include soundness of mind, moderation, prudence, and self-restraint, has no exact English equivalent. I have either left it untranslated or, depending on the context, translated it as "moderation" or "sound-mindedness."

22. On Glaucon's sexual appetite see 468b–c, and cf. 403a. That Glaucon has a lover who sings his praises in poetry (368a)—possibly Critias (Nails, *People of Plato*, 155, following Schleiermacher; Munn, *School of History*, 239)—suggests that he is handsome in body as well as soul.

23. Socrates addresses Glaucon as Ariston's son at 580b (cf. Craig, *War Lover*, 44) and Adeimantus at 427c; cf. 368a. Cf. Rosen's assertion that, "for all his intelligence," Glaucon is incapable of "rising up to philosophy" (*Plato's Republic*, 165).

24. Nalin Ranasinghe is an exception: he remarks that Socrates has in mind Glaucon and Charmides as well as Alcibiades (*The Soul of Socrates* [Ithaca and London: Cornell University Press, 2000], 19).

25. On the oligarchic *hetaireiai* see Lysias 12.55, and cf. 365d. Xenophon mentions the Thirty's measures against Socrates at *Mem.* 1.2.33–35. Plato seems ironically to echo one of their injunctions when Socrates tells Glaucon that, in Callipolis, no one under the age of thirty will be exposed to dialectical argumentation (537d, 539a–b). On the arrest of Leon, see *Ap.* 32c–d with Xen. *Hell.* 2.3.39.

26. Cf. Craig, who asserts that, while Glaucon is not indifferent to honor, he is more of a "nikocrat" (victory lover) than a timocrat (*War Lover*, 113).

27. The philosopher is said to "mind his own business" at 496d; on Socrates in particular, see *Ap.* 17d with *Euthphr.* 2a, and note the anecdote related at Diog. Laert. 2.21. In *Socrates' Second Sailing: On Plato's Republic* (Chicago and London: University of Chicago Press, 1989), Seth Benardete observes that the father of the future timocrat is indifferent both to money and to his wife (194; cf. 549d); this also describes Socrates (see *Ap.* 23b–c with *Phdo.* 60a). Adeimantus's vehement affirmation of Socrates' description of the mother's criticisms (549e) may imply that his own mother expressed similar attitudes. Craig suggests that Adeimantus and Glaucon together "illuminate the multifaceted nature of the Timocrat" (*War Lover*, 45).

28. The Greek word *mousikē* refers to any activity performed under the auspices of the Muses, and includes poetry and dance as well as well as tunes and songs. In the traditional Greek conception, which informs Socrates' account of education in the *Republic*, *gymnastikē* or physical exercise is the counterpart to *mousikē* in a well-rounded education. (*Gumnos* means "naked"; many forms of exercise were undertaken in the nude.)

29. Because the seer went on to sacrifice his life in order to ensure victory for his side, this particular prophecy was well known; Xenophon quotes from it, and even identifies the location of the man's tomb (*Hell.* 2.4.18–19).

30. And indeed, Glaucon's defense of injustice in the Ring Myth is so well-crafted that it is extremely unlikely he is not at least somewhat persuaded by it. Cf. Rosen, *Plato's Republic*, 62. Socrates is forced to assume that the brothers

are not so persuaded only on the basis of their character, "since on the basis of the speeches themselves I would distrust you" (368b; cf. 358c). One wonders just how close the analogy with Oedipus's sons might have been. Might Adeimantus have fought with the party of the Piraeus, opposite Glaucon and the Thirty? Could he have played Eteocles to his brother's Polyneices? (I thank Paul Rahe for suggesting this possibility.)

31. According to Homer, Eriphyle, whose name means "Tribal Strife," received jewelry in exchange for compelling her husband to take part in the siege of the Seven (*Od.* 11.326–27). Socrates' mention of gold and jewelry at 589d–90a may also be meant to remind us of a fact on which Lysias places great emphasis in *Against Eratosthenes*, namely, that one of the Thirty greedily ripped a pair of gold earrings from the ears of Polemarchus's wife (Lys. 12.19).

32. Socrates calls him by name at 608b, 609e, 611d, 612b, 615a, 618b, and 621b.

33. *Aeschylus: Fragments* (Loeb Classical Library 505), ed. and trans. Alan H. Sommerstein (Cambridge, MA: Harvard University Press, 2008), 24.

34. As it happens, Critias uses the masked dramatic figure of Sisyphus to communicate his own conception of godlike political wisdom. See ch. 3, herein.

35. On *chrusochoein*, "to smelt ore for gold," see James Adam, ed., *The Republic of Plato*, 2 vols. (Cambridge: Cambridge University Press, 1902), *ad loc.* 450b.

36. This last remark is apparently ironic. See Adam, *Republic, ad loc.* 451b.

37. *Anth. Graeca* XVI.223, cited in Davide Stimilli, *The Face of Immortality: Physiognomy and Criticism* (Albany: State University of New York Press, 2005), 182 n. 17.

38. Plutarch accordingly identifies Adrasteia with Atropos, the Fate and "daughter of Necessity" whom Socrates associates in the Myth of Er with the irreversible future souls choose in the lottery of lives (617b, 620e; Plut. *De Stoic.* 47).

39. Sonja Tanner, "Prostrating Before Adrasteia: Comedy, Philosophy, and 'One's Own' in *Republic* V," *Angelaki* 21.3 (2016): 35–53, at 37. "Like [Aeschylus's] Adrastus," Tanner adds, "Socrates is about to launch an attack against a city, but his attack will come in the form of speech." On the Phrygian Adrastus, son of Midas, see Hdt. 1.35–45. The second homicidal error of Adrastus is a literal act of *hamartia*: he kills Croesus's son Atys with a lance he had aimed at a boar (1.43.2).

40. Douglas M. MacDowell, *The Law in Classical Athens* (Ithaca: Cornell University Press, 1978), 110.

Chapter 2: Socrates' Music

1. *Politeia* "denotes citizenship, form of government, constitution, and regime," and first appears at Hdt. 9.33–35 in connection with Sparta (Paul A. Rahe, *The Spartan Regime: Its Character, Its Origins* [New Haven: Yale University Press, 2016], xii). The scholium on *Leg.* 625a explains that *politeia* refers to

"the one way of life of a whole *polis*." In a specifically political sense, the regime is "the dominant portion (be it few or many) of the citizenry" (Thomas Pangle, "Socrates' Argument for the Superiority of the Life Dedicated to Politics," *Interpretation* 42.3 [2016]: 437–58, at 442).

2. The spirit of Socratic piety seems to me to be captured in the assertion of Emmanuel Levinas, perhaps the greatest modern advocate of the translation of Jewish sources into "Greek," the language of philosophy, that "the existence of God . . . [is] the sacredness of man's relation to man, through which God may pass" (*Face to Face with Levinas*, ed. Richard A. Cohen [Albany: State University of New York Press, 1986], 18). Like Socrates, Levinas emphasizes the philosophical primacy of the ethical relation of discourse. See *Totality and Infinity: An Essay on Exteriority*, trans. Alphonso Lingis (Pittsburgh: Duquesne University Press, 1969) and *Nine Talmudic Readings*, trans. Annette Aronowicz (Bloomington and Indianapolis: Indiana University Press, 1990); and cf. Francisco J. Gonzalez, "Levinas Questioning Plato on Eros and Maieutics," in *Levinas and the Ancients*, ed. Brian Schroeder and Silva Benzo (Bloomington and Indianapolis: Indiana University Press, 2008), 40–61. Gonzalez argues that Levinas and Plato share a dialogical conception of truth; "truth has its being only in dialogue . . . in the addressing of one person by another" (43).

3. Nicole Loraux, *The Divided City: On Memory and Forgetting in Ancient Athens* (New York: Zone Books, 2002), 17, 18.

4. Cf. Jean-Jacques Rousseau, *Discourse on the Origin of Inequality*, in *The Basic Political Writings of Jean-Jacques Rousseau*, ed. and trans. Donald A. Cress, 2nd ed. (Indianapolis: Hackett Publishing Company, 2012), 72–74. Rousseau assigns this sweetness, however, to a stage of human existence prior to concentrated agriculture and the division of labor. His opinion about the happiness available to hunter-gatherers has recently been echoed in Yuval Noah Harari, *Sapiens: A Brief History of Humankind* (New York: Harper, 2015), 48–52.

5. Cf. Søren Kierkegaard, "The Lily in the Field and the Bird of the Air," in *Without Authority*, ed. Howard V. Hong and Edna Hong (Princeton: Princeton University Press, 1997), 44: "all true prayer . . . prays itself joyful and more joyful and unconditionally joyful."

6. Leo Strauss calls the True City "the city *par excellence* . . . [which] exhibits the fundamental character of the best city" (*The City and Man*, 95). While Rosen maintains that the True City is "not fully human," he later suggests that its peace and health are associated with "primitive humans" (*Plato's Republic*, 81, 94). The Virtuous City is identified with Adeimantus, and Callipolis with Glaucon (427c–d, 527c); the True City would seem to be Socrates'.

7. The expedition won broad support among "the great throng and the soldier," who aspired "to earn money in the present, and to acquire in addition the power to accrue a never-ending wage" (Thuc. 6.24.3). Speaking against the expedition, Nicias warned the Athenians not to be "sick with desire [*duserōtas*] for things that lie far away" (6.13.1), yet Alcibiades' counter-arguments helped to produce "an *erōs* for the expedition [that] fell upon [*enepese*] everyone alike"

(6.24.3); the verb *piptein* may signify the attack of an enemy or of disease (cf. 2.49.4). W. Thomas Schmid connects this *erōs* (and Thuc. 6.24) with the beginning of Plato's *Charmides,* where the Athenians' extreme passion about the war is linked with Socrates' sexual excitation; see *Plato's Charmides and the Socratic Ideal of Rationality* (Albany: State University of New York Press, 1998), 5–6; cf. *Chrm.* 153a–b, 155d.

8. Consider that Socrates uses the word *sunousia* to refer to philosophical conversation. See esp. *Tht.* 150d4, e5.

9. Cf. Rahe, *Spartan Regime,* 14–15.

10. Stamping: 377b; molding: 387c; tuning: 410e, 411e–2a; dyeing: 430a–b. The Noble Lie is a device or mechanism (*mēchanē*) that belongs to "the lies of which we were just now speaking" (414b)—a "preventative drug" to treat "madness or some sort of folly" (382c; cf. 389b). Cf. my article "Plato's *Republic* and the Politics of Convalescence," *American Dialectic* 1.1 (2010): 1–17.

11. Homer displays the functions of Hermes as messenger and psychopomp at *Od.* 5.28–148 and 24.1–10. In Plato's *Cratylus,* Socrates remarks that "this name 'Hermes' seems to be somehow concerned with speech, and to be the interpreter [*hermēnea*] and the messenger, and that which is thievish and wily in speeches, and an able trader; all this business is concerned with the power of speech" (407e–08a).

12. This important passage is illuminated by Jenny Clay in "The *Planktai* and *Moly*: Divine Naming and Knowing in Homer," *Hermes* 100.2 (1972): 127–31.

13. Glaucon's dismissal of the True City as a city of pigs (*huōn*) underscores its effeminate character. Observing that *hus* is "a Greek slang term for female genitalia," Marina McCoy writes that Glaucon in effect calls Socrates' healthy *polis* a "city of cunts" ("The City of Sows and Sexual Differentiation," in *Plato's Animals,* ed. Jeremy Bell and Michael Naas [Bloomington: Indiana University Press, 2015], 149–160, at 151).

14. Odysseus, with whom Socrates and Critias (see ch. 3, herein) are both in their own ways associated, is thus a deeply questionable figure in the *Republic.*

15. In the event, however, Adeimantus takes over as Socrates' interlocutor as soon as the matter of education is raised (376d). Glaucon reenters the conversation only after poetry has been purged of content detrimental to the formation of virtue (398c).

16. In book 4, Socrates explains that justice in the city and soul consists in each part minding its own business; conversely, a man behaves unjustly when, "inflated by wealth or multitude or strength or some other such thing . . . [he] tries to do all of these things [i.e., the work of the other classes] at once" (434a–c, 441d–e). The inflation of a part into a spurious whole is central to Aristotle's conception of tragic error and catharsis; see Michael Davis, *Aristotle's Poetics: The Poetry of Philosophy* (Lanham, MD: Rowman & Littlefield, 1992). Aristotle associates tragic error specifically with the self-assertion of *thumos;* see Carnes Lord, *Education and Culture in the Political Thought of Aristotle* (Ithaca

and London: Cornell University Press, 1982), 159–74. I discuss Davis and Lord in the context of an extended reflection on the political significance of tragedy in "Aristotle on Tragedy: Rediscovering the *Poetics*," *Interpretation* 22.3 (1995): 359–404.

17. On the Spartan education or *agogē*, see Rahe, *Spartan Regime*, 13–30. As Rahe observes, competition for distinction did not cease for those accepted as Spartan peers, but intensified (25).

18. The Spartans seem not to have followed the normal Greek practice of memorizing passages of Homer. They instead competed in chanting the verses of Tyrtaeus, who "rejected the Homeric precedent and radically altered the heroic ethic" in praising nothing but "prowess in battle" (Rahe, *Spartan Regime*, 20–21). Socrates' comparable purification of Homer, discussed below, runs from 379c–98b. In Plato's *Laws*, the Spartan Megillus claims that Homer portrays an Ionian rather than a Laconian way of life (680c–d); Glaucon rejects Ionian harmonic modes as unsuitable for warriors (398e–99a). On hunts and horse races see 412b. Battery of tests: cf. 413e–14a with Rahe, 18–19, 23–26. "Going to a common mess [*sussitia*]," Socrates asserts, the citizens "will live together like soldiers on campaign" (416e). The *sussitia* at Sparta instilled moderation in drinking and eating and strengthened bonds of fellowship; see Plut. *Lyc.* 10.2 with Xen. *Lac. Pol.* 5.5–7, and cf. Dion. Hal. *Ant. Rom.* 2.23.3 (cited at Rahe, 25). Forbidden practices: cf. 396a–b, 397e, and 416e–17a with Rahe, 9.

19. While Spartans could—and did—possess wealth, including useful or "handy" (*procheira*) as well as necessary items stocked in private storehouses (Plut. *Lyc.* 9.4; Rahe, *Spartan Regime*, 30–31), Socrates allows no private property among the auxiliaries and guardians beyond what is "altogether necessary." He states in the same passage that there is to be no house or storeroom in the Virtuous City into which "everyone who wishes may not enter" (416d)—a considerable extension of the Spartan practice of seeking out forbidden gold and silver and punishing its possessor (Xen. *Lac. Pol.* 7.6).

20. Rosen, *Plato's Republic*, 9. The major contemporary example is surely John Rawls, *A Theory of Justice* (Cambridge, MA: Harvard University Press, 1971).

21. See the discussion of Tyrtaeus in Paul A. Rahe, *Republics Ancient and Modern: Classical Republicanism and the American Revolution* (Chapel Hill and London: University of North Carolina Press, 1992), 145–52.

22. At *Crat.* 411e he derives the term *sōphrosunē* from *sōtēria phronēseōs*, the "salvation of practical wisdom." Aristotle offers the same etymology at *Eth. Nic.* 1140b11–12.

23. On the difference between *sōphrosunē* and self-restraint (*enkrateia*), see Leo Strauss, "The Spirit of Sparta or the Taste of Xenophon," *Social Research* 6.4 (1939): 502–36, at 514. Strauss establishes that Xenophon's *Constitution of the Lacedaemonians* attributes to the Spartans only "manliness [*andreia*] not accompanied by wisdom, moderation or justice" (520–21). See also Noreen Humble, "*Sōphrosynē* Revisited: Was it Ever a Spartan Virtue?" in *Sparta: Beyond the*

Mirage, ed. Anton Powell and Stephen Hodkinson (London: The Classical Press of Wales and Duckworth, 2002), 81–109. Humble shows that, while "laconizing oligarchs" like Critias attributed *sōphrosunē* to the Spartans and claimed it for themselves, the Greek philosophers agreed that this virtue "was not cultivated in Sparta at any time, past or present" (97–98; cf. 90, where she cites Aristotle's assertion at *Pol.* 1334a9–10 that "the lawgiver did not educate them [the Spartans] to be capable of being at leisure").

24. Plut. *Cleom.* 9.1–2; Rahe, *Spartan Regime*, 11–13 with 32–33.

25. Rahe, *Spartan Regime*, 30–31; cf. *Alc. 1* 122e with *Rep.* 555c.

26. Socrates does something similar in describing the decay of the best regime: he speaks of "auxiliaries" and "guardians" (545d, 546d), but not philosopher-kings.

27. Adam, *Republic, ad loc.* 414c; cf. the reference to "earth-born men" at 415d. The Spartoi sprang from the teeth of a dragon killed by Cadmus, a Phoenician (Apollod. *Bibl.* 3.4).

28. The word *harmonia* (harmonic mode) "signified a combination of features which together denoted a certain type of musical discourse: not only a particular disposition of the intervals but also specific pitch, modulation, color, intensity, and timbre, all the elements which distinguish the musical output of a particular geographic and cultural environment" (Giovanni Comotti, *Music in Greek and Roman Culture*, trans. Rosaria V. Munson [Baltimore: Johns Hopkins University Press, 1989], 25). Socrates resembles the Spartans in being able to identify politically serviceable *harmonia* without (like Glaucon) knowing the names of these modes. See 399a with Arist. *Pol.* 1339b2–4 and Rahe, *Spartan Regime*, 14.

29. Socrates attempts in the *Memorabilia* to persuade Xenophon of the excellence of just such a moderate and disciplined political life (Pangle, "Socrates' Argument"). G. R. F. Ferrari takes Socrates to be doing something similar in the *Republic*. Ferrari maintains that the ascent of "the lower orders in politics" in Periclean Athens imposed a choice on the elite: oligarchic opposition to the democracy or political quietism (*apragmosunē*). Glaucon, he asserts, chose the latter (having outgrown the youthful ambition Xenophon portrays in the *Memorabilia*), and Socrates now attempts "to deflect the brothers from the feeling that quietism is the best recourse in their imperfect world" (*City and Soul*, 22; cf. 35). But Glaucon's initial quietism does not allow us to infer, as Ferrari does, that he took no part in Critias's coup (13). To the contrary: in rekindling his early political ambition (cf. 23), Socrates dramatically increases the risk that he will be attracted to political extremism. Only a proper appreciation of Socrates' teaching could protect him from this danger; on the evidence of the *Republic*, however, this is precisely what he lacks.

30. On the corruption of Spartans when abroad, see the sources cited at Rahe, *Spartan Regime*, 160–61 n. 73, and cf. Xen. *Lac. Pol.* 14.2–7.

31. Rahe observes that the Spartans "thought of themselves quite literally as a breed apart" (*Spartan Regime*, 9).

32. This is in striking contrast with the Virtuous City, in which Socrates forbids poetry that portrays the gods as sexually immoderate (390b–c, 391c–d). What is more, incest between brothers and sisters is allowed in Callipolis (461d–e). Given that size, strength, and other physical attributes desirable in warriors run in families, the probability of incest in a city with such eugenic practices will necessarily increase over time. I thank Destiny Hrncir for this observation.

33. The word *stasis* specifically connotes political faction. In the Virtuous City, Socrates had hoped to persuade the young that "no citizen ever behaved hatefully toward another"—let alone toward his own father—"and that to be so is not holy" (378c). In the present context, however, he allows only that it is "likely" that a younger man would not attempt to assault or strike an older one (465a).

34. Glaucon takes a more neutral stance when Socrates points out that it is he who has caused him to be attacked (474a–b).

35. Freedom to indulge in adultery: Strauss, "Spirit of Sparta," 506, commenting on Xen. *Lac. Pol.* 1.7–9; on the eugenic purpose and efficacy of these arrangements, see 1.5–6 and 1.10. Unavoidability of incest: Strauss, 511. Common exercise: see Strauss, 505 n. 3 (on Xen. *Lac. Pol.* 2.11) with Eur. *Andr.* 595–600, where Peleus proclaims that "Not even if she wanted to could one of the Spartan girls become chaste [*sōphrōn*]—they who leave their houses in the company of young men, with naked thighs and loose garments; they have running-tracks and wrestling schools in common [with boys] in a way I cannot endure." Spartans raised in an *agelē*: cf. *Leg.* 666e with Plut. *Lyc.* 16.7. Paternal authority at Sparta: Xen. *Lac. Pol.* 6.1–2. Rival teams: Xen. *Lac. Pol.* 4.5–6. Socrates seems to be envisioning a similar practice at 464e; cf. his reference at 465a to an authority figure resembling the Spartan *paidonomos*, on which see *Lac. Pol.* 2.2. Xenophon describes these rival cohorts as being motivated by "the most god-beloved and most political strife, in which what must be done in relation to the good is shown forth" (4.5). Read in connection with his many implicit criticisms of the Spartan regime (concerning which see Strauss, "Spirit of Sparta"), this remark seems highly ironic.

36. Arlene Saxonhouse, "Comedy in Callipolis: Animal Imagery in the *Republic*," *American Political Science Review* 72.3 (1978): 888–901, at 890.

37. Jean Ducat notes that "Spartan education provides most of the background" of the Old Education (*tēn archaian paideian*) praised by Strong Argument (or Just Speech) at *Clouds* 961–1023 (*Spartan Education: Youth and Society in the Classical Period*, trans. Emma Stafford, P.-J. Shaw, and Anton Powell [Swansea: The Classical Press of Wales: 2006], 36). While Strong Argument emphasizes that the Old Education inculcated *sōphrosunē* (962), he himself conspicuously lacks this virtue, as he cannot conceal his lust for pubescent boys (see esp. 973–78). Weak Argument (Unjust Speech) ultimately forces him to admit that virtually everyone is *euruprōktos*—possessed of a "wide anus," or "buggered"—including "this long-haired fellow I see" (1101); the Spartans had long

hair. In defeat, Strong Argument sheds his cloak and deserts to the other side (1102–04); the *Clouds* was produced in 423, less than two years after the surrender at Sphacteria. Ducat observes the "striking" similarity between *Clouds* 961–83 and ch. 2 of Xenophon's *Constitution of the Lacedaemonians* (37); Strauss, "Spirit of Sparta," argues that Xenophon's treatise satirizes Critias's straightforward praise of Spartan customs in his work of the same name (528–29).

38. Alcibiades secured enthusiastic support for the Sicilian Expedition, which he commanded along with Nicias and Lamachus. He then betrayed his city when he fled to Sparta after his political enemies succeeded in recalling him to stand trial, and roused the Spartans to actions that would lead to the crushing defeat of the Athenians at Syracuse (Thuc. 6.8–24, 6.88–93).

39. Referring to learning and truth, Socrates repeats the fundamental progression "all," "every kind," and "the whole" at the beginning of book 6 (485b and d and 486a).

40. Erasmus opines that something like philosophy as Plato understands it "must have been, I think, in Homer's mind, when Mercury arms Ulysses against Circe's witchcraft with the herb called moly" (*The Education of a Christian Prince*, ed. Lisa Jardine [Cambridge: Cambridge University Press, 1997], 2).

41. See the passages cited by Roslyn Weiss, *Philosophers in the Republic: Plato's Two Paradigms* (Ithaca and London: Cornell University Press, 2012), 5.

42. Weiss exhaustively develops the distinction between the "philosophers by nature" Socrates introduces at the end of book 5 and the "philosophers by design" who rule in Callipolis. Speaking of the latter, Weiss observes that "nothing is left to chance in the regime discussed after 502c" (*Philosophers in the Republic*, 32).

Chapter 3: Tyranny, Poetry, and Science

1. Cf. Doyne Dawson, *Cities of the Gods: Communist Utopias in Greek Thought* (Oxford: Oxford University Press, 1992), 31: "so far as we know he [Critias] did not mention installing anything like the *agoge* and the *syssitia* during his brief dictatorship, but he had written much about these institutions, and we may suppose the idea lay somewhere in the background." Krentz notes that the goals of the oligarchy remain obscure because "after the restoration of democracy, no one . . . was interested in the Thirty's point of view" (*The Thirty*, 9).

2. *Gerousia*: cf. Munn, *School of History*, 259. Ephors: Xen. *Hell.* 2.3.34; cf. Lys. 12.43. Lash-bearers: Whitehead, "Sparta and the Thirty Tyrants," 124; cf. Roger Brock, "Athenian Oligarchs: The Numbers Game," *The Journal of Hellenic Studies* 109 (1989): 160–64 (at 163 n. 32). List of 3,000: Xen. *Hell.* 2.3.19; Krentz, *The Thirty*, 65–66. The list, supposedly naming the "best" (*beltistoi*) and "noble and good" (*kaloi kai agathoi*) Athenians, remained long unpublished, and was revised as circumstances required; cf. Arist. *Ath. Pol.* 36.2. 3,000 Spartan peers in 404: Krentz, 65; Whitehead, "Sparta and the Thirty," 127. Note also that, at Xen. *Hell.* 2.3.38–39, Theramenes twice refers to well-born Athenians (*kaloi*

k'agathoi) executed by the Thirty as *hoi homoioi*, the Lacedaemonian term for Spartiates. Expulsion of Athenians: Xen. *Hell.* 2.3.20, 2.4.1. The *perioikoi* were "non-Spartiate Lacedaemonians who resided in the subject villages of Laconia and Messenia and retained in privilege a measure of local autonomy" (Rahe, *Spartan Regime*, 11). The Thirty's murder of metics or resident aliens may also have been inspired by the Spartan practice of *xenēlasia*, the periodic expulsion of foreigners; see Whitehead "Sparta and the Thirty," 127–30, with Dawson, *Cities of the Gods*, 29.

3. Spartan garrison: Arist. *Ath. Pol.* 37.2. *Epikouroi* and *phulakes*: Lysias 12.94.

4. Krentz, *The Thirty*, 62–63.

5. Aeschin. *In Tim.* 173; Xen. *Mem.* 1.2.12. The dual verbal forms of the latter passage indicate that Critias and Alcibiades were regarded as birds of a feather. Speaking later in his own voice, Xenophon uses the dual form to express the same idea: "They [Critias and Alcibiades] set out straight from the beginning to be the leaders of the city" (*Mem.* 1.2.39). The two are also paired in the historical record: Critias sang Alcibiades' praises in poetry, and proposed his return from exile in 408. See DK frag. 4 and Munn, *School of History*, 166, with Plut. *Alc.* 33.1.

6. The Critias who appears in the *Timaeus-Critias* was traditionally assumed to be the leader of the Thirty, who plays a central role in the *Charmides* and appears in the *Protagoras*; he is identified as such by Diogenes Laertius (3.1) and Proclus (*In Ti.* 1.70). John Burnet was perhaps the first to suggest that this Critias, who claims that Solon "was a relative and really close friend of our great-grandfather Dropides" (*Tim.* 20e), must be the notorious oligarch's grandfather (*Early Greek Philosophy*, 3rd ed., [London: A. C. Black, 1920], 203 n. 3); see Laurence Lampert and Christopher Planeaux, "Who's Who in Plato's *Timaeus-Critias* and Why," *Review of Metaphysics* 52.1 (1998): 87–125, with the discussion of contemporary scholarly debate in Luc Brisson, trans., *Platon: Timée/Critias* (Paris: Flammarion: 1992), 326–35. Alternatively, Critias—for good Platonic reasons—"may have dropped a generation in tracing the story [about Solon]"; see Zuckert, *Plato's Philosophers*, 429–30 n. 24, citing J. K. Davies, *Athenian Propertied Families, 600–300 B.C.* (Oxford: Clarendon Press, 1971), 325–26. Problems of chronology to one side, Plato strongly invites the traditional assumption; absent any clear indication to the contrary, he can hardly have expected readers to distinguish persons of the same name who are virtually identical in character and thought.

7. Ducat, *Spartan Education*, 15; cf. Schmid, *Plato's Charmides*, 11.

8. Critias was descended from early rulers of Athens (Nails, *People of Plato*, 108), and Socrates tells Charmides that his paternal line has been celebrated "by Anacreon and by Solon and by many other poets as being preeminent in beauty and virtue and all the rest of what is said to be happiness" (*Chrm.* 157e–58a). Herodotus presents Solon, one of the Seven Sages (cf. *Prt.* 343a), as a man of godlike wisdom (1.29–33, 1.86–87); Athenian children chanted his poetry at a public festival (*Tim.* 21b).

9. Except where noted, I have followed the Greek text of Malcolm Davies, "Sisyphus and the Invention of Religion," *Bulletin of the Institute of Classical Studies of the University of London* 36.1 (1989): 16–32, which differs only slightly from that of DK frag. 25.

10. I have retained *agōn*, rejected in Davies, "Sisyphus."

11. Albrecht Dihle, "Das Satyrspiel *Sisyphus*," *Hermes* 105.1 (1977): 28–42. In reply, Davies ("Sisyphus," 25–26) notes that Dihle overlooks Epicurus, cited at Philodemus *On Piety* 519–33 (in Dirk Obbink, *Philodemus On Piety, Part 1: Critical Text with Commentary* [Oxford: Clarendon Press: 1996], 143), who seems to have assumed that Critias authored the fragment, and that Critias is named as an atheist also by Sextus Empiricus, Cicero, and Theophilus. Cf. Walter Burkert, *Greek Religion*, trans. John Raffan (Cambridge, MA: Harvard University Press, 1985), 467 n. 22 with Jan N. Bremmer, "Atheism in Antiquity," in *The Cambridge Companion to Atheism*, ed. Michael Martin (Cambridge: Cambridge University Press, 2006), 16–17. Dana Sutton, "Critias and Atheism," *The Classical Quarterly*, New Series 31.1 (1981): 33–38 furthermore maintains that stylistic features argue against Euripidean authorship (34 n. 19). Patrick O'Sullivan, "Sophistic Ethics, Old Atheism, and 'Critias' on Religion," *Classical World* 105.2 (2102): 167–85 cites the literature on both sides of the debate, observing that "an increasing number of scholars has favored Critias as author at least of fr. 19" (167 n. 1); cf. Laurence Lampert, *How Philosophy Became Socratic: A Study of Plato's Protagoras, Charmides, and Republic* (Chicago: University of Chicago Press, 2010), 188 n. 74.

12. Sutton, "Critias and Atheism," 36.

13. At *Chrm.* 163d, Socrates says that he understands what Critias has just said because he has heard Prodicus make similar distinctions; Brann surmises that Critias studied in Prodicus's school ("Tyrant's Temperance," 77). Philodemus writes that "Epicurus reproaches Prodicus, Diagoras, and Critias, among others" for their "compete [atheistic] madness" (*On Piety* 519–27 [Obbink, *Philodemus*, 143]). Like Critias, Prodicus authored an account of the origins of religion in which, as in the Sisyphus fragment, the gods are understood to be a "by-product of human society" (Albert Henrichs, "Two Doxographical Notes: Democritus and Prodicus on Religion," *Harvard Studies in Classical Philology* 79 [1975]: 93–123 [at 112]; cf. Davies, "Sisyphus," 25).

14. O'Sullivan, "Sophistic Ethics," 174; Lampert, *How Philosophy Became Socratic*, 188. Cf. Zuckert, *Plato's Philosophers*, 242.

15. Critias, too, prided himself on poetic innovation: "And now I will crown the son of Cleinias, an Athenian / Hymning Alcibiades in new ways. / For it was not possible to fit his name into elegy; / But now in iambics it will lie, not unmetrically" (DK frag. 4).

16. Dawson, *Cities of the Gods*, 22; cf. 23. Dawson also observes that both Solon and Lycurgus of Sparta were "reforming lawgiver[s] . . . partly modeled on the oikist lawgiver" (22). A similarly experimental and ecumenical perspective is reflected in Critias's comparison of Spartan customs with those of other

Greek and barbarian communities, as well as in his list of the various technical innovations for which different nations are responsible (DK frags. 2, 6, 33–35; cf. 31).

17. On pre-Socratic cosmology, see Arist. *Metaph.* 1.3. In a drama of disputed origin, Critias echoes the thought expressed in lines 33–34 of the Sisyphus speech: "Time—indefatigable and filled with an eternal flowing—revolves, itself begetting itself" (DK frag. 18).

18. O'Sullivan notes that "Protagoras' πολιτικὴ τέχνη has, in effect, the same consequence as the invention of religion does in Critias' fragment" ("Sophistic Ethics," 173). This is because Protagoras's political art includes not just *dikē*, but also reverence for customary beliefs and practices (*aidōs*), the equivalent of the fragment's "fear of gods" (*Prt.* 322c).

19. DK frag. 37; Dawson, *Cities of the Gods*, 29. The Greeks commonly supposed that freedom for their own cities presupposed the domination of others. See J. A. O. Larsen, "Freedom and its Obstacles in Ancient Greece," *Classical Philology* 57.4 (1962): 230–34.

20. Xen. *Hell.* 2.3.50–51; cf. Arist. *Ath. Pol.* 37.1. After he was condemned to death, Theramenes is said to have clung to the altar in the Bouleuterion, proclaiming that "by the gods, I am not unaware that this altar will not help me in any way, but I want to demonstrate this: that these men [the Thirty] are not only the most unjust in relation to human beings, but also the most impious in relation to the gods" (Xen. *Hell.* 2.3.53).

21. See Seth Benardete "On Interpreting Plato's *Charmides*," *Graduate Faculty Philosophy Journal* 11.2 (1986): 9–36 (see esp. 25–27); Schmid, *Plato's Charmides*, 37–38; Lampert, *How Philosophy Became Socratic*, 185–89; and David Lawrence Levine, *Profound Ignorance: Plato's Charmides and the Saving of Wisdom* (Lanham, MD: Lexington Books, 2016), 176–81. Cf. Zuckert, *Plato's Philosophers*, 242–43. Sutton is too quick to dismiss Critias's atheism ("Critias and Atheism," 37 n. 28).

22. Cf. Ronna Burger, "Socrates' Odyssean Return: On Plato's *Charmides*," in *Socratic Philosophy and Its Others*, ed. C. Dustin and D. Schaeffer (Lanham, MD: Lexington Books, 2013), 217–35. On Socrates' service at Potidaea and elsewhere, see Mark Anderson, "Socrates as Hoplite," *Ancient Philosophy* 25.2 (2005): 273–89. Theramenes intriguingly alleges that Critias was "with Prometheus" in Thessaly, "establishing democracy and arming serfs against their masters" (Xen. *Hell.* 2.3.36)—an activity that suggests his embrace of aristocracy (or oligarchy) was not entirely principled. Theramenes was probably referring to the god Prometheus; I have been unable to find a historical figure with that name. Prometheus (Forethought) claims in Aeschylus's eponymous drama that "all the arts [*technai*] for mortals come from Prometheus" (*PB* 506); he also plays a significant role in Protagoras's myth (*Prt.* 320d, 321c–22a).

23. Besides the third wave of the *Republic*, examples include the doctrine of the non-arithmetical mean at the arithmetical midpoint of the *Statesman* and the Eleatic Stranger's parricide of Parmenides in the *Sophist*. See How-

land, "*Republic*'s Third Wave," 633–36, which develops the observations of Leo Strauss.

24. The *Charmides* begins at 153a and ends at 177d, making it almost 24 Stephanus pages long. The center of the dialogue would be 165a. The speech in which Critias discusses Delphi runs from 164c to 165b.

25. Benardete, "Interpreting Plato's *Charmides*," 27. As Benardete observes, Critias does not construe "Know thyself" as "an ellipsed binary construction" in which *hōs ouk ei theos*, "because you are not a god," goes without saying (27).

26. Schmid, *Plato's Charmides*, 37–38. Levine aptly characterizes Critias's interpretation as his "liberation theology" (*Profound Ignorance*, 179).

27. In the *Phaedrus*, Socrates explains that "I am not yet able, according to the Delphic inscription, to know myself; it therefore seems laughable to me, as I am still ignorant, to inquire into things that do not belong to me" (229e–30a). Later in the same dialogue, he makes amends for having offended against the gods by presenting philosophy as the endeavor to recollect transcendent being and truth under the guidance of divine erotic madness (242b–57a). In the *Apology*, the Delphic oracle focuses and validates Socrates' desire for wisdom, directing him to the knowledge of ignorance (20e–23c, discussed in my *Kierkegaard and Socrates: A Study in Philosophy and Faith* [Cambridge: Cambridge University Press, 2006], 59–68).

28. The dramatic date of the *Timaeus* can be reckoned only approximately. Socrates was at Potidaea from 432 to 429, and an earlier date for the *Timaeus*—Debra Nails places it in the late summer of 429 (*People of Plato*, 326), Laurence Lampert and Christopher Planeaux in 421 ("Who's Who in Plato's *Timaeus-Critias*," 93–95), and Catherine Zuckert after 411 (*Plato's Philosophers*, 429 n. 23)—is extremely unlikely. A date of 429 would support the intriguing suggestion of Warman Welliver that the *Timaeus*'s "missing fourth" (17a) is Pericles, just taken ill with the plague that was to kill him (*Character, Plot and Thought in Plato's Timaeus-Critias* [Leiden: E. J. Brill, 1977], 44).

29. The Athenians fought three battles against the Locrians in 426–25; the Locrians entered into a treaty with Athens in 422, but in 415 closed their city to the Athenian fleet that sailed against Syracuse (Thuc. 3.99.1, 3.103.3, 5.5.3, 6.44.2). Locri possessed a legal code known for its unusual strictness (*Plato's Timaeus*, trans. Peter Kalkavage [Newburyport, MA: Focus Publishing: 2001], 50 n. 2); Socrates echoes the Athenian Stranger of Plato's *Laws* (at 638b) in asserting that Locri has "most excellent laws" (*Tim.* 20a). Hermocrates was among the first to recognize the Athenian threat, against which he rallied the Syracusans and attempted to unite the Greek cities of Sicily (Thuc. 4.58–4.65, 6.32.3–6.41, 6.72–73, 6.75–6.80); Thucydides praises him as "a man otherwise lacking nothing in comprehension, and in war both well-experienced and conspicuous in courage" (6.72.1).

30. In "The Genre of the Atlantis Story," *Classical Philology* 72 (1977): 287–304, Christopher Gill argues that Atlantis is primarily to be understood as "the dream or ideal Periclean Athens had about itself" (296); cf. Gill, *Plato: The Atlan-*

tis Story (Bristol: Bristol Classical Press, 1980), xvii–xx. Jean-François Pradeau reviews the tradition of reading the Atlantis story as a political allegory containing a criticism of contemporary Athens (*Le Monde de la Politique: Sur le récit atlante de Platon, Timée (17–27) et Critias* [Sankt Augustin: Akademia Verlag, 1997], 71–110).

31. Socrates' summary in the *Timaeus* mentions the separation of the warriors from the artisans; the principle of one man, one job; the need for warriors to be spirited toward enemies and gentle toward friends; their education in gymnastic and music; the requirement that they not regard gold or silver as their own private possession; and matters pertaining to women and children, with special emphasis on the deception of the marriage lottery and the secret removal of inferior offspring from the warrior class (17c–19a). The summary removes certain limitations implicit in the corresponding parts of the *Republic*. Socrates does not forbid the warriors to possess money, but assigns them "a measured wage for sound-minded men," which they are to spend in common (18b); he also says that the natures of the women are to be tuned and assimilated to the men (18c); this is not stated in the *Republic* (cf. 455d). Nathalie Nercam notes also that Socrates makes no mention of the Noble Lie and its myth of autochthony, which emphasizes the brotherhood of all citizens and binds them to a particular, well-defined territory ("L'introduction problématique du *Timée*," *Plato Journal* 15 [2015]: 41–57). On the timing of the festivals see John Sallis, *Chorology: On Beginning in Plato's Timaeus* (Bloomington: Indiana University Press, 1999), 21–23.

32. Nercam argues that this city is cut to the measure of his oligarchic interlocutors; in addition to testing their philosophical potential, it is designed to explore the tension in their souls between wealth and virtue ("L'introduction problématique du *Timée*," 43–44).

33. Cf. Kalkavage's remark that Socrates' silence in the *Timaeus* "make[s] a receptive space for the designs of men who think of truth in terms of doing and making" (*Plato's Timaeus*, 10). The distinctly practical orientation of Timaeus's philosophizing prepares the ground for Critias; Kalkavage emphasizes that his cosmology presents mathematics not as a means to turn the soul around "from Becoming and utility to Being and contemplation," as in the *Republic*, but as "a form of productive practice or moral demiurgy" used "to give order to the world and to the soul" (19).

34. The role of Hermocrates in this plan is never made clear.

35. Welliver, *Character, Plot and Thought*, 13.

36. "Precision" (*akribeia*), an important element of competitive expertise in late fifth-century Athens, was closely associated with access to written texts (Munn, *School of History*, 191–92).

37. As Welliver observes, Critias does not initially claim even that the story came down from Solon; he says only that Solon told Dropides that the Athenians had performed "great and marvelous" exploits (*Character, Plot and Thought*, 12 n. 10). Critias's implausible assertion that the poems of Solon were

new at the time he recited them at the Apatouria (21b) similarly collapses the distance between himself and his illustrious ancestor.

38. Catherine Osborne, "Space, Time, Shape, and Direction: Creative Discourse in the *Timaeus*," in *Form and Argument in Late Plato*, ed. Christopher Gill and Mary Margaret McCabe (Oxford: Clarendon Press, 1996), 188. "On balance," Nercam writes, what Critias "takes to be 'veridical' is simply that which *doxa* [opinion] affirms to be such: a fact lived and past, guaranteed by the authority of one or more wise men" ("L'introduction problématique du *Timée*," 50). Cf. Pradeau's observation that Critias "never considers the existence of man outside of the temporal and geographic limits of the city" (*Monde de la Politique*, 56).

39. Solon evidently assigned the date of the Coureotis, "making provision for reception of children in [the month of] Pyanepsion" (Edward Greswell, *Origines Kalendariae Hellenicae*, vol. 6 [Oxford: Oxford University Press, 1862], 607).

40. Critias's penchant for what Levine calls "doxastic inflation" (*Profound Ignorance*, 78) is equally visible in his effusive praise of his ward (*Chrm.* 157d). In the *Timaeus*, Critias pays homage to his heritage through a kind of patricidal emulation. He embraces a crucial assumption that Solon's extant writings reject, namely, that scientific and technical knowledge can control the contingencies of human life and produce happiness. See David Roochnik, *Of Art and Wisdom: Plato's Understanding of Techne* (University Park: The Pennsylvania State University Press, 1996), 27–33. Solon's wisdom regarding the problem of happiness is dramatically confirmed in Herodotus's story of his visit to Croesus and Croesus's subsequent fate (1.29–33, 86–87). When at the point of death Croesus recognizes his folly, he thrice cries out "Solon!" (1.86); his miraculous rescue from the burning pyre on which Cyrus has bound him closely identifies Solon with the Delphic Apollo. The Egyptian priest's "Solon, Solon!" (22b), uttered in a very different vein, implicitly invites readers to read Critias's tale of Saïs against the backdrop of Herodotus.

41. Cf. Nercam, "L'introduction problématique du *Timée*," 45–46, where it is also observed that Critias omits the "rule of intergroup mobility explicitly imposed by Socrates at the beginning of the *Timaeus* [19a]."

42. Aristotle defines *phronēsis* as "a true disposition of acting with reason in matters of good and bad for human beings," and he identifies the art of legislation as its architectonic form (*Eth. Nic.* 1140b5–6, 1141b25). In Plato's *Statesman*, the Eleatic Stranger indicates that *phronēsis* is the goal of philosophy (272b–c).

43. Munn, *School of History*, 259. There is another, ironic sense in which Solon's and Socrates' speeches are enacted, and thus completed, within the framework of the *Timaeus-Critias*. Recalling that the Apatouria celebrated an act of deceit that led to an Athenian military victory, Welliver shows that Critias joins with Hermocrates to violate their agreement with Timaeus in order to defeat him in a war of words and claim the prize for the best speech (*Character, Plot and Thought*, 18–21). Welliver argues that the manifest failure of this treacher-

ous attack, which echoes the defeat of the swollen armies of Atlantis, Persia, and Athens at the hands of lean and virtuous opponents, is the primary action of the *Timaeus-Critias*, and that it dramatically fulfills Socrates' desire to see "the perfect citizens of his imagination come to life in a noble exemplar [i.e., Timaeus] and win a victory befitting their education and training" (32; cf. 39–45).

44. Kalkavage notes that Timaeus's cosmology "has inspired and instructed such diverse thinkers as Proclus, Plotinus, Dante, Montaigne, Kepler, Leibniz, Vico, Schelling, Goethe, Whitehead and Heisenberg" (*Plato's Timaeus*, ix); for the full story, see Novotný, *Posthumous Life of Plato*. Welliver gives a good account of the vanity and jealousy Timaeus's speech arouses in Critias, and of the churlishness of his response (*Character, Plot and Thought*, 22–28); see also Jacob Howland, "Partisanship and the Work of Philosophy in Plato's *Timaeus*," *Review of Politics* 69.1 (2007): 1–27.

45. I compare the world-making of the Demiurge with that of the God of Genesis in "Cosmos and Philosophy in Plato and the Bible," *Nova et Vetera*, English Edition, 13.3 (2015): 669–92.

46. See Pierre Vidal-Naquet, "Athens and Atlantis: Structure and Meaning of a Platonic Myth," in *The Black Hunter: Forms of Thought and Forms of Society in the Greek World*, trans. Andrew Szegedy-Maszak (Baltimore: The Johns Hopkins University Press,1986), 263–84. Vidal-Naquet effectively confirms Welliver's suggestion that the *Critias* is a "parable" about "a good city and a city gone bad"—the former being the Athens that defeated the Persians (a victory celebrated at the Panathenaea), the latter, the city Athens became as it "grew into the part of Atlantis, [and] the role of the small and virtuous land power which she had deserted was filled by Sparta" (*Character, Plot and Thought*, 40–42).

47. Vidal-Naquet, "Athens and Atlantis," 270 (where it is also noted that "the country [of pre-historic Athens] is surrounded by sea, but there are no harbors"); cf. 268–69. Perhaps to underscore the contrast between proto-Athens and Atlantis, Critias indicates but does not dwell on the technical capabilities of the ancient Athenians: their land was "decorously ordered" by accomplished farmers (111e), they engaged in "the greatest acts of building" (111c), and "always . . . administering their own land and Hellas with justice, they were held in repute over all Europe and Asia, and most famous for beauty of body and the manifold virtue of their souls" (112e).

48. Vidal-Naquet, "Athens and Atlantis," 270, 272.

49. Nine archons: see 114a with Diskin Clay and Andrea Purvis, *Four Island Utopias* (Newburyport, MA: Focus Publishing, 1999), 40. Temples and harbors: 116c–e, 117d–e with Vidal-Naquet, "Athens and Atlantis," 268–69, 275; cf. Clay and Purvis, *Four Island Utopias*, 40. On Hermocrates' comparison of Athenians to Persians see Thuc. 6.33.5–6, 6.76.4–77.1. The trick whereby Hermocrates ensures that the Athenian generals fail to retreat when they might have gotten away (Thuc. 7.73.3–7.73.4) mirrors Hdt. 8.75, where Themistocles deceitfully convinces the Persian commanders that the Greeks are going to retreat from Salamis. The historical pendulum that connects Athens and Atlantis resembles

the alternating motion of heavenly bodies described by the priest of Saïs (*Tim.* 22d), which Clay and Purvis compare to the Eleatic Stranger's description of "two phases in the rotation of heavenly bodies around the earth: one from west to east, the other from east to west ([*Stsm.*] 269D–274E)" (63 n. 26); in both cases, this cosmic reversal of motion brings great destruction to the earth.

50. Lys. 12.5; Pl. *Epist.* 7.324d.

51. As Vidal-Naquet remarks, when "Athens meets and vanquishes Atlantis . . . she really overcomes herself" ("Athens and Atlantis," 268).

52. The temple of Poseidon stands at the center of the Phaeacians' agora (*Od.* 6.266). The god nevertheless cuts the Phaeacians off completely from the rest of the world by piling a mountain around their town.

53. In these respects, Atlantis eerily prefigures Nazi Germany (Brann, "Tyrant's Temperance," 70–71).

54. The *Charmides* takes place in the early summer of 429, immediately after the return of the Athenians from Potidaea following their defeat in the battle of Spartolus, in which more than four hundred Athenians were killed (Thuc. 2.79.7; Anderson, "Socrates as Hoplite," 278–79 n. 11; Nails, *People of Plato*, 311–12). Socrates does not assume that his unidentified audience knows about this famous battle (153b), which suggests that he is speaking decades later to a person (or persons) young enough never to have heard of it. Because Socrates tells the story of the *Charmides* in a way that foreshadows the depredations of the Thirty, we are perhaps meant to infer that the narrative frame is set somewhere around the time the oligarchy was overthrown. On the dramatic date of the *Timaeus*, see n. 28 above.

55. See Anderson, "Socrates as Hoplite," which lays out the history of Socrates' military service at Potidaea and elsewhere.

56. Brann describes him in this scene as "*sophrosýne* incarnate . . . a model of modesty" ("Tyrant's Temperance," 73).

57. Nails, *People of Plato*, 90.

58. Chaerephon's remark thus introduces "the tension between individuality and anonymous universality that will unfold with sinister implications over the course of the conversation" (Burger, "Socrates' Odyssean Return," 219).

59. While "the desire of each for Charmides is confirmed and watered by the desire of all the others," Socrates is "the only one to look anywhere else" (Lampert, *How Philosophy Became Socratic*, 159). Perhaps his military service and intimate familiarity with death have helped to distance him from Athenian values.

60. But even if his soul is *eu pephukōs*, or "has grown well by nature," it will be out of balance with his body, which in its beauty "exceeds nature" (*huperphuōs*: 154d). Timaeus teaches that such imbalances produce illness (*Tim.* 87e–88b).

61. Levine observes that Critias's guardianship of Charmides, as "an instance of rulership," offers a preview of his later political governance. In taking Charmides under his wing, Critias furthermore positions himself as "the

educator of the promise of the city (an 'advisor to princes')" (*Profound Ignorance*, 40–41).

62. The men and boys at the school of Taureas know that Socrates has just returned from Potidaea, and Charmides later tells him that "there is no little talk of you among our agemates" (153a–b, 156a). Their talk surely concerned his courage and coolness in combat, as well as his toughness in the face of the unusual hardships of the Potidaean campaign (cf. *Symp.* 219e–21c). It should be noted that nature has equipped Charmides with a body made for the hand-to-hand combat of hoplite warfare, for his physique is massive as well as perfectly formed: when he joins Socrates and Critias, *two* men are forced off the bench to make room for him (155c).

63. One is reminded of the poet of Plato's *Ion*, who cannot make poetry until he is "out of his mind, and intelligence is no longer in him" (534b). Socrates' word *ephlegomēn*, "I became inflamed" (i.e., erect) recalls the Feverish City (*phlegmainousan polin*, *Rep.* 372e).

64. There is no food, Socrates says in the *Republic*, from which the tyrant will abstain (571d, 574e).

65. *Aidōs* is often indistinguishable from *aischunē*, and at *Chrm.* 160e–61b it designates the "heteronomous quality" of Charmides, who "has his eye on how he will look to others" (Schmid, *Plato's Charmides*, 27). But the inward sense of modesty that restrains Socrates in Charmides' presence seems to be the same as the *aidōs* that restrains "the horse that is obedient to the charioteer"—which, as a part of the soul, is invisible to others—from leaping on the beloved in the *Phaedrus* (254a).

66. The "leaf" with which Socrates identifies the medicine is probably the papyrus plant, which was beaten into scrolls. In the *Phaedrus*, Socrates invents an Egyptian myth to argue that writing is a *pharmakon* that is useless if it is not accompanied by internal recollection or *anamnēsis* (274c–75b); perhaps we are to understand that such recollection is induced by music.

67. Socrates' reference to precision (*akribeia*)—an important element of competitive expertise in late fifth-century Athens (Munn, *School of History*, 191–92)—anticipates the role of *technē* (art) and *epistēmē* (science) in Critias's account of *sōphrosunē*, and begins to suggest the influence of sophistry on both of his interlocutors.

68. This sentence contains the first mention of *sōphrosunē* in the *Charmides*.

69. This negative core is captured by the Eleatic Stranger's description of a "noble" educator who attempts to purify human beings of vice by refuting their presumed wisdom (*Soph.* 226b–31b). See my book *The Paradox of Political Philosophy: Socrates' Philosophic Trial* (Lanham, MD: Rowman & Littlefield, 1998), 198–206.

70. Socrates models such introspection while on campaign in Potidaea, where (to the amusement of some soldiers from Ionia, the land of scientific cosmologists) he once stood silently from dawn to dawn thinking about something (*Symp.* 220c–d).

71. Weiss discusses the basic identity of these virtues in detail; see *Philosophers in the Republic*, 173–81.

72. The bad and unlearned man, as Socrates observes, is also unjust: he tries to outdo everyone, knowers and ignorant alike (349b–50c). As Schmid points out, Charmides also does his own things—the things proper to one of subordinate role or station—"by withdrawing and having his guardian tested" (*Plato's Charmides*, 31).

73. Socrates later uses the same epithet of Critias (174b). If translated as "bloodstained," as Levine does in *Profound Ignorance, miare* anticipates the political future of both men.

74. Schmid plausibly suggests that Socrates draws Critias into the conversation because he recognizes that "whatever influence he may have on Charmides can only come about through the refutation and hence diminishment of the authority of Critias" (*Plato's Charmides*, 70). Burger opines that Critias becomes angry because he realizes that Socrates has "peeled Charmides away from the authority of his guardian" ("Socrates' Odyssean Return," 225).

75. Hes. *WD* 311; Xen. *Mem.* 1.2.57.

76. On this understanding of self-knowledge, as Burger notes, "the individuality of the self vanishes" ("Socrates' Odyssean Return," 227).

77. Socrates remarks on the impurity of philosophy at *Tht.*196e–97a. In the *Cratylus*, this impurity is shown to be rooted in the unavoidable circularity of speech; see Howland, *Paradox of Political Philosophy*, 136–49. On the impossibility of philosophy in Critias's "technocratic beehive," see 173d with Burger, "Socrates' Odyssean Return," 231 (where it is also noted that Socrates' conversation with Charmides could not have occurred "under the omniscient eye of the ruling science of *sōphrosunē*," for Socrates would have been exposed "as a quack" when he claimed to be a doctor).

78. Cf. Schmid, *Plato's Charmides*, 56–57. Schmid observes that Critias's conception of *sōphrosunē* as science looks like a version of the familiar Socratic teaching that virtue is knowledge, stripped of the distinction Socrates draws between moral knowledge and "the kind of truth sought by . . . practical arts and theoretical sciences" (50). Once again, Critias seems to be plagiarizing Socrates, but without having understood his meaning.

79. Cf. Terry Penner, "Socrates and the Early Dialogues," in *The Cambridge Companion to Plato*, ed. Richard Kraut (Cambridge: Cambridge University Press, 1992), 149 n. 14. In wondering whether his dream "has come through horn or thorough ivory," Socrates echoes Penelope, who does not know whether her dream of Odysseus's return and slaughter of the suitors is lying or truthful (173a; cf. Hom. *Od.* 19.562–67). He seems thereby to imply that "it is Critias who some day, like Odysseus, will set out to make real something like the order Socrates now imagines" (Burger, "Socrates' Odyssean Return," 230).

80. Brann, "Tyrant's Temperance," 81. Observing that totalitarian regimes promote "one schematic idea . . . [that] certifies itself and all other knowledge

as within or without its pale," Brann adds that Critias's master science, "objectless because indifferent to the object's truth, has one true intention: power" (81).

81. Socrates uses the dual grammatical form here.

82. Welliver, *Character, Plot and Thought*, 27; Schmid, *Plato's Charmides*, 33–34, 81, 102. The observations of Welliver and Schmid have generally escaped the notice of Plato scholars; cf. the remarks Levine cites at *Profound Ignorance*, 51 n. 57. While otherwise sensible on the subject of Critias, W. K. C. Guthrie claims that Plato shows him "respect and affection" and offers "no hint that he was worse than the rest" of Socrates' associates (*A History of Greek Philosophy, Vol. 3: The Fifth-Century Enlightenment* [Cambridge: Cambridge University Press, 1969], 299). Gabriel Danzig goes even further in "The Use and Abuse of Critias: Conflicting Portraits in Plato and Xenophon," *Classical Quarterly* 64.2 (2014): 507–24, asserting that Plato produced a "remarkably positive portrait of Critias" (!) out of a desire to protect his own reputation and to "bring some retrospective glamour to Socrates' otherwise unhappy career" (511–12). Danzig fails to distinguish the erotic philosopher from the lover of honor, or to grasp that "where there is thinking there are no inadvertent loyalties" (Brann, "Tyrant's Temperance," 71).

83. Schmid, *Plato's Charmides*, 129.

Chapter 4: Channeling Critias

1. The word "enemies" in this section is not the relatively neutral *polemioi*, enemies in war, but *echthroi*, those who are hateful. Craig points out that Socrates connects this word with civil strife or faction (470b–d), and that there are many more references to *echthroi* in the Republic than to *polemioi* (*War Lover*, 55–56).

2. On the identification of *to meson* with the political community itself, see Rahe, *Republics Ancient and Modern*, 42 with 812 nn. 80–86.

3. Xen. *Hell.* 1.3.2–12; Donald Kagan, *The Fall of the Athenian Empire* (Ithaca and London: Cornell University Press, 1987), 176, 275–86.

4. Thuc. 5.89, trans. Richard Crawley, in *The Landmark Thucydides*, ed. Robert B. Strassler (New York: The Free Press, 1996).

5. In analyzing *Rep.* 522b–25c, Roochnik observes "a basic feature of Platonic techne: it relies on mathematics" (*Of Art and Wisdom*, 279).

6. See ch. 1, n. 19 with ch. 3, nn. 13 and 22, herein.

7. Cleitophon, who is reported to have praised Thrasymachus and disparaged Socrates in conversation with Lysias, similarly objects when Socrates' companions tell him that the just man is able to produce "the advantageous . . . the needful . . . the beneficial . . . the profitable" (*Cleit.* 406a, 409c).

8. Munn, *School of History*, 70–71.

9. Cf. Søren Kierkegaard, *Philosophical Fragments*, in *Philosophical Fragments/Johannes Climacus*, ed. Howard V. Hong and Edna Hong (Princeton:

Princeton University Press, 1985), 49–54. While in the cited passage it is dogmatic philosophy that takes offense at the paradoxical claims of faith, erotic, Socratic philosophizing and faith ultimately converge in Kierkegaard's writings. See my *Kierkegaard and Socrates.*

10. White rightly observes that Thrasymachus's account of justice is not normative but descriptive, "an empirical generalization of what he sees happening everywhere: the stronger simply *do seek* their own advantage" ("Thrasymachus the Diplomat," 321, emphasis in original).

11. Cf. *Stsm.* 294a–c; Arist. *Eth. Nic.* 1137b11–32.

12. Aristotle argues that human beings are the most political of animals, for they alone possess speech and have "a perception of good and bad and just and unjust and other things [of this sort], and partnership in these things is what makes a household and a city" (*Pol.* 1253a16–17).

13. See Introduction, n. 9.

14. At 342a–b, Socrates poses an alternative: (1) the arts are all defective, in which case either (a) each art needs another art to consider its own advantage (producing an endless regress), or (b) each art considers its own advantage by itself; (2) no art is as such defective, in which case the problem of advantage does not arise. He does not contemplate the possibility that there is a ruling art which provides for the advantage of all other arts.

15. The Greeks conflated *Ploutōn*, the god of the underworld, with *ploutos*, wealth, perhaps because Hades grows ever richer in souls.

16. Thrasymachus accordingly blurs the difference between being *called* "happy and blessed" and actually being so (344b–c).

17. Thus G. M. A. Grube translates *hiera kai hosia* as "sacred objects or temple property" (*Plato's Republic* [Indianapolis: Hackett Publishing Company, 1974]).

18. Cf. White, "Thrasymachus the Diplomat," 323.

19. Cf. Weiss, *Philosophers in the Republic*, 127.

20. All but the nine Archons and the heads of the Council were to serve without pay for the duration of the war (Arist. *Ath. Pol.* 29.5).

21. This willingness is also characteristic of Aristotle's equitable man (*ho epieikēs*); see *Eth. Nic.* 1136b20–12.

22. Like Thrasymachus, Socrates overlooks the stochastic character of particular medical treatments, about which even expert doctors regularly disagree.

23. Ranasinghe remarks that Glaucon's "perfectly unjust man would be a practitioner of the kind of master science that so fascinated . . . Critias in the *Charmides*" (*Soul of Socrates*, 10). Plato clearly intends for us to regard the tale of Gyges' ancestor as Glaucon's own invention. Cf. Andrew Laird, "Ringing the Changes on Gyges: Philosophy and the Formation of Fiction in Plato's *Republic*," *Journal of Hellenic Studies* 121 (2001): 12–29.

24. It is noteworthy, however, that Socrates infers this "from the rest of your character, since according to your speeches alone I would distrust you" (367e–68b).

25. The noun *timē*, "esteem" or "honor," is audible in the verb *timōreisthai*, "to avenge."

26. Cf. 377e–78a with the discussion of the Noble Lie in ch. 5, herein.

27. There is no visible inside to a chunk of marble: breaking it open just produces more surfaces. This exteriority, too, resonates in the Greek word for "license," with its suggestion of that which lies outside (*ek*) the particular kind of being (*ousia*) we are *qua* human: a being that is inseparable from community (*sunousia*).

28. Candaules' use of the vocative form *Gugē*, which occurs twice in the Gyges story, may be meant to call attention to the resemblance between Gyges' name and the word *gunē*, "woman" or "wife."

29. The importance of *aidōs* in this context is underscored by the fact that the word occurs nowhere else in Herodotus (Seth Benardete, *Herodotean Inquiries* [The Hague: Martinus Nijhoff, 1969], 12).

Chapter 5: Disgracing the Song

1. Sophocles' *OT* has 1530 lines; Oedipus narrates the slaying of Laius at lines 800–813.

2. The resemblances between the legends of Oedipus and Periander are explored in detail in a seminal article to which my reflections in this chapter are particularly indebted: Jean-Pierre Vernant, "From Oedipus to Periander: Lameness, Tyranny, Incest in Legend and History," *Arion* 15.1 and 2 (1982): 19–37. Polynices and Eteocles kill each other in combat over the rule of Thebes, while Lycophron, Periander's only competent heir, is murdered by the Corcyreans (D.L. 1.94–95). Corcyra was a colony and longtime enemy of Corinth, and its citizens—like Lycophron, who had taken refuge among them when Periander disinherited him—hated and feared the tyrant, who in his old age had agreed to switch places with his son.

3. Phaethon is said by Hesiod at *Theog.* 986–87 to be the son not of Helios but of Eos (Dawn) and Cephalus (Head), a genealogy that might also be taken to suggest the theme of ideological tyranny.

4. Which god may have dispatched the dolphin to rescue Arion is another matter. Apollo, Dionysus (who takes over from Apollo at Delphi during the winter months), and Poseidon have all been advanced as possible candidates (Vishwa Adluri, "Plato's Saving Mūthos: The Language of Salvation in the *Republic*," *The International Journal of the Platonic Tradition* 8.1 [2014]: 3–32, at 11–12). On the role of the Delphic oracle in Socrates' philosophizing, see *Ap.* 20e–23c with *Phdr.* 229e–30a.

5. "Localized melodic idiom": Gregory Nagy, *Pindar's Homer: The Lyric Possession of an Epic Past* (Baltimore: Johns Hopkins University Press, 1990), 88, cited in Timothy Power, *The Culture of Kitharōidia* (Washington, DC: Center for Hellenic Studies, 2010), 216. Aristotle speculates that songs called *nomoi*

were so named "because before they learned letters, they sang the laws, so that they might not be forgotten, as is indeed still the custom among the Agathursi" (*Pr.* 19.28).

6. Power, *Culture of Kitharōidia,* 223. At 449a, Socrates calls the Virtuous City good and right (*agathēn . . . kai orthēn*).

7. Cf. Power, *Culture of Kitharōidia,* 223 n. 87. Land trade from northern Greece had to go through Corinth, while the city also captured maritime trade by hauling goods from ship to ship across the isthmus, enabling merchants to avoid what could be a dangerous passage around the Peloponnesus.

8. The "noble shipowner" of the image is bigger and stronger than everyone else, but is also hard of hearing, somewhat shortsighted, and largely ignorant of seamanship (488a–b). That Socrates is describing the *dēmos* is later confirmed when he compares the many to a great beast, and insists that it is impossible for a multitude to be philosophical (493a–94a).

9. Power, *Culture of Kitharōidia,* 4–5, 11–17.

10. In place of Periander Socrates numbers Myson the Chenaean in his list of the Seven Sages in the *Protagoras* (343a–b).

11. Seth Benardete notes that the letter lambda "resembles an uneven gait." See "Sophocles' *Oedipus Tyrannus,*" in *The Argument of the Action: Essays on Greek Philosophy and Poetry,* ed. Ronna Burger and Michael Davis (Chicago and London: University of Chicago Press, 2000), 75.

12. Vernant writes that "Greek tradition makes Periander, the model tyrant, a new Oedipus; he supposedly has sexual intercourse in secret with his mother, Crateia" ("From Oedipus to Periander," 29; cf. D.L. 1.96).

13. Hdt. 5.92.η. The story that Herodotus tells at 5.92.ζ about Thrasybulus is repeated, in a slightly different form, in Livy, who attributes a similar esoteric communication to Tarquinius Superbus (Liv. 1.54.5–8).

14. In utterly confounding what is public and what is private, Periander also displays what Xenophon regards as the extreme of barbarism (*An.* 5.4.34); cf. Vernant, "From Oedipus to Periander," 30.

15. 5.92.β–γ. The Noble Lie, discussed below, predicts the destruction of the city when a man of iron or bronze soul becomes its guardian (414c).

16. Cf. *Phdo.* 62c with Adam, *Republic, ad loc.* 378a and the sources cited in *The Knights of Aristophanes,* ed. Robert Alexander Neil (Cambridge: Cambridge University Press, 1901), *ad loc.* Ar. *Eq.* 648.

17. Froma Zeitlin, "Thebes: Theater of Self and Society in Athenian Drama," in *Nothing to Do With Dionysos? Athenian Drama in its Social Context,* ed. John J. Winkler and Froma I. Zeitlin (Princeton: Princeton University Press, 1990), 130–67, at 148.

18. 361b, 362a–b; cf. 550c. Zeitlin argues that Thebes functions in the theater as an "anti-Athens" where "events . . . and the characters who enact them both fascinate and repel the Athenian audience, finally instructing the spectators as to how their city might refrain from imitating the other's negative example" ("Thebes," 145).

19. In book 8, Socrates says that carelessness in mating results in guardians who begin to pay too little attention to music and gymnastic; their own unmusical children will be inadequate to conduct the proper tests, resulting in a mixture of "iron with silver and bronze with gold" (546e–47a).

20. Vicki Hearne's philosophical, Xenophon-inspired essay "How to Say 'Fetch!'" (in *Adam's Task: Calling Animals by Name* [New York: Alfred A. Knopf, 1986], 42–76) sheds invaluable light on these matters.

21. On the relationship between the *Assemblywomen* and *Republic* book 5, see the appendix of Adam, *Republic,* vol. 1, 345–55, and cf. Saxonhouse, "Comedy in Callipolis."

22. Plut. *Comp. Lyc. et Num.* 3.2, quoted at Rahe, *Spartan Regime,* 26.

23. He seems already to be contemplating the possibility of incest: the term "sacred marriage" (*hieros gamos*) referred to the nuptials of Zeus and Hera, who were brother and sister. See Adam, *Republic,* and Bloom, *Republic of Plato, ad loc.* 458e.

24. Cock-fighting was practiced in Athens since at least the time of the Persian Wars, and is said to have been institutionalized in a yearly public ceremony after Themistocles encouraged his soldiers to imitate the birds' pugnacious spirit (Ael. *VH* 2.28).

25. Socrates pointedly overlooks this problem when he says that the warriors "will be free from faction, to the extent, at any rate, that human beings divide into factions on account of the possession of property, or of children and relatives" (464d–e).

26. On the Spartan *paidonomos* or superintendent of youths, see Xen. *Lac. Pol.* 2.2 with 4.6–7.

27. Aristotle alleges that that the Thirty feared Theramenes "would become leader of the people and break up their political dominance" (*Ath. Pol.* 36.1). Cf. Critias's discussion of the hostility of the multitude at Xen. *Hell.* 2.3.24–25, when Theramanes' fate is decided.

28. The tyrant is always parricidal in relation to the pre-existing regime and its fathers; tyranny differs from despotism in that the former is exercised over unwilling citizens, the latter over willing, slavish souls, as in the great barbarian nations of Egypt and Persia (Arist. *Pol.* 1285a).

29. See *Civilization and Its Discontents,* trans. David McLintock (New York: Penguin Books, 2002), 45 (where Freud quotes Schiller).

30. Odysseus hears the tale of Ares and Aphrodite when he visits the Phaeacians (Hom. *Od.* 8.266–366). Ruled by King Mighty-Mind and Queen Prayed-For, married blood-relatives of penetrating intelligence (Alcinous is Arete's uncle: *Od.* 7.63–66), the island of the Phaeacians is in significant respects a Homeric protoype of Callipolis. Hephaestus's automata are mentioned at Hom. *Il.* 18.375–78; Vernant connects his lameness with that of the Cypselids and Labdacids ("From Oedipus to Periander," 21).

31. The Athenians honored Olympic champions with meals in the *Prutaneion,* the city's hearth.

32. In Sparta, too, "the city's champions were treated like the demigods honored in her hero cults" (Rahe, *Spartan Regime,* 22).

33. On Glaucon's attraction to Callipolis, cf. Ranasinghe's comparison of "the life of the Guardian of the just city" with the unjust life Glaucon describes in connection with the Ring Myth (*Soul of Socrates,* 15).

34. Cf. Rosen's discussion in *Plato's Republic,* 201–06.

35. Cf. Vernant, who follows Lévi-Strauss in connecting lameness with stuttering and forgetting: all are "failures, distortions or blockages of communication" ("From Oedipus to Periander," 20).

36. Cf. *Ap.* 23b with *Tht.* 151c–d.

37. These men would soon be at odds with each other: Thrasyboulos went into exile under the Thirty, and led the force that overthrew them.

38. Munn argues that Socrates' objection to the collective trial of the generals had no statutory basis (*School of History,* 186). It is also worth noting that Socrates' refusal to arrest Leon of Salamis under the Thirty involved disobeying a legally constituted authority.

39. 477b1, b5, b7, b10, d7, e5, e8; 478a6, a10, b1, c7, d7, d9.

Chapter 6: Philosophy in Eclipse

1. Rosen, *Plato's Republic,* 9. Rosen observes that this crucial dimension of the *Republic* "is regularly missed by commentators" (163).

2. Cf. Eva Brann, "Plato's Theory of Ideas," *St. John's Review* 32.1 (1980): 29–37.

3. Cf. *Euthphr.* 11b with *Meno* 80a–b. Observing that the argument of the *Republic* is "wide open to development, to challenge, to reconsideration, and to doubt," Diskin Clay opines that "it is difficult to think of another Platonic dialogue in which what Socrates says is challenged as often as it is by the very *structure* of the dialogue in which he speaks" ("Reading the *Republic,*" in *Platonic Writings, Platonic Readings,* ed. Charles L. Griswold, Jr. [New York and London: Routledge, Chapman & Hall, Inc., 1988], 21, emphasis in original).

4. *Soph.* 230b–d. In this, the Stranger observes, the Socratic educator resembles a physician who purges bodies before attempting to nourish them.

5. *Theoeidos* is far more common in Homer than *theoeikelos.* The latter occurs twice in the *Iliad,* both times in reference to Achilles. In the *Odyssey,* it occurs three times: Telemachus is called *theoeikelos* at 3.416, Deiphobus at 4.276, and Alcinous at 8.256.

6. Socrates' language here recalls the beginning of the great myth of the *Phaedrus,* in which he describes the soul's journey to the roof of the cosmos in order to nourish itself on the sight of the beings: "All soul is immortal" (245c).

7. On the connection between *nomisma* and *nomos,* see Arist. *Eth. Nic.* 1133a30–31.

8. Socrates' extraordinary fecundity is emphasized by Alcibiades, who portrays him in the *Symposium* as bursting with images "divine and golden and altogether beautiful and amazing" (217a).

9. My understanding of the work of the Good owes much to David Lachterman, "What is 'The Good' of Plato's *Republic*?" In *Four Essays on Plato's Republic*: *St. John's Review* 39 (1989–90): 139–71.

10. Tad Friend, "Vermin of the Sky," *The New Yorker*, February 28, 2011, 24.

11. The Phaethon myth is told (albeit only in surviving fragments) in *Euripides: Phaethon*, ed. James Diggle (Cambridge: Cambridge University Press, 1970).

12. Phaethon's imprudent behavior should be compared with Telemachus's great self-restraint in refraining from stringing Odysseus's bow when he is on the point of doing so: while his apparent failure makes him look like the son of another, success would have interfered with the surprise slaughter of the suitors who have stolen his patrimony (*Od.* 22).

13. See Rahe, *Spartan Regime*, 23.

14. The absence of music in the philosophical curriculum is noted by Weiss, *Philosophers in the Republic*, 83. On the limitations of the "exclusively mathematical curriculum" of the philosopher-kings, cf. Roochnik, *Beautiful City*, 69–77.

15. 519c–d, 520a, 539e–40b; cf. Weiss, *Philosophers in the Republic*, 56–57, 69, 73–77.

16. Roochnik's assertion that Callipolis is "a city in which citizens are transformed into units" (*Beautiful City*, 38) thus applies especially to its rulers.

17. Sherwood Belangia, "Thinking Through *Doxa*: The Erotic Remainder in the Dialogues of Plato," paper delivered at the Ancient Philosophy Society Annual Meeting, Portland, Maine, April 29, 2016.

18. As Socrates observes, all those who are slow in calculation become sharper if given gymnastic in it (526b).

19. Perhaps it is unnecessary to add that pure ontology, the formal science of being and the Good with which Socrates identifies the song of dialectic, is highly unlikely to yield anything like concrete guidance in ethical and political matters. Cf. Arist. *Eth. Nic.* 1097a8–14.

20. Cf. Ferrari's observation that the philosopher-king is "a new kind of model" for "the most manly Glaucon . . . to measure himself against" (*City and Soul*, 29).

21. Cf. Blondell, *Play of Character*, 211–12.

22. This episode seems to furnish evidence for Rosen's assertion that the philosopher is torn between the desire to rule and not to rule, and more specifically, that the *Republic* is a "catharsis of the philosophical compulsion to rule" (*Plato's Republic*, 9; cf. 82, 166; on the desire of philosophers to see wisdom prevail over ignorance, see esp. 229–31). This compulsion must be purged, Rosen argues, because it is a form of decadence or sickness no less than an antidote to decadence: Plato teaches in the *Republic* that "every attempt to enact the truth in human affairs without compromise leads to a reversal of that truth" (6). I reviewed Rosen's dense but exceedingly rich study of the *Republic* in *Society* 46.2 (2009): 195–98.

23. Weiss, *Philosophers in the Republic*, 79.

24. On Alcibiades' violent and unpredictable behavior as a boy and a youth, see Plut. *Alc.*, esp. 2.2–3, 4.5, 7.1. According to Martin Ostwald, the word *paranomia*, "lawlessness," was applied most frequently in the fifth century to Alcibiades (*From Popular Sovereignty to the Sovereignty of Law: Law, Society, and Politics in Fifth-Century Athens* [Berkeley: University of California Press, 1986], 116).

Chapter 7: Socrates Reborn

1. "He chose it [the dialogue form], we say, because the dialogue is a kind of cosmos. For in the same way as a dialogue has different personages each speaking in character, so does the universe comprise existences of various natures expressing themselves in various ways; for the utterance of each is according to its nature. It was in imitation, then, of God's creation, the cosmos, that he did this. Either this is the reason, or it is that the cosmos is a kind of dialogue. For just as in the world there are superior and inferior existences and the soul during her stay in the world sometimes conforms to the superior, sometimes to the inferior, so the dialogue also has its characters, the questioners and the questioned, and our soul, sitting in judgment, now sides with the questioners, now with the questioned." *Anonymous Prolegomena to Platonic Philosophy*, ed. and trans. L. G. Westerink (Amsterdam: North-Holland Publishing Company, 1962), 14.3–8.

2. So profoundly does necessity, "the wandering cause" (48a), interfere with the purposeful pursuit of the good that the Demiurge is obliged to use force even in fashioning the soul of the cosmos. Timaeus explains that the Same and the Other, of which all soul is composed, are "loath to mix" (35a). The *Timaeus* implies that matter is far easier to master than the human psyche: politics is more difficult than any "hard" science.

3. The dependence of intellect on order in Timaeus's account produces, however, what may be a vicious circle. Timaeus asserts that the intellect is impaired when it becomes embodied: as though "bound within a prodigious river," the "circuits of the immortal soul" are assailed by a flood of sensations, emotions, and desires and "washed over" by a "food-supplying wave" together with a "stream of increase and nutriment" (42a, 43a–b, 44b). Subject to these multiple affections, which cause "the most widespread and greatest [internal] commotion," the soul "becomes unintelligent" (44a–b). Although Timaeus presents *thumos* as the handmaid of intellect, the spirited mastery of disorderly motion in the soul is in fact a precondition of intelligence. What is worse, an intellect whose internal motions are disturbed through its connection with the body can never be sure that it is capable of forming adequate judgments about the world; like a computer with defective software, it may be prone to systematic error. For further discussion, see Howland, "Partisanship and the Work of Philosophy."

4. The imperfection of human perfection is a central theme of Michael Davis's work; see most recently *The Soul of the Greeks: An Inquiry* (Chicago and London: University of Chicago Press, 2011).

5. Perhaps philosophy in the True City consists in theoretical contemplation of the order of creation. In the *Timaeus*, this is the original activity of intellects prior to incarnation, and perhaps their future activity as well (41e–42d; note the Demiurge's promise that one who lives well would "journey back to the dwelling of his lawful star, and have a happy life that is habitual to him"). Maimonides posits that Adam and Eve engaged in such contemplation in Eden; see *The Guide of the Perplexed*, vol. 1, trans. Shlomo Pines (Chicago and London: University of Chicago Press, 1963), 1.2.

6. Socrates strongly reinforces this message at 618b–19d. Cf. 344d–e, 358d, and 450b with Rosen, *Plato's Republic*, 64.

7. On the sophist as an angler, see *Soph.* 221d–23a. Socrates implicitly appears in two of the Eleatic Stranger's definitions of the sophist; cf. 226b–31b with 265a–68d.

8. Cf. the discussion of moral weakness at *Eth. Nic.* 7.4 (esp. 1148a27–32), examined in my article "Aristotle on Tragedy"; see esp. 382, 394–95. In achieving increased self-knowledge through painful experience, Socrates illustrates the tragic watchword *pathei mathos*, "learn by suffering."

9. Polemarchus, Plato suggests, was open to philosophical persuasion in a way that his brother Lysias, who is present in the *Republic*, was not. That it is just to harm hateful men is the fundamental moral principle upon which Lysias rests his case in *Against Eratosthenes*, a courtroom speech in which, years later, he would call for revenge against those who arrested his brother and took his life. In putting Eratosthenes on the dais for questioning, Lysias goes so far as to ignore the risk of pollution in addressing an unpurified murderer. "My view is this," he explains, "I believe that to talk to another about this man, if it is for his benefit, is unholy, but to talk to him, if it is for his harm, is pious and holy" (12.24). For further discussion see Howland, "Plato's Reply to Lysias."

10. The myth's teaching of philosophical salvation is discussed in Eric Voegelin, *Plato* (Baton Rouge: Louisiana State University Press, 1966), 45–134; Charles Segal, "'The Myth Was Saved': Reflections on Homer and the Mythology of Plato's *Republic*," *Hermes* 106.2 (1978): 315–36; and Adluri, "Plato's Saving Mūthos." The distinction between "philosophers by nature" and "philosophers by design" is drawn from Weiss, *Philosophers in the Republic*.

11. Homer and Hesiod speak of Hades as bounded by Ocean and the river Styx, while the land of the dead in the Myth of Er lies across the river of Carelessness (612a). The adjective *peraios*, in turn, means "on the other side"; *Hē Peraiē* is the Beyond-Land—"the land beyond the river that was once thought to have separated the Peiraic peninsula from Attica" (Brann, "Music of the *Republic*," 118).

12. Said to be "close kin to the gods" (Hom. *Od.* 5.35), the Phaeacians used to reside in Hyperia or Overland; having fled the violence of their neighbors the Cyclopes, they now live on the island of Scheria, Cut-Off Land (6.4, 6.8). These names are suggestive of their fantastic remoteness from the ordinary cares and necessities of human life, and anticipate the fate they suffer when Poseidon

punishes them for transporting Odysseus to Ithaca by physically blocking them from all further contact with outsiders (13.159–87).

13. Stephen Halliwell notes that the myth's "veneer of historicity" and relatively undistinguished protagonist (an "ordinary barbarian soldier") gives it an "*anti*mythologial and antipoetic slant" ("The Life and Death Journey of the Soul: Interpreting the Myth of Er," in *Cambridge Companion to Plato's Republic,* 448–49, emphasis in original).

14. John Man, *Kublai Kahn: The Mongol King who Remade China* (London: Bantam Books, 2006), 360.

15. On these details of the image discussed in this paragraph, see Griet Schils, "Plato's Myth of Er: The Light and the Spindle," *L'antiquité classique* 62.1 (1993): 101–14. In existing independently of any star, the light Er sees is comparable to the light God calls into being in the Hebrew Bible, prior to the creation of the heavenly bodies (Gen. 1:3).

16. "Of one thing only is even a god deprived: to make undone whatever has been done." Quoted at Arist. *Eth. Nic.* 6.2.1139b10–11.

17. See Sarah Iles Johnston, *Ancient Greek Divination* (Malden, MA and Oxford: Wiley-Blackwell, 2008), 33–75.

18. Halliwell notes that Socrates interprets what in the myth was a "once-for-all choice" of life as "a vitally recurring imperative" ("Life and Death Journey," 464).

19. This notion recalls Aristophanes' *Frogs,* in which the chorus of frogs in Hades refers to the Athenian Archedemus as "a demagogue among the corpses above" (419–20). In presenting philosophy as the means of escaping the Cave, Plato refutes Aristophanes' suggestion that Socrates and his companions are themselves dead souls (cf. *Clouds* 103, 119–20, 504, 508).

20. On Atalanta, see Apollod. 1.8; on Epeius, see Hom. *Od.* 8.492–93 with *Laws* 796a; on Thersites, see Hom. *Il.* 2.212–77.

21. *Laws* 829d–e; Sophocles, frag. 245 (in *Sophocles: Fragments* [Loeb Classical Library 483], ed. and trans. Hugh Lloyd-Jones [Cambridge, MA: Harvard University Press, 1996], 105.

22. On Thamyras as king of the Thracians, see Power, *Culture of Kitharōidia,* 222. On the sorrow of the nightingale, cf. Aesch. *Ag.* 1143–45 with Power, 299 n. 303. Power notes that one version of Thamyras's contest with the Muses, going back "at least to the fifth century BCE," stipulates that "if he should defeat the Muses in the *agôn,* he is permitted to have intercourse with each of them" (49).

23. Burkert, *Greek Religion,* 296–301.

24. *Aeschylus: Fragments,* 18–19.

25. See Malcom Davies, *The Greek Epic Cycle* (London: Bristol Classical Press, 1989), 48, 66–67, and 73; on the Palladium, cf. Verg. *Aen.* 2.163–70.

26. The remark also recalls Leucothea's instruction to Odysseus to turn away when he throws his veil into the sea as he steps, reborn, onto the shores of Scheria (Hom. *Od.* 5.350). One thinks also of Lot's wife, whose crushing sorrow

over the daughters she has left behind in Sodom prevents her from heeding the angels' warning not to look back (Gen. 19:17, 26).

27. Andoc. 1.90. Andocides praises the Athenians for their civic-minded restraint: "When you came back up from the Piraeus, although it was in your power to exact vengeance, you were determined to let go of the past, and you judged it better to save the city than to avenge private wrongs, and it seemed best not to recall past wrongs against one another" (1.81).

28. See Thomas Clark Loening, *The Reconciliation Agreement of 403/402 B.C. in Athens: Its Content and Application*, Hermes 53 (Stuttgart: Franz Steiner Verlag, 1987).

29. Munn, *School of History*, 239.

30. "What is ideology if not the extreme politicization of philosophy? And is not the *Republic* one of the most influential, perhaps *the* most influential, of the causes of the deterioration of philosophy into ideology?" (Rosen, *Plato's Republic*, 229).

31. Halliwell observes that the *Republic*'s "denial of a final reaction to Glaucon functions as a signal of its own philosophically incomplete status" and "enacts a silence that is both dramatic and metaphysical" ("Life and Death Journey," 472).

Acknowledgments

Professors are strange and profligate animals. The ones I know are always getting pregnant, have had miscarriages and abortions, and are quick to abandon their offspring if they do not measure up to expectations. The child you hold in your hands is to be congratulated for having made it this far: while no less robust than its older siblings, it suffered a more laborious birth. I am therefore especially pleased to acknowledge the many friends and students who helped me to bring this book to light and life.

My greatest debt is to Paul Rahe, who buoyed me with encouragement and counsel when I spent a pleasurable afternoon visiting him at the Hoover Institution in Palo Alto just before Christmas in 2013, and when he later read the first draft of the manuscript. In my first years as an assistant professor at the University of Tulsa, I audited Paul's courses on the comedies of Aristophanes and Plato's *Laws*, and I joined him in an extraordinary summer seminar on Greek tragedy taught by Froma Zeitlin of Princeton and Charles Segal of Harvard. As the *Republic* suggests, intellectual genealogy is not an exact science; Paul has been something like a great-uncle and godfather of several of my books, including this one.

Nalin Ransinghe and James Murphy also generously read the manuscript, and I thank both for their kind words and helpful criticism. Lenn Goodman invited me to speak about Glaucon's fate at Vanderbilt in 2012; a similar invitation from May Sim and the Boston Area Colloquium in Ancient Philosophy brought me to Assumption College in 2013. Adriel Trott invited me to deliver a lecture on the *Republic*'s True City at a lovely undergraduate philosophy conference she organized at Wabash College in 2014, and Leon Botstein and Garry Hagberg invited me to talk about my book project at Bard College in 2016. I thank all of the aforementioned for the opportunity to share my ideas with sympathetic but critical audiences.

Lenn Goodman, Paul Rahe, and Roslyn Weiss (author of the invaluable *Philosophers in the Republic*) helped me to secure an NEH Summer Stipend in 2015, and I am grateful to all three. Beatrice Rehl, my former editor at Cambridge University Press, offered me good advice at a critical stage of my project. Paul Dry did the same for my Introduction, and accepted the book on the advice of Eva Brann of St. John's College, the tutor of my *Doktorvater* (with Stanley Rosen), David R. Lachterman. I thank Paul and Eva for their dynamic teamwork and sound criticism of more than one of my manuscripts. The staff of Paul Dry Books has done outstanding work; my debt to them is as inexhaustible as my gratitude. I also wish to thank Dean Kalpana Misra and the University of Tulsa for a sabbatic leave in 2015–2016, and the Chapman Trusts, which underwrite my research as McFarlin Chair of Philosophy.

I am grateful to my colleagues in the Department of Philosophy and Religion at the University of Tulsa for their friendship, intellectual community, and remarkable *esprit de corps*: Matthew Drever, Stephen Gardner, Jane Hittinger (of blessed memory), Russell Hittinger, and Michael Futch. I am also deeply indebted to the past and present participants in the Tulsa Plato Seminar, generous and learned companions who happily agreed to study the *Timaeus* and *Charmides* with me: Aaron Bell, Jared Burden, Denise Dutton, Jim Ford, Frank Grabowski, Nora Greening, Bruce MacQueen, Avi Mintz, Matthew Oberrieder, Julianne Romanello, Regan Rule, and Victor Udwin.

Last but not least, I am delighted to acknowledge the extraordinary students—including mathematicians and poets, combat veterans and political activists, athletes, journalists, feminists, medievalists, a fashionista and a Southern gentleman—in my Spring 2015 undergraduate seminar on the *Republic*: Nicholas Cox-Steib, Lauren Delucchi, Kelsey Erwin, Destiny Hrncir, Maggie Lane, Clara Langley, David Lepine, Austin McDaniel, Shadi Nadri, Daryl Simmons, Kyle Walker, and Walker Womack. Our dialogue was lively, joyful, and brilliant.

Index

Jacob Howland is McFarlin Professor of Philosophy at the University of Tulsa, where he has taught since 1988. He earned a B.A. from Swarthmore and a Ph.D. in philosophy from Penn State in 1987. A past winner of the University of Tulsa Outstanding Teacher Award and the College of Arts and Sciences Excellence in Teaching Award, Howland has received research grants from the National Endowment for the Humanities, the Littauer Foundation, and the Earhart Foundation. He has lectured in Brazil, Denmark, England, France, Israel, Norway, and Romania, and at colleges and universities around the United States. His essays have appeared in *Commentary, The New Criterion*, and *A Public Space*, and he has published roughly fifty scholarly articles on subjects ranging from the political philosophies of Plato, Aristotle, Xenophon, and Aristophanes to Richard Wright's *Black Boy* and Claude Lanzmann's *Shoah*. His other books, three of which have been or are being translated into Chinese, are *Plato and the Talmud, Kierkegaard and Socrates: A Study in Philosophy and Faith, The Paradox of Political Philosophy: Socrates' Philosophic Trial,* and *The Republic: The Odyssey of Philosophy*. He also edited *A Long Way Home: The Story of a Jewish Youth, 1939–1948,* by Bob Golan.